François Kersaudy

# KERSTEN'S LISTS

## A SAVIOUR IN THE DEPTHS OF HELL

*Translated from the French by
the author*

MLP

Originally published in French as *La Liste de Kersten*
in 2021 by Librairie Arthème Fayard
First published in Great Britain in 2024 by Mountain Leopard Press

This paperback edition published in Great Britain in 2024 by
Mountain Leopard Press
an imprint of
HEADLINE PUBLISHING GROUP

2

Cataloguing in Publication Data is available from the British Library

ISBN (PB) 978 1 80069 906 9

Offset in 10.35pt/15.64pt Minion Pro by Jouve (UK), Milton Keynes

Printed and bound in Great Britain by Clays Ltd, Elcograf S.p.A.

This book is supported by the Institut Français (Royaume-Uni)
as part of the Burgess programme

HEADLINE PUBLISHING GROUP
An Hachette UK Company
Carmelite House
50 Victoria Embankment
London EC4Y 0DZ

The authorised representative in the EEA is Hachette Ireland, 8 Castlecourt
Centre, Dublin 15, D15 XTP3, Ireland (email: info@hbgi.ie)

www.headline.co.uk
www.hachette.co.uk

# CONTENTS

# DRAMATIS PERSONAE

**Berger, Gottlob**, General, chief of S.S. Hauptamt (Central Office), in charge of recruitment and training within the S.S.

**Bernadotte, Count Folke**, nephew of King Gustav V and vice-president of the Swedish Red Cross

**Bormann, Martin**, Hitler's secretary and chief of the National Socialist Party's chancellery

**Brandt, Rudolf**, private secretary to Heinrich Himmler

**Ciano, Galeazzo**, Italian foreign minister and Mussolini's son-in-law

**Dönitz, Karl**, Grand Admiral and head of the Kriegsmarine from 1943; Hitler's successor-designate in April 1945

**Goebbels, Josef**, Reich propaganda minister

**Göring, Hermann**, Reich Marshal and commander-in-chief of the Luftwaffe

**Günther, Christian**, Swedish foreign minister

**Hess, Rudolf**, Führer's deputy for party affairs

**Hewitt, Abraham**, President Roosevelt's special envoy and O.S.S. agent in Stockholm

**Heydrich, Reinhard**, Himmler's deputy and head of the Reichssicherheitshauptamt (Central Office for Reich Security or R.S.H.A.)

**Himmler, Heinrich**, Reichsführer of the S.S.

**Kaltenbrunner, Ernst**, successor to Reinhard Heydrich as the head of the R.S.H.A.

**Kersten, Arno**, second son of Felix Kersten

**Kersten, Felix**, doctor in manual therapy

**Kersten, Irmgard**, wife of Felix Kersten

**Kivimäki, Toivo**, Finland's ambassador to Berlin

**Lüben, Elizabeth**, "adoptive sister" of Felix Kersten

**Masur, Norbert**, deputy to Hillel Storch as representative of the World Jewish Congress in Stockholm

**Müller, Heinrich**, head of section IV (Gestapo) within the R.S.H.A.

**Mussert, Anton**, chief of the Dutch national socialist movement (N.S.B.)

**Nagell, Baron Justinus van**, former Dutch ambassador to Stockholm

**Posthumus, Nicolaas**, professor of economics and founder of the Dutch Institute for War Studies (N.I.O.D.)

**Quisling, Vidkun**, chief of Nasjonal Samling, the Norwegian collaborationist party

**Rangell, Johan**, prime minister of Finland, 1941–43

**Ribbentrop, Joachim von**, Reich foreign minister

**Richert, Arvid**, Swedish ambassador to Berlin

**Ryti, Risto**, president of Finland, 1940–44

**Schellenberg, Walter**, chief of section VI (foreign intelligence) of the R.S.H.A.

**Seyss-Inquart, Arthur**, Reich commissioner for occupied Netherlands

**Storch, Hillel**, representative of the World Jewish Congress in Stockholm

**Terboven, Josef**, Reich commissioner for occupied Norway

**Witting, Rolf**, Finnish foreign minister, 1940–43

**Wulff, Wilhelm**, professional astrologer and "adviser" to Reichsführer Himmler

# INTRODUCTION

Just about everyone knows the story of Oskar Schindler, who saved a thousand Jews from Nazi extermination during World War II. Yet Felix Kersten did better than that: as early as 1947, a memorandum from the Swedish section of the World Jewish Congress stated that Kersten had saved in Germany "100,000 people of various nationalities, including some 60,000 Jews, at the risk of his own life". And yet, having closed this book, the reader will no doubt regard such numbers as a considerable underestimate.

One of Joseph Kessel's lesser known and most moving novels was entitled *The Man with the Miraculous Hands*. As early as 1960, it revealed the exploits of Himmler's doctor, who demanded as payment for his services the liberation of victims of the regime sentenced to imprisonment or death – with the reader being left to decide how much of the story could be assigned to Kessel and how much to Kersten. Admittedly, the latter seems to have been viewed by Western historians with the same condescending incredulity that once greeted Otto Strasser, Hermann Rauschning and Hans-Jürgen Köhler – three highly knowledgeable political refugees who gave detailed inside accounts of Hitler's regime as early as the late thirties.[i] But in the case of Kersten, the astonishing

i   The very same happened in the case of the Soviet Union: during Stalin's lifetime – and even long thereafter – such insiders as Kravchenko, Krivitski or Bajanov faced the same resolute scepticism from Western historians.

fact remains that most historians who deny him the slightest value as a witness or actor tend to quote him extensively in their own works . . . To which can be added that their scepticism comes up against several indisputable facts: first, both the appointment diary and the correspondence of Heinrich Himmler show that he benefited more than two hundred times from medical treatment by Felix Kersten between March 1939 and April 1945 – for an hour at a time. Second, Himmler's assertions as noted immediately after these sessions and reproduced in Kersten's memoirs in 1947 are strikingly similar to the views expressed by senior Nazi leaders, as evidenced by the transcripts published between five and thirty-three years later. Third, numerous original documents signed by Himmler or his secretary Rudolf Brandt bear clear witness to Kersten's remarkable accomplishments – as do the public testimonials and personal memoirs of friends and foes alike. Fourth, American, British, Dutch and Swedish diplomatic correspondence during the last two years of the war unambiguously shows that ambassadors and foreign ministers, not to mention Franklin Roosevelt and Winston Churchill, were all informed of Felix Kersten's humanitarian undertakings. Last but not least, most of the latter's recollections are verifiable, and should they prove inaccurate or exaggerated – which happens not infrequently – the reasons can most often be readily explained.

Reviving the memory of Felix Kersten is no easy task. He came from a German family settled in an Estonian province of the Russian Empire, he became Finnish without really ceasing to be German, and by the late thirties he had become Dutch at heart – before the vagaries of World War II induced him to opt for Swedish citizenship; his memoirs cover four volumes written in as many languages over a period of ten years; his diary, sought by historians for three-quarters of a century, eventually proved non-existent; correspondence, affidavits, testimonials, sworn statements and findings of commissions of inquiry pertaining to his wartime actions are in German, English, Swedish, Danish, Norwegian, Finnish and Dutch; the secrecy that was so necessary to the success of his humanitarian undertakings during the war persisted during the immediate post-war period, and, with few exceptions, the hundreds of thousands he had saved were never to know who their saviour was. Finally, due to the extreme confusion that reigned during the last few months of the war, the precise number of people saved by his interventions is well-nigh impossible to ascertain.

The challenge was thus to prevent such difficulties from hampering the present narrative. How, for instance, can one provide translations, explain institutions, set out implications, specify locations and constantly refer to the progress of the war raging all around? Excluding them might make the story incomprehensible, but including them might make it unreadable. I have thus chosen to reference them in footnotes, where they can be consulted at leisure. It will be seen that this story includes numerous conversations as quoted by Felix Kersten, General Schellenberg, Count Bernadotte, Himmler's astrologer Wulff, Swedish foreign minister Günther and various post-war commissions of inquiry. How can one be sure that such dialogues are entirely authentic? Apart from the commissions of inquiry that had stenographers, no-one – not even the spies – was equipped with portable tape recorders at the time. The accounts of actors and eyewitnesses had therefore to be taken at face value, after cross-examining archives and testimonies, evaluating context and verisimilitude, and applying plain common sense.

Besides opening up various interesting historical prospects, this rather amazing foray into the dark and baffling maze of the Third Reich may serve to remind us that three passions reigned supreme at the top of this evil and ephemeral regime: the disguised yet mortal hatred dividing Himmler, Ribbentrop, Goebbels, Bormann, Göring and Rosenberg, which was so skilfully exploited by Felix Kersten to ensure the success of his undertakings; the blind fanaticism that united them all, under the demonic influence of the Führer, which caused Marshal Göring to confess: "I have no conscience. My conscience is called Adolf Hitler"; and of course fear – an abject fear that preyed upon them relentlessly, as overtly expressed by the self-same Marshal Göring: "When I enter Hitler's office, my heart invariably sinks into my boots."

All along this hectic and horribly dangerous journey in the footsteps of Felix Kersten, the reader will discover that humour sometimes emerges in the midst of the most tragic situations. This may cause some outrage, since we now have to contend with vocal minorities of professional indignants. But most readers will no doubt look beyond that[ii] and enjoy the satisfaction of having met one of those exceptional characters who occasionally reconcile us with human nature.

---

ii  With the encouragement of Sergueï Obraztsov, the great Russian artist who used to say: "*Iumor, eto serioznoïe dielo*" – humour is a serious thing.

# 1

## ONTO THE SCENE

This story begins at the end of the nineteenth century near Yurieff in Livonia – one of the three Baltic governorates of the Russian Empire. Here came to life in September 1898 one Felix Alexander Eduard Kersten. The newborn baby's godfathers were three prominent local figures and great friends of his father, who gave him his three Christian names: Eduard of Livron, minister of the tsar; Alexander Westberg, private physician to the tsarina, and Gustave Lannes, Marquess of Montebello[iii] and French ambassador to St Petersburg. But the latter, instead of giving him his own Christian name, chose to name him Felix, in honour of the then French president, Félix Faure.

This was but one part of the highly cosmopolitan atmosphere surrounding Felix Kersten's early childhood. For in the very imperfectly Russified Livonia of the time, the common people were Estonian, the civil servants Russian and the tradesmen Jewish,[iv] but the landowners remained predominantly German, as was the case with young Felix's mother, Olga, and his father, Friedrich Kersten, who came from a long lineage of Brandenburg farmers dating back to the sixteenth century. Once old enough to enter school, their son

iii   And a grandson of Marshal Lannes.
iv   For the Russian imperial administration, as for that of the Soviet Union afterwards, there existed a Jewish "nationality".

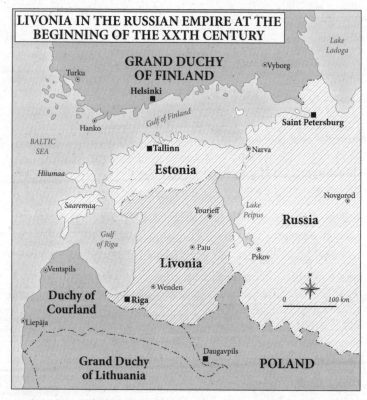

## LIVONIA IN THE RUSSIAN EMPIRE AT THE BEGINNING OF THE XXTH CENTURY

GRAND DUCHY OF FINLAND

Lake Ladoga

Turku

Vyborg

Helsinki

Hanko

Saint Petersburg

BALTIC SEA

Gulf of Finland

Tallinn

Narva

Estonia

Hiiumaa

Novgorod

Saaremaa

Yourieff

Lake Peipus

Russia

Gulf of Riga

Paju

Pskov

Livonia

Ventspils

Wenden

N

Duchy of Courland

Riga

0          100 km

Liepāja

Daugavpils

Grand Duchy of Lithuania

POLAND

*Livonia within the Russian Empire at the beginning of the twentieth century*

therefore found himself among German pupils, but also Russian, Estonian, Finnish, Ingrian[i] and Jewish ones; as he was to say many years later: "There we learned early on to discern in people of such diverse origins, languages and conditions only their value as human beings."[1]

Did he learn much more than that? Probably not, as he was himself to admit: "I was far from being a model pupil."[2] Indeed, he was mainly noticed by his teachers for his gluttony, negligence and indolence – much to the chagrin of his parents, who sent him in 1907 to the German-speaking boarding school of Birkenruh, near Wenden. He went on to complete his schooling in Riga, with no particular distinction – and no matriculation. Nevertheless, having inherited from his father a passion for agriculture, Felix Kersten then entered the Jenfeld school of agronomy in German Holstein. There he seems to have found his calling: after graduating two years later, he underwent a practical training period as a domain administrator at Giersleben, in the Duchy of Anhalt. "This I greatly enjoyed," he later said, "for I am greatly attracted to country life."[3]

But it was now 1917, the Great War had been raging for three years, and whatever their place of birth or residence, the Kerstens were recognised as German citizens. As a result, the Russian authorities had exiled Friedrich and Olga Kersten to Kazakhstan as early as 1914, and the German army proceeded to draft their son in the autumn of 1917. But Felix Kersten was not sent to the trenches of France or the battlefields of the Balkans; according to his military service certificate, he was first recruited into the 8th reserve battalion of Infantry Regiment 93, then, on November 22, 1917, into the 3rd reserve machine gun company stationed at

i   A Finno-Ugric language mainly spoken around St Petersburg.

Halle. In September 1918, he was sent to Estonia, where he was demobilised one month after the end of the Great War.

Yet, at that time, there was another war going on: having expelled the Red Army from her territory at the end of 1918, Finland sent two regiments of volunteers southwards early the next year to join in the liberation of the Baltic countries: the 1st Finnish Independent Group and the Pohjanpojad Regiment[ii] under Lieutenant-Colonel Kalm. Kersten chose to join the latter force; now aged twenty, he was a tall, stout and sturdy lad, with more than a year of German military training. He was therefore appointed sergeant, and at Paju, on January 31, 1919, he took part in the first great battle against the Latvian riflemen of the Red Army; he then joined in the liberation of his birthplace, Yourieff, soon to regain her ancient name of Dorpat. The Finns and their Estonian allies making up for their numerical inferiority by a superior mobility, much of the fighting was done on horseback, and Sergeant Kersten invented a device that allowed light machine guns to be mounted on horses.[4]

Yet Kersten was not to see the end of the Estonian liberation campaign; in the course of a particularly fierce encounter, he was forced to lie in a swamp for a whole day and night, which left both his legs paralysed by acute rheumatoid arthritis. What followed is best narrated by Kersten himself: "I was therefore directed to a military hospital in Helsinki; having served in the Finnish army, I had acquired Finnish nationality,[iii] and it was therefore on crutches

ii   Literally "The Lads of the North" or "The Lads of Bothnia".
iii  This is not quite clear: in a memorandum written on September 30, 1945, Kersten was to state that he had acquired Finnish nationality in 1920 – which seems more plausible.

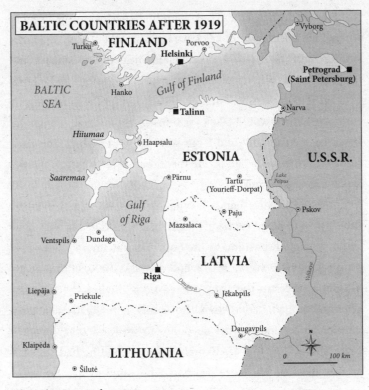

**BALTIC COUNTRIES AFTER 1919**

FINLAND

Turku

Porvoo

Helsinki

Vyborg

Petrograd
(Saint Petersburg)

BALTIC
SEA

Hanko

Gulf of Finland

Hiiumaa

Haapsalu

Talinn

Narva

ESTONIA

U.S.S.R.

Saaremaa

Pärnu

Tartu
(Yourieff-Dorpat)

Lake
Peipus

Gulf
of Riga

Paju

Mazsalaca

Pskov

Ventspils

Dundaga

LATVIA

Riga

Daugava

Liepāja

Priekule

Jēkabpils

Velikaya

Daugavpils

Klaipėda

LITHUANIA

N

Šilutė

0          100 km

*The Baltic States after 1919*

that I joined my new fatherland. For months I remained in hospital, where I felt bored as only a sick person can feel bored. [. . .] When my strength returned, I occasionally helped Dr Ekman, the hospital's senior physician, during his massage sessions. In Finland, massage therapy was held in high regard, and for the most difficult cases, Dr Ekman would take over himself. On my first attempt, he observed me carefully, and I can still hear him saying: 'You have real treasure in your hands.' He therefore offered to teach me the art of massage therapy."[5]

"Treasure in your hands"? What Dr Ekman's expert eye had detected were powerful hands, extremely sensitive fingertips and an obvious predisposition to use both. Here at any rate were new prospects for this young man who did not know what to do with his life: a career in the army offered no attraction, the Estonian government had nationalised the family homesteads just after independence, and he had no desire to work on other people's lands. Besides, he told Dr Ekman that as a child he had seen his mother massage and cure peasants who came to her for assistance – and his mother had confided that her own mother had done likewise. The doctor answered: "There, you see: it runs in the family! Pick up your crutches and follow me to the polyclinic; I'll give you your first lesson there, in the presence of patients."[6]

From then on, Kersten began to learn his craft, while assisting the medical officers who attended to Finnish soldiers wounded during the campaign. He had a definite gift for the exercise, since within a month the soldiers were asking to be treated by him rather than by the professional practitioners! And when Dr Ekman introduced him to his colleague Dr Colander – an authority in his field – the latter was sufficiently impressed to take Kersten on as a pupil. The chronology then becomes somewhat muddled, since by December 1919, Kersten was back on active service, first as master sergeant in the Tavastland cavalry regiment, then in the national guard at Ikaalinen, in Northern Satakunta province.[7] Granted, this was not far from Helsinki, but between 1920 and 1921, medicine could hardly have been the young officer's major concern . . .[iv]

By January 1922, however, Kersten had resigned from the army, and though he now had more time to devote to medical studies, he also had to provide for his subsistence; he thus worked successively as longshoreman, waiter, dishwasher and house cleaner: "Come evening, in my little room, I was to be found bent over my books – which were mainly on anatomy. For two whole years, I strove to acquire as much knowledge as possible, all the time performing my practical training with Dr Colander."[8] An effort that clearly paid off, since in 1921 he duly obtained an official diploma in "scientific massage". But the very next year, his professor advised him to go hone his skills in Berlin, where the practice was even more advanced.

It was clearly inadvisable to arrive destitute in the Berlin of 1922, whose inhabitants had hardly recovered from the four years of the Great War, the two years of revolutionary agitation that followed and the runaway inflation that had raged ever since. Our young student therefore had to accept more odd jobs: dishwasher again, film extra and even interpreter for Finnish businessmen visiting Berlin. Accommodation was no problem, however, for an old friend of his parents, the widow of Professor Lüben, resided in

iv   Kersten himself was to shed precious little light on these two years of his life, which later gave rise to some of the most outlandish conspiracy theories (see Bibliography, p. 406).

Berlin with her daughter Elizabeth; the latter, twelve years older than Felix Kersten, was a most dedicated woman, and this was the beginning of a lifelong friendship; Kersten was to refer to her as a sister or as a mother, adding that he could never have made his way in life without her.

Meanwhile, Kersten assiduously pursued his training, attending courses at medical school in Berlin and simultaneously following the practical teachings of the renowned physicians who had been recommended to him: Professor Binswanger from Leipzig; Dr Cornelius, a specialist in neuralgic points massage, and Professor Bier, a highly regarded Swiss vascular surgeon. In fact, it was at the latter's home that Kersten met someone who was to have a lifelong influence on him; Professor Bier introduced him to one Dr Kô, a diminutive East Asian of respectable age and remarkable background: born in China, he had been educated from the age of seven in a Tibetan monastery as a novice, then as a monk and finally as a lama, with fourteen years of instruction in Chinese and Tibetan medical sciences. Aged twenty-one, he was sent to Britain in order to study Western medicine; he enrolled in medical school in London, and, after graduation, opened a medical practice in the capital; his reputation having travelled far and wide, he was invited to come and practise in Berlin after the war.

Duly intimidated, Felix Kersten shared his own far more limited medical background, but Dr Kô, clearly interested in his case, invited him to his modest flat in the Ansbacherstrasse. There, he undressed and asked him to demonstrate what his masters had taught him. Kersten having surpassed himself, the little doctor got dressed without a word, made some tea and eventually said with a smile: "My young friend, you know nothing yet – nothing at all. But I have been expecting you for thirty years. [. . .] According to my horoscope, drawn up in Tibet when I was but a novice, I was to meet this very year a young man who knew nothing and to whom I would have to teach everything. I propose that you become my disciple."[v][9]

Thus it was that Felix Kersten became a disciple of Dr Kô, while simultaneously attending lectures at medical school and doing odd jobs to ensure his subsistence. For three years, between 1922 and 1925, he observed the master's technique, became his assistant, witnessed cures that seemed well-nigh miraculous, and was initiated into a science that went far beyond simple massage. Much later, he was to explain the fundamental principles of a practice he named "manual therapy" or "physioneural therapy": "It is about the treatment and maintenance of nervous tissue by adequate manual pressure. [. . .] One could almost speak of an in-depth nervous therapy, inasmuch as the skin, the subcutaneous tissue and the muscle tissue, with their blood vessels and their nerves, are grasped and stretched. [. . .] Most indispositions due to a restricted blood flow – with resulting congestions and insufficient nutriment of the nerves and other tissues – [. . .] are specific indications for physioneural therapy. From a biological point of view, there is a close relationship between the blood flow and the nervous system. Circulatory disturbances may trigger headaches, migraines and peripheral pain symptoms: neuralgia, neuritis and nervous disorders in the functions of internal organs, such as cardiovascular diseases, digestive complaints, etc., as well as psychic disorders

v   The versions of Kersten's confessor, Achim Besgen, and of Joseph Kessel published the same year coincide very closely. Admittedly, Kersten told them the story at about the same time, shortly before his death.

possibly leading to deep neurosis. Conversely, psychophysical manifestations such as agitation, fear, worries, overwork and depression exert a constant and often noxious effect on the vaso-motor activity of blood vessels, and thereby on blood flow, metabolism, digestion and internal secretion."[10]

In other words, in order to relieve the main organs – heart, liver, stomach, lungs, kidneys and even brain – one must drain, by means of pressure, kneading, stretching and sliding with the hand's palm and fingers, all the deposits and congestions of the circulatory system obstructing the supply of fresh blood – and thus of oxygen – to the nervous and subcutaneous tissues. By no means did Kersten claim that such a therapy could cure everything; on the contrary, he observed that it was strictly counter-indicated in cases of major inflammation, tumour formation, heart failure or advanced atherosclerosis.[11] But of course, the range of illnesses arising from nervous and circulatory disorders was broad enough for numerous patients to be relieved almost miraculously by Kersten's treatment. All the more so as Dr Kô's assistant had a remarkably sensitive touch, allowing him to localise in the depths of the abdomen all densifications, congestions, nodules and adhe-sions that were at once his cues and his main targets. Over time, he was to progress still further, until he was able to say that with fingers alone, eyes closed, he could "see" the entirety of a patient's neural pathways.[12]

This called for an exceptional degree of concentration – obvi-ously acquired under the guidance of Dr Kô. Kersten was to speak of "a degree of concentration so extraordinary that it could almost be compared to the state of trance attained by some Indian yogis". Such concentration was indeed at the heart of his old master's teachings, featuring various aspects of Tibetan, Chinese and Indian medicine and centred on the meridians, the twelve pulses and the 761 (main) acupuncture points. The teaching also included breathing exercises, training in meditation and an almost total degree of asceticism, without which the required degree of concentration could never be attained: no tobacco, no alcohol, no stimulant of any kind, and strict observance of rest hours in order to conserve energy.[vi] And then there was the whole initiatory component – the most difficult to grasp for a Western mind: the relation of body and mind to the cosmos, the invisible nervous system, the doctrine of Three Principles with its therapeutic implications – so many elements that Kersten was to remember as "infinitely problematic" – while adding that they opened before him "the way of truth".[13]

Felix Kersten would no doubt have long pursued a hectic life divided between initiatory journey, therapeutic sessions, medical school lessons, odd jobs for survival and gallant adventures, had it not been for that morning in the autumn of 1925 when Dr Kô told him that he was about to depart. According to what Kersten told Joseph Kessel in confidence, the master took his leave in the following terms: "Tomorrow, I shall return to my monastery. I must begin to prepare for my death, as I have only eight more years to live. [. . .] The date appeared in my horoscope long ago."[14] After which the old master assured an incredulous Kersten that he now had all the knowledge required to take over his practice and his patients.

vi   Nonetheless, sexual abstinence was not recommended – the master himself setting an example. But to Kersten's astonishment, he only set his sights on South-East Asian women – no doubt a matter of taste rather than religious prescription. Kersten seems to have been more eclectic in his choices.

All this may seem strange to a Western mind, but it should be remembered that astrology as conceived in Tibet, Nepal and Bhutan is regarded as a science on a par with astronomy, and has but a distant connection with the kind of commercial astrology practised in the West. Be that as it may, Kersten's life was thus transformed overnight: "When in 1925 Dr Kô went back to China,[vii] I took over part of his practice. From then on, I was provisionally free from financial anxieties. Many of my patients were quite well-off, and soon came an influx of new ones, from the leading circles of industry."[15]

At the age of twenty-seven, for the first time in his life, Felix Kersten thus began to earn a decent income – more than decent, actually, since it allowed him to rent a spacious apartment on Rüdesheimer Platz, in the fashionable Berlin district of Wilmersdorf. There he also opened his practice, and the whole was managed by Elisabeth Lüben, his faithful "adoptive sister"; he also bought an expensive car and hired a chauffeur. All this was something of a revenge on five years of poverty, as well as an opportunity to discover some hitherto unfamiliar medical complaints: "I became acquainted with a new type of people, who suffered from various ailments caused by excessive physical and mental efforts. These could be called occupational diseases, resulting from a life of overwork. [. . .] Such men made economic success their life's goal. In fact, their motivation was no longer to make money, but rather to set up large businesses, "*Konzerne*", that would enable them to maintain and strengthen their economic power. [. . .] One might say that their human feelings were repressed by something of a power complex. When coming to see me, they sought

vii  Which is literally correct, as Tibet was already under Chinese sovereignty at the time.

24

neither assistance nor relief, but only wanted to recover their physical strength in order to wield more power."[16]

Actually, such "occupational diseases" usually occur in the form of chronic migraines, abdominal or chest pain, neuralgia, circulatory disorders, rheumatism, sciatica, tachycardia, severe insomnia, impotence, dizziness and generalised exhaustion. As all these symptoms pertained *par excellence* to Kersten's field of competence, he undertook to treat patients who were at the height of their power but were consumed by ambition, crushed by responsibilities, exhausted by overwork – and abandoned by their doctors. Among them: Carl Bosch, administrator of I.G. Farben; August Rosterg, managing director of Wintershall Konzern;[viii] August Diehn, head of Kalisyndikat – the potash syndicate; Carl Friedrich von Siemens, chairman of Siemens & Halske electrical engineering company; Gustav Knepper, director of Gelsenkirchener Mining Society; and Friedrich Flick, all-powerful boss of the main German coal and steel conglomerate.

Where the best physicians had failed, the Finnish masseur and disciple of Dr Kô succeeded brilliantly: in a few weeks, a few months at most, all these men were freed from their ailments – temporarily at least, since they often fell back on the habits that had caused their overexertion in the first place. But that was precisely what made their saviour indispensable, for they could always come back to him for renewed treatment. Hence Kersten's fame spread by word of mouth: within the business community, these influential men boasted of their return to health and whispered the address of the practice on Rüdesheimer Platz – which saw a renewed influx of well-off patients.

viii   Specialised in the exploitation of potash, oil and gas deposits.

Kersten's reputation was soon to extend beyond the German borders. After benefiting from his care, Grand Duke Adolf Friedrich von Mecklenburg-Schwerin recommended him to his brother Prince Hendrick, who was the husband of Queen Wilhelmina of the Netherlands. The prince suffered from congestive heart failure, and his doctors had given him a life expectancy of six months at best; since then, Prince Hendrick, overwhelmed by pain, had been prostrate in his palace. In the spring of 1928, Kersten examined him in The Hague, and although aware of the gravity of his condition, he agreed to treat him. A letter sent by the prince to his benefactor on October 27 of that year gives an idea of the results obtained: "I wish to thank you for the miraculous results of your arts of manual therapy. [. . .] I am now entirely free from all the nervous pains that tormented me."[17] Prince Hendrick, though considerably overweight and prone to a somewhat dissolute way of life, went on to live pain-free for another six years – which indeed verged on the miraculous! Thereupon, a grateful royal court invited Kersten to come and settle in the Netherlands.[ix]

This he did towards the end of 1928, opening a medical practice in Scheveningen, an affluent district of The Hague – after which the address of 18 Badhuisweg[x] soon became famous within the upper circles of Dutch finance, industry, politics, diplomacy and aristocracy. Just as in Germany, most of his new patients showed characteristic symptoms of overexertion: too many responsibilities, too many business meetings, too much tobacco, too much

ix    As both the Germans and the Dutch used "Holland" and "the Netherlands" indiscriminately, the same practice will be followed here. Likewise, the translation of documents will respect the German wartime habit of saying and writing "England" and "English" for "Britain" and "British".

x    "Path of the public baths" – Scheveningen being a seaside resort.

alcohol, too many social gatherings in the evening, too little rest at night . . . Ever since 1925, Kersten had become something of an expert in this field, and the results he obtained were little short of amazing. "Relieving them of their ailments made me a happy man,"[18] he was later to say. With a course of treatment lasting between two and three months, he could only treat eight patients simultaneously – approximately forty per year. The fees he charged well-off patients were high, but the poorer ones recommended to him he treated for free. One of his wealthiest patients, J.L. Doedes, head of the Dutch Concrete company, was later to remember that "Kersten refused to take charge of patients he had no hope of curing, though he could have made much money thereby. But in one case, he spent several Sundays treating a friend of mine who was destitute."[19]

Not that his German patients were neglected, for Kersten had kept his practice on Rüdesheimer Platz, to which he duly returned each year from January to April; after that, he spent six months in The Hague and the rest of the year in Switzerland, Italy, Austria or the Riviera – without ever failing to visit his parents in Estonia. In The Hague, his patients came from the Dutch East Indies, the United States, France and Great Britain. For Kersten, who was *persona gratissima* at the Royal Palace, dined at the most exclusive tables and left few ladies indifferent,[xi] these were years of unalloyed happiness: "I felt a very strong bond with the Dutch people, I learned their language[xii] and I soon felt at home in their country. [. . .] Holland was for me something of a revelation. The landscape

xi   Including Queen Mary of Romania, which did much to enhance his reputation as a ladies' man.
xii   At least he tried – though he never quite succeeded.

attracted me, the circle of my patients widened constantly, and financial worries were a thing of the past."[20]

Yet dark clouds were gathering over Germany: in January 1933, after four years of political agitation, President Hindenburg finally agreed to call for Adolf Hitler, and from then on, the new chancellor proceeded to destroy his political opponents, suppress civil liberties, annihilate opposition, stifle the Länder, eliminate the trade unions, bring the churches to heel, muzzle the Reichstag and set up a ferocious police state. By the summer of 1934, the death of President Hindenburg and the elimination of the top S.A. leaders[xiii] made Hitler the sole master of Germany.

As a Finnish citizen and Dutch resident, Felix Kersten was hardly affected by these political upheavals, though rather more so by their economic consequences: indeed, as the Reichsmarks he had received from his patients for the past nine years were no longer exchangeable and could only be used in Germany, Kersten decided to invest them in the purchase of a domain seventy-six kilometres north of Berlin: the estate of Hartzwalde. "Thus materialised a long-standing desire to have a piece of land that would be my very own, and where I could spend my leisure time far from the crowd, with all its din and turmoil. Besides, it offered an opportunity to revert to my initial training in my father's craft. The house being somewhat dilapidated, I had it entirely rebuilt, with the addition of electricity, running water and telephone. [. . .] And just as when I was in Berlin, I longed to be back in Holland, when I was in Holland, I impatiently looked forward to spending my holidays at Hartzwalde."[21]

---

xiii  And particularly their chief, Ernst Roehm, in the wake of the Night of the Long Knives.

*Hartzwalde*

Soon came a time when he no longer went there alone; for in February 1937, at the house of friends, he had met Irmgard Neuschäffer; she was the daughter of the forest warden of the Grand Duke of Hesse, and the wedding took place in Darmstadt four months later. From then on, the new Mrs Kersten was to follow her husband in his commute between Berlin, Hartzwalde and The Hague, and would bear him a son one year later.

In Berlin, as in The Hague, the success of Kersten's treatments continued unabated: doctors who treat are readily found, but doctors who heal are always in demand. Moreover, it happened more than once that some renowned professor of medicine would refer a patient he could not cure to this humble practitioner in Finnish massage; and when that patient was relieved or healed by Felix Kersten, he seldom failed to let it be known. Thus it was that one of his German patients, Count Wilhelm von Hochberg, introduced him to the wife of the Italian ambassador to Berlin, Elisabeth Cerruti, who was suffering from myocardial ischaemia. After a prolonged treatment, Kersten succeeded in healing her, after which she lost no time in recommending him to a noble compatriot, the Duke of Spoleto, Prince of Savoy-Aosta and cousin of King Victor-Emmanuel III of Italy. The duke's medical case was a delicate one: a motorboat accident had left him with a quadruple fracture of the right leg, complicated by a deep vein thrombosis – to such an extent that the best doctors in Paris had prescribed amputation. But upon the recommendation of Elizabeth Cerruti, the duke consulted Felix Kersten, who declared after auscultation that he could spare him an amputation.[xiv] Sure enough, the duke of Spoleto

xiv   It is noteworthy that, just as in the case of Elizabeth Cerruti, this was a problem of insufficient oxygenation of the tissues, resulting from obstruction or congestion

was able to walk with a cane three months later, and was completely healed after six months! Thus was Kersten to enjoy a highly flattering reputation in Italian high society as well.[22]

Although this magician in the art of deep massage displayed little interest in politics, he could hardly fail to see the dark war clouds gathering over Europe after 1937: Germany was rearming at breakneck speed and bringing increasing pressure to bear on Austria and Czechoslovakia; the Reich's diplomatic rapprochement with Italy and its intervention in the Spanish Civil War were clear harbingers of the great confrontations to come, and the Führer's henchmen – Goebbels, Göring, Ribbentrop, Hess, Rosenberg and Himmler – seemed to be competing in bellicose rhetoric. In the spring of that year, General Willem Roëll, commander-in-chief of the Dutch army – whose son had been saved by Kersten after his doctors had given him up – appeared in person at 18 Badhuisweg and went straight to the point: "Listen, Kersten, you have high-level connections in Germany. Try to get close to the highest Nazi dignitaries. We must know what they intend to do. One of these days, they are going to attack us. We know precious little, for none of our people have succeeded in approaching them."[23]

General Röell apparently thought that Kersten was looking after high dignitaries of the regime – which the latter promptly denied: his German patients were almost all businessmen and magnates in the fields of finance, chemistry, iron and steel, mining, automobiles, aeronautics and shipping. These business moguls were forced to hide their views in public, but before a complacent ear, in the secrecy of the practice on the corner of Rüdesheimer Platz, most

of the circulatory system – a perfect indication for the kind of "manual therapy" practised by Felix Kersten.

31

of them concealed nothing of their hatred for the criminal and corrupt character of Hitler's regime.[xv] Which is why, while promising General Roëll that he would do his best all the same,[24] Kersten doubted that he would ever be able to give him satisfaction. Yet in history, just as in life, the most unexpected is usually the most likely to happen . . .

---

xv  Many of them had supported Hitler financially before his rise to power – and became disillusioned soon thereafter.

# 2

# ON A SLIPPERY SLOPE

By early 1939, the international situation had considerably deteriorated by dint of the latest initiatives of Nazi Germany: Austria and Sudetenland had been absorbed by the Reich, and it was clearly understood in every European chancellery that the invasion of the rest of Czechoslovakia was only a matter of time. In anticipation of his future conquests, Hitler had launched a huge rearmament programme that affected all sectors of the economy, while German society as a whole was gradually being brought under control: the Gauleiters, Reich governors in the Länder, were already acting as local satraps and lording it over their subjects; a centralised secret police had been set up, under the authority of a "Reichsführer S.S. and chief of the German police"; persecutions against the Jews rose apace and climaxed during the Kristallnacht of November 9, 1938; systematic harassment and imprisonment also targeted socialists, communists, religious orders, gypsies, homosexuals, Freemasons, intellectuals, the disabled and "antisocial elements", while almost every month saw the opening of a new internment camp: Sachsenhausen, Buchenwald, Flossenbürg, Neuengamme, Ravensbrück, Mauthausen – with the result that close to twenty thousand Germans had been imprisoned by late 1938.

None of this had escaped Felix Kersten, who was still commuting between his practices in The Hague and Berlin. In the German capital, his patients, most of whom had become faithful friends, told him all that was rumoured in the local business community: Joachim von Ribbentrop, the new foreign minister who was equally presumptuous and incompetent, seemed to be doing his best to draw the Führer into a war against England; Marshal Göring, the plump morphine addict in charge of the four-year plan, was seeking to control the whole of German industry on behalf of the general rearmament effort; Joseph Goebbels, venomous dwarf, fanatical orator and foremost Reich satyr, was the organiser of the regime's worst acts of violence, from the Reichstag fire to the infamous Kristallnacht; Robert Ley, supremely alcoholic head of the Arbeitsfront,[i] had made corruption into a high-yield industry. Yet Heinrich Himmler, the former agronomist and chicken farmer turned Reichsführer S.S. and chief of the German police, remained the most feared man in Germany – and rightly so: his 280 S.S. men had been the Führer's original security detail; his S.S. Leibstandarte,[ii] twenty times as numerous, had led the bloody 1934 purge known as the Night of the Long Knives; his Sicherheitsdienst,[iii] headed by the ruthless Reinhard Heydrich, tracked down all potential enemies of the regime; his Gestapo arrested and tortured them; detachments of his Sicherheitspolizei[iv] had just spearheaded the occupation of Austria and the Sudetenland; his Totenkopfverbände (Death's Head Units) guarded the concentration camp inmates and systematically abused them.

i   Labour front.
ii  Personal bodyguard.
iii  S.S. intelligence service, known by its initials S.D.
iv  Security police, abbreviated as Sipo.

Hence Felix Kersten's surprise and fright when in early 1939, the head of Wintershall Konzern, August Rosterg, one of his oldest patients and friends, asked him to examine Heinrich Himmler – and even, if possible, to treat him! The ageing magnate allegedly hoped that a man capable of alleviating the Reichsführer's ailments could also persuade him to abandon the project he had conceived with Ley and Göring of nationalising German heavy industry.[v] Kersten first baulked at the proposal: "Once drawn into this, I'll never get out!"[25] But August Rosterg could be quite persuasive, and the man with the golden hands eventually relented: he would accept an "invitation".

Thus it was that on the morning of March 10, 1939, Felix Kersten crossed the threshold of the building no ordinary citizen would have willingly entered: the Prinz-Albrecht Palais, residence of the notorious S.S. leader.[vi] One can easily imagine his state of mind when stepping into this lair, but Kersten was only to state: "I was highly sceptical when entering for the first time the abode of this feared and hated man, of whose bloody misdeeds I had heard countless whispered accounts."[26] Having passed the huge sentries in black uniform, the man with the burly figure and the gentle gaze was led to the top floor and shown into the antechamber of

v   This is Kersten's version, and it is clearly intended to avoid embarrassing Rosterg's family in the post-war years. The truth is more probably that Rosterg, who belonged to the Freundekreis Reichsführer S.S. (Circle of Friends of the Reichsführer S.S.), wanted to ingratiate himself with Himmler by introducing him to a skilled practitioner.

vi  Joseph Kessel depicted Kersten entering 8 Prinz-Albrecht-Strasse, and even "treading the ground above the cells where the Gestapo torturers were conducting merciless interrogations". However, No. 8 was only the Gestapo headquarters, whereas the Reichsführer S.S. had his office and residence in the palace at the corner of Prinz-Albrecht-Strasse and 102 Wilhelmstrasse.

Himmler's office. "In the room where I waited to be shown in, I had a look at the shelves, which were crammed with books. Apart from the ubiquitous *Mein Kampf* and the usual Nazi propaganda booklets, there were many history books [. . .] mainly dealing with the history of Germany and that of the Middle Ages. [. . .] Next to these, many books on Islam, biographies of Muhammad, and so on."[27]

Once led into Himmler's office, Kersten was in for another surprise: "I found myself in front of a man whose appearance in no way corresponded to the idea one generally had of a Reichsführer and chief of the secret police. Here was a little man[vii] who looked at me with a keen eye from under his pince-nez; one could almost say that there was something oriental in his round face and high cheekbones; he had nothing of the athlete. [. . .] My first impression: here was a nobody. [. . .] Looking at him, I could easily picture a schoolmaster[viii] – a pedantic one who would readily apply the cane. However, I could see nothing in him to recall the farmer, though he had previously been one. In fact, nothing in his appearance seemed to betray the slightest contact with nature. Here was obviously a pedantic and mystical figure who read a lot – a strange man, and a sick man."[28]

Indeed, Himmler began by listing his various illnesses: paratyphoid in infancy, two bouts of bacterial dysentery followed by jaundice, and a recent food poisoning with tainted fish from which he had not entirely recovered. But worst of all were the stomach

vii  Like Hitler and Göring, Himmler was 1.74 metres tall. But Kersten presumably sized him up relative to his own height (1.80 metres).
viii  A judicious appraisal: the son of Professor Gebhard Himmler always felt a strong urge to teach.

cramps that had tormented him ever since the Great War. These exhausted him and instilled in him a mortal fear of the cancer from which his father had died. He was being treated with injections and narcotics that no longer had any effect.[29] Himmler added: "I have heard of your miraculous cures. Do you think you can rid me of those recurrent abdominal pains that are plain agony to me? Herr Professor, do help me!" To which Kersten replied:

"I'm not a professor."

"But you're a great physician. I've heard of your abilities. What can you do for me?"

"We must see."[30]

Kersten asked him to remove his shirt and lie down on the long sofa facing the desk, after which he took his place behind the pallid body, with its drooping shoulders, weak muscles and nascent paunch. The therapist's stubby and extremely sensitive fingers brushed against the flaccid skin, followed the nerve pathways towards the heart, liver, kidneys and stomach, and occasionally pressed upon some densifications, drawing grunts and moans from the patient. The diagnosis was quickly established: "It was a dysfunction of the sympathetic nervous system; I immediately saw that this belonged to my field of competence, and that no-one else could help him."[31]

A quarter-hour of treatment followed, during which Kersten's fingers and palm sank into the patient's belly and reached through the skin, subcutaneous tissues and deep muscles to grasp and knead the nerve clusters. This drew some gasping and panting, a few cries of pain, but when the hand finally withdrew, an amazed Himmler realised that his stomach cramps had vanished. He muttered: "Your hands acted like a balm," followed by: "You can and must help me!" To which Kersten replied: "I shall try."[32] But he was later to note: "I promised him no miracle treatment. In fact, I didn't think I could heal him completely; I considered that I could relieve him of his pains periodically, but nothing more. Nonetheless, I thought it would be unreasonable to deny him my care."[33] Unreasonable, and above all terribly dangerous . . .

Actually, Himmler proposed that he remain entirely at his service, there and then offering to make him a colonel in the S.S. – which Kersten politely declined, on the grounds that he had many patients to treat in Berlin, and many more in The Hague, where he had his main residence.[34] But since he was to remain another fortnight in Berlin, he agreed to return daily in order to relieve the Reichsführer of his pains.

That treatment was to prove sporadic, since by March 15, 1939, Himmler was in Prague with the Führer, celebrating in Hradcany Castle their bloodless triumph over what remained of Czechoslovakia. Yet celebration was not the main item on Himmler's agenda: he had come first and foremost to supervise the action of his Security Police, who were entrusted with the widespread arrests of communists, Jews and German emigrants. Meanwhile, in Berlin, Kersten had gone to the Finnish embassy in order to inform his compatriots of the responsibilities he had just assumed – probably hoping to secure his recall to Finland as well. To his great surprise, Edvin Lundström, counsellor at the embassy, strongly encouraged him to pursue his activities in Berlin: Finland, being threatened by the Soviet Union, was in dire need of people with privileged access to the upper echelons of the German ruling elite.[35]

Back in The Hague on March 25, our physician turned Finnish intelligence agent visited some of his Dutch friends; one of them,

P.J. Schijf, was to state much later: "Kersten told me that he had accepted Himmler as a patient, then he added: 'The Nazis cannot be regarded as normal people.'"[36] To General Willem Roëll, at any rate, Felix Kersten was able to announce that he had kept his promise of getting close to one of the uppermost Nazi dignitaries – albeit highly unwillingly.[37]

On April 5, 1939, Kersten returned to look after the Reichsführer, this time in his villa at Gmund on the Tegernsee, south of Munich. The results obtained a month earlier having proved ephemeral, Himmler had begun once again to suffer, so his benefactor went back to work. In just two days, he was able to relieve him of his chest pains, until they disappeared almost entirely. Thereupon, Himmler addressed the delicate issue of remuneration: what fees did Kersten charge? The latter's reply seemed spontaneous: "Yes, yes, we'll settle that later."[38] Actually, he intended to charge him nothing at all. "Himmler was not rich; on an income of 24,000 marks per annum, he lived in fairly modest circumstances."[39] This was true enough: curious though it may seem, Himmler was one of those very rare non-corrupt dignitaries of the Third Reich, and his income was indeed paltry compared to that of such notorious swindlers as Ribbentrop, Goebbels and Göring.[ix] Besides, Kersten could afford to be magnanimous, as his German patients usually paid him 25,000 marks for a treatment of eight to ten weeks – slightly more than the Reichsführer's salary for a whole year – and he had at least forty patients a year. But Kersten, naturally, had other reasons: by not being paid, he retained a certain degree of independence from Himmler; conversely, in a country where

ix   The latter earned 10,000 marks a year officially, 700,000 marks unofficially, and at least double that in "gratifications" (bribes).

arbitrariness ruled supreme, the benevolence of a Reichsführer S.S. and chief of the police was worth far more than any remuneration, especially for someone who had a family and in-laws to protect.

By late April 1939, Kersten was back in The Hague. Once again, the treatment he had given Himmler had proved only marginally effective, which was hardly surprising in view of the highly peculiar lifestyle of this notorious predator, executioner, sycophant, bureaucrat, schemer and workaholic; he toiled sixteen hours a day, seldom exercised and never went to bed before 2 a.m. Even that was bound to worsen, for by early May, Himmler was frantically preparing for the great offensive soon to be launched against Poland. To be sure, his S.S. had a key role to play in the scheme, which involved simulating a Polish attack against the German transmitting station of Gleiwitz as a pretext for initiating hostilities.[x] Immediately thereafter, his Einsatzgruppen – the militarised political police – as well as three regiments of his Totenkopfverbände were to hunt down behind the front all "hostile elements", a fairly extensive concept that included communists, Freemasons, Jews, priests, intellectuals and aristocrats. Considering that Himmler had already been entrusted by the Führer with the future "creation of new territories for German settlement through population displacements" and that the Reichsführer S.S. was in almost permanent conflict with Goebbels, Göring, Rosenberg, Bormann, Ley, Darré and Ribbentrop – while living in permanent fear of displeasing his Führer – it stands to reason that his nervous disorders had little chance of lasting improvement.

x   Convicts dressed in Polish uniforms and pushed forward by S.S. officers duly attacked the transmitting station a few hours before the beginning of the September 1 offensive – and were subsequently executed one and all.

Sure enough, when on August 26 Kersten returned to Berlin from a journey to Estonia, he was called upon urgently to treat Himmler, whose stomach cramps had flared up again. Only after the second session did Kersten succeed in relieving him, and during a pause in the treatment, he alluded to the German–Soviet pact of August 23, and to the major troop concentrations he had noticed while passing through Königsberg and Stettin. Did this mean that war was about to break out? After some hesitation, Himmler admitted that the Reich was about to invade Poland, in order to punish "the English Jews" who had guaranteed the integrity of the Polish borders. Appalled at what he heard, Kersten argued that such an action would plunge the world into a global war, but Himmler scoffed at this: once again, England and France would not budge, and the whole affair would be over in ten days.[40]

On September 1, 1939, Hitler duly unleashed the invasion of Poland. Everything went according to plan, but then the unforeseen happened: on September 3, the French and British leaders, under pressure from their parliaments and public opinion, declared war on Germany. To Hitler, this came as an unpleasant surprise,[xi] but he managed to conceal it; indeed, when Kersten returned to treat Himmler on September 11, his patient appeared unruffled, and was as usual his master's voice:

"The England that declared war on us is not the decent England – it's the England of the English Jews. That is what reassures the Führer. But England is bound to suffer from this war; the Führer is firmly resolved to let the Luftwaffe raze city after city, until the decent elements in England understand where the Jews have led

xi   He had originally intended to open hostilities in the West between 1943 and 1945 – when his Wehrmacht was to be sufficiently armed and equipped for a world war.

# Der Reichsführer-ſſ

### und
## Chef der Deutschen Polizei
#### im Reichsministerium des Innern

Berlin SW 11, den 25. August 1939
Prinz Albrecht-Straße 8

Bestätigung

Der Massage-Therapeut und Landwirt, Herr Felix K e r s t e n ,
geboren 30.9.1898 zu Dorpat, ursprünglich deutscher, zurzeit
noch finnischer Staatsangehöriger, ist mir persönlich wohlbe-
kannt.

Ich bitte die Behörden, ihm behilflich zu sein und in jedem
Zweifelsfalle bei mir anzufragen.

Attestation délivrée à Felix Kersten le 25 août 1939 par le Reichsführer SS et chef de la police allemande.

« Le masseur-thérapeute et agriculteur Herr Felix Kersten, né le 30.9.1898 à Dorpat, Allemand d'ori-
gine et actuellement sujet finlandais, m'est bien connu personnellement. Je prie les autorités de-lui
porter assistance et de m'en référer en cas de doute.

Signé : Heinrich Himmler. »

*The pass issued by Himmler to Kersten*

their country. And when they call for an end to hostilities, they will be granted a generous peace in exchange for the delivery of all the Jews to Germany. This done, Germany will give England its rightful place in the world. The English belonging to the Germanic race, the Führer will treat them as brothers."

Kersten voiced some doubt in that respect; it could well be that the Führer underestimated the capacity and determination of the English people to defend their country.

"England has never lost a war, and she has all the necessary raw materials at her disposal."

Himmler guffawed.

"That will be of no use to her during this war, for the German submarines will sink all her supplies. Nothing will reach England, not even a mouse. As for the rest, the Luftwaffe will take care of it . . ."

Kersten mildly pointed out that it was always easier to start a war than to finish one, but Himmler pursued his monologue:

"First we'll strike down the external enemy, and after that we'll deal with the enemies within . . ."

"Tell me, who are the enemies within?" Kersten asked.

"All those large industrialists, the senior officers, the big landowners, the high-ranking civil servants and the academics. These we will deal with after the war. Heavy industry will be nationalised, just like large landholdings – and after that, Germany will be a good place to live in."

Kersten pointed out that this looked a lot like communism, but Himmler disagreed.

"No, no, absolutely not! Germany will never become communist. The Führer is against communism. But some aspects of it will be introduced if we deem them advantageous; we will remain national socialists, but include some components of capitalism – which the Russians do not have."[41]

In mid-September 1939, with Kersten back in Holland, Himmler and his evil genie Heydrich followed in the tracks of the Wehrmacht that was systematically crushing Polish military concentrations, surrounding Warsaw and reaching the Bug – where Soviet intervention on September 17 sealed the fate of the Polish army. Behind the front lines, the three S.S. Totenkopf regiments, the seven Einsatzgruppen of the Sipo-S.D. and the militarised Leibstandarte terrorised the population, burned down the synagogues and killed tens of thousands of Polish Jews, aristocrats, officers and intellectuals. Admiral Canaris, head of the Abwehr, loudly protested to his superior, General Keitel, but in vain: these were the Führer's orders, and Himmler was both the executor and the executioner of his dirtiest deeds.[xii]

Was Kersten aware of all this when on November 6, he joined in Berlin a Reichsführer who was obviously exhausted by his abdominal spasms? No-one knows, but it seems unlikely: on-the-spot liquidations were carried out in the utmost secrecy, and a stringent rule of silence prevailed among Himmler's entourage. On the other hand, Himmler told Kersten that Hitler would be in Munich on November 8 for the annual commemoration of the aborted 1923 coup attempt, and would deliver a major speech at the Bürgerbräukeller. Himmler therefore invited Kersten to join him in Munich for the occasion, and offered to secure him a seat in one

---

xii   But on orders from Admiral Canaris, the Abwehr discreetly removed to Romania and Switzerland a number of Catholic and Jewish Poles – including Chief Rabbi Joseph Isaac Schneerson.

of the front rows, so that he could fully appreciate the Führer's remarkable eloquence. Kersten agreed, but the next day, Himmler had changed his mind: "You're a foreigner and you're not a party member. You had better not come with me tomorrow."[42] Had Himmler learned of something important since the previous day? The fact remains that at one o'clock on the morning of November 9, upon returning to the Vier Jahreszeiten Hotel in Munich, Kersten heard the news that a bomb had exploded at the Bürgerbräukeller, in the immediate vicinity of the platform from which Hitler had been addressing the audience; the Führer had left thirteen minutes earlier with his staff after having cut short his speech, but there were seven fatalities among the party members seated in the front rows. Kersten learned nothing more at the time – he was only to understand five years later.[xiii] [43]

In the meantime, Felix Kersten was to have numerous opportunities to observe his peculiar patient, which enabled him to draw a few early conclusions: Himmler was basically a weak man who did his utmost to appear strong; a bureaucrat who dreamed of being an army officer; a puny creature who aspired to physical prowess; a swarthy, dark-eyed Bavarian who only admired blond, blue-eyed people; an indecisive character with a constant drive to action; a thug with the mindset of a school teacher and amateur

xiii   In December 1944, he overheard a conversation between S.S. officers from which he deduced that this bomb attack had in fact been organised by the Gestapo, in order to show the population that "Providence" was protecting the Führer. A short time later, he received confirmation from Himmler himself, who added that this "really brilliant idea" had originated with Joseph Goebbels. If true, this would validate the arguments of Pastor Niemöller and of the British prisoners Best and Stevens concerning a Gestapo manipulation of Georg Elser, who had carried out the bomb attack. The latter was held incommunicado until April 9, 1945, when he was executed at Dachau.

historian; a rabid anti-clerical activist fascinated by all sorts of religions – and above all, a man entirely under the devilish influence of Hitler. "Whenever Hitler was on the telephone," Kersten noted, "Himmler would begin to stammer, and he suddenly became an entirely different man: *'Ja – Ja – Ja – Jawohl, mein Führer, ganz meine Ansicht.*'[xiv] It took him at least half an hour to recover from the fact that he, Heinrich Himmler, had been called by the Führer, the greatest mind in the world."[44] This, of course, was just another contradiction: Himmler never did what he wanted to do, but only what he thought the Führer wanted him to do. Hence this preliminary diagnosis by his physician: "His severe abdominal convulsions were not, as he surmised, due to a frail constitution or an excess of work. They were rather the result of an entire life of contradictions and psychological tensions. Which is why I had realised early on that I could relieve his pains temporarily, and even help him for long periods, but that I would never be able to heal him completely."[45]

For hundreds of thousands of people, this was to prove an unadulterated blessing, but Kersten could not possibly know it at the time . . . By early December 1939, he was back in The Hague, where the atmosphere was thick with apprehension; for after the invasion and occupation of Poland, Holland and Belgium had come squarely into the line of fire: in late October, Major Sas, the Dutch military attaché in Berlin, was informed by his contact within the Abwehr, Colonel Oster,[xv] of "Instruction no. 6 for the conduct of the war", issued by the Führer on October 9, which included the following ominous passage: "In the northern sector of

xiv  "That is precisely my point of view." Kersten also observed that on such occasions, Himmler frequently stood at attention before the telephone.
xv  Head of Abwehr section Z (administration), Hans Oster was one of Admiral Canaris' closest deputies – and at the heart of the plot against Hitler within the Abwehr.

the western front, an offensive operation through the territories of Belgium, Luxembourg and Holland is to be prepared. This attack must be launched as quickly and as brutally as possible."[46] The Dutch general staff was therefore fully aware of German intentions, and when Kersten met his old friend General Roëll, he was told bluntly: "There is a possibility that we will be occupied by the Germans, but England and France will liberate us in the end. Meanwhile, you, being at Himmler's side, must strive to help Holland as much as possible."[47]

Kersten promised once again, but he had no idea at this juncture how he could possibly help Holland. Besides, this was not an issue in December 1939: due to bad weather, technical constraints and the reluctance of his generals,[xvi] Hitler was compelled to postpone his western offensive until the spring – the more so since he had other concerns: on his northern flank, a war had just broken out between Finland and the Soviet Union, while according to some sources, there was an imminent threat of British landings in Norway;[48] on top of that, Hitler had not fully digested his Polish conquest: the initial measures of expulsions and resettlement between the Warthegau and the General Government[xvii] tended to overlap, get in each other's way and end up in stalemate. Matters were only made worse by turf wars between Himmler, who had on October 7 been appointed "Reich Commissar for the strengthening

xvi   And of Marshal Göring.
xvii   The Warthegau, a vast region extending from Poznan (Posen) to Lodz (Litzmannstadt), was supposed to be incorporated into the Reich, while Polish and Jewish populations would be expelled towards the regions of Lublin and Warsaw, in the General Government. Simultaneously, Germans from the Reich were to settle in the Warthegau. But in both cases, transport and housing capacities had proved sorely deficient.

of the German race", the minister of agriculture Walther Darré and the master of the four-year plan Hermann Göring. Last but not least, the continued exactions and arbitrary executions carried out by the S.S. Einsatzgruppen against the Jews and the Poles in the occupied regions caused clashes with the Wehrmacht and sparked renewed protest from such generals as von Bock, Petzel, Ulex and Blaskowitz.

In her strenuous but successful effort to contain the Red Army, Finland could count on the help of Kersten, who mobilised all his connections in Germany, Holland, France and Italy to obtain the necessary money, clothing, medication and materials – and did so with such success that his adoptive fatherland shortly thereafter bestowed upon him the title of Medizinalrat – in Finnish Lääkintöneuvos.[xviii] Of course, there was another less advertised reason for such a prestigious award, as Foreign Minister Henrik Ramsay later recalled: "Through his position with Himmler and Ribbentrop, Kersten could both acquire significant intelligence and exert a certain influence on their views and measures."[49] Both Heydrich and "Gestapo Müller" always suspected Kersten of being a British agent. They were wrong: he was a *Finnish* agent.

On December 21, 1939, Kersten went to spend the holiday season at Hartzwalde with his wife Irmgard and his 88-year-old father.[xix] Felix and his father shared a passion for agriculture and cattle breeding; the fields of the estate were modest in size, but the

---

xviii   Literally "Medical Councillor" – the highest honorary title that could be given to a physician in Finland. Conferred by the president of the Republic and ratified by Parliament, it had been granted only four times in the country's history.

xix   Who had been forced to leave Estonia, a country that was to be absorbed into the Soviet Union under the terms of the German–Soviet pact. His wife Olga had died in 1936.

wooded areas were immense and the family thoroughly enjoyed riding through them on horseback or by horse-drawn carriage. It felt good to live in a place so completely insulated from the turmoil of the world outside!

Yet back in Berlin, where the mood had become tense since the beginning of the war, Kersten's patients were more numerous than ever, and among them was the most impatient of all: Heinrich Himmler, who was periodically laid low by his abdominal pains. Of course, the Reichsführer's stomach cramps were something of a state secret, so that even his immediate subordinates were left in the dark as to the reason for the presence at headquarters of this eccentric civilian with his easy-going attitude, his bulky frame and his strong Baltic accent. Mystery breeds mistrust and mistrust can easily arouse hatred – which was especially true of the formidable chief of the R.S.H.A.,[xx] Reinhard Heydrich, and of the head of its section IV, the sinister "Gestapo Müller". But fortunately for Kersten, their subservience to the Reichsführer was commensurate to the Reichsführer's subservience to Hitler . . .

At any rate, these therapeutic care sessions remained for Kersten unique opportunities of political edification and psychological observation. To Himmler, on the other hand, they provided both a physical salvation and an emotional outlet; he had always felt a strong urge to pontificate, and was delighted to have an interlocutor coming from outside his usual circle of cronies, which was

xx  The R.S.H.A. or Reichssicherheitshauptamt (Central Office for Reich Security) included from the autumn of 1939 the Gestapo (Amt IV), the Kripo (criminal police, Amt V), the S.D. Inland (counterespionage, Amt III) and the S.D. Ausland (foreign intelligence, Amt VI).

characterised by distrust, careerism and denunciations. In addition, as so often in relations between a doctor and his patient, the relief induced by his benefactor's treatment encouraged him to indulge in confidences. The session of February 6, 1940 seems typical in that respect. Once again, Himmler broached the topic of England, which clearly remained a subject of concern for Germans during the ongoing "phoney war" that threatened to last forever. "Today," noted Kersten, "Himmler was in excellent humour. He told me that the Führer had received very favourable news concerning the current state of mind of the British people, namely that they did not want war, and everything pointed to the fact that England was about to make peace proposals. These would certainly not be rejected, but on the contrary would be greeted by us as an expression of great Germanic solidarity. 'The Führer will be magnanimous in his treatment of England. Germany has no intention of undermining England's position as a great power. Quite the reverse, England must be one of the pivots of this Germanic Europe. [. . .] A conflict between the two peoples cannot be justified from a great Germanic point of view. There is enough room in the world for the two peoples to live together in peace. The advantages of such a cooperation are obvious: Germany can protect England with her land forces and safeguard her colonial possessions, whereas England can afford Germany the protection of her powerful fleet. Together, they form a block capable of resisting any attack and of extending their rule into the very heart of Europe.'"[xxi] Having noted these words, Kersten commented: "I would have liked to shake this frail ideological construction

xxi  These are almost word for word the views of the resolutely anglophile Adolf Hitler – which Himmler probably heard dozens of times.

somewhat, but Himmler had hardly any time left, and he was frequently interrupted during the treatment."[50]

All the same, no argument was likely to undermine the conviction of this fanatical patient under powerful Hitlerian influence – as evidenced by the next day's session, when he concluded: "*Mein lieber Herr Kersten*, you will see that Adolf Hitler, Führer of the greatest Germanic land power, will be received on the occasion of an official visit to London by the king of England, Führer of the great Germanic maritime power; and as equal partners, they will forge a just peace to protect the Germanic race throughout the world."[51]

Apparently disregarding the call of the Germanic race, the British were just then waging a merciless war on German submarines and surface raiders, all the while reinforcing their expeditionary corps in northern France; moreover, April 1940 saw the first land, air and sea confrontation between the Franco-British forces and the Wehrmacht in central Norway. That month, Felix Kersten, having almost completed his cycle of treatments in Germany, was about to return to Holland, so on April 28, he submitted to Himmler's office the usual application for an exit visa. "Alright," said the Reichsführer, "go to Hartzwalde, and you'll be able to leave around May 1." The events to follow were thus recounted by Kersten himself: "That same evening, Himmler called me back on the phone and said: 'For technical reasons, I cannot give you that visa.' I naturally asked him what these technical reasons were, but he just answered that he did not want me to leave Hartzwalde during the following days. I argued that I was expected in Holland, but he replied: 'No, nothing doing.' I said: 'What do you mean, nothing doing? I'm a Finnish national, you cannot detain me.' Whereupon he retorted: 'You can be sure that Finland will not declare war on us on your account!' – and he hung up."[52]

Kersten was dumbfounded. "I was thus prevented from leaving my estate, nor could I contact the Finnish embassy to ask for help, since after this conversation with Himmler, my telephone line was cut off for twelve days. Finally, on May 10, my phone rang again: Himmler was inviting me to Berlin. I went there with mixed feelings. Himmler welcomed me most amicably and apologised politely for having caused me such inconvenience. He explained that unfortunately he had been unable to avoid it. 'The reason is,' he continued, 'that German troops entered Holland last night, in order to save her from the Jewish capitalists.' I could not therefore go back there and had to stay in Germany. He asked nothing more of me than to continue treating him; he was even willing to recruit me into the S.S., where I could start with the rank of Standartenführer.[xxii] I answered that, as a Finnish citizen, I had no intention of serving Germany, and I added that since I regarded Holland as my second homeland, I was deeply indignant at what had just happened. 'The best thing,' I concluded, 'is for me to leave for Finland with my family.' Himmler was extremely put out by this, and he shouted at me: 'Finland will soon be part of the great German Reich. For us, there are only two sorts of men, Germans and traitors. The English and the Dutch are now among the traitors."[53]

But Himmler had another card up his sleeve: "He assured me that he did not want to pressure me in any way, but he had received information about my in-laws that could prove dangerous for

xxii  Equivalent to a Wehrmacht Oberst (colonel).

them,[xxiii] and no-one could protect them better than I could – by continuing to look after him. I could thus ensure that nothing happened to them. It was patently clear what he meant by that."[54] It was indeed perfectly clear: sheer blackmail! Hence Kersten was forced to yield. "It dawned on me that I was henceforth under his thumb. The vagaries of war had chained me to the man who, apart from Hitler, was considered to be the most powerful and the most dangerous of them all."[55] Nothing could have been truer . . .

xxiii   Kersten's father-in-law, Chief Forest Warden Neuschäffer, was indeed known for his outspoken opposition to national socialism.

# 3

# THE FELIX NETWORK

Felix Kersten's state of mind during that fateful month of May 1940 can easily be imagined; being detained in Germany was distressing enough, but feeling fivefold stateless was perhaps worse still: the Holy Russia of his birth had been replaced by a savage dictatorship that was about to absorb the Estonia of his youth; Germany, his parents' original fatherland, was enslaved by a criminal and predatory regime; Finland, his adoptive country threatened by two dictatorships, had ordered him to remain in Germany; Holland, his country of choice, had just been overrun by the Hitlerian hordes; and now France, the country that had given him his Christian name and was so dear to his mother's heart, was invaded in turn and struggled to defend herself . . .

An appalling situation, but what could be done? Felix Kersten realised that he was effectively chained to Himmler when on May 15 the Reichsführer, who was about to leave for the combat zone, ordered him to get ready to accompany him: his services might be needed during the campaign. During the following weeks, therefore, Kersten was to live in Himmler's private train, stationed close to the Belgian border. That train, the "Sonderzug Heinrich",[i] though modest compared to Marshal Göring's mobile palace, was

i  "Special train Heinrich".

nonetheless quite impressive: coupled to the locomotive was a platform truck with a six-barrelled anti-aircraft gun, a freight car, Himmler's saloon carriage, an office carriage for the secretaries and assistants, two sleeping cars, a radio and telegraph wagon, a dining car, four more sleeping cars, a freight car for supplies and a second platform truck with a six-barrelled anti-aircraft gun to protect the rear. This long, mechanised headquarters was staffed by forty-eight officers and N.C.O.s, in addition to the main heads of S.D., Gestapo and S.S. Amt III (counterespionage).

For thirty-five days, the victory cries of all these men were to inform Kersten that the Germans had broken through at Sedan, occupied Amiens and Calais, then crossed the Seine; soon thereafter, that Italy had entered the war, while the Wehrmacht had reached the Loire and the Saone; then came the coup de grâce: the armistice of June 22. In the meantime, Kersten had been looking after Himmler, but also after Rudolf Hess, the Vertreter des Führers,[ii] who suffered from sharp abdominal pains – probably made worse by his wounds from the Great War, his overwork and his general frustration with life. On June 24, when both men had left the train to take up residence in Bad Godesberg, Kersten recorded the following: "I have been here for more than a week with Rudolf Hess in the Hotel Dreesen.[iii] Hess is very busy and excited about recent events – the French armistice – and suffering in consequence from severe stomach pains. Meanwhile he has been in Compiègne forest[iv] and came back yesterday. During the

ii  The Führer's deputy, entitled to represent him on all matters concerning the party.
iii  A hotel of sinister memory: Hitler had stayed there on June 29, 1934, just before flying to Munich in order to supervise the bloody purge of the Night of the Long Knives.
iv  The clearing of Rethondes, where the armistice was signed.

treatment, still charged with tension, he sketched to me the course of recent events, and spoke of the future, which he envisaged as an era of fruitful Franco-German cooperation." Kersten having asked him how England fitted into this optimistic scheme, Hess replied enthusiastically: "We'll make peace with England in the same way as with France. Only a few weeks back, the Führer again spoke of the great value of the British Empire in the world order. Germany and France must stand together with England against the enemy of Europe, Bolshevism. That was why the Führer allowed the English army to escape at Dunkirk. He did not want to compromise the possibility of an understanding.[v] The English must see that and seize their chance."[56]

Kersten appears to have felt some sympathy for the naivety and idealism of his rather strange patient: "In Hess, I encountered a man who was quiet, friendly and grateful. He frequently spoke of his home in Egypt, for which he longed.[vi] He often said that he would be happiest if he could retire to the loneliness of the Bavarian mountains. But he emphasised even more that he had only one wish: to meet a hero's death while flying.[vii] But the Führer had forbidden him to fly, so he was condemned to sit at his desk. Hess was a good and helpful person, very modest in his way of life. He was a vegetarian, surrounded himself with clairvoyants and astrologers, and despised official medical views. [. . .] Once, when

v  A representation of facts that was widely circulated at the time, in order to bolster the Führer's reputation of infallibility. Actually, the *Haltbefehl* (order to stop) given by Hitler to his divisions at the time was meant to enable the Luftwaffe to carry out its mission of preventing the British evacuation by sea – which it had been unable to accomplish.

vi  Rudolf Hess, born in Alexandria, had spent the first fourteen years of his life in Egypt, of which he had a fond memory.

vii  Hess was a virtuoso pilot.

headquarters were in Belgium and Hess had to go to an interview with Hitler, he asked me to accompany him. We drove through towns and villages which had been shelled during the recent heavy fighting. Later, Hess said to me with tears in his eyes that it was horrible to see these once flourishing areas so laid waste. The war should not last any longer. The world must come to see that Germany was unconquerable. And he, Hess, had to stretch out his hand, to bring about a reconciliation between Germany and the other nations. [. . .] Another time, he told me that he had to concentrate all his powers and harden himself – he needed all his strength for the deed that would secure the salvation of Germany. When I asked what he meant by this 'salvation', Hess replied that he could not tell me, but that he was preparing for an act of historic importance."[57] What exactly this act was meant to be, Kersten and the world were only to learn eleven months later . . .

Meanwhile, these five weeks of promiscuity with the occupants of "Special Train Heinrich" had enabled Kersten to get better acquainted with Himmler's entourage. It took him little time to ascertain the hostility of the senior officers towards him – beginning with Standartenführer S.S. Willy Suchanek, aide-de-camp for police matters, who was firmly committed to exposing the "English spy" Kersten, and hoped to be rewarded with a vast estate in the eastern territories if he succeeded; there was also Oberführer[viii] Horst Bender, expert in legal issues and notorious thug; Brigadeführer[ix] Oswald Pohl, head of the central S.S. office for economy and administration, and his deputy Richard Glücks – the two equally corrupt – not to mention the notorious "Gestapo

viii   Intermediate rank between colonel and brigadier.
ix   Brigadier.

Müller" and his superior, Gruppenführer[x] Reinhard Heydrich, for whom Kersten was quite simply the man to be killed at the earliest opportunity.

Yet among the lower ranking officers nearest to Himmler, Kersten did find some more decent characters, such as Sturmbannführer[xi] Josef "Sepp" Tiefenbacher, who commanded the convoy; Detective Kirrmayer, Himmler's bodyguard; Sturmbannführer Franz Lukas, his personal driver; and Untersturmführer[xii] Werner Grothmann, his young aide-de-camp. All these Bavarians were civilians in uniform with no interest in politics; they did their job routinely and without questioning, only looking forward to the end of the war, when they could at last go back home. Such men regarded with a mixture of sympathy and indifference that bizarre, bulky Finn in civilian garb, who was always ready to give medical assistance and seemed to enjoy the Reichsführer's special favour. And then there was Untersturmführer Rudolf Brandt, an apparently insignificant little man, but also a virtuoso stenographer and a doctor of law, who held the key position of private secretary to Heinrich Himmler. At the latter's request, Kersten treated Brandt in his carriage, and discovered in him a discreet, decent and obliging idealist who rejected all brutality and was in fact secretly opposed to both Hitler and Himmler.[58] During that bleak month of June 1940, a complicity was thus to develop between Kersten and Brandt, with far-reaching consequences . . .

On the evening of June 28, "Special Train Heinrich" was back

---

x   Major General. (All these ranks were conferred "for police purposes only", as distinct from those of the Waffen S.S.)
xi   Major.
xii   Second Lieutenant.

in Berlin, allowing Kersten to return to his practice on the Rüdesheimer Platz, and then to his Hartzwalde estate, which was more prosperous and extensive than ever. The height of bliss: his wife was expecting a second child in the month of August! But in the outside world, events were picking up momentum: between June and August, the Soviet Union occupied the Baltic countries, and 190,000 Estonians, Lithuanians and Latvians were deported or liquidated; in the west, after the failure of his peace offers to Great Britain, Hitler ordered the implementation of Operation Adler,[xiii] a massive air attack against England – the first stage of an invasion plan code-named Seelöwe.[xiv] Himmler expressed his confidence: the British would not fail to follow the French example by capitulating after the first serious bombings. Had not the Führer said so?

In mid-August 1940, as the Battle of Britain was just beginning, Felix Kersten was visited in Berlin by his friend August Rosterg; the industrialist had come to ask him to intercede on behalf of his foreman, an elderly social democrat recently arrested by the Gestapo and sent to a concentration camp. Nor was this the only case: that summer, Kersten had received several pleas to intercede, and he was at a loss as to what to do with them. But on August 26, Himmler had a new attack and his therapist was urgently summoned to the Prinz-Albrecht Palais. He succeeded fairly quickly in relieving the pains of the Reichsführer, who remained sprawled on the sofa, still panting and exuding gratitude. What followed is best told by his saviour: "I had in my pocket a list of five or

xiii   Operation Eagle.
xiv    Sea Lion.

six people, Germans[xv] and perhaps a Dutchman too. Himmler said: 'Listen, Kersten, we have never broached the financial aspect. I know that your services are very costly, of course, *aber zahlen muss ich* – I must pay.' I answered: 'You know, Reichsführer, I'm glad to help. You are in need, and I know that you cannot pay. Let's leave it at that. Let there be a friendship between us with no money matters attached.'[xvi] He then said: 'Thank you very much. You know, I have no friends; I am so lonely . . .' Then and there, the words came to me and I blurted out: 'Have a look at this, Herr Reichsführer,' and I showed him my list. He immediately exclaimed: '*Das darf ich nicht!* – I have no right to do that!', and I answered: 'But, Herr Reichsführer, between friends, many things are allowed. Just sign, then all will be settled!' And he signed."[59]

Was Kersten aware at the time that he had thus triggered an inexorable process? He did not say so, yet it is more than likely. Three days later, Himmler, having recovered both his health and his aggressiveness, bitterly blamed him for having kept his house in The Hague. Kersten agreed to move, provided he was allowed to supervise the relocation himself. Himmler was forced to consent, but he set some stringent conditions: immediate departure, only ten days' stay in The Hague, and an obligation to report every day at the office of Hanns Albin Rauter, Höhere S.S. und Polizeiführer[xvii] for the Netherlands. But shortly before departing for The Hague, Kersten obtained an exceptional favour, thanks to the

xv   Including his old friend the industrialist Friedrich Flick, suspected of working covertly for the Allies and about to be sent to a concentration camp with his wife.
xvi   Whether Kersten was to receive no payment for his services during the rest of the war is less than certain. Ribbentrop, for one, paid him handsomely; Hess and Ley certainly did likewise.
xvii   H.S.S.P.F. – Supreme S.S. and Police Commander.

assistance of Secretary Brandt: the possibility of receiving his mail at the Reichsführer's address: military postal sector 35 360, the only one in Germany that was entirely free of censorship.[xviii] [60] Now of course, Kersten would not have made such a request without an ulterior motive . . .

Once in The Hague with his wife on September 1, 1940, Kersten was struck by the atmosphere of desolation that pervaded the city; it had suffered very little from the bombings, but ten weeks of occupation had sufficed to transform it entirely: many shops were closed, access to the seafront was prohibited, the inhabitants hunkered down and the N.S.B.[xix] militiamen patrolled the empty streets. But news of the wonder doctor's return spread like wildfire, and during the next few days, some of his former patients discreetly returned to 18 Badhuisweg; they told Kersten of the first requisitions conducted by Reichskommissar Seyss-Inquart, the exclusion of Jews from public sector jobs, the arrests of opponents ordered by Polizeiführer Rauter and the imprisonment of General Roëll – one of the main heads of the resistance organisation Ordedienst, who thus faced a death sentence.

Kersten took note of these unfortunate events, but he did rather more than that, as later recalled by a young officer freshly returned from the Dutch East Indies, Jacobus Nieuwenhuis: "In September 1940, I contacted Mr Kersten. His name was known to me because my in-laws had been patients of his and had befriended him. My wife and I had therefore received an introduction to Mr Kersten,

xviii   It would appear that Brandt had obtained that favour by telling Himmler that Kersten wanted to receive letters from his Dutch mistresses unbeknown to his wife. The Reichsführer, who maintained a second family himself, had been understanding.
xix   The collaborationists of the Nationaal Socialistische Beweging in Nederland – the Dutch national socialist movement, headed by Anton Mussert.

as well as several presents for him. [. . .] We accordingly visited him several times and we eventually came to talk of the German occupation and its consequences. During one of these conversations, I told Kersten that I had been a member of the N.S.B. during my stay in India,[xx] but that, due to the turn of events, I had lost all interest in the movement, and after my return to Holland, I had no longer sought to contact them. [. . .] Mr Kersten gave us a glimpse of what Holland faced under German occupation, since he was quite familiar with Nazi policy. He told us among other things that he had been ordered to leave Holland and remain for the time being at his Hartzwalde estate, and also that he had been pressed into treating Himmler, as well as a few others."

Whereupon, no doubt after having discreetly sounded out his interlocutor,[xxi] Kersten got right to the point: "Then he told me that, if I or one of my friends and acquaintances were to have troubles with regard to the occupation, he could use his influence on Himmler in order to help us. During subsequent conversations, the idea emerged that we ought to organise and even extend that connection, by passing on to him any important fact that would come to my knowledge. From that point of view, Kersten reckoned that my having been a member of the N.S.B. could prove a valuable asset, since it would allow me to obtain information from within the movement. He therefore told me that I absolutely ought to remain a member of the N.S.B. Although I was sceptical at first, Kersten was able to convince me to follow his idea, adding that I could thereby achieve more than by staying quietly at home to

xx    The Dutch East Indies, now Indonesia.
xxi   Understandably so, when faced with a man who had formerly belonged to a national socialist movement.

await the end of the war. I thus promised to keep him regularly informed of any event that might affect the cause of Holland or of the Dutch, and he promised to use his influence to see that things evolved favourably. I was very strictly advised to tell no-one about my contact with him, and above all to always remain in the background – to be a member of the N.S.B. in name only. I was to write to him at the address of military postal sector 35 360, with the assurance that these letters would evade censorship."[61]

The intention was quite clear: Kersten's aim was not just to lend assistance – he also wanted to set up an intelligence service. Besides, how could one lend assistance without receiving intelligence? Actually, Jacobus Nieuwenhuis was by no means the only former patient to receive such a proposal: there was also the lawyer Reyes and Professor Schijf – who was to state eight years later: "All of Kersten's patients in whom he had confided would have gone through fire for his sake."[62] Yet the therapist's stay in The Hague was to be drastically curtailed: on the morning of the fifth day, a friend arrived breathless to warn him that the house of the antiquarian and auctioneer Bignell was being searched, and that his arrest was imminent. Now Bignell, who had sold some paintings to Kersten in the past, had become a close friend, and the news spurred him into action; he immediately made for Gestapo headquarters and asked to see Hanns Albin Rauter, the all-powerful head of the S.S. and police for occupied Netherlands. To this seven-foot giant glaring at him, Kersten quietly said: "I can vouch for Bignell's innocence. He did nothing against the Germans. Release him!" Rauter gasped in disbelief, but maintained enough composure to reply with a blunt refusal and some thinly veiled threats. Yet he remained speechless when Kersten calmly asked him to ring

Himmler; this was of course highly irregular, but in the snake pit of the Third Reich, only those with powerful connections could afford to speak with such impertinence. Somewhat taken aback, Rauter complied, and once the connection had been established, he was dumbfounded to hear the Reichsführer say: "Put me through to Kersten!" The latter informed him in a few words of his friend Bignell's arrest, adding that he could vouch for his innocence and was demanding his release. Fortune favours the bold: Himmler, beset anew by his abdominal pains, urged him to return to Berlin forthwith. But Kersten reminded him that he was allowed to stay five days more, and that if he returned without Bignell having been freed, his morale would be so affected that his treatments would become completely ineffectual.

This was the very first time Kersten resorted to such blackmail, and it proved remarkably effective. Himmler asked to speak to Rauter again; the latter took the receiver, listened in awe for a while, then replied obsequiously: "*Zu Befehl,*[xxii] Herr Reichsführer!" Having put down the telephone, he said to Kersten: "Himmler ordered me to release Bignell. I know that the man is a traitor, *aber Befehl ist Befehl* – but orders are orders."[63]

Felix Kersten had just made another formidable enemy, who would not fail to refer to his superior, Gruppenführer Reinhard Heydrich. But for now, our doctor turned attorney had won the day: his friend was released on the spot, he himself was able to leave The Hague without having completed his relocation, and he had just measured the extent of his power over the man who terrified Holland's chief executioner . . .

xxii   As you command! Actually, Bignell had probably been arrested for black marketeering rather than for activities connected with the resistance.

Back in Berlin, Kersten lost no time in using that power on behalf of his old friend and mentor Willem Roëll. Now the general's case was particularly serious: identified as a major figure in the underground movement, the former commander-in-chief of the Dutch army had just been sentenced to death. But Kersten, having harassed the ailing Reichsführer for several days, managed to wrest an inordinate concession from him: instead of being shot, the old general would be held prisoner, and then placed under house arrest![xxiii] That autumn, several Germans were also to benefit from Kersten's intervention – and so did at least one Dutchman, according to later testimony by officer Jacobus Nieuwenhuis: "As I had nothing special to do, being still on leave from the army, I enrolled in a course of studies at the Amsterdam Colonial Institute. I was thus almost immediately able to send Kersten an important piece of information: one fine day I heard it said that one of our main instructors, Professor Gerke, had been arrested. This I relayed forthwith to Kersten, who replied that he would deal with the matter, and that Professor Gerke would no doubt be back home soon. [. . .] Sure enough, the professor was set free shortly thereafter."[64]

In a letter sent to a friend after the war, Felix Kersten explained his *modus operandi*: "I could help people above all when Himmler was very ill. In such cases, he was defenceless [. . .] and easily influenced. I therefore had to come with my lists at the beginning of his attacks. At such times, he would sign just about anything that was laid before him. But once he had recovered, it was well-nigh impossible to have him sign anyone's release. [. . .] One could

xxiii  Since Himmler refused as a matter of principle to renege on his commitments, General Roëll was to remain unharmed until the end of the war. He died of old age in 1958.

obtain nothing from these Nazi dignitaries by logic or rationale –
on the contrary, it made them suspicious. The mentality of these
people had sunk to such depths that one felt separated from them
by a sheer abyss."[65]

Doubtless, but positive results could also be obtained by ex-
ploiting their inner feuds and hatreds; that autumn, for instance,
Kersten answered a call for help from weapons manufacturer Willy
Daugs, who had emigrated to Finland four years earlier:[xxiv] his
wife was under surveillance in Germany by Gestapo agents, who
had orders to arrest her as soon as she attempted to leave the
country. Kersten thereupon raised the matter with Foreign Minister von Ribbentrop, who jumped at the opportunity of playing
a nasty trick on his arch-rival Himmler – and promptly delivered
an exit visa to Frau Daugs![66] Subsequently, Kersten's exploitation
of the appalling relations between Himmler, Goebbels, Göring,
Rosenberg and Bormann enabled him to secure more than a few
near-miraculous releases . . .

That, however, was not the end of the matter, since once the
orders to release the prisoners had been obtained, Kersten also had
to make sure that they were carried out; for the junior S.S. officers
and N.C.O.s all too often answered: "It has not been possible
to locate the prisoner," or else: "The man is not detained here," or
even: "He is probably dead." In such cases, Kersten was compelled
to use bribes in order to "grease the wheels", and he was later to
note: "My rescue work cost me approximately 380,000 to 400,000
marks,[xxv] used to win over the Nazis by the distribution of presents

xxiv   Where he had become majority shareholder in the Finnish armaments
corporation Tikkakoski Oy.
xxv    About sixteen and a half times Himmler's annual salary . . .

in the form of gold cigarette cases, rings and diamond-set brooches, gold bracelets, gold watches and sometimes even silverware, radio sets, master paintings and stamp collections – all of them purchased on the black market. To be sure, Himmler, Brandt and Schellenberg[xxvi] were incorruptible, but all the others reached out for bribes."[67]

Kersten was simultaneously handling his other patients in Berlin, and their confidences, as well as the marked absence of the usual triumphalism in Himmler's statements, led him to suppose that Hitler had already abandoned his plans to invade the British Isles – which was indeed the case since mid-September. But two weeks later, that strategic failure was eclipsed by a diplomatic success: Germany, Japan and Italy solemnly signed the Tripartite Pact in Berlin.[xxvii] This was when Kersten met Count Galeazzo Ciano, the Italian foreign minister and Mussolini's son-in-law. Now it so happened that the count was a friend of Ambassador Cerruti, whose wife had benefited from Kersten's care, and an acquaintance of the Duke of Spoleto, who had benefited even more. Since both of them had lavished praise on the unique talents of the Finnish physiotherapist, Ciano, himself somewhat unwell, invited Kersten to the Italian embassy on September 29, two days after the signature of the Tripartite Pact. Kersten summed up his initial impressions of Count Ciano in the following words: "A handsome man, and perfectly aware of it. With his vivacious and exuberant temperament, he looked the typical Italian; the Germans thought so too and disliked him. [. . .] He was a great

xxvi   See below, p. 111.
xxvii   Whereby the three countries were committed to establishing a "new order" in Europe and Asia, and pledged mutual assistance in case of attack by a third power.

lover of French theatre and admirer of French culture in general. He spoke French well, English passably[xxviii] and German very badly. Count Ciano had been everywhere – either on his consulate's service or for his own pleasure. He knew Shanghai, New York and Rio; he knew Paris and London quite well . . . A conversation with him was like a waft of fresh air coming from the outside world."[68]

Meanwhile, Kersten had had the opportunity of examining his new patient and of presenting a preliminary diagnosis: "I concluded that I could help him, but that the cure would take a long time."[69] Thereupon, Ciano proposed that he settle in Rome for a while, and even promised to obtain him a chair at the university! Kersten having replied that for all intents and purposes, he was detained in Germany and could not leave the country even for a few days without Himmler's permission, Ciano undertook to settle the matter personally with the Reichsführer. Sure enough, diplomatic propriety on the morrow of the Tripartite Pact would have made it difficult to refuse this little service to Mussolini's son-in-law, so Kersten received permission to stay in Rome from November 27 to December 16. The sequel was thus remembered by press correspondent, S.S. officer and interpreter Eugen Dollmann, who had been asked by Himmler to look after Kersten's personal needs in Rome: "The miracle-worker arrived, plump and gentle as a Buddha, and was installed in ex-King Alfonso's suite at the Grand Hotel. I am quite sure the Bourbon monarch never had as many visitors. [. . .] Ciano was delighted with Kersten, whose drawing room in the Grand Hotel was soon crowded with

xxviii   An intriguing comment, coming from someone who spoke neither French nor English.

ladies from the golf club.[xxix] Kersten was discretion itself, so I never learned what they were all suffering from [. . .] He was far less interested in relics of the Ancient World than in sweet shop windows, which displayed treasures no longer obtainable in Hitler's Germany. Sweets and chocolates were Kersten's ruling passion, and it was not long before his patients were bringing him *pralinés* by the pound in the hope of keeping him sweet, both before and during treatment. These he would devour with evident satisfaction while his hapless victims waited for their next bout of torture. [. . .] He certainly caused me some pain during a nerve massage which only a masochist could have described as enjoyable [. . .]. However, he did save me from having to undergo a dangerous operation which had been recommended by a number of more conventional specialists, and I am eternally indebted to his skill and that of his great Chinese mentor."[70]

What followed was best told by the miracle-worker himself: "I stayed at the Grand Hotel, as a guest of the Italian government. I was thus able to continue my treatment of Count Ciano, who recommended me to other important people, including his friend Guido Buffarini, the interior minister; the latter was the very type of the burly Roman caesar, who distrusted the Nazis and was opposed to the policy of the Axis. He said that whichever way things went, it would turn out badly for Italy: if the Axis lost the war, Italy would be ruined; but if the Axis won it, Italy would be occupied by the Germans and ruined in another way. Nothing to win, everything to lose! For Italy, entering the war had been a mistake."[71]

xxix  The Acquasanta golf club, an unofficial annexe of the Palazzo Chigi, where Foreign Minister Ciano transacted most of his diplomatic business – and met most of his mistresses.

Kersten was more than mildly surprised to hear such words spoken by one of the main ministers of a government that had resolutely committed itself to support Germany two months earlier. But more was to come: "Ciano expressed himself more and more openly as my treatment relieved him, and he went even further: he harboured a deep distaste for the Nazi chiefs. [. . .] He told me one day that he considered national socialism to be a forgery of fascism – and even a very bad forgery. He did not believe in a German victory and regarded the Germans as barbarians, such as they had been described in Roman history. But he saw no possibility of breaking with Germany so long as his father-in-law Mussolini was in power.[xxx] He said that the latter was very much afraid of the Nazis, for they had set up a whole network of secret agents in Italy."[72]

Who, even among the best-connected diplomats, ever heard these two pillars of the regime express themselves so openly as early as November 1940? In Rome, a doctor – and a Finnish one to boot[xxxi] – clearly attracted sympathy, and even confidences. In fact, Kersten was to add: "I noticed among other high-ranking fascists the same distrust of the Third Reich; they appeared generally convinced that Hitler was an adventurer who had an unfortunate influence on Mussolini."[73] Of course, Kersten could not see beyond appearances, nor could he know that all these fascist leaders who privately vented their Germanophobia were simultaneously counting on Germany to supply them with raw materials

xxx   An interesting and little-known harbinger of what was to happen in July 1943, when Ciano voted in favour of Mussolini's destitution.
xxxi   Finnish resistance against Soviet aggression during the Winter War had made the Finns extremely popular in Italy.

and transport planes, in order to help them out of the disastrous situation into which they had blundered by attacking Greece.[xxxii] In this respect, Count Ciano was just as schizophrenic as all the others . . .[74]

Nevertheless, Kersten clearly enjoyed every minute of his stay in Rome: "On December 12, a few days before my departure, a farewell dinner was given in my honour, during which Ciano personally awarded me the Grand Cross of Commander of the Order of Mauritius and Lazare." Interpreter Eugen Dollmann described the after-dinner atmosphere as well: "The Buddha-like guest of honour devoured mountains of sweetmeats and entertained his malicious audience by gossiping, with my assistance, about the members of royal and princely houses whom he had treated, with special reference to the legendary meanness of the Dutch Queen Mother. He prudently skirted the subject of Himmler, but left us in no doubt as to the power he wielded over him. [. . .] Kersten left Rome *sans* cash but no poorer. Berlin had not forbidden him to accept presents, so his private suite became heaped with bolts of silk for shirts, framed photographs, items of male apparel, gift parcels from the ladies of the golf club, and box after box of his favourite chocolates and marrons glacés from Rosati's in the Via Veneto."[75]

But all good things must come to an end, and Kersten returned to Berlin on December 16. "I found the German capital rustling with rumours about a new front that would be opened somewhere

xxxii   Attacked on October 28, the Greeks pushed the Italians back into Albania, and at the time of Kersten's visit, the Italians were even struggling to maintain themselves in Albania. In addition, General Graziani's forces in Libya suffered a serious setback against the 8th British Army on December 10.

in the Balkans. There were important troop movements in that direction." Kersten, for one, had to deal with the home front: "Himmler's health was far from satisfactory on my return, and he complained bitterly about my prolonged absence. The news from Holland was bad, and through other channels I received frightful and depressing news about what was happening there. I therefore had to go back to work."[76]

Over the next few weeks, that work consisted mainly in treating the Reichsführer and in presenting him with lists of condemned individuals to be pardoned, released or placed under house arrest; he also had to complete his studies, for, incredible though it may seem, Kersten had attended during these two hectic years all the required courses at the medical school, and, having passed all the necessary examinations, he duly received on February 25, 1941 the official title of *Artzt für Naturheilkunde* – naturopathic physician.[77] But our newly qualified doctor was simultaneously to experience a rather close call: in the course of one session, Himmler asked him abruptly if he took notes of their conversations, adding that he would like to know what they consisted of; the Gestapo was obviously keeping close watch on this highly suspect physician, and its chief would stop at nothing to discredit him in Himmler's eyes. Sensing the danger and feeling that a denial would be useless, Kersten replied placidly: "It's true, Herr Reichsführer, I always jot down the conversations I have with you and your collaborators." Himmler's reply was highly unexpected: "Well, keep on doing that; you will thus be the only one to know what is happening here, while we're making world history. You will be a witness for posterity of the way in which the great German Reich was founded."[78] Saved by his patient's conceit! Kersten's relief must have been immense, but it had really been a close shave . . .

Actually, Himmler was proving rather uncommunicative as to his personal contribution to the foundation of the great German Reich; perhaps he sensed that it was not entirely avowable, or that his benefactor, being unduly influenced by outdated moral or religious prejudices, would have been unable to appreciate it – and might even have taken offence. For as Reichsführer S.S., head of the Office for Race and Settlement, and Reich Commissar for the Strengthening of the German Race, Himmler had already supervised the elimination by carbon monoxide of Polish psychiatric patients, organised the first deportations of Jews and Poles to the General Government, and contributed to the successive projects of the Final Solution, including deportation to Madagascar, setting up of ghettos in the east and removal of the Jews to peripheral regions that were to remain unmentioned at this stage – since they were linked to a plan whose knowledge was restricted to the chiefs of staff and the main dignitaries of the Reich: Barbarossa.[79]

On February 26, 1941, however, Himmler was faced with an unforeseen event: the citizens of Amsterdam had gone on strike en masse for two days, and 300,000 workers had taken to the streets to protest against the first great roundups of Jews.[xxxiii] The S.S. were taken by surprise and forced to postpone deportations temporarily, but the following weeks witnessed widespread arrests and executions of presumed leaders – measures of such rapidity and brutality that Kersten was unable to intervene. Yet this was precisely the setting for an episode that is well known to all readers

xxxiii   This solidarity strike, unique of its kind in occupied Europe, is still commemorated in the Netherlands under the name of *Februaristaking* – the February strike.

of Josef Kessel's *The Man with the Miraculous Hands.*[xxxiv] On March 1, 1941, at the S.S. headquarters mess, Kersten overheard a conversation between Heydrich and Rauter, who were discussing the impending deportation to Poland of the whole Dutch population! A highly upset Kersten asked for confirmation of this project from Secretary Brandt, who presented him that very evening with an envelope labelled "Most Secret". And Josef Kessel went on to write: "Kersten had before his eyes, black on white, detail after detail, paragraph by paragraph, the condemnation of a whole people."[80] The following twenty pages of Kessel's book include a breathtaking narrative of Kersten's efforts to induce Himmler to give up on such a crazy project – or rather to persuade Hitler to postpone that deportation until the end of the war. By cleverly taking advantage of the Reichsführer's excruciating pains that only he could relieve, Kersten succeeded after six weeks of constant pressure in getting Himmler to yield and agree to raise the issue with Hitler – who accordingly renounced his project on April 18, 1941, shortly after the Yugoslav campaign.

The whole affair, narrated with all of Kessel's literary flair, was one of the most moving passages in his book. Alas! More than a few readers will be cruelly disappointed on hearing that this episode was entirely fictitious – even if Joseph Kessel told it in good faith: after all, he had heard of it from Kersten, who recounted it himself in three of his four books of memoirs.[xxxv] Yet it is precisely

xxxiv   Joseph Kessel, *The Man with the Miraculous Hands*, Ayer Co. Pub, 1961.
xxxv   *Samtal med Himmler* (*Dialogue with Himmler*), Ljus, Stockholm, 1947; *Klerk en Beul, Himmler van nabij* (*Clerk and Executioner, Himmler Seen Up Close*), Meulenhoff, Amsterdam, 1948; *The Kersten Memoirs,* Macmillan, New York, 1957. But the whole episode of the Dutch deportation plan had entirely disappeared in the German version: *Totenkopf und Treue,* Robert Mölich, Hamburg, 1952.

in these books – and in Kersten's declarations to the commissions of inquiry after the war – that the flaws in the narrative begin to emerge: too many successive and incompatible versions, too many impossibilities in the dates and the places mentioned, too many documents that could not be found, too many successive truths, too many contradictions, too many suspicious and contradictory testimonies. But the reader will have to wait fifty-three more months before understanding the reasons for this surprising invention . . .[xxxvi]

Actually, Kersten had no reason to add a new act of heroism to his record of achievements: he already had quite a few amazing exploits to his credit, and was to have many more in the four years to come. But that spring, the danger threatening him was anything but imaginary, for the man involved in the dramatic events of May 11, 1941 was none other than one of his patients: Rudolf Hess himself. It will be recalled that a year earlier, the Führer's representative had told Kersten that he was preparing for "a mission of historic importance". Sure enough, on May 10, 1941 around 5 p.m., Hess had taken off from Augsburg on his "peace mission" at the controls of a Messerschmitt 110 fighter plane,[xxxvii] and parachuted into Scotland six hours later. At the Berghof, Hitler was only informed the next morning, and his reaction was extremely violent;[xxxviii] but even once he had regained his composure, he

xxxvi   With perhaps some basis in reality nonetheless, since Bormann seemed to have hatched such a plan in the spring of 1941, and though it was not seriously considered, Kersten may well have seen it at the time.

xxxvii   Already an exploit in itself, since the Messerschmitt Me 110 Zerstörer was a heavy fighter plane normally manned by two pilots.

xxxviii   Apart from the enormous loss of prestige for the Reich, there was the maddening fact that Hess was one of the very few dignitaries who knew of the impending attack against the Soviet Union.

kept on bringing up the event before his entourage: "Hess has always had crazy ideas. [. . .] His obsessions were reinforced by his mingling with soothsayers and other quacks dabbling in the supernatural. [. . .] His act was clearly inspired by the astrological phantasmagorias he revelled in. It is therefore high time we made a clean sweep of this noxious welter of nonsensical divination."[81]

No sooner said than done: all over the Reich, mages, spiritists, psychics, soothsayers, anthroposophists, magnetisers and therapists of various descriptions ended up in jail. For Gruppenführer Heydrich, this was a unique opportunity to get rid of the accursed Finn and English spy who had such deleterious influence on his superior. Was he not a practitioner of alternative medicine, who had treated Rudolf Hess to boot? Nothing could be more consistent with the Führer's orders than to get rid of him for good! In the early afternoon of May 14, Felix Kersten was therefore summoned to Heydrich's office. After having instructed the S.S. officer on duty to warn Himmler, who was in Munich at the time, Kersten left for Prinz-Albrecht-Strasse with some apprehension.

The supreme head of Sipo and S.D. had decided to conduct the interrogation himself, no doubt with considerable relish – but not without caution, for this was no ordinary suspect. Heydrich began by asking Kersten if he had mentioned England in his conversations with Rudolf Hess, and if he had not perchance encouraged him in his undertaking; in fact, Heydrich went so far as to insinuate that Kersten had helped Hess plan his escape – to which the good doctor replied that, as a rule, he only talked to his patients about medical matters and never broached political or economic issues, of which he knew nothing anyway. Heydrich made it clear that he didn't believe a word of it, then added:

"I know that you're not on our side. One fine day, you'll understand that you must speak the truth."

The "conversation" then shifted to Holland, and Heydrich expressed his astonishment that Kersten was so well informed about what was happening there. This must have brought Kersten out in a cold sweat, but he didn't let on at all:

"Perhaps I'm a psychic!"

"Perhaps I'm a psychic too," answered Heydrich. "In fact, I'm beginning to guess who you are . . ."

This duel with kid gloves went on for almost five hours. The Gruppenführer was a fencing champion, both literally and figuratively, but a telephone ringing in the next-door office interrupted the unequal contest. Heydrich rose to answer, came back after a few minutes and said to his "guest":

"You may leave. The Reichsführer has just called. He vouches for your innocence and will carry on your interrogation himself another time. Meanwhile, you must remain at our disposal and you are not to leave Berlin, except on the Reichsführer's orders."[82]

For all his devilish cunning, Heydrich had forgotten two things: first, Himmler himself routinely resorted to "astrological phantasmagorias" and to "quacks dabbling in the supernatural".[xxxix] Second, the Reichsführer's state of health was such that he could not possibly do without the ministrations of Felix Kersten . . .

---

xxxix Definitely: by his own admission, Himmler never took an important decision without consulting at least two astrologists.

# 4

## EASTWARD HO!

In the spring of 1941, it was the best-kept secret in Germany: only the top dignitaries of the Reich and the main heads of the armed forces knew that the greatest invasion of all times was about to be launched in the east. Felix Kersten was not supposed to know more than any German citizen, for, like all the Nazi hierarchs, Heinrich Himmler was obsessed with secrecy; but with the relief induced by the care of his doctor, the Reichsführer became more talkative as the deadline drew nearer. During morning treatment on March 20, as the conversation centred on Finland and the scant help afforded her by Germany during the Winter War against the Soviet Union, Himmler suddenly said: "Wait, Herr Kersten, many things are going to change in the east. Unfortunately, our Führer's hands have been tied until now, but the day will come when German and Finnish troops shall fight side by side in the east." Kersten said that he thought this unlikely, since a year earlier, the Führer had "stood at attention" while Finland was being deprived of one tenth of her territory by the Soviet Union. But Himmler went on: "Don't be so harsh in your judgment, Herr Kersten; Finland will recover everything she has lost, and more besides."[83] The message was crystal clear . . .

What Kersten could not possibly suspect was the intensity of dealings and confrontations behind the scenes, where everyone seemed to be sharing the spoils of the Soviet Union before having conquered it: Reichsleiter Rosenberg had indeed been appointed minister for occupied eastern territories, but he was already competing with Marshal Göring, grandmaster of the four-year plan, who strove to pre-empt the economic exploitation of all areas to be conquered; he was also at odds with Heinrich Himmler, who insisted that he had a "special mission from the Führer" to maintain law and order in the future "eastern colonies"; and he was at loggerheads with Foreign Minister von Ribbentrop, who intended to monopolise relations with all future "autonomous territories" ranging from the Baltic countries to the Caucasus[84] – not to mention his squabbles with Minister of the Interior Frick, Minister of Agriculture Darré and Hitler's Brown Eminence Martin Bormann, all of whom wanted to have their say in the matter! As usual, Hitler refused to decide between these competing claims, since power conflicts between his acolytes were the best guarantee of their subservience towards the Führer. Be that as it may, such wrangles could hardly appease Heinrich Himmler's nervous spasms – and this at a time when the eastern conquest was only at the planning stage!

The military, on the other hand, had done their job with varying degrees of enthusiasm[i] but typical Prussian *Gründlichkeit*,[ii] so that at daybreak on June 22, 1941, three army groups set off from the Baltic to the Carpathian mountains: 3.5 million men in 190

---

i   Marshal Göring, for one, had shouted to General Kammhuber: "This is the worst we could do. It's an economic blunder, a political blunder and a military blunder!"
ii   No satisfactory English equivalent: something between great meticulousness and extreme thoroughness.

divisions, 3,350 tanks and 2,465 planes crossed the Soviet borders. In three weeks, their armoured columns had made deep inroads into the country, and their vast turning movements resulted in the capture of hundreds of thousands of prisoners. In the north, Marshal von Leeb's army group sliced through the Baltic countries and reached the Luga, a bare one hundred kilometres from Leningrad; in the centre, Marshal von Bock's armoured columns captured Minsk and then Smolensk, less than four hundred kilometres from Moscow; in the south, General von Manstein's armies were already on the outskirts of Kiev on July 11. These three army groups included six Waffen S.S. divisions, as well as four Einsatzgruppen[iii] – the notorious task forces that had terrorised the Poles, and were presently operating behind the front lines against isolated Soviet units, political commissars, civilians in general and Jews in particular.

Hence the Reichsführer's presence in the vicinity of Hitler's campaign headquarters in East Prussia: Himmler, who greatly valued his military role, wanted to stay as close as possible to the supreme commander, and Hitler had set up his permanent headquarters in the Wolfsschanze (the Wolf's Lair), a bunker complex near Rastenburg, in the Görlitz forest. The *Sonderzug Heinrich* was thus stationed thirty-two kilometres to the east, in a pine forest near Lötzen. Himmler had naturally insisted on the presence of Kersten, who thus described the S.S. chief's new facilities: "So long as his headquarters was established in East Prussia, it was designated by the code name 'Hochwald'. [. . .] A side track led to a wood, and the Reichsführer's train was stationed at the end of that track. About twenty metres away, four large bunkers had

iii   Einsatzgruppe A in the Baltic countries, B in Byelorussia, C and D in Ukraine.

## OPERATION BARBAROSSA (June-November 1941)

🅖 Hitler's General H.Q.    ⟶ German axes of attack    ·⌒· Marsh

*Operation Barbarossa, June–November 1941*

been set up as shelters in case of an aerial attack.[iv] All around the train, twenty wooden barracks were used by the S.S. as both lodgings and offices. The Reichsführer's barracks was about seventeen metres long by eleven metres wide; he had a spacious office with a large light-brown walnut table in the middle, and the seats with their green seat covers gave the whole a mildly diplomatic aspect; alongside the wall, a safe where Himmler stored his secret files. [. . .] In front of Himmler's seat, on the opposite wall, a picture of Hitler; next to the office, his bedroom, with the Quran on the bedside table as usual. [. . .] The dining room too was furnished with simplicity and tastefully arranged; there were a few good reproductions of paintings by Dürer and Breughel. The corridor leading to these rooms could be cordoned off by an iron gate, which Himmler commanded electrically from his office, but I never saw it closed – it only served in case of emergency. In Himmler's barracks, there were also rooms for Dr Brandt,[v] the secretaries, the orderlies and his detective, who followed him everywhere."[85]

But Kersten did more than observe the interior architecture; as Himmler remained his principal focus of interest, he was able to note many contradictory aspects in the character and behaviour of his rather sinister patient: "Himmler had been influenced by the ancient Germanic gods and ideals that came back into fashion around 1900; he had in his blood the mentality of a teacher, the meticulousness of a civil servant and a genuine infatuation with

iv These bunkers can still be seen today near the village of Pozezdrze, now in Polish Masuria.
v Doctor of Law, that is. The Germans attach the greatest importance to academic titles.

police and military affairs. [. . .] To the dismay of his assistants, he worked every day until 2 or 3 a.m., and many of his meetings with them were held at night. He used to say: 'History will not ask if Heinrich Himmler slept well, but rather what he was able to accomplish. [. . .] The Führer must have at least one man on whom he can depend implicitly, and I must be that man.' All this gave the impression that he absorbed himself far too much in details [. . .] instead of sticking to an overall control. He immersed himself in an ocean of red tape [. . .] and matters of secondary importance."[86]

Having ascertained that this peculiar Nazi dignitary was "personally incorruptible", despised luxury and often stated that his greatest ambition was to "die in poverty", Kersten went on: "The modesty and simplicity of the man were reflected in his lifestyle; he ate and drank very moderately. [. . .] At his table, there was never any talk of service matters or trivialities: he liked to discuss historical subjects – the kingdoms of the Goths, the Vandals, the Vikings, the Varangians and the Normans; the transformation of Europe by the three great movements of Germanic tribes; the settlement policy of King Henry I; Genghis Khan and his methods of government; the great empire builders, etc. But as a rule, he did not monopolise conversation; quite the contrary, he welcomed contributions to the discussion by colleagues or guests – though he reserved the right to expound all the practical conclusions to be drawn from the exchange. [. . .] I was able to observe Himmler closely during his talks with various categories of people; unless he had special reasons to be angry, he was invariably polite, concerned with propriety and often very friendly"[87] – the perfect host, as it were!

But mundanities aside, Kersten also noted some of the Reichs-führer's more baffling practices: "Himmler used to compel those he had summoned to his headquarters to wait for two or three days before being received. The S.S. generals and chiefs of police, who would arrive with heaps of demands and recriminations, had counted on unloading them as quickly as possible; and since they were not told when Hitler could receive them, they had only to wait quietly. After three or four days, they had considerably softened; it was then that they were presented to Himmler, who asked them curtly what they wanted, then swiftly interrupted them and barked out a few brief orders. This whole comedy, played with an air of stiff impatience, allowed Himmler, who was basically an irresolute man, to strike a posture of omnipotence. Brandt himself had told me that Himmler always postponed decisions as long as possible; fear was his prime motor, and he would take no decision without having internally delegated responsibility for it to Adolf Hitler. [. . .] There was something spasmodic in all he did. [. . .] With all his inner duality and weakness of character, he preached toughness and took measures that were entirely foreign to his temperament, simply because his Führer had ordered them."[88]

Now this is hardly the way one usually pictures the supreme master of the S.S., but the fact is that Himmler went almost daily to the Wolfsschanze, from which he returned each time as if trans-figured; in the course of endless monologues in his massive and sinister command bunker, Hitler had assured his entourage that the conquest of the Soviet Union would take no more than three to four months, and upon returning to his own headquarters, Himmler said to Kersten: "The war will last two months at most – three at the extreme limit. [. . .] It will be a walkover."[89] Hitler's interpreter, Paul Schmidt, was later to call Himmler *"Eine Gramophonplatte"* – His Master's Voice.[vi]

To be sure, the Reichsführer did not tell Kersten what instructions he had received in Hitler's lair, yet the secret one was also the most horrific: his S.S. Einsatzgruppen were expected to make the conquered regions *Judenfrei* – free of Jews; hence the abominable massacres of Augustovo,[vii] Brest-Litovsk, Minsk, Kiev,[viii] Krivoï Rog, Mogilev, Novgorod, Kovno and Riga between July and October 1941. On August 15, Himmler personally witnessed the mass murder of about a hundred Jewish "spies and saboteurs" perpetrated by Einsatzgruppe B[ix] in the vicinity of Minsk; the victims were forced to lie face down in a pit about two metres deep, and, at the officer's command, a firing squad of twelve men shot several salvoes at the prostrate men. Karl Wolff, the Reichsführer's chief of staff, saw his superior turn pale, then green, after which he staggered at the edge of the pit, wiped with a trembling hand the parcel of human brain that had spattered his cheek, and turned around to vomit.[90] Cold heart but soft guts? Kersten himself duly noted that Himmler could never have killed anyone with his own hands, as "he was far too cowardly for that".[91]

Yet if the Reichsführer was incapable of killing people himself,[x]

vi  He was to say the same about Göring and Ribbentrop – with as much justification.

vii  In the north-eastern part of Poland; it had been recovered from the Soviets at the end of June.

viii  Scene of the carnage at Babi Yar, where 33,800 Jews were murdered in two days.

ix  Under the command of S.S. Gruppenführer Arthur Nebe, chief of the criminal police – and a member of the secret opposition to Hitler . . .

x  Unlike another less industrial butcher named Ernesto Che Guevara, who greatly enjoyed killing prisoners himself, publicly bragged about it, and has remained the idol of naive youths and "progressist" adults ever since.

he never ceased to goad his men into doing so – for such were Hitler's orders. Actually, just after the Minsk massacre, he had sufficiently regained his composure to address the men who made up the firing squad, telling them that he personally assumed all responsibility for an act that was "repulsive, but necessary".[92] This he was to repeat in one form or another during his inspections of Einsatzgruppen A, C and D – all the while striving to find more effective ways of achieving his master's insane ambition; for the liquidation process was deemed far too slow, and the S.S. executioners, even fanaticised and plied with alcohol, were nervously affected by their task and became uncontrollable; besides, these public slaughters shocked many Wehrmacht soldiers and generated protests from some of their officers – protests that were often relayed abroad.[xi] The basic problem was that the Führer had ordered the elimination of hundreds of thousands of additional "undesirables": officers of the Red Army, political commissars, Ukrainian nationalists, gypsies, the mentally ill, Soviet Jews, Polish Jews, German Jews and Jews from all the conquered countries of western Europe . . . Now, "artisanal" methods such as the massacres perpetrated in Poland, Byelorussia and Ukraine clearly could not meet requirements in this respect, which was why, in early October, Himmler had entrusted the S.S. und Polizeiführer for the Lublin region, Odilo Globocnik, with the building of two extermination camps south of Lublin, Majdanek and Belzec, to which two more camps were to be added further north during the winter: Treblinka and Sobibor. But in early September, in the concentration camp

---

xi   Notably through the intervention of Admiral Canaris, who protested personally to his superior, Marshal Keitel. But most of the senior officers, like von Manstein and von Reichenau, approved the massacres or refused to condemn them.

of Auschwitz[xii] near Kraków, S.S. Hauptsturmführer[xiii] Karl Fritzsch, deputy to camp commander Rudolf Höss, had experimented with the gassing of six hundred Soviet prisoners by means of Zyklon B – crystals of prussic acid hitherto used for rodent control. The success of the operation, immediately communicated to his superiors, was to open up for Reichsführer Himmler some entirely new prospects . . .

Was Felix Kersten informed of all this? It seems most unlikely, for among Himmler's staff, only allusions, rumours and obscure code names circulated. "In certain circles," wrote Kersten, "there was some whispered talk of the abominations that were constantly taking place in these camps, but it was all shrouded in a thick veil of secrecy. My impression was that those who were in the know remained silent, and every time I tried to learn more either from Himmler or his entourage, I invariably got the answer that these were rehabilitation centres, where wrongdoers were turned into honourable and socially useful citizens; I was also assured that the inmates of these camps were properly treated. [. . .] At any rate, I was warned more than once against bothering Himmler with these concentration camp matters, since he could have taken it amiss coming from a foreigner."[93]

Ever since the war, a number of sensation-seeking journalists have tried to establish that Kersten accompanied Himmler on his tours of inspection to Polish and Ukrainian concentration camps.[94] However, they have invariably run up against three major obstacles: first, whereas all the Reichsführer's movements were profusely filmed and photographed, not a single picture or film could be

xii   Set up in the spring of 1940 on the emplacement of a Polish artillery barracks.
xiii   Captain.

produced that showed a burly civilian among the visiting S.S. officers; second, Himmler always jotted down in his appointment diary the names of those who joined him on these occasions, and Felix Kersten's is nowhere to be found. Last but not least, there is a question of plausibility: the Reichsführer, knowing perfectly well the humanistic and altruistic dispositions of his doctor and being extremely anxious to keep his esteem, would never have invited Kersten to cross the threshold of his industrialised inferno – even supposing that Kersten had agreed to follow him there. But to this citizen of an allied nation,[xiv] Himmler never concealed his ultimate aims – and above all those of his master: "The precondition for a satisfactory permanent understanding with Finland is that she solve her Jewish problem according to the Nuremberg laws. For at the end of this war, Europe must be free of Jews! He who opposes the Führer's clearly stated orders, or even expresses compassion for the Jews, is a traitor to the cause of the Germanic people. [. . .] If Finland wants to enter the great community of the Germanic people after the war, she must introduce German racial laws and hold herself ready to deliver unconditionally all Finnish Jews to Germany as soon as the latter demands it." To which Kersten commented: "When I asked him if all this also reflected his personal point of view, he replied significantly that, for someone in his position, personal opinions were irrelevant: it was only a matter of implementing the Führer's orders."[95]

Thus, all the European Jews had to be delivered to Germany, and at the end of the war, Germany was to be free of Jews . . . The

---

xiv   Co-belligerent to be precise: the Finns had only agreed to cooperate with Germany against the Soviet Union in order to win the back the territories occupied by the Soviet Union as a result of the Winter War.

conclusion was easy to draw, but Kersten was to wait another three months before obtaining confirmation from Himmler himself: "The destruction of the Jews is imminent." Faced with his interlocutor's indignation, the Reichsführer conceded that "the extermination of peoples is a non-Germanic practice", but he added immediately that "this was the eternal conflict between will and duty".[96] Actually, Himmler could perfectly well have endorsed the following peremptory statement: "I have no conscience; my conscience is called Adolf Hitler!" – provided of course he did not know that its author was none other than his sworn enemy, Hermann Göring!

In East Prussia that summer, Kersten kept receiving letters from all over the Reich, Holland, Belgium and Finland. One of them came from his second correspondent in The Hague, P.J. Schijf, who informed him in mid-September of the arrest of former Dutch prime minister Hendrikus Colijn.[97] For all his rather fluctuating political positions,[xv] the old statesman remained a respected figure in his country, and Kersten felt bound to intervene; he asked Brandt to show him the prisoner's file, and thus learned that Colijn was accused by both Reichskommissar Seyss-Inquart and Höhere S.S. und Polizeiführer Rauter of having spied on behalf of England; furthermore, the man was a devout Catholic who belonged to circles that were particularly hostile to Germany. Kersten having asked Brandt what penalty he faced, the little secretary and doctor at law replied without a moment's hesitation: "Death." Kersten

xv   In June 1940, Colijn, indignant at the flight of the government and the queen to London, had authored a brochure entitled *Op de grens van twee verelden* (*At the border between two worlds*), in which he predicted a long period of German hegemony over Europe, that the Dutch would have to put up with. But quickly disillusioned with the new order, he had joined the resistance movement.

thereupon undertook to gather as much information as he could, and during the next session of treatment, he mentioned Colijn's case to his patient. Himmler, who had just read the man's file, answered that this was a clear case and that the accused being "a stooge of the Pope's anti-German activities" was absolutely indefensible. Kersten immediately countered: "How can you believe such rubbish? Rauter deceived you!" Himmler, stung to the quick, exclaimed: "No-one can lie to me!" But Kersten calmly went on: "Well, in this case, Rauter brazenly lied to you [. . .] about Colijn's religious denomination, which never was Catholic – he's always been a Protestant; moreover, he belongs to a Protestant political party that has always fought against the Catholic church . . ." Himmler, clearly taken aback, said that he could not decide on the spot, but that he would think about it.

During the next session six days later, Kersten returned to the charge by reminding Himmler that the S.D. in The Hague and Reichskommissar Seyss-Inquart had obviously tried to play on his anti-Catholic feelings in order to induce him to accept Colijn's elimination. A pensive Himmler replied: "You may be right. I had the matter looked into, and it turns out that Colijn has nothing to do with the Catholics. It was a misunderstanding." Yet for all that, the case was not won, since Himmler added: "But the Protestants are at least as dangerous . . ." Nevertheless, the Reichsführer seemed to be somewhat shaken in his convictions, for he then added: "Maybe Colijn is not as bad as we were told [. . .] But one thing's for sure: if he and his followers had been a bit better disposed towards the Germans and had given some support to the Führer, I would now have 600,000 more Dutch volunteers engaged in the campaign against Russia." To which Kersten retorted that the discussion was not about reinforcements for the eastern front, but about whether Colijn – "of good Germanic blood, like you and the Führer" – was innocent and had been wrongly accused. Himmler eventually relented. "What do you suggest?" Kersten replied unhesitatingly: "Set him free immediately!" But for his patient, things were not so simple. "I cannot let him go back to Holland. Colijn has many enemies in the N.S.B. who could take it out on him." After another day of reflection, the Reichsführer finally came to a decision: "We'll release him, but place him under house arrest in one of our residences for distinguished individuals in the Rhineland" – after which he started to tremble at his own daring. "I have just gone against the leadership of the party, the S.D. and the N.S.B. My decision is going to appal them."[98]

Between the summer and the autumn of 1941, Kersten was to take up cudgels for many more people caught in the wide web spun by the Gestapo; in fact, rumours of his accomplishments had begun to circulate in the immediate vicinity of Hartzwalde, as was later recalled by Countess Clara von Arnim, who lived in the neighbouring estate of Wiepersdorf; the two daughters of her acquaintance Professor Schrader had been arrested by the Gestapo[xvi] and since then, nothing further had been heard from them. Count and Countess von Arnim thereupon called on Kersten at Hartzwalde: "We found him at home, he listened to the whole story and took a few notes. A week later, the parents were informed that their daughters were detained in the Potsdam Gestapo jail, and that they could visit them and bring them food and clothes. After four weeks, the two ladies were released."[99]

xvi   Under suspicion of spying for the Soviet Union. Actually, one of them had been in love with a Ukrainian refugee.

There were to be many others: Albert Plesman, director of the Dutch aviation company K.L.M., the family of the Jewish diamond dealer Aascher, the chairman of Unilever-Germany, Hendricks, his daughter Inez van Dijk and dozens of others, for whom Kersten eventually obtained, if not immediate release, at least a waiver of enforcement. And yet, among the people imprisoned that Kersten was later to mention, one at least makes surprising reading: that of Baroness Ella van Heemstra; for not only was her arrest undocumented, but it would have made no sense at all: the Baroness, who had met Hitler in 1935 and found him charming, remained in 1941 an active supporter of the N.S.B. and an enthusiastic collaborationist.[xvii] There was probably a confusion here, since the name Heemstra was widespread in Holland; but it pointed to a crucial fact: other than those who had a high public profile, his former patients and their families, Kersten did not know the great majority of the people whose release he was requesting – even if he often presented them to Himmler as personal friends. Another of his techniques consisted of gradually discrediting their accusers in the eyes of the Reichsführer . . .

Much later, our would-be advocate was to explain how the game was played on such occasions: "It was often a genuine case of horse-trading. [. . .] If, for instance, I had a list of twenty people jailed by the Gestapo for one reason or the other, and on whose behalf friends or relations had asked for my intervention, I took advantage of the treatment sessions to bring their case before

xvii   Ella van Heemstra, incidentally Audrey Hepburn's mother, became disillusioned with the Nazis after the execution of her brother-in-law, Count Otto van Limburg Stirum, in August 1942. She then approached the underground resistance, but still escaped arrest.

Himmler. [. . .] I dwelt on the honourable and even remarkable character of the people concerned, and suggested to Himmler all sorts of motives for which a release appeared desirable. Most of the time, Himmler did not even ask what had brought these people to jail, but rather who was interested in their case. He would quickly glance at the list of names, then say: 'You want to have twenty released? What's in it for you? What will my men think of it? You can have five. Be content with that – or else you'll have nothing at all.' He occasionally authorised the liberation of the first five on the list, sometimes also the last one, and that arbitrarily, quite haphazardly. Most of the time, I handed my list to Dr Brandt, whom Himmler usually entrusted with these matters, and I asked him not just to carry out Himmler's decision, but to add names to the list before submitting it to him – which was usually what happened. At that stage, Himmler was no longer concerned with the number of names, and he swiftly signed the document just as Brandt had drawn it up."[100]

This then was what went on behind the scenes of this most uncommon feat. But Kersten does not dwell on another aspect of his activity during that autumn of 1941, after his return to Berlin; hence the need to resort to his other informant in Holland, Jacobus Nieuwenhuis – the man who had renewed his membership of the N.S.B. in September 1940 in order to keep Kersten informed of everything that was being said among the heads of that collaborationist party. In July 1941, two S.D. agents had come to inform Nieuwenhuis that his application for a visa to enter Germany had been granted; he was greatly puzzled, until he received a letter from Kersten with a request to join him in Berlin in mid-September. "On September 15, 1941," Nieuwenhuis later testified, "I thus arrived in

Berlin, at Kersten's home, where he told me in confidence that he had conceived a new plan: he had been informed that the Germans intended to proceed with the massive purchase of goods on the black market in Holland, Belgium and France, for the benefit of the German Reich. This was to be done within the framework of Göring's four-year plan. [. . .] As Kersten considered that this scheme would be extremely detrimental to Holland – since it would be tantamount to fleecing her entirely – he deemed it essential to be informed of it as precisely as possible, so that he could torpedo it through his intercession with Himmler. He had given a lot of thought to the matter and decided to bring me in to the circuit. He had told Himmler that he was seeking employment for me, and that, since I had a business background, he suggested that I join this new venture. When I arrived in Berlin, Kersten was already far advanced in his preparation of the affair. As it implied my participation in an entirely German undertaking, I asked for some time to consider the matter, but at Kersten's urgent request, I ended up accepting on October 15. Kersten told me that I would probably have to begin by working in Berlin for a time, but that later on he would see to it that I was transferred to Holland. That is precisely what happened: starting November 15, I received preliminary training in Berlin, within the framework of the S.S. Wirtchafts-Verwaltungsamt.[xviii] Two months later, I was transferred to The Hague and employed in the Dienstelle für Auftragsverlagerung,[xix] with its seat at 2b Javastraat.[xx] [. . .] As had been agreed with

xviii   S.S. main office for economic administration.
xix   S.S. service for the transfer of orders. As usual in national socialist adminis-trative terminology, such insignificant titles were meant to conceal the real activities of the offices in question.
xx   Java Street.

Kersten, I sent him each week a short report on the most important business."[101]

Actually, it was an attempt by Kersten to anticipate events, since this ambitious and potentially disastrous project could only be launched in the spring of 1942: for the time being, the German leaders had more pressing preoccupations; indeed, the eastern campaign, far from being "a walkover", was slowly turning into an ordeal of gigantic proportions. Sure enough, after their great summer offensives, the Germans were on the threshold of Leningrad, west of Kiev, east of Smolensk and less than four hundred kilometres from Moscow; but at that stage, Hitler was constantly hesitating between the northern, central and southern objectives, while combat attrition, logistic problems and the stubbornness of Soviet defence were fatally delaying all renewed offensives – the latter being further hampered by the Führer's untimely interventions, changes of mind and neglect of distances, ground conditions, supply problems, manpower exhaustion, equipment wear and enemy potential. When at long last he decided to unleash the main offensive on Moscow at the beginning of October, two months had been lost, his troops were scattered on a 3,600-kilometre-wide front between Lapland and Crimea, and weather conditions were about to deteriorate . . .

This is precisely what happened in mid-November 1941, as seventy-seven divisions of Army Group Centre were beginning to encircle Moscow: temperatures sank to -20°C, then -30°C, planes could no longer take off, tank turrets got stuck, machine guns jammed, motor oil froze, locomotives came to a standstill, supply convoys could no longer get through, fuel began to run out, and German infantrymen, clad and equipped for summer conditions, had every difficulty coping with such extreme conditions. At day-break on December 6, 1941, as the Wehrmacht was immobilised all along the front, sixteen Soviet armies commanded by General Zhukov suddenly launched a counteroffensive north and south of Moscow. The whole German centre was thus forced to retreat hastily westward, soon followed by Army Groups South and North in front of Rostov and Leningrad. Although the Führer categorically forbade any further retreat and ordered the formation of "hedgehogs" around the occupied districts, the fact remained that by mid-December 1941, the Wehrmacht had experienced its first real setback.

Heinrich Himmler, constantly on tours of inspection from Poland to Estonia and Ukraine, was deeply disappointed with the turn of events. Not only had this campaign suffered a humiliating reverse, but it threatened to last indefinitely, and, possibly worse still, the S.S. divisions of which he was so proud had not lived up to his expectations; to be sure, they had displayed both courage and ferocity, but this could not make up for their lack of training, armament and leadership; set up too hastily, they had no doubt distinguished themselves by perpetrating innumerable massacres against civilian populations in Byelorussia and Ukraine, but once confronted with a pugnacious and resolute enemy, they had quickly shown their limits: by July 6, the Totenkopf division was reporting abnormally high losses: 1,700 men in less than three weeks;[102] on July 13, the S.S. brigade Nord was severely mauled near Salla, on the Murmansk front – compelling Himmler to consider the replacement of its commander, Obergruppenführer Karl Maria Demelhueber;[xxi] in September 1941, the Totenkopf division again

xxi  Which was to prove impossible until April 1942, for lack of a competent successor.

suffered unacceptable losses in the fighting around Demiansk –
during which two of its regiments disbanded and fled before
a Soviet counteroffensive; seven weeks later, the S.S. divisions
Leibstandarte Adolf Hitler and Wiking found themselves in great
difficulty in southern Ukraine, mainly for lack of artillery – after
which the S.S. division Reich suffered in turn what was described
as "inordinately high losses" during the fighting at Rjev, north-east
of Smolensk. In addition, there were numerous instances of failings
in discipline within all these units: theft, alcoholism, corruption,
mistreatment of subordinates – offences that were all punishable
by death within the S.S. – and Hans Himmler, the Reichsführer's
nephew himself, had just been tried and sentenced to death by an
S.S. tribunal for homosexuality.[xxii] [103]

Heinrich Himmler naturally avoided discussing such things
with his favourite doctor, who noted at the time: "When events
cast a shadow over values such as 'honour', 'comradeship' and
'loyalty' within the S.S., he was as silent as the grave."[104] Actually,
what the Reichsführer feared most was the loss of prestige that
such setbacks could cause him vis-à-vis Hitler, and the opportunity
it offered his many enemies in high places to tarnish his reputation
as a great military leader – an utterly undeserved reputation no
doubt, but one that he valued immensely. However, all this was
to be relegated to the background by a stunning turn of events:
on December 7, 1941, Japan burst into the war by bombing the
American naval base at Pearl Harbor. The Japanese had warned
no-one – not even their German allies – and under the terms of
the Tripartite Pact, Berlin had no obligation to come to Tokyo's
assistance: the signatories of the pact had pledged to rescue each

xxii   Himmler upheld the sentence – to set an example.

other "in case of attack by a third power" – whereas in this case it was Japan herself that was attacking a third power. Never mind! On December 11, Hitler declared war on the United States . . .

There is no evidence that the Führer ever consulted his ministers, diplomats or military men before taking such a fateful decision; as usual, he had acted on inspiration – and under the influence of a few enduring prejudices: he greatly overestimated Japan's military potential, fatally underestimated that of the United States, and predicted that the latter would be unable to intervene militarily in Europe for at least a year; in fact, he rejoiced at the prospect of being able at last to attack American supply convoys headed for Great Britain across the Atlantic. As usual, his main acolytes Ribbentrop, Goebbels, Ley, Rosenberg, Göring and Himmler, though taken utterly by surprise, bowed to this abrupt initiative and rushed to justify it; on the morning of December 12, when Himmler proudly told him of the declaration of war, Kersten asked:

"Was it really necessary?"

"Of course," answered his patient. "We could no longer bear the provocations of that Jewish stooge Roosevelt . . ."

"And what do the German people think of that?"

"They are not asked. They have only to obey. Anyone who speaks out against this decision will be immediately crushed by the Führer. The American Jews and their mercenaries have sided with the English and Russian Jews, which is why they must be annihilated."

"But there are not only Jews in the United States . . ."

"I know, but the non-Jews in America are degenerate and flabby; they let the Jews lead and rule. In America, the dollar rules and it is in Jewish hands. Once we win the war, our only peace conditions will be: 'Deliver all Jews to Germany.' We will ask nothing more from the United States. With the other Americans, we'll soon get along quite amicably!"[105]

Once again, Himmler had only been his master's voice; it was therefore without the slightest regret or apprehension that the Nazi leaders slid into the new year – and into what had just become an outright world war . . .

# 5

# THE UNSPEAKABLE

On September 24, 1941, Reinhard Heydrich was appointed deputy governor of Bohemia Moravia,[i] with an eloquent title: Stellvertreter des Reichsprotektors. Now, in the literal sense, a *Stellvertreter* is less a deputy then a substitute – and that is precisely what it was all about: Reichsprotektor Constantin von Neurath having been considered too lenient, Hitler had decided to replace him with an iron man. In Hartzwalde, where Heydrich was feared like the devil himself, the news was greeted with intense relief; within Himmler's close entourage as well, where Heydrich was unanimously hated. But everyone was quickly disillusioned, for the new master of Prague, promoted Obergruppenführer,[ii] remained in charge of the R.S.H.A. – the Third Reich's ubiquitous security service. In fact, it was in this capacity that he chaired on January 20, 1942 the Wannsee conference, at which thirteen Nazi officials designed the plan for a "final solution of the Jewish question in Europe". During the following months, he was therefore to be the grand organiser of a deportation and elimination scheme unequalled in the sinister register of human crimes – to such an extent that German historian Eberhard Jäckel was later to write:

i    The present-day Czechia.
ii   Lieutenant General.

"The supreme architect of the genocide was not Himmler, but Heydrich. He goaded Hitler himself."[106] Whereas the first sentence is perfectly true, the second is definitely not, for no-one goaded Hitler – least of all from such a subordinate position: Heydrich was only an executor – admittedly a dreadfully efficient one . . .

That efficiency was of course highly valued by his direct superior; in fact, Himmler never tired of praising his Grand Inquisitor in front of Kersten – who nevertheless gained the impression that the relationship between these two men was more complex than met the eye: "Heydrich behaves towards Himmler, who always treats him with the most open friendliness, with quite inexplicable servility. He addresses Himmler as 'Herr Reichsführer' – a thing absolutely forbidden throughout the whole S.S. – instead of simply 'Reichsführer'. Heydrich's side of the conversation between them goes like this: 'Certainly, Herr Reichsführer, if that is the Herr Reichsführer's wish, I will have the necessary arrangements made at once and report back to the Herr Reichsführer. Yes, certainly; yes, yes, indeed!'[iii] Doubtless, as a politician, Heydrich is far more dynamic than Himmler. He knows it and shows his superiority in mustering his arguments; Himmler just isn't in the same class. On the other hand, Heydrich draws back at once the moment Himmler manifests any opposition or puts forward a different point of view. Himmler seems to possess some sort of secret power over Heydrich, before which Heydrich submits unconditionally."[107]

What exactly that secret power was, Himmler did not tell Kersten in February 1942, and he would have to wait a few more months before discovering it. However, the Reichsführer entrusted

iii  And all this in a high-pitched tone, since this colossus had the voice of a pre-pubescent girl.

him with a far more momentous secret on the morning of February 8:

"I shall need all my strength during the weeks to come. [. . .] New missions await me."

Kersten having pointed out that he was hardly in a fit state to increase his workload, Himmler continued nonetheless:

"During the next few weeks, Sweden will be incorporated into the Reich."

A slight pause, then:

"Yes, yes, it will be a pleasant affair. Did you really think that we could tolerate much longer being pushed around by this nation of parasites? We must drain that abscess in the middle of our Great German *Lebensraum*. It is the centre of world espionage; the entire Swedish press constantly lashes out at Germany,[iv] and besides, we need more iron ore – double what they are supplying us at present. [. . .] Once in Sweden, after having razed Stockholm to the ground, we shall soon teach the Swedes what Germanic thought is all about . . ."

At this, Kersten protested:

"But that's completely idiotic! If you occupy Sweden, you won't get any iron ore at all . . . The Swedes will destroy their mines, or at least render them unusable. [. . .] What's more, there will be a wave of sabotage all over the country that will paralyse all activity. Even if you execute hundreds of people, it will do you no good."

"We have our methods to force people to work . . ."

But Kersten remained adamant.

iv  True enough: most Swedish papers were extremely critical of the Reich, which outraged Hitler.

"I'm sure you're getting it wrong. These are things you can perhaps do with Russians or people from the Balkans, but not with Germans. Once the Swedish food reserves are exhausted, you'll have to feed the Swedish population yourselves [. . .], since you can't let them all starve."

Seeing that he got nowhere with such arguments, Kersten tried another approach:

"I simply cannot understand how you, who usually think so logically and intelligently, can contemplate making such a mistake. You will only have trouble in occupied Sweden, whereas a free and independent Sweden would deliver all the supplies promised."

This was clearly more intelligible to Himmler, who replied:

"I see; since you come from these Baltic countries, you perhaps know Sweden personally . . ."

Kersten confirmed that he had indeed gone through Sweden several times on his way to Finland, and that the Swedes struck him as a hard-working, courageous and above all respectable people – and incorruptible too.

"Yes," Himmler admitted, "we noticed that: with offers of bribes, we get nowhere. Their foreign policy is so bland that diplomacy is useless . . ."

An encouraging admission, which led Kersten to push his advantage.

"I think it would rather be in Germany's interest to leave Sweden alone."

"You really think so?" Himmler inquired. "Göring, who knows Sweden well, has a different opinion."

Kersten, who was well aware of the fierce antagonism between

Himmler and the paunchy Reichsmarshall, asked Himmler innocently if he was henceforth going along with Göring's views. The effect was instantaneous.

"By no means! That stupid swine can go to hell . . ."

"Göring," Kersten went on, "may have personal motives to advocate an invasion of Sweden – perhaps in order to satisfy his own egotistical interests . . ."

"It's not impossible; I hadn't thought of that. [. . .] I must see the Führer this evening, so we will discuss that Swedish question."[108]

Kersten then noted that on February 14, he went to the Finnish embassy, in order to inform his friend Ambassador Kivimäki of what he had just heard.

Did such a plan for the invasion of Sweden exist at the time, and did the two men really hold such a surrealistic conversation? The first objection seems obvious: Hermann Göring would certainly *never* have advocated an invasion of Sweden, his "exclusive preserve"[109] – in fact, he would have spared no effort to prevent it. But that is hardly a compelling argument, since Himmler, albeit one of the best-informed men in the Reich, could not have had the slightest idea of what had passed between Hitler and Göring; for the Führer only received his acolytes individually and carefully compartmentalised his confabulations:[v] *Divide et impera!*[vi] The last Reich council of ministers had been held in 1938, and ever since then, the dignitaries of the regime could only speculate as to their rivals' stances before the Führer – and they tended to give

v   "My principle is to tell the people only what they ought to know, and only when they ought to know it." (Adolf Hitler)
vi  Divide and rule.

greater credence to fanciful rumours than to reliable information.[vii]

On balance, there is only one way to establish the veracity of all this: if Kersten did indeed warn the Finnish embassy, then the Finnish diplomats could not have failed to pass on such vital information to their Swedish counterparts. If so, this would necessarily have left some traces in the archives of the Swedish foreign ministry; and sure enough, such traces clearly turn up in the diplomatic correspondence for February 1942 between Swedish ambassador in Berlin Richert and the head of the political section in the Swedish ministry of foreign affairs, Söderblom – as well as in the ensuing deliberations within the Swedish government, which include the following mention: "Rumours and diffuse information concerning an imminent action – or at least one at the planning stage – on Germany's part were relayed by our Berlin embassy during the first weeks of the year. [. . .] In mid-February, these rumours intensified and were reported to our embassy by usually reliable sources."[110] Now what source could be more reliable than the Finnish embassy, with which the Swedish diplomats were in continuous contact? And in mid-February to boot, when one recalls that Kersten went to the Finnish embassy precisely on February 14! At any rate, the Swedish government clearly took the information seriously, since only a few days later they announced a mobilisation of the air force, anti-aircraft defence and coastal artillery, as well as a reinforcement of the land forces by the conscription of some one hundred thousand men.[111]

That things did not go any further may well have been due to

vii   Thus, Hermann Göring, probably the best-informed man in the Reich, was convinced that Ribbentrop and Goebbels had persuaded Hitler to invade the Soviet Union – whereas in fact, neither of them had been in favour of the undertaking.

this immediate partial mobilisation, to a personal message sent to Hitler by King Gustav V on February 24, and above all to the fact that the German general staff had just estimated that thirty divisions would be required to conquer Sweden.[112] In view of his plans for an imminent offensive in Ukraine and the Caucasus, the Führer quite probably found the prospect of a new Scandinavian adventure excessively costly at that stage.[viii] [113] Be that as it may, it appears clearly that the notes taken by Kersten at the time owed nothing to his imagination – even if he would have been entirely deluded in thinking that, once persuaded himself, Himmler would have convinced the Führer to give up his invasion projects; for in matters of strategy, Hitler listened to none other than himself – after which he decided "with the assurance of a sleepwalker".[ix]

But Kersten being remarkably single-minded, he was simultaneously fighting yet another deleterious Nazi undertaking: the plan to corner the black market in France, Belgium and the Netherlands, whose preparation had proceeded apace since September 1941. "I chose," wrote Kersten, "to return relentlessly to the subject at every opportunity – to adopt something of a harassment tactic. [. . .] I succeeded in convincing Himmler that the Dutch were *au fond* favourably disposed towards Germany, but that they would inevitably become hostile if the country were submitted to economic pillage. 'What advantage would Germany draw from a Holland that was entirely fleeced, either during or after the war?' I

---

viii   Himmler did not reveal to Kersten – or perhaps he did not know himself – the reasons for this invasion project: ever since the end of 1941, Hitler had feared a British landing in Norway – possibly in cooperation with the Swedes, who could attack the German occupation troops from the rear. At least concerning Sweden, this was a rather paranoid view of things – but not an unusual one in the Führer's case.

ix   The expression is Hitler's own.

asked. That Holland which, after all, was Germany's natural spearhead against England, ought to be preserved in all its might, etc. etc."[114] Yet it was all in vain, for if Himmler could be persuaded, he had no more power over the Reich's economy than over its strategy: that baneful central buying office being set up in The Hague, Paris and Brussels depended not on his S.S., but on the *Vierjahresplan* – Marshal Göring's four-year plan.

Kersten thus felt understandably depressed by the poor results of his efforts at the time – the more so as he was sorely tried by the loss of his father, who had just died at the ripe old age of ninety-one; in addition, a bout of sickness left Kersten bed-ridden for several days in early March. Yet even then, he pursued his task unwaveringly; the following message addressed to Rudolf Brandt on March 5 refers to an unknown affair, yet it is quite revealing as to the *modus operandi* of our humanitarian Stakhanovist: "Your telephone call frightened me greatly. I don't know if you understood me right, which is why I am sending my sister to Berlin with this letter. I am still in bed with fever [. . .]. Therefore I beg of you to withhold this report by Rauter, and under no circumstances to present it to the Reichsführer before I can talk to him about it and muster counter-arguments. [. . .] This message is to be destroyed, lest it fall into the wrong hands."[115]

But sickness could not keep Kersten away from his patients for long – especially the foremost among them, from whom he managed to obtain a few additional liberations, even by correspondence; thus, on June 15, 1942, this letter to Himmler: "Thank you for accepting the liberation of the twelve Dutch officers; also my thanks for the liberation of the six Frenchmen and the three French women. I appeal to your humanitarian compassion and to your

Germanic sense of equity."[116] Kersten having been "invited" to join Himmler during his stay in Holland between May 16 and May 20, Standartenführer Harster, deputy to Obergruppenführer Rauter, was later to give a good idea of the results obtained: "Kersten came here for eight days,[x] and five days after his departure came the first liberation orders. On several occasions, we received orders from the Reichsführer S.S. to release people who had been arrested. I said to Rauter: 'Look at this – yet another list of cursed people that this confounded Finnish doctor Kersten succeeded in massaging out of the Reichsführer.'[117] "*Herausmassiert*": the verb did not even exist in German, but the S.S. in Holland invented it especially for Felix Kersten! A tribute as grudging as it is eloquent . . .

Precisely about Kersten's attachment to the Netherlands, S.S. Standartenführer Sepp Tiefenbacher, the stern commander of Himmler's special train, had this to say: "In this matter, Herr Kersten was disarmingly uncomplicated. He didn't care if his direct interventions resulted in clashes with the Reichskommissar for the Netherlands; he was only interested in the Dutch and their tribulations." To which Tiefenbacher added these revealing comments: "Himmler's indulgence towards Herr Kersten was astonishing and sometimes incomprehensible. The only explanation I could find was that Himmler wanted to show the civilian Kersten that he also had a human side.[xi] There is no doubt at all that Herr Kersten did much good and helped a huge number of people. He hated war and repeatedly used his position for humanitarian

x   Five, actually – but Harster probably found the time somewhat longer.
xi   A reasonable but very incomplete explanation, which goes to show that even Tiefenbacher, one of Himmler's closest Bavarian acolytes, was unaware of the Reichsführer's dependency on Kersten's ministrations.

purposes. In this respect, he felt more like a Dutch or a Finn than like a German. Just one example: in early 1942, I reminded Herr Kersten of Hitler's strict order to conserve petrol, to which he replied literally: 'It's your war, not mine. I'll drive wherever I please. After all, I didn't come to Germany of my own free will – I was summoned.'"[118]

That spring of 1942, boundless confidence prevailed at the headquarters in Berlin and Rastenburg; for during the last five months, the Soviets, counter-attacking everywhere, had failed to break through anywhere. The Führer therefore considered that his decision to forbid any retreat had been the right one, and he kept on bragging about having "avoided a Napoleonic debacle". The fact that he had also ruined his military transport aviation and considerably weakened his army in the process was apparently deemed secondary. Besides, everywhere else that spring, the conflict seemed to turn in favour of the Axis: in Malta, Libya, Malaya, Burma, in the North Atlantic as in the South Pacific, the British and their allies were either on the defensive or in full retreat. With Rommel at the gates of Egypt and the Japanese at the confines of India, the greatest optimism seemed justified: *Deutschland siegt an allen Fronten!*[xii]

But on May 27, the news struck like a bombshell – one that had been carefully prepared in London: Reinhard Heydrich, "deputy" Reichsprotektor of Bohemia-Moravia, fell victim to a bomb attack perpetrated by Czech agents of the S.O.E.[xiii] Over the last eight

xii   "Germany is victorious on all fronts!" A recurrent slogan of Dr Goebbels' propaganda – until the spring of 1945.

xiii   Special Operations Executive, a secret British organisation whose mission, determined by Churchill, was to "set Europe ablaze" by supporting and monitoring local resistance movements and carrying out attacks, sabotage and disinformation operations.

months, Heydrich had imposed a rule of terror on the country by having thousands of opponents arrested and executed; but the "henchman of Prague" had also succeeded in winning over the workers of Czech factories producing weaponry for Germany, mainly by boosting their pay and improving their living conditions. For British strategists, this was what made him really dangerous – the more so as he was about to apply the same methods in occupied France. His fatal error was to stick invariably to the same route between his residence and his office in the centre of Prague, on board an open and non-armoured Mercedes, without an escort.[xiv] Around 10.30 in the morning of May 27, parachutists Jozef Gabcik and Jan Kubis stopped his car at a bend in the road, failed to shoot him, but threw an anti-tank grenade that exploded in the rear of the vehicle, projecting debris from the door and seat into Heydrich's back; he drew his pistol, jumped out of the car, but almost immediately collapsed. Rushed to a hospital, he underwent surgery and his life did not seem to be in danger; but the seat upholstery that had penetrated his back contained horsehair, an infection soon set in, and he died of septicaemia on June 4, 1942, aged only thirty-eight.[xv]

Berlin awarded him a grand state funeral; with the disappearance of Reinhard Heydrich, Hitler lost the supreme organiser of the Final Solution, Himmler a most zealous assistant, and Felix Kersten a sworn enemy. On June 9, after the funeral ceremony, Himmler received the main section chiefs of the R.S.H.A. and told

xiv  Pure bravado: the aim was to show that he had nothing to fear from the Czech population.
xv  The reprisals against the resistance and the Czech population were horrific: more than 1,200 killed and the village of Lidice razed to the ground.

them: "It is impossible for another man to ever lead the gigantic apparatus of the R.S.H.A. [. . .] as Heydrich would have wished." Therefore, "with the Führer's agreement, I will personally take over the leadership of the R.S.H.A., pending the appointment of a suitable successor."[119] Shortly thereafter, Himmler received the head of section VI of the organisation (foreign intelligence), and told him the following: "I have conferred on several occasions with the Führer on the subject of Heydrich's succession. You yourself are not being considered; the Führer thinks you are too young[xvi] and I think you are not tough enough." After which Himmler abruptly changed the subject: "Tell me quite frankly what was the nature of your relations with Heydrich recently . . ." And without awaiting a reply, he went on: "Did you try to persuade Heydrich that he was the only man capable of succeeding the Führer? Heydrich himself hinted at something of the sort, albeit fleetingly. Be so good as to explain."[120]

Schellenberg had no difficulty in explaining that in view of his extremely tense relations with Heydrich, the last thing he would have desired was to see the latter accede to supreme power. Yet the Reichsführer's question was quite revealing: behind a facade of great cordiality and harmonious cooperation, Himmler was extremely wary of Heydrich, to whom he owed his meteoric rise to power, but who, being far more capable than himself, might one day supplant him in his functions – or even in higher functions; Himmler therefore kept a thick file replete with compromising documents on his subordinate Heydrich, who in turn had collected equally compromising documents on his chief Himmler. Which is why, during Heydrich's agony, the Reichsführer had rushed to his

xvi   Standartenführer Schellenberg was only thirty-two.

bedside – in order to retrieve the keys to his safe![121] The reader should always be reminded that he is here in the midst of a veritable snakepit.[122]

All this gave Schellenberg ample time to justify himself, after which Himmler, apparently reassured, went on: "Whoever the person appointed to head the R.S.H.A., you will remain chief of section VI, and you will answer directly to me. [. . .] Try to live an abstemious life. Henceforth, my personal physician, Kersten, will take care of you; he'll examine you, and, if he deems it appropriate, he will treat you regularly, as he does me. He has already worked miracles, and his treatment should surely benefit you. Kersten is Finnish and he is devoted to me; you can therefore trust him. Perhaps you'll have to be a bit careful, because he sometimes talks too much; in addition, he is very curious. But apart from that, he's quite a good egg and he's extremely helpful. Well, you'll see for yourself!"[123]

In taking over Heydrich's duties, Himmler found himself more deeply involved in the implementation of the Final Solution; in addition to his various roles as a channel for the Führer's orders, an inspector, a spur and a propagandist, he was now to become an organiser. This was not his favourite role: no doubt a fanatical executor and a nebulous theorist, he lacked the practical sense of the master builder. Unlike Hitler, he could issue perfectly clear orders, but being a hesitant, finicky, pedantic, overworked and procrastinating theorist, he tended to issue them out of sequence, and without really caring whether they were compatible or implementable – the essential criterion being that they satisfy the Führer. This did not escape Kersten, who was later to assert: "Himmler was capable of ordering, but not of achieving."[124] Yet at this stage, the foundations of Heydrich's industrial extermination apparatus were already extremely strong; the Jews and gypsies of the Reich, Poland, Bohemia-Moravia, Slovakia, Ukraine and the Baltic countries had already been deported and crammed together by tens of thousands in the main eastern ghettos: Theresienstadt, Warsaw, Kraków, Kovno, Vilna, Grodno, Bialystok, Lodz, Lublin, Minsk, Czestochowa and dozens of others. From there, many were transferred to the *Arbeitslager,* the labour camps of Mauthausen, Auschwitz I, Kaunas, Riga, Janowska, Plaszow and numerous secondary camps, where they were joined by Soviet war prisoners, Polish intellectuals, homosexuals, socialists, Jehovah's Witnesses, communists and resistance fighters. Such camps had abominable living conditions and a horrendous mortality rate. Yet the ultimate in horror was attained with the commissioning of the new extermination camps: Auschwitz-Birkenau, Belzec, Sobibor and soon Treblinka;[xvii] by June 1942, most of the deportees from France, Belgium, Holland and Luxembourg were sent directly to these death camps.

On July 17, Himmler personally inspected the facilities of Auschwitz, and witnessed the gassing of 449 Jews arrived from Holland that same morning. The camp commandant, Rudolf Höss, was to state much later: "He observed the extermination process in complete silence and made no comment."[125] But shortly thereafter, he issued several peremptory orders: "Corpses must be burned rather than buried;"[xviii] "The working capacity of the survivors must be increased, in spite of the reduction in rations;" "Even if

xvii   In addition to the two camps already functioning since the previous winter: Chelmno and Majdanek.
xviii   Crematoria were only to be installed the following year.

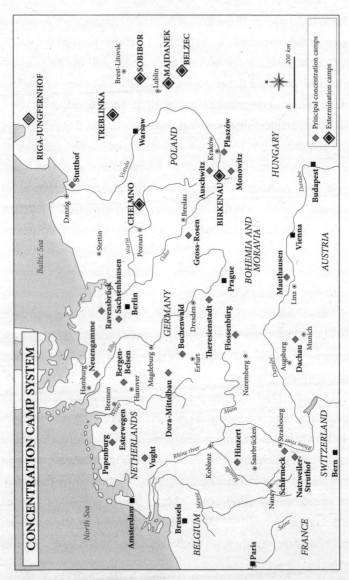

The Concentration Camp System

some of the camp guards are to be withdrawn for front duty, escapes must be prevented at all costs." Yet at the evening dinner, the man seemed utterly transformed: brimming with amiability, gallant with the ladies, holding forth on child-rearing, art, literature, travel, religion and philosophy. "I had never seen him like this," commented Rudolf Höss.[126] Yet this was indeed the other side of that two-faced Nazi Janus – the side he always took pains to show to Felix Kersten . . .

At Auschwitz and everywhere else, Himmler, having kept in place all the staff appointed by Heydrich, merely urged the police to conduct a more ferocious repression, the labour camp commanders to increase productivity,[xix] the executioners in the death camps to show even greater diligence, the rogue doctors to conduct ever more horrific experiments,[xx] and all the S.S. officers to respect the most absolute silence about what was happening in these antechambers of hell.

By the end of 1941, Himmler had expressly forbidden the photographing of executions – "except for reasons of service"[127] – and in accordance with Hitler's stringent order, he imposed on all his subordinates the exclusive use of a *Tarnsprache* – "camouflage language"; thus, there could be no oral or written mention of liquidations, but only the use of euphemisms such as "deportations", "work assignments", "transfers", "special treatments", "sidelining",

---

xix   Armament, munitions and vehicle industries were being set up next to the labour camps of Buchenwald, Neuengamme and Auschwitz I.

xx   Specifically designed to evaluate the degree of human resistance to extreme conditions of cold and lack of oxygen – all this for the (theoretical) benefit of the Wehrmacht and Luftwaffe. There were also experiments in massive sterilisation, and many others that seemed mostly designed to satisfy the sadistic instincts of the practitioners.

"appropriate solutions", "departures", "enforcement actions", "implementing measures", "removal", "Action Reinhard", "evacuations", "special actions", "displacements", "distancing", et cetera, *ad nauseam*.[xxi]

Although this rule of silence was strictly enforced, Kersten could not entirely ignore that less than five hundred kilometres from Berlin, in the eastern part of occupied Poland, unspeakable abominations were being committed – particularly as eight months earlier, Himmler had told him of Hitler's genocidal intentions concerning the Jewish people; yet Kersten logically and optimistically believed that the Nazi leaders, absorbed as they were by the war effort, would wait until after the war to carry out such a massive elimination. As for the "ordinary" camps in Germany herself – *Konzentrationslager, Arbeitslager, Sammellager, Durchgangslager*[xxii] – he believed the Reichsführer and his entourage when they assured him that these were merely "rehabilitation centres, where wrongdoers were properly treated and turned into honourable and socially useful citizens".[xxiii]

Only in July 1942 did Kersten see the light, in circumstances he was later to explain: "It so happened that my Hartzwalde estate was short of labour force and the harvesting season was nearing. Thereupon, I learned that some of my neighbours had obtained workers from the Ravensbrück concentration camp. I therefore applied directly to the agricultural commissioner for the loan of

---

xxi   The meaning of other camouflage terms such as *Endlösung* (Final Solution) or *N.N.* (*Nacht und Nebel* – Night and Fog) only became obvious to all after the Reich's downfall.
xxii   Concentration, work, transit and "short stay" camps.
xxiii   See above, p. 87.

some of them, and on July 27, 1942[xxiv] I received ten women for one week. [. . .] As an exceptional favour, they were allowed to stay the night, for my estate was located rather far from the railway track, and the twenty-two kilometres of road leading to the camp were very poorly maintained. [. . .] These women belonged to the sect of Jehovah's Witnesses. Due to their religious beliefs, they had always refused to adhere to the Nazi party, and even to give the Nazi salute. [. . .] Since they considered war to be sinful, they also refused to participate in work that could be used for war purposes, which had exposed them to the worst retribution: locked in isolation cells, they were whipped and endured all sorts of humiliations. [. . .] Once their shoes were worn out, they received no others and had to walk barefoot in the snow during the winter; they were forced to work until they dropped, and to join in brisk marches which even the most vigorous soldiers would hardly have survived. On top of that, they had been fed famine rations for years; they were skeleton-thin and suffered from numerous sicknesses due to malnutrition and lack of hygiene."[128]

Yet the tales they had to tell were more frightening still. "They asked me for one thing only: absolute silence, for if it were known that they had talked, they would meet certain death. I gradually got to learn more details that made me understand why the German people knew so little about the concentration camps; for in the camp itself, the detainees often lived without any knowledge of the murders that were constantly perpetrated against their companions in misfortune. Thus, for instance, one of the women

xxiv   As so often, the date is untrustworthy: it must have happened before July 17 or between July 20 and July 23, since Kersten was not in Germany from the 17th to the 20th, and he was no longer there after the 24th.

who had worked for years in the camp's clothing barracks [. . .] noticed one day that the clothes of several women who had gone to work in the morning had been returned to her in the evening, whereas the women themselves had disappeared. What had become of them? After a few days, this woman, who had asked one of the guards, received an unambiguous reply, together with an injunction to keep absolutely silent about it – if she valued her life."[129]

Kersten was astounded. "I was enlightened; the sinister forebodings of the last few years, the fears and preoccupations of my friends, all this was thus confirmed and surpassed a hundredfold. I knew I had to do something, but what? I resolved to ask Himmler for confirmation of these atrocities at the earliest; but for that, I had to await a favourable opportunity."[130]

That opportunity was slow in coming, since the eastern front was ablaze once again. In accordance with his plan Blau, conceived during the spring, Hitler intended to set forth from Kursk and Kharkov, strike east towards Vononezh, then attack south and south-east in order to destroy the Soviet armies concentrated between the Don and the Donets; next, he would build a vast line of defence stretching from Voronezh to Rostov and Stalingrad on the Volga, before occupying the Caucasus with all its oilfields. Between May and early July 1942, after having won three crushing victories at Kharkov, Sebastopol and Voronezh – and captured more than five hundred thousand prisoners in the process – Hitler duly launched two armies towards Rostov and a third towards Stalingrad and the Volga. On July 16, he set up his headquarters in a pine forest twelve kilometres from Vinnitsa, south-west of Kiev; from a camp of log huts perfectly camouflaged in the forest, the Führer henceforth personally directed the campaign in its minutest details, and virtually overnight he undertook to change his strategy: on July 23, he ordered that the offensives towards the Volga and the Caucasus be carried out *simultaneously*. This amounted to dividing his forces and making them fight on two opposite fronts – separated by more than seven hundred kilometres of steppes, forests and mountains!

The truth is that the Reich's foremost strategist remained untroubled by considerations of distance, terrain, weather, road conditions, supply situation, manpower exhaustion and equipment attrition; besides, he relied on his intuitions alone, scorned intelligence reports, despised his generals and rejected their advice, wanted to strike everywhere at the same time, blindly believed in the omnipotence of willpower and constantly underestimated the enemy. All this was true enough, but by late July 1942, between Don and Donets, the Wehrmacht was advancing relentlessly and the Red Army was in full retreat.

## THE WEHRMACHT'S SUMMER OFFENSIVE, 1942

|  |  | | |
|---|---|---|---|
| 🗲 Hitler's General HQ | → German offensive | | ⋯ Marsh |
| ⋯⋯ Borders of the German progression, May 1942 | | 🛢 Oil areas | |

*The Wehrmacht's Summer Offensive, 1942*

# 6

# CREST LINE

Once Hitler had established his headquarters in Ukraine, Himmler
lost no time in joining him; on July 24, 1942, he set up camp
with his staff near Jitomir, about one hundred kilometres north
of Vinnitsa – and he was of course accompanied by his regular
practitioner, who described their new living conditions as follows:
"The Jitomir headquarters was installed on the premises of a Soviet
military school, so it had not been necessary to reconstruct or
modify it. The first floor of the main building was one immense
hall, perfectly suited to meetings and conferences. I was the only
civilian, and my movements were rather restricted. In East Prussia,
I could go for long walks in the forest, but around Jitomir this was
ruled out. I had to be content with roaming around the shooting
range, which was about a hundred metres long and surrounded
by barbed wire. [. . .] I could only walk around in circles like a
prisoner, stopping from time to time to observe the soldiers' shooting practice. It was my first stay in Russia, and I was irritated by
these restrictions to my freedom of movement. 'If you wore a
uniform, you'd be able to go wherever you please,' Himmler told
me, but I refused the offer, as usual.[i] Seeing that all this did not

i   It was surely not that simple: a month later, probably at Himmler's insistence,
Kersten was to write to the Finnish minister of foreign affairs, asking for permission

suit me, Himmler put a car at my disposal from time to time, and on market days I could also drive to Jitomir, under protection.[ii] The countryside we were going through seemed to me quite unreal: flat, yellow, infinite stretches of land, scorched by the burning summer sun. At the market, the people looked picturesque in their multicoloured garments, yet they seemed oppressed and fearful; they moved slowly and ponderously, as if in a dream. I talked with a few of them[iii] and bought sunflower seeds from them."[131]

Himmler, for one, had no time to stroll: "On July 27," Kersten noted, "he came back from the Führer's headquarters at five in the morning. It had been an important meeting, at which the participants discussed the partition of the European part of Russia after victory. According to Himmler, the Führer was absolutely convinced that Russian resistance as a whole was about to collapse, and that now was the time to prepare the partitioning of Russia."[132] As a result, Himmler had reserved the fertile soils of Ukraine for his S.S., and he generously offered to give Kersten an estate in that region – which the latter politely refused, on the grounds that he intended to retire in Finland at the end of the war. Himmler then addressed more momentous issues: "Hitler wants all Finnish Jews to be brought to Poland – to Majdanek. He considers that, as the war will soon be over, one must act quickly in order to eradicate the Jews. [. . .] The moment is particularly appropriate to compel

to wear the uniform of a German military doctor. Permission was granted, but no-one seems ever to have seen him decked in such a garb.

ii   In another version, he recalled going there alone and without protection, after which he was severely reprimanded by Himmler's security service. The admonition was doubtless justified: three months later, Himmler's pilot Carl Schnäbele, on the same jaunt, was murdered by Ukrainian partisans.

iii   No doubt with the Russian he had learned at Yourieff some four decades earlier.

Finland to make concessions over the Jews, for that country presently suffers from an acute shortage of grain for bread. The German government has let it be known that it is willing to supply this grain, provided the Jews are delivered to Germany. Indeed, the Finnish grain supplies will last only until September, and without the importation of about 30,000 tons, the Finns will inevitably face a serious food crisis."[133]

Such was the bargain that Himmler was about to propose – or rather to impose – during his trip to Helsinki two days later. Kersten lost no time in informing Finnish ambassador Kivimäki,[iv] who beseeched him to dissuade the Reichsführer from undertaking such a trip – and in case of failure, to accompany him at all costs. "The next day, I said to Himmler that the state of his health did not allow him to embark on such a tiring trip. But my patient replied that Hitler's pressing demand made the voyage imperative – the more so as he intended to inspect the Waffen S.S. units in northern Finland. Thereupon he proposed that I accompany him, in order to pursue the treatment."[134] Himmler apparently added that Kersten could also act as an interpreter during that visit.

On the morning of July 29, the Reichsführer therefore took off for Finland, accompanied by Kersten, his aide-de-camp Karl Wolff and the usual security personnel. But shortly after their landing in Helsinki, Himmler was once again tormented by his abdominal cramps, and Kersten had to treat him on the spot. He described what followed in these terms: "As we were alone, I undertook to persuade him that an impromptu discussion of the Jewish question with the Finnish government was inopportune. When in the throes

iv   It is not known how he did this, since all his telephone conversations were listened to, and he was strictly forbidden to speak any language other than German.

of pain, he was more malleable than usual, and he eventually agreed to let me establish preliminary contact with a few senior Finns. Once the treatment was over, Himmler, Wolff and I went to lunch with President Ryti and his spouse. Owing to his indisposition, Himmler returned to his hotel immediately after the meal, so I was able to discuss the object of his visit with Foreign Minister Witting. We agreed that the first thing to do was to try to have the Jewish problem dealt with by procrastination. There were several possibilities in this respect; the simplest was to tell Himmler that the Jews could not be surrendered without the Finnish parliament's consent; at that time, however, Parliament was in recess and would not be meeting again until November. Without defining the precise attitude of the Finnish government, we had to let it be understood that the government was ready to call an extraordinary session of Parliament, but, at the same time, we would point out that such a convening in the middle of a war might arouse political passions and raise a host of other unwelcome questions. In addition, Himmler would be told that handing over the Jews could lead to a deterioration of Finnish opinion towards Germany – the more so as during the Winter War and the present campaign a number of Jews had heroically sacrificed their lives for Finland. No Finn would understand how one could agree to surrender the mothers and wives of such men. On the other hand, however, one had to take into account the fact that Finland was hamstrung by her grain shortage. In the light of these considerations, we decided that Witting would reply along these lines as soon as Himmler raised the Jewish question; in the meantime, I would use my influence with Himmler to support Witting's stance."[135]

What followed is less clear, for in the various editions of his memoirs, Kersten gave a number of incompatible versions – some of which were also chronologically aberrant. However, on the basis of plausibility and of Himmler's appointment diary, the following version[v] can be retained: "Once back at my hotel, I told Himmler [. . .] that the Finnish government agreed in principle with his proposal concerning the Finnish Jews. But I added that the practical implementation of the plan faced certain difficulties, and I presented things in such terms that Himmler, instead of being disappointed and upset, expressed complete satisfaction. He immediately asked to be put in telephone communication with Hitler's headquarters, and reported to the Führer that negotiations were progressing favourably – which Hitler was content with for the moment."[136]

That communication must have taken place in the evening of July 29,[vi] and the next day, Himmler paid a visit to Marshal Mannerheim at his headquarters in Mikkeli – after which he was to spend four days on inspection tours to Wehrmacht and S.S. units in northern Finland, from Oulu to Rovaniemi. The civilian Kersten was left behind in Helsinki, and in the afternoon of July 31 he was invited to the house of President Risto Ryti, together with minister Rolf Witting. In the course of a long conversation, the three men agreed that "the Finnish vessel ought to move away from German waters slowly and discreetly". When Kersten asked whether Finland ought not to break completely with Germany, Witting replied: "Unfortunately, it's impossible for the time being; Finland cannot surrender to the Russians. But the ideas and proposals

v   As set out in the Swedish version of his memoirs: *Samtal med Himmler*, published in 1947.
vi   Or at night: Hitler was an insomniac.

brought by Himmler are appalling;[vii] Finland is a free country, whose policy is governed by honour and justice. It cannot extradite its Jews and refuses to do so."[137]

Having returned from his tours of inspection, Himmler was received on August 4 by Prime Minister Rangell, with whom he immediately raised the question of the Finnish Jews. Upon receiving the glacial reply "*Wir haben keine Judenfrage*",[viii] [138] the moderately courageous Reichsführer promptly backpedalled: "I wanted to bring the Finnish Jews back with me immediately, but Medizinalrat Kersten explained to me that this would raise technical problems for the time being, and as I have always been opposed to measures that stir up too much emotion among the public, I felt that it would be more judicious to wait until the question was dealt with more discreetly during the ordinary session of Parliament in November."[139] Of course, no such thing was to be discussed in November, but the Finns duly received their grain, the Jews were not extradited, and Felix Kersten was awarded the Finnish Order of the White Rose – in recognition for something more than his services as an interpreter. [ix] Ambassador Kivimäki was later to confirm that Kersten had originally informed him of Himmler's plan to have all Finnish Jews deported to Poland, adding that Kersten's intervention "contributed to the fact that the plan was not seriously brought up". Foreign Minister Henrik

vii  It would seem that in the course of a face-to-face conversation, Himmler had also proposed to Witting that Finland initiate a conflict with Sweden, thus giving Germany a pretext to invade the latter country. Without showing it, Witting had been indignant at the dishonesty of the proposal.

viii  "We have no Jewish question."

ix  Actually, such services had not been required: in Finland, the president, the prime minister, the foreign minister and Marshal Mannerheim all spoke perfect German.

Ramsay hinted just as discreetly that "in the important matter of Finland's supply of grain from Germany, Herr Kersten intervened forcefully to forestall all difficulties and delays".[140]

On August 6, during the return trip, Himmler may already have understood that he had been duped, for he confided to Kersten: "That Ryti is an English *Sir*, he went to school in England and, what's more, he's a Freemason. He will never be a friend of national socialism and he is certainly anti-German.[x] I even consider him a very dangerous man. [. . .] Besides, I never trusted these Freemasons Ryti and Mannerheim,[xi] and now I see that I was right."[141]

In Jitomir, Kersten resumed the routine of life at headquarters with its scorching daytime heat, biting night-time cold and relentless assaults by voracious mosquitoes. The Reichsführer's health still leaving much to be desired, Kersten's ministrations remained necessary, and he supplied them with dedication – yet without forgetting his resolutions of the previous month about the concentration camps: "Perhaps a doctor ought to limit himself to the practice of healing . . . But it appeared to me quite clearly that if I wanted to keep my peace of mind, I had to act. [. . .] I thus conceived a plan that was likely to help me in dealing with Himmler. Summoned to headquarters a few days later, I immediately took the offensive by asking with feigned naivety if it was true that concentration camp inmates were systematically tortured and murdered. Himmler replied with a laugh: 'Well then, Kersten, you seem to have fallen victim to enemy propaganda! They are really

x There was much truth in all this: Risto Ryti had briefly been an Oxford student, he was a Knight Commander of the Royal Victorian Order, undeniably a Freemason, far more Anglophile than Germanophile and absolutely hostile to national socialism.

xi Mannerheim was not a Freemason.

cunning in spreading false rumours about us!' I retorted that these were not rumours: what I had heard came from reliable sources . . . Himmler immediately wanted to know what these sources were, so I answered: 'Some time ago, at the Finnish legation, I met some Swiss people who were about to leave for Sweden. They had photographs of concentration camps that they had bought from S.S. guards . . .' Himmler fell headlong into the trap, and he interrupted me: 'That's impossible! Did you really see these photographs of concentration camps? Are these gentlemen still in Germany? If so, I must speak to them forthwith!' I replied that the Swiss gentlemen were no doubt in Sweden already, and added that those reports on the concentration camps were obviously not mere propaganda. He then said: 'I admit that regrettable things may happen there from time to time – but all that is distorted and exaggerated. For heaven's sake, tell me: is there no way these photographs can be bought back?' When I answered that this was out of the question, Himmler seemed quite preoccupied."[142]

Thus enlightened, Kersten set out to learn more, by eliciting the confidences of Himmler's entourage. "I gradually succeeded in overcoming their reluctance, and, swearing me to silence, they told me things that not only tallied with the frightening descriptions of the women from Ravensbrück, but surpassed them by far. Most of them were ashamed of such deeds, [. . .] very few attempted to justify them, and almost all agreed that the German people were entirely ignorant of conditions prevailing in these camps. [. . .] But when I asserted that they themselves held positions that would enable them to intervene, they merely shrugged: they were powerless – and besides, it was none of their business. [. . .] When I asked them why they didn't refuse to participate in such atrocities, they gave me a bewildered look and replied: 'We must obey, or else we'll be killed ourselves.'"[143]

By mid-August 1942, the greatest optimism prevailed at the headquarters of Vinnitsa and Jitomir: General Paulus' Sixth Army, moving forward at full speed, encircled and destroyed two Soviet armies before Kalach, only seventy kilometres east of Stalingrad; in the south, Marshal List's Army Group A crossed the Kuban plains to occupy Stavropol, Armavir and Maïkop. On August 19, Hitler told Goebbels that the great assault against Stalingrad was about to begin and that the city would be taken in eight days, then it would be "razed to the ground". He added that he intended to capture the Caucasus oilfields during the summer, thus securing his oil supplies and cutting off those of the enemy, after which he would "burst into the Near East, occupy Asia Minor and invade Iraq, Iran and Palestine, thus depriving Britain of its oil supplies".[144] The Führer clearly remained untroubled by considerations of time, distance and logistics . . .

Himmler, for one, preferred to focus on the organisation of regions already conquered; he had presented Hitler with his ideas on the setting up in Russia of villages inhabited by "soldier peasants",[xii] and the following morning, Kersten found him in a state of great excitement. "You cannot understand how happy I am, Herr Kersten! The Führer not only listened to me, he even refrained from interrupting constantly, as he usually does. [. . .]

xii   *Wehrbauern.* In *Totenkopf und Treue,* his "journal" published in 1952, Kersten asserts that this conversation took place on July 16, 1942, which seems unreasonable: at that date, the Reichsführer S.S. had not even established his headquarters in Jitomir! Based on Himmler's appointment diary, the most probable date is August 10, taking into account the following entry: "Lunch with Hitler at Vinnitsa August 9, 14h–15h. Treatment by Kersten at Jitomir, August 10, 9 a.m."

And he approved the proposals I submitted to him,[xiii] asking questions and drawing my attention to important details I hadn't thought of. [. . .] It's the happiest day of my life!"

Kersten asked him to lie down so he could begin the treatment, but Himmler wasn't listening, and he went on: "I linked the arguments I presented to the Führer with the idea of defending Europe's living space, which I know the Führer particularly values. Villages inhabited by an armed peasantry will be the basis of the settlement in the east – and simultaneously of its defence; they will be the kernel of Europe's great defensive wall, which the Führer must set up after the victorious conclusion of the war. Germanic villages inhabited by a military peasantry and filling a belt several hundred miles wide – just imagine, Herr Kersten, what a magnificent idea! [. . .] Once he has accomplished that, Adolf Hitler's name will be the greatest in Germanic history – and I am the one to whom he has entrusted the task!"

Himmler took out a document from a pile of records and presented it to his astounded practitioner.

"Look, Herr Kersten, here is the ground plan of a Germanic *Wehrbauern* village, as it will be laid out in the east. Such a village will include thirty to forty farms; each farmer will receive up to three hundred acres of land, more or less according to the quality of the soil. Thus will develop a class of financially powerful and independent farmers. [. . .] The head of this farming community will at the same time be the military commander of the *Wehrbauern* village."

xiii   Sure enough, Hitler had already expressed his interest in that project back in April 1942. See Henry Picker (Ed.), *Hitlers Tischgespräche*, Ullstein, Berlin, 1989, p. 202.

"Then it would also be a military unit?" Kersten asked.

"But of course. That is one of the most important tasks to be entrusted to these villages of military peasants. [. . .] Each village, with its forty farms, its farmers, their sons and labourers will have roughly the battle strength of a company, and the company commander will occupy the estate. They will all be fighting for their own farms and their own hearths; everyone will know that any measures taken have not been ordered by a distant bureaucracy, but by autonomous farmers, men subject to the laws they have themselves enacted."

Though still taken aback, Kersten raised an initial objection:

"I can well imagine the actual installation of the settlement itself, but to connect it with the military problem seems to me pure fantasy. After all, we are no longer living in the age of Gustavus Adolphus, who could fight with peasant armies and for whom the most primitive weaponry was enough. But today, one operates with tanks, flamethrowers, aircraft, etc. Seen in that light, all this appears to me as just a fine piece of Germanic romanticism."

"We are no longer living in the age of Gustavus Adolphus . . ." How could Kersten guess that, on the contrary, the Führer was living entirely in the spirit of the Thirty Years' war? That, on his own admission, one of his greatest ambitions was to "liquidate the Treaty of Westphalia"?[145] Indeed, his *Pressechef*, Otto Dietrich, was to describe Hitler as "a figure out of the past",[146] and Himmler was no more than his ventriloquist puppet. But Kersten having the mindset of a more rational – and more civilised – century, comprehension between the two men was by no means easy.

"So, Herr Kersten, you want to be cleverer than the Führer [. . .]. He has stipulated that every *Wehrbauer* must take his rifle home with him, together with his steel helmet and other equipment. The smallest unit will possess machine guns, automatic weapons and grenades; there will be tanks at battalion level."

Kersten remained doubtful.

"But will men enjoy always having to play at soldiers? Young men will like it well enough for two years, and will gladly take part in training exercises, but they certainly won't enjoy being permanently under this military pressure."

"Leave us to worry about that," Himmler replied. "We'll soon fix it by psychological methods. It's merely a question of training – which is right up our street. [. . .] Cowards are born in towns, heroes in the country. We just have to create the preconditions, and a new nation of heroes will arise in the east."[147]

Yet all good things must come to an end, and Kersten noted:

"Once again, Himmler had forgotten all the people who were waiting to see him – and his treatment too; I therefore proposed to postpone it until the evening.

'My God,' Brandt said as I came out of the room, 'you really gave the Reichsführer a long treatment today!'

'Not at all,' I replied, 'today he gave *me* a treatment. My head is still swimming with all the talk about military peasantry, farm settlements, farmer-sniper units, tank and parachute units, etc. [ . . .]'

'Don't you think it's a good idea, then?' Brandt asked. 'The Führer seems to be taken with it too . . .'

'I won't express any judgment on it,' I answered, 'but the Reichsführer does not understand the farmers, he paints himself an ideal picture of a Germanic military peasantry that cannot exist in reality. The farmer is primarily an egoist; he will doubtless be glad to take a farm in the east, but if he then has to play at war all the time, the Reichsführer will soon find how much opposition he has brought upon himself and what resistance will grow against him. The farmer is wholly occupied with the job of farming, and regards everything that keeps him away from it as useless fiddling about. He will gladly ride and shoot here and there on Sundays as a kind of social activity, but not under military compulsion. I would like to see farmers ruining their own fields by running tanks over them!'"[148]

Sure enough, we have just witnessed a conversation between two former agronomy students, one of whom still had his feet on the ground and the other who was given to flights of ideological fancy . . .

Kersten could thus hardly be blamed if he had the impression of being trapped inside a lunatic asylum administered by its most dangerous inmates; but he had seen nothing yet, as he noted a few days later. "August 20, 1942.[xiv] Today, I treated Himmler, who was suffering from exceptional pains. Once finally relieved, he relaxed and what I had so often experienced happened once again: his pent-up thoughts now poured out, and in his relief, he confided them to me. Talk turned to Heydrich's death. Hitler had been severely shaken by it. Heydrich's death meant 'more to him than a lost battle'. [. . .] A really tragic fate. It would be very difficult to find a substitute for this highly gifted man. Hitler had had other great tasks in view for him. He, Himmler, would have great

xiv   Here too, the indication of date is unreliable: on August 20, Himmler was on an inspection visit between Lvov (Lemberg) and Lublin – without Kersten. This conversation must have taken place at Jitomir on August 11, 12 or 13 – the three dates of treatment entered in the Reichsführer's diary. (The most likely explanation is that Kersten had omitted most dates in the notes taken at the time, and had to try to reconstruct the chronology several years after the war.)

difficulty in appointing his successor from within the police."[149] Kersten seized the opportunity to ask him a question:

"According to certain rumours, Heydrich was not entirely Aryan, but that can hardly be true, can it?"

"Yes, it's true enough."

"Did you know that before, or have you only learned of it since his death? And does Herr Hitler know about it?"

"I already knew it when I was still head of the Bavarian political police. I reported it to the Führer at the time; he had Heydrich brought before him, talked to him for a long time and was very favourably impressed by him. Later, the Führer informed me that Heydrich was a highly gifted but also a very dangerous man, whose gifts the movement had to retain. Such people could only be used if they were kept under close control, and in this respect his non-Aryan origins were extremely useful; for he would be eternally grateful to us that we had held on to him and not expelled him, and he would obey blindly. That is indeed what happened . . ."

And Kersten added: "While Himmler talked, I remembered the servile way in which Heydrich had always approached him, and my eyes were opened."

But Himmler went on:

"The Führer could confidently entrust Heydrich with tasks that no-one else would care to take on, and rest assured that he would carry them out perfectly – even the action against the Jews."

Kersten could not repress a movement of indignation.

"Then you have made use of one of their own people, whom you had under your thumb, to exterminate the Jews? That's a really devilish trick!"

134

"What do you mean? Just read Machiavelli and his teachings on *raison d'Etat*, and you'll find much more than that. Do you think that times have changed? Methods have just become more refined. Machiavelli wouldn't have behaved a whit differently if it was a question of saving the state and employing forces which he could keep permanently under control."

"Thereupon," wrote Kersten, "I remained silent, and Himmler ended the conversation by asking me to keep quiet for the time being about what he had just told me."[150]

Since nowadays most historians agree on the fact that Heydrich had no Jewish ancestors, one might conclude that the above conversation was purely imaginary. But this would be forgetting that the actors of 1942 did not feel bound by the conclusions of historians from 2024; indeed, the former were rather influenced by information and rumours circulating before the war, which taken together told the following story: in the early thirties, a baker from Halle had revealed that Heydrich's paternal grandmother, whom he knew well, was named Sarah and was Jewish. Reinhard Heydrich sued the baker and won his case, since the "slanderer" had been unable to produce "material proof of his allegations". But in the course of the review procedure, the baker had requested that the ecclesiastical and civil registers of the city of Halle be consulted, and it appeared that on both registers, the pages for the month of March 1904 had disappeared.[xv] Between 1935 and 1937, Heydrich had sued two other men who claimed to have proof of his Jewish ancestry, but before their case went to trial, the first one had recanted and the second had "disappeared mysteriously". By 1939, rumour also had it that in the Leipzig cemetery, Sarah

xv   Reinhard Heydrich was born in Halle on March 7, 1904.

Heydrich's tombstone had been replaced by another, simply bearing the inscription "S. Heydrich".[151]

Whatever the value of such information, the fact remains that it was taken very seriously at the time. Actually, it had fed numerous files kept by the main hierarchs of the Nazi party[xvi] – and even by a few military men; thus General Hans Piekenbrock, chief of Abwehr section 1,[xvii] later recalled that his chief, Admiral Canaris, kept a full copy of the proceedings of the three above-mentioned trials, as well as the invoice of the marble worker who had changed Sarah Heydrich's tombstone.[152] Indeed, the admiral had even informed her grandson Reinhard of the fact, in order to secure something of a "life insurance" – which was an extremely common practice in the Third Reich.[153] Another chief of intelligence confirmed this: S.S. Colonel Walter Schellenberg, the head of R.S.H.A. section VI and therefore Heydrich's immediate subordinate: "Canaris told me after Heydrich's death that he possessed proof of Heydrich's Jewish ancestry."[154] Admittedly, when the section chiefs of two intelligence services as well informed and implacably antagonistic as the Abwehr and the S.S. agreed on something, it was difficult not to take it seriously – which is clearly what Heinrich Himmler had done.

This self-same Walter Schellenberg was summoned to Jitomir by Himmler on August 12, 1942; the Reichsführer had several missions to entrust to him, but Schellenberg in turn had a rather unexpected proposal to make: the S.S. intelligence chief, having

---

xvi   Very much including Martin Bormann, to whom Heydrich represented a permanent threat.

xvii   In charge of foreign military intelligence.

studied at length the economic and military capacities of the United States and the U.S.S.R., had already concluded by January 1942 that a war against these two allied powers simply could not be won; he had therefore decided to ask Himmler for permission to initiate secret communications with the Allies, in order to assess the possibility of a compromise peace! After asking him if he had gone mad, the Reichsführer went through various emotional stages – indignation, incredulity, uncertainty, anxiety, resignation – eventually leading to a conditional assent; after all, there had to be a way out in case the Führer's military adventure went awry. All the same, it was a risky business, the more so as in order to negotiate with some hope of success, Ribbentrop would have to be removed from the foreign ministry. Schellenberg was eventually allowed to establish exploratory contact with some intermediaries in neutral countries; but fear quickly gaining the upper hand, Himmler added the following characteristic caveat: "If you make a serious mistake in your approaches, I'll drop you like a hot potato."[155]

According to Himmler's diary, Schellenberg was indeed received at lunch with seven other officers on August 12 at 14.00, and again at 16.45 for a face-to-face interview. Now the next visitor, at 18.30, was none other than Felix Kersten.[156] The two men must therefore have run into each other . . . Actually, they did rather more than that: the previous evening, Schellenberg, on his chief's recommendation, had gone to visit Kersten for a medical examination; his health was admittedly a cause for concern, since he was getting markedly thinner for no apparent reason – which the S.S. doctors had ascribed to ill-defined liver or gallbladder disorders. Had Kersten and Schellenberg met before? They were

137

to contradict each other more than once on the subject,[xviii] but on that same evening, Schellenberg gave us an interesting description of the man he was to rub shoulders with more than once during the next few years: "In appearance, he was a rather unattractive man: round and fat, weighing by my estimation more than 200 pounds. His massive hands would never have led one to suspect the extreme sensitivity of his fingertips. In addition, he had an unusual black ring around the iris of his light blue eyes,[xix] which could often disturb the observer, since it gave him at times an almost reptilian look. [. . .] On the whole, he was good-natured and kindly, even jovial most of the time."[157]

Kersten was to give us the other half of the double portrait: "Schellenberg struck me with the correctness of his demeanour; he was not a rabid national socialist, but an intelligent officer who nourished an instinctive aversion to the brutality of the system. [. . .] Once satisfied that this aversion was perfectly genuine, I decided to associate him with my undertaking."[158] Sure enough, the two men conversed all night and quickly sympathised.

"After a long conversation," recalled Schellenberg, "I was sure that Kersten entirely agreed with my ideas regarding an early termination of the war. He even agreed to use all his influence with Himmler to that effect. [. . .] For my part, I promised Kersten to protect him against Müller."[xx] [159]

A sound basis of agreement – almost immediately sealed by therapy: that same evening, Medizinalrat Kersten, having diagnosed

xviii  Thus, Schellenberg was to state in his memoirs that they had already met the previous year, but he had said the opposite to his British interrogators in 1945.
xix  Something of a mystery, since Kersten's son Arno told this author that he had never noticed the slightest black ring in his father's eyes.
xx  Heinrich "Gestapo" Müller, chief of R.S.H.A. section IV.

a functional dysphrenia[xxi] coupled with strong tensions around the duodenum,[160] relieved his new patient with the first treatment – and rid him of all pains by the fifth![161] Such things naturally nurture friendship; their common interests were soon to foster complicity as well . . .

xxi   A malformation of the diaphragm, which could cause breathing difficulties.

# 7

# THE SHADOW OF A DOUBT

By the autumn of 1942, triumphalism had somewhat regressed among the Nazi leaders; at Stalingrad as in the Caucasus, Soviet resistance had considerably stiffened, and as Joseph Goebbels wrote in his diary on September 16: "One has to admit that in this instance the Bolsheviks are demonstrating a defensive energy of which very few would have thought them capable."[162] Indeed . . . All the more so as Hitler's main objective, the oil fields of the northern Caucasus, had been sealed or set alight before the withdrawal of Soviet troops, so that the Wehrmacht could not draw a single drop of petrol from that source. In addition, Allied bombing raids over Germany had considerably intensified, and those of September against Karlsruhe, Bremen, Düsseldorf, Frankfurt and Munich had caused serious damage to their industrial installations; in Egypt, Marshal Rommel's German-Italian army had been brought to a standstill a hundred kilometres from Alexandria, in front of a coastal locality called El-Alamein; in the South Pacific, Japanese expansion had also been blocked south of the Solomon Islands, near a small island called Guadalcanal.

All this notwithstanding, Hitler remained highly optimistic that September of 1942: the fall of Stalingrad was only a question of days, after which the city would be razed to the ground – along with its remaining inhabitants; as for the occupation of the Georgian coast up to Batumi, it would be a mere formality: "The difficulties can be overcome. [. . .] We must first conquer the road. After that, the way to the plains of the South Caucasus will be open, and once there, we'll be able to quarter our armies at leisure and set up supply bases. [. . .] Then, with minimal forces, we can liberate Persia and Iraq; the Indians will give our divisions a triumphal welcome."[163]

Did Himmler share this enthusiasm? As a slavish and unconditional admirer of the Führer, he had not the slightest doubt as to Hitler's strategic genius – which was made easier by the fact that Heinrich Himmler's military aptitude was quite comparable to Hermann Göring's economic skills. For all that, the Reichsführer could not help but register a few troubling facts: the successive defeats of the Soviet armies over the last fifteen months did not seem to have seriously affected their ability to resist – witness the disproportionate losses suffered by his S.S. divisions; the exploitation of the agricultural, mining and energy resources of Ukraine and Byelorussia had also proved disappointing, mainly due to the scorched earth policy ordered by Stalin,[164] and the strength of partisan movements in regions that had greeted the Germans as liberators a year earlier was a growing cause for concern.[i] Last but not least, it seemed hardly reassuring that the Führer had deemed necessary to dismiss in less than a month both his chief of staff, General Halder, and the head of Army Group A in the Caucasus, Marshal List. In view of some

i   But Himmler's fanaticism probably prevented him from understanding that the causes were both the horrific massacres perpetrated by his Einsatzgruppen and the cruel incompetence of Alfred Rosenberg's Reichkommissars.

recent precedents,[ii] one might suspect that they were being used as scapegoats . . .

Perhaps for all these reasons, the Reichsführer refrained from boasting of the Wehrmacht's triumphs during his morning therapy sessions between September 8 and September 23, 1942.[165] In fact, Kersten was the one who spoke most of the time – usually to extol the merits of all the people whose liberation he was requesting: Belgians, Luxembourgers, Estonians, Latvians, Dutch, French . . . and Norwegians. Two of the latter had been particularly recommended to him by Finnish Ambassador Kivimäki: the banker and honorary Finnish consul in Oslo Johannes Sejersted Bødtker and the rector of Oslo University Didrik Arup Seip[iii] – both arrested a year earlier and sent to concentration camps. During the next few weeks, the latter, detained in Sachsenhausen, was to be the subject of intense bargaining, as Kersten recalled: "Himmler gave me dilatory answers. However, I eventually learned [. . .] that there could be no question of releasing Professor Seip, because he had been caught stealing! I inquired as to the real reasons and, thanks to Dr Brandt, I finally learned that during the unloading of a supply of carrots, Seip had taken a few, for which he had been sentenced to five beatings with a stick! I reported this to Himmler; he had the information checked and it proved to be true. Whereupon I asked him if it was compatible with Germanic dignity that Professor Seip – a man of the same race – should receive a corporal punishment. Himmler seemed much affected by the whole affair;

ii   Nine months earlier, after the Soviet counteroffensive of December 1941, the Führer had already dismissed thirty-five generals, the head of the three army groups operating in Russia and the army commander-in-chief, Walther von Brauchitsch.
iii   Unbeknown to the Germans, Rector Seip was one of the ten members of the council of Norwegian civil resistance known as *Kretsen* – the Circle.

at any rate, he ordered that the camp commander apologise to Seip. [. . .] In the end, he declared himself ready to release him, but refused to let him go back to Norway: he would be allowed to work in a Munich library and could be joined by his wife."[166]

On October 31, 1942, in Sachsenhausen concentration camp, where 16,000 prisoners of all nationalities were crammed together and thousands died each month of deprivation, exhaustion and ill-treatment, a very emaciated Rector Seip was picked up by two S.S. officers and driven to Berlin. His new place of detention was to be the *Hausgefängnis*[iv] located at 8 Prinz-Albrecht-Strasse – the seat of the Gestapo – which clearly did not bode well. But from then on, the rector was to go from astonishment to amazement: he was asked whether he preferred an individual cell, and his questioning sessions turned into interviews, during which he was asked about his early years, his studies and his travels abroad! More incredible still: on December 23, he was visited in his cell by a "General Müller" in full uniform,[v] who apologised to him for the abuse he had suffered, and added: "I wish to inform you that those responsible have been punished."[167] And on Christmas Eve 1942, Seip was escorted to a train bound for Munich and put up at the Vier Jahreszeiten – the best hotel in Munich; three days later, he was joined by his wife and informed that he was authorised to pursue his research work in the Munich University library.[168]

Like all prisoners released on orders from Himmler, Rector Seip had no idea to whom he owed his good fortune; but after the war, he wrote in his memoirs, *Hjemme og I Fiendeland*:[vi] "In December

iv  "Internal prison".
v  Obviously Gruppenführer Heinrich Müller, a.k.a. "Gestapo Müller".
vi  *At home and in enemy country.*

1945, Ambassador Richert told me more: in 1942, while he was staying in Sweden, Prinz Eugene[vii] had beseeched him to do everything possible to have me released. Richert had answered that at this stage he had no influence in Berlin, but that he would ask his Finnish colleague Kivimäki to take up the case. The latter had attempted to negotiate with the German foreign minister, but in vain. Thereupon, he had applied to the Baltic-German of Finnish nationality, Medizinalrat Felix Kersten, who had persuaded Himmler to deal with my case."[169] The rest is history.

But although he could not know it, Rector Seip was far from safe. "I thought the matter was settled," remembered Kersten, "but shortly thereafter, thanks to Dr Brandt, I learned that the Reichskommissar in Norway, Terboven,[viii] had written to Himmler to express his indignation at the release of Seip and demand his execution, on account of the great danger he represented. In his letter, Terboven suggested that the man be 'shot while trying to escape'.[170] For Kersten, this constituted a cruel dilemma: how could he raise the matter again with Himmler without revealing that he often read the Reichsführer's mail before the latter had seen it? On the other hand, allowing Rector Seip to be shot was out of the question. Kersten would therefore have to outdo himself – and resort to a few tricks that had worked in the past. "Alleging that I had heard it said in Finnish circles that Terboven considered Seip a great enemy of his administration, I asked Himmler what he would do if Terboven demanded the execution of Seip; Himmler,

vii    Prinz Eugene Bernadotte, the youngest brother of Swedish King Gustav V.
viii   Josef Terboven, former Gauleiter of Essen and protégé of Marshal Göring, was a dangerous and alcoholic hoodlum, whose tense relations with Norwegian "minister-president" Quisling were quite comparable to those of Seyss-Inquart and Mussert in the Netherlands.

who rather disliked my question, answered that the matter was settled, and that Terboven would certainly not make such a demand – but that if, contrary to all expectation, he were to do so nonetheless, he, Himmler, would refuse for sure."[171]

This was an attitude that Kersten had observed time and again: once he had made a commitment, even most reluctantly, Himmler insisted on honouring it. So it was that the honourable Norwegian rector was able to quietly pursue his research in the Munich University library, and afterwards in Berlin's, without ever being threatened.

His compatriot Bødtker, on the other hand, was by no means out of the woods: detained in the sinister concentration camp of Grini, near Oslo, he was at the mercy of Reichskommissar Terboven and his days were clearly numbered, as Kersten later recalled: "When Himmler confirmed to me the liberation of Professor Seip, he added that I had to be content with that, for in the case of Bødtker, there was nothing he could do. According to him, the theatre strike had been organised by the British secret service,[ix] and Bødtker had taken part in it; he wouldn't escape the noose. I drew his attention to the fact that the hanging of a Finnish consul general at the present time would do little to promote good relations between Finland and Germany. After long negotiations, Himmler eventually agreed to talk the matter over with Reichskommissar Terboven, whom he was soon to meet in Berlin."[172] A stay of execution, so to speak, but Kersten did not intend to let go of the case ...

ix   This five-week strike had broken out in Oslo, Bergen and Trondheim in May 1941, in retaliation for the withdrawal of the work permits of six actors who had refused to contribute to broadcasts of the Norwegian national radio N.R.K., controlled by the Nazis.

And yet he had many other commitments at the time, as witnessed by his main "correspondent" in The Hague, Jacobus Nieuwenhuis: "Kersten asked me to return to Berlin, and once again he took care of my visa. In Berlin [. . .] he informed me that the action against the black market was to begin shortly; he had already tried to persuade Himmler to intervene, but so far without success – mainly because the action was to be undertaken within the framework of Göring's four-year plan. I had accordingly to keep him precisely and punctually informed of the action, for if armed with precise facts, he could certainly obtain better results."[173]

Nothing could be less certain, as Kersten himself was not slow to recognise: "For a long time, Himmler refused to budge; he kept on repeating that the matter concerned Hitler and Göring, and was outside his scope. I rather had the impression that he was not personally opposed to the undertaking, quite simply because there was something there to be gained by the Third Reich. After all, I had once found at Himmler's headquarters a book brazenly entitled *The Law of the Strongest in the Middle Ages*. I thought this went a long way to explain the background of this black-market business . . ."[174]

But these were by no means Kersten's only commitments during that particularly busy autumn of 1942; another one was the Kieschke case – a glaring instance of how institutions functioned under the Third Reich: in the spring of 1942, Hitler had complained bitterly about malfunctions in the transportation system towards the eastern front, and Secretary of State Kleinman had been held responsible. But as the man was an *alter Kämpfer*,[x] a prominent party activist and a fierce careerist, he could not be dismissed

x   A former "comrade in arms" (in the struggle for power before 1933).

without adequate compensation; indeed, he had only agreed to step down if he were placed at the head of Mitropa – the European company of dining and sleeping cars. That company had been run for seventeen years by a director named Werner Kieschke, who, though not a member of the National Socialist Party, had quite conscientiously carried out his duties. Yet that was beside the point: anonymous reports began to circulate concerning the inefficiency of the company, a series of mysterious accidents broke out, and Secretary of State Kleinman, supported by Parteiminister Bormann, demanded the arrest of Werner Kieschke.

In desperation, Kieschke turned to Felix Kersten – a very old friend of his – who later told the rest of the story. "Would I agree to take up cudgels for him? Of course I would! The incriminating evidence against him as transmitted to Himmler was fourfold: Kieschke was not a party member, he had shown contempt for certain national socialist theories in the presence of witnesses, he had on several occasions treated his subordinates in a way that was incompatible with the principles of the Third Reich, and – worst of all – his grandmother's mother was a Jewess. Kleinman himself produced evidence to back up all four charges; he claimed that Kieschke and his wife were a danger to the German people and demanded their arrest and internment in a concentration camp. I asked Himmler to intervene personally in the matter. Kieschke was compelled to resign as head of Mitropa, since Himmler considered that the Jewish great-grandmother constituted an insuperable obstacle to his remaining in office. But he promised me that all subsequent proceedings against Kieschke and his wife would be dropped. Kieschke and I agreed that this was the most favourable outcome that could be hoped for."[175]

Such was indeed the case, in that nightmarish country where even the Nuremberg laws were exceeded[xi] and the authorities had created "Jews in spirit", "honorary Aryans", "economically useful Jews"[xii] and even "counterfeit Aryans".[xiii] But concerning the treatment meted out to so-called "full-blooded Jews", Kersten had to admit that he was powerless, which clearly affected him. "I wondered what I could do [. . .] for these unfortunate people who were threatened with complete annihilation. I knew that in this solitary struggle, there was no superior instance on which I could rely. I did try to intervene in favour of German and Dutch Jewish patients and acquaintances who had asked for my help, but the results were minimal. [. . .] When I tried to assist them, I encountered only derision and found myself under attack. [. . .] Thus, I was told more than once that I must have been bribed by Jews; it was also suggested that I had Jewish blood myself. My behaviour appeared highly suspect to those for whom it was impossible that any person with a race consciousness should intervene in favour of such dregs of mankind. Little by little, I succeeded in obtaining the liberation of a few, or at least in bringing them help in one form or another, but all in all, the results of my endeavours remained derisory. In the case of Jews, one came up everywhere against the most obstinate rejection."[176]

In early October 1942, Kersten travelled to Rome with his wife; Ciano had sent him a pressing invitation, and Himmler, who was

xi  "Article 2.2: Whoever has one or two grandparents who are full-blooded Jews is a half-Jew. Article 5.1: whoever has at least three grandparents who are racially full-blooded Jews is a Jew."

xii  *Wirtschaftlich Wertvoller Jude* (W.W.J.).

xiii  Such as Erhard Milch, indispensable to the Luftwaffe, for whom Marshal Göring had found a substitute and impeccably Aryan father.

himself to go there on October 11, agreed to it without difficulty. Once on the spot, Kersten discovered that the atmosphere had changed markedly since his last visit: "The country was teeming with Germans and seething with discontent. After the terrible defeats of Graziani and the Duke of Aosta in Africa, confusion reigned in Italy among civilians and military alike, and the demands for peace made for a stormy atmosphere. The Duce's *guerra fulmine*[xiv] was dragging on and turning into a war of attrition."[177]

This was precisely what galled the Führer, and his faithful subordinate broached the subject with Mussolini on the very evening of his arrival in Rome. The next day, October 12, Kersten was told of the results by the Reichsführer himself: "The aim of my trip," he said, "was to put these Italian affairs in order. The Italians put up a passive resistance to the war everywhere; the peace party, to which Ciano belonged, was steadily gaining in numbers and influence. But the Führer was firmly resolved to support the Duce and, if necessary, to disarm the Italian military and occupy the country;[xv] Italy as it was at present no longer had the right to exist. The royal house and the nobility were on England's payroll. Himmler added that he had sorted things out with the Duce, but the latter had requested that we give up the idea of an occupation for the time being: he would take matters into his own hands."[178]

That same evening, a reception was given in Himmler's honour at the Hotel Ambassadore, and Kersten noted at the time: "Ciano also invited me. All the Fascist party leaders and every member of the Italian government were on the guest list. After the meal, Buffarini and I joined Himmler and Ciano, who told Himmler

xiv "Lightning war" – the (much slower) Italian version of the German blitzkrieg.
xv A little-known prefiguration of what was to happen eleven months later.

what extraordinary benefits he had derived from my treatment. Himmler replied that he did not know how he would be able to live without my help. 'Kersten's treatment is quite unique,' he said. 'He is a great magician, a Buddha, and we all have reason to be grateful to him. He has succeeded where all other doctors have failed in immediately overcoming my stomach pains and enabling me to get down to my work.' Himmler went on: 'All I reproach him for is that he will not accept any recognition or honours.' Ciano replied with a laugh: 'Then we Italians must be proud that he's accepted the Maurice Cross from us.'[xvi] All this was very disagreeable to me. I said that satisfying my patients and helping those who stood in need was the only honour I desired. Himmler then said: 'Our Buddha often causes me great anxiety, however. He comes to me with a list of names in his hand and asks me to release men who are opposed to the war and to the Führer's great conceptions. Most of them are Dutchmen, Jews and German traitors. And he's so incredibly obstinate and persistent that I always have to give in to him.' Ciano laughed and said: 'Yes, nobody can refuse Kersten anything.' And Himmler added: 'Our Buddha is well aware of that, and that's why he always returns to the charge.'"[179]

Count Ciano did indeed mention in his diaries "*il dottor Kestner* [sic], whom Himmler calls the magic Buddha, and who cures everything with massages".[180] Ciano had even extolled before his father-in-law all the exploits of that prodigious therapist, but the Duce, though suffering cruelly from a stomach ulcer, remained uninterested – so Kersten was never to count Benito Mussolini among his patients.

After Himmler's departure two days later, Ciano, Buffarini and

xvi  The Cross of Maurice and Lazarus, see above, p. XXX.

several other ministers confided to Kersten their concern over German interference – and over the course taken by the war. Their alarm was fully justified, for in Libya as in Egypt, the Italian soldiers, treated by officers of the Afrika Korps as subordinate allies, suffered almost as much from German contempt as from English shelling; in the Mediterranean, thousands of Italian sailors perished when their convoys bound for Tripoli and Benghazi were torpedoed by Royal Navy submarines; to make matters worse, intense aerial bombings had been devastating Torino, Milan, Genoa and Brindisi for more than a month.

But the Italians had seen nothing yet; in early November 1942, Kersten was still in Rome when news came that the Afrika Korps had been routed at El Alamein – the Italians, short of fuel and abandoned by their German allies, making up the great majority of the 31,800 men taken prisoners. But for Italians and Germans alike, the worst was still to come: on the morning of November 8, British and American troops landed in Algeria and in Morocco. That day, Ciano said to Kersten: "The Allies chose the wrong spot; they ought to have landed at Genoa![xvii] Then Italy would have been out of the war . . . Now that they are in Africa, we must keep on fighting, and this means that the war will drag on for us. Many more Italians will have to die – and for what? Not for Italy, but for Nazi Germany."[181]

And with little gratitude: on November 18, two days after his return from Rome, Kersten was told the following by the Reichsführer: "I'm beginning to think that with one exception – that of Mussolini – all Italians are traitors to the Axis cause. But just you

xvii   A rather perilous undertaking! Winston Churchill himself, though a reckless strategist, would not have risked it that year.

wait! One of these days, the S.S. will take Rome and capture the Pope! [. . .] I'll be sure to attend when he hangs with all his nice vestments and his tiara on his head. When he swings on the gallows and the tiara falls from his head to roll in the dust, that will be the symbol of the fall of Rome. [. . .] The Catholics and the Jews are working hand in hand to rule the world. [. . .] Our hands are tied just now, and for diplomatic reasons we must conceal our real intentions; but once we have won the war, Hitler will settle accounts with Italy and the Roman Catholic church . . ."[182]

Maybe so, but in the meantime, there were more pressing matters to attend to: the Allied landings in North Africa had compelled the Germans to launch Operation Anton for the occupation of the free zone in France,[xviii] and to mount an airlift from Sicily that poured 50,000 men into Tunisia, thus beating the Allies to the post. From north to south and east to west, it was a race against the clock to plug the most gaping holes; for on the eastern front as well, the situation had considerably worsened since that month of September when Hitler had boasted that "the Russians are at the last extremity" and that "resistance at Stalingrad may be considered as a purely local affair".[183] Since then, the twenty-two divisions and 280 panzers of General Paulus' Sixth Army had indeed entered a city reduced to rubble by the aerial bombings of the previous August, but the Soviet soldiers under General Tchouikov had entrenched themselves in the great factories on the western banks of the Volga; repeated offensives during the month of October had proved powerless to dislodge them, and the whole of Army Group B, with its lines of communication stretched to the limit between Voronej and Stalingrad, found itself in early

xviii   Mainly in order to secure control of France's Mediterranean coast.

winter as immobilised as Army Group A, blocked in the Caucasus on the heights of the Terek and before the forests of Sochi. So, as early as mid-October, General Paulus had recommended a halt to military operations in Stalingrad and the Sixth Army's withdrawal west of the Don. But Hitler had replied by issuing Operational Order no. 1, strictly prohibiting any retreat. Paulus was thus forced to pursue his costly attacks against the last Soviet strongholds along the Volga, until November 19, 1942, when his forces were overwhelmed by the counteroffensive of a million men and nine hundred tanks that enveloped Stalingrad from the north-west and the south-east – a gigantic pincer whose jaws closed near Kalach on November 22. For a very few days, retreat west of the Don remained possible, but Hitler opposed it once again, and the 270,000 men of the Sixth Army were pushed back eastwards – towards a city they had methodically devastated for the last three months. As a result, Paulus now had to face an all-out siege among the ruins of Stalingrad, in the very heart of the Russian winter.

Towards the end of his stay in Rome, Kersten had met a general of the former Tsarist army[xix] who had confided to him: "The Germans are courting disaster; they have already lost the war in the east," for "they have made in Russia all the mistakes possible." Kersten asked him if there was really nothing that could be done, and the general replied: "Oh yes, there is, but on one condition: the Germans must raise a Russian national army.[xx] Out of the

xix   Kersten did not give his name, but the man was doubtless General Prince Anton Turkul, who was living in Roman exile at the time.

xx   With a few months' anticipation, this was General Vlassov's project of a Russian Liberation Army (*Russkaja Osvoboditielnaja Armija*). In fact, General Turkul was later to serve as one of its councillors.

three million Russian prisoners of war,[xxi] perhaps 10 per cent of them are genuine communists – these must be set aside; but the others would be glad to fight for a free Russia, should the project be presented to them in that light."[184]

Kersten had asked the general to put his ideas in writing, and on the next day, he was presented with a detailed memorandum that he brought back to Germany with him. Having rejoined Himmler at his "field headquarters" at Aigen Castle[xxii] near Berchtesgaden, he initiated a new series of treatments and noted on November 21: "This morning, Himmler was in the best of humours. Yesterday's treatments had done him good and he had slept excellently. He spoke with great contempt of Italy; the situation in Russia was rather serious.[xxiii] I regarded this as the right moment and handed him the memorandum. After a quick glance through it, he said: 'This is extremely interesting.' After supper, Himmler said to me that he had read the memorandum and spoken to Hitler about it the same afternoon. Hitler had torn the proposal from his hand in a frenzy and shouted as he asked whether now, when he was master of Russia, the victory should be snatched from him. There could be no question of that. The difficulties on the Stalingrad front would be overcome in a few weeks, and then Russia would fall into his lap like a ripe apple. 'We are the only people who know the psychology for dealing with Russia' were, it seems, his words. Himmler thought that this was

xxi   He could not know that almost two million of them had already died of cold and hunger in German prison camps.
xxii   Code name "Bergwald" – no doubt in imitation of Hitler's Berghof, which was close by.
xxiii   Something of a euphemism, two days after the formidable Soviet counter-offensive around Stalingrad.

the end of the matter. Apart from this, he told me in detail what Hitler intended to do with Russia. He would incorporate the land up to the river Ob in the Reich.[xxiv] The area between the river Ob and the river Lena he would hand over to be administered by the English; Hitler hoped soon to come to an understanding with the English. England would realise that this war was not being waged against her position in the world, but against the world's enemies, the Jewish Bolsheviks. The United States of America would receive the area between the River Lena, Kamchatka and the sea of Okhotsk."[185]

This time, Kersten must really have thought that he had strayed into a lunatic asylum, but he did not let on, for he had another request to make of the Reichsführer. "I took advantage of this favourable moment to hand him a list with the names of twenty Dutchmen, six Germans and four Norwegians who were said to be held under suspicion of a crime for which the penalty was death, and asked for their release. Himmler glanced through the list and said: 'Really, I oughtn't to do that!' I replied: 'I know, but your human feelings will make you sign a release for these men.' To this Himmler said: 'So be it. But these people don't deserve it.' He signed, rang for Dr Brandt, and in my presence gave orders for the immediate liberation of the people on the list."[186]

If, at the end of this rather surrealistic conversation, Kersten had wondered about the Führer's mental balance, he was to find the beginning of an answer less than three weeks later. Indeed,

xxiv   That is to say far east of the Urals, and practically up to the foothills of the Altai mountains!

during a session of treatment on December 12,[xxv] Kersten was asked by the Reichsführer whether he would agree to take on a new patient – "a man suffering from severe headaches, dizziness and insomnia". Kersten answered noncommittally that he would have to examine the man before giving a definite opinion. Himmler swore him repeatedly to secrecy, then fetched a black portfolio from his safe, and after another moment of hesitation he said: "Alright, here is the report, see for yourself. But you must promise me to tell no-one what you read in it." Kersten went on: "There-upon, he placed a blue file on the table. I said that, of course, I was not in the habit of disclosing medical secrets. He again hesitated a little, then handed me the file. I leafed through it; it comprised twenty-six typewritten pages – the whole being a detailed report on Hitler's medical record. 'Read it immediately, while I'm here,' Himmler said. Unfortunately, I could not take notes in his presence, [. . .] but this is what I gathered from the report: Hitler indeed suffered from headaches, dizziness and insomnia, as well as from a mild tremor in the left arm[xxvi] [187] and a slight stiffness in the left leg. During World War I, he had remained blind for several days after a poison gas attack; the gas had affected his throat, causing him speech problems; a polyp was excised from his vocal cords; as a soldier, he had contracted syphilis that had been incompetently treated, so that his eyes had been affected and he

---

xxv   The date was obviously added afterwards, for on December 12, 1942, Himmler was on an inspection visit between Peenemünde and Friedrichsruh, without any treatment session being mentioned in his diary. This conversation must have taken place between December 3 and December 8, when Kersten treated him daily.

xxvi   Spot on: it was exactly at that time that Hitler's valet noted the first tremors of his left hand "which he had much difficulty in controlling".

156

was constantly at risk of becoming blind. When released from hospital, he was considered cured, and subsequently his health had been satisfactory until 1937, when several symptoms reappeared. By the beginning of 1942, his health had worsened, and as a result of thorough medical investigations, a diagnosis of progressive paralysis had been established. All the symptoms pointed in that direction, except for two: the pupils were still reactive and the speech problems had disappeared. For several months, he had only been able to work thanks to daily injections by his physician – injections obviously containing all sorts of things,[xxvii] except morphine, which he categorically rejected. [. . .] There had been several instances of tuberculosis in his family, as well as cases of cancer. Once, in his youth, he had been hospitalised for pneumonia. Hitler's medical history also showed that he had been suffering from impotence for years and was thus unable to have sexual intercourse with women. It was stated that homosexuality was absolutely ruled out, and also that Hitler could derive sexual satisfaction when he spoke before a large audience – he himself having said that he had at times had orgasms on such occasions. There were also some details about his diet, which was strictly vegetarian, with the additional information that he neither smoked nor drank any alcohol."[188]

Kersten reread a few passages, then silently returned the file to Himmler, who asked: "Well, Kersten? Will you take on this patient?"

"I answered that I did not have the necessary competence to treat Hitler's illness, which was essentially of a mental nature; I added that what Hitler needed was a psychiatrist, and I recused

xxvii   Nothing could be truer: all in all, *ninety* different drugs over a period of eight years.

myself. [. . .] Himmler said that he regretted it, but I had the impression that he had expected such an answer. On the other hand, when I went so far as to say that, in my opinion, Hitler's capacity of judgment was probably altered and that it might be necessary to relieve him of his duties as Führer, Himmler got angry and practically shouted: 'That's impossible! The party depends on Hitler entirely . . . Everything humanly possible must be done to preserve his working capacity!'"[189]

Having somewhat calmed down, Himmler inquired what could be done in such a case. Before venturing an opinion, Kersten asked if Hitler was receiving medical care; to which Himmler answered:

"Certainly. Morell is giving him injections, which he asserts will check the progress of the disease, and in any event maintain the Führer's ability to work."

"What guarantee is there that this is true?", Kersten put in. "There is no acknowledged cure for progressive paralysis in the present state of medical science."

"Of course, I've considered that too," Himmler replied. [. . .] "When I reflect how the Führer was sent to us by Providence, I just cannot believe that there is no way of saving him from the consequences of syphilis. And now along comes Morell and declares that he can help the Führer. There is nothing in the facts of the case to contradict him, for when he's had the injections, the Führer is astonishingly clear and logical, and his thoughts are as original as ever they were in the old days. [. . .] That's the reason why I have decided to trust Morell and let him have his way. I'll see to it that nothing happens. The great thing will be if he manages to keep the Führer going until we have won the war. Then we'll see, and the Führer can retire for a well-earned rest."

"Thereupon," Kersten concluded, "Himmler put the documents back in the black portfolio and locked them in his safe – once again impressing upon me the need for absolute secrecy."[190]

Once out of Himmler's office, Kersten, somewhat bewildered by what he had just learned, asked Brandt two questions: how many people knew the secret, and who could have written this report? The secretary, visibly frightened that a foreigner had been given access to "our greatest state secret", finally answered that, apart from Himmler, only Bormann and probably Göring knew of it. As for the author of the report itself, Brandt refused to give his name, only specifying that he was "a man with a very deep sense of responsibility, a person whose integrity could not be doubted".[191] Kersten had to be content with that.

The reader too. However, he is left with a number of clues: the author of the report clearly had access to one of Hitler's medical files, as before and during the war, Hitler's fits of dizziness, his impotence, the nature of his treatments and even the excision of a polyp in 1935 were all considered state secrets. However, the "man of integrity" probably could only consult older medical documents,[xxviii][192] so he had had to pad his report with backstage rumours and second-hand information, from which he had concocted a synthesis of his own. Thus, it is difficult to see how a man who carefully avoided sexual intercourse with women could have contracted a venereal disease.[193] Besides, the few symptoms mentioned in the report could easily have been related to other causes, and no-one among Hitler's doctors ever mentioned a

xxviii    Armed with a more recent medical file, he would surely have mentioned the diagnosis established in the summer of 1942: "progressive sclerosis of the coronary arteries".

"progressive paralysis". Above all, there is no diagnosis of syphilis in the detailed notes of Dr Morell, although he specialised in dermatology and venereal diseases.[xxix] [194] All in all, as was often the case, Himmler had allowed himself to be misled by one of his informants, only to end up somewhat puzzled as to what he could do with the intelligence thus obtained. Indeed, the Reichsführer was to tell Kersten on the morrow of that conversation that "it will be time enough to act once it's established that the report is correct"[195] – which means that he was far from sure of it.

All things considered, the diagnosis established at a distance by Dr Kersten appeared to be the most reliable: Hitler's disease was essentially of a mental nature. Even then, our physician could not know all the phobias of a Führer who was afraid of lifts, nights, loneliness, immobility, treason, tobacco, alcohol, altitude, heat, attacks, sports, cats, germs, anaesthesia, physical contact, constipation, obesity, journalists, sunshine, meat, bathing, navigation, horses and of course poisoning . . .

xxix  Not to mention that a man whose Wassermann, Kahn and Meinicke tests were negative in 1940 could hardly have had a long history of syphilis. The very fact that Morell ordered such tests, however, indicates that he had at least envisaged such a possibility. In the end, it was only in April 1945 – *very* late in the day – that the real problem was diagnosed: Parkinson's disease.

# 8

## PITCHING

By the end of January 1943, the slow agony of the Sixth German Army was coming to a close; since the previous November, the Soviet noose had been tightening inexorably around Stalingrad, rendering any sally from the city most improbable and any prolonged resistance highly uncertain. By ordering General Paulus to stand his ground and await reinforcements, Hitler had fatally overestimated the defensive capacities of twenty-two much depleted divisions, trapped in the ruins of a city far from their home bases, without adequate supplies, in the heart of the Russian winter and for an indefinite period of time. In mid-December, Marshal von Manstein had attempted a breakthrough from the south in an effort to lift the siege of the city, but he was forced to retreat in all haste when his 4th Panzer Army was pushed back in the north, threatened in the east and without protection in the west. Thereafter, in Stalingrad surrounded by ninety Soviet divisions, 120,000 men were forced to hunker down for forty more days among the rubble, with increasingly precarious provisioning, in -30°C and under murderous artillery fire. Finally, on January 10, 1943, the Red Army launched Operation Koltso:[i] 57 divisions, 270,000 men and 457 tanks, covered by 7,000 cannons, mortars and katyuchas,

i   Operation Ring.

surged towards the city. The defenders held their ground for twenty more days, but on January 31, 1943, Marshal Paulus[ii] surrendered with his staff, and 45,000 ragged, frozen, exhausted and famished soldiers emerged from the rubble, piled up their weapons on Red Square and marched into captivity; left behind were the corpses of 110,000 comrades in arms.

It was the German army's first major defeat; the setback before Moscow in late 1941 could still be explained away as a tactical withdrawal, but the annihilation of a whole army, with its pathetic climax filmed at length by Soviet propaganda, was nothing less than an utter disaster. For another three days, the news was hidden from the German people, and Kersten recalled: "On February 3, 1943, I happened to be at Hochwald, Himmler's headquarters in East Prussia, when the radio announced the capitulation of the German armies in Stalingrad. Himmler was very ill at the time, and his treatment was rather laborious. When I asked him why this defeat had been made public so late – after all, the German people had been aware of the Stalingrad debacle for quite some time – Himmler answered that it was for propaganda reasons. Besides, there could be no talk of defeat, but rather of the greatest German victory in history: thanks to the brave resistance of the German soldiers in Stalingrad, the Russian armies had been contained and utterly crushed; their great assault against Europe had thus been delayed and thwarted. Only a master of war with the historic dimension of Adolf Hitler was capable of choosing the right moment to deal such a blow and prevail. Only in the centuries to come would the German people be able to understand the background of this exploit – but the time had not yet come. Of course,

ii   His promotion had been announced the day before.

it was regrettable that all these soldiers had fallen in combat, but considered in a historical perspective, these losses were trifling. [. . .] Actually, it was a pity that the Führer never had an opponent who could match him, and that all his life he had only fought nonentities."[196]

There may well have been a touch of truth in the midst of all these wild rantings, but Kersten could not know it: the desperate resistance of the Sixth Army in Stalingrad had allowed General von Kleist's whole Army Group A, blocked in the Caucasus and threatened with encirclement from the south and east, to retreat post-haste towards Kharkov in mid-January, and rejoin the main German defence line between Dnepr and Donets. But for Himmler to mention this would have amounted to recognising that the Führer had committed a major strategic blunder by dividing his forces and venturing them 700 kilometres too far south, in the steppes and mountains of the Caucasus.[iii]

For all that, Kersten noted with quiet satisfaction that even in Himmler's entourage, most officers dismissed Dr Goebbels' propaganda and fully appreciated the scope of the Stalingrad disaster. But almost simultaneously, another piece of news somewhat dampened their morale: a successor had finally been found for Reinhard Heydrich. No doubt on orders from the Führer, who trusted only his compatriots,[iv] the new chief of the R.S.H.A. was to be Ernst

iii   In addition, Himmler, who had a permanent liaison officer at Hitler's H.Q., was no doubt aware that it was only upon the interventions of Chief of Staff Zeitzler and Marshal von Manstein that the Führer had authorised the retreat of Army Group A towards Rostov. Even then, he had rescinded that order shortly thereafter – but too late: the retreat had become irreversible.

iv   Provided of course they had amply given proof of their complete absence of scruples.

Kaltenbrunner, a massive, malevolent, brutal, blinkered, arrogant and alcoholic Austrian policeman. He was far less intelligent than Heydrich, but no less dangerous; in association with his subordinate "Gestapo Müller" and his acolyte Oswald Pohl,[v] he would henceforth pose a permanent threat to Felix Kersten and to all his undertakings.

For the time being, at least, these undertakings appeared to prosper; thus, Himmler had at long last been persuaded to grant a reprieve to Johannes Sejersted Bødtker: the Norwegian banker and Finnish consul general who "wouldn't escape the noose" was sent back to Grini concentration camp and discreetly released seventeen months later. At Hartzwalde, Kersten had succeeded in obtaining five additional Jehovah's Witnesses to work on his estate – and persuaded his neighbours to hire others. He also had the considerable satisfaction of learning in February 1943 that the German authorities had given up their project of taking over the black market in France, Belgium and the Netherlands – a renunciation that owed nothing to Kersten's efforts. Marshal Göring's amateurishness, along with persistent disagreements between his representative in France, Ambassador Otto Abetz, and the Militärbefehlshaber in Frankreich, von Stülpnagel, had effectively killed the whole scheme.

On the other hand, it was undeniably Kersten's intervention that proved decisive in the case of the arrest by Kaltenbrunner of his old friend and patient Adolf Friedrich zu Mecklenburg, former governor of Togo and brother-in-law to Queen Wilhelmina;

v Who had by then been promoted S.S. Obergruppenführer (lieutenant general), inspector of concentration camps and head of the central S.S. office for economics and administration.

Kersten was not treating Himmler at the time, but on March 2, he wrote to him: "In the present case, your new Gestapo chief, Dr Kaltenbrunner (whom by the way I regard as one of your enemies), seems to be fishing in murky waters. [...] This *alter Kämpfer*,[vi] who already has two criminal convictions, is also a notorious alcoholic. He accuses the prince of spying for the queen and toasting Allied victory with champagne every evening while spitting on a portrait of the Führer ... It is rather the informant who ought to be locked up in a concentration camp." And Kersten ended his letter by reminding Himmler of his May 20, 1940 promise not to retaliate against members of the princely family of Mecklenburg – to which he added this rather rash postscript: "I enclose a list with the names of three Estonians, four French and eleven Dutch women, two Belgians and three Norwegians. I strongly urge you to release them."[197] The most extraordinary thing is that this was actually done – and that the Gestapo apologised to Prince Adolf Friedrich zu Mecklenburg, before inviting him most courteously to return to his castle!

The other case which Kersten had to handle that month could seem commonplace, in view of the political practices prevailing under that criminal regime: in Warsaw, eight months earlier, the Gestapo had arrested seven Swedish businessmen: Herslow and Widén, directors for Poland of the firm Svenska Tändsticksbolaget,[vii] Gerge, Grönberg and Lagerberg, engineers in the same company, as well as Berglind and Häggberg, the two managers of the L.M. Ericsson telephone company. The accusation of espionage was

vi   See above, p. 146.
vii  Swedish match company.

practically routine in such cases,[viii] but these men had indeed been in close contact with the Polish underground. However, the real reason for their arrest was to be sought elsewhere: in May 1942, Sven Norman, regional director for the Swedish firm A.S.E.A.,[ix] had managed to leave occupied Poland with full documentation on the manner in which 70,000 Jews had been murdered, and on the experiments conducted in Auschwitz and Treblinka to find the best means of secretly liquidating many more – beginning with the 500,000 Jews of Warsaw. These documents were duly forwarded to London and made public by the B.B.C., causing amazement in the world and consternation in Berlin. Viewed in that light, the arrest of the Swedish businessmen left in Poland appeared as an act of impotent rage – one that was potentially devastating . . .

During the summer of 1942, the seven Swedes had been sent to Germany, held incommunicado and mercilessly interrogated. But as their two companies had a certain amount of influence and their country wielded considerable economic leverage,[x] they were entitled to a lawyer – who also happened to be an old friend of Kersten:[xi] "My friend Dr Karl Langbehn, who had been hired by the two firms to defend the accused, visited me in February 1943 together with Axel Brandin, director of the Tändsticksbolaget, and that is when I received full information on the identity of the men arrested and the charges against them. [. . .] Those against

viii   Under the Third Reich, you were not arrested because you were a spy; you were a spy because you were arrested.
ix   Allmena Svenska Elektriska A.B. – General Corporation of Swedish Electrical Engineering.
x   Sweden supplied the Reich with much of its iron ore and most of its precision ball bearings, which were essential to the armaments industry.
xi   And also of Heinrich Himmler: their daughters were classmates, which had brought their parents together.

Grönberg and Lagerberg were relatively insignificant, but the accusations levelled at the five others were so damning that they faced a death sentence. [. . .] I promised to do my best and started by presenting the whole case to Schellenberg, so that he was on my side from the start. This was an auspicious beginning, for as head of the intelligence service, this "espionage affair" discovered in Warsaw was within his purview. Thereafter, I never undertook anything in this matter without prior agreement with Schellenberg."[198]

So be it, but Schellenberg was only an executor, and some higher intervention was clearly needed. "When I placed the matter before Himmler for the first time, he refused even to discuss it, on the grounds that he could not intervene; this was a matter of international importance, which only the foreign minister could deal with – Ribbentrop in the event. But he gradually began to take an interest in the case and to consider the seven Swedish internees with rather more sympathy. He agreed to receive Brandin and Möller[xii] in order to hear their version of the affair, after which he contacted Justice Minister Thierack, from whom he obtained the documents of the case. I finally succeeded in extracting his promise that he would help to gain a reprieve for the seven Swedes – but only on condition that Ribbentrop agreed."[199]

This was to be no easy task – particularly as there was an additional obstacle: Langbehn was very close to the underground opposition, and he was not particularly discreet, as Kersten later recalled: "In the meantime, Dr Brandt gave me to understand that it would be preferable for my friend Langbehn to withdraw from the case, as the Gestapo was just then collecting evidence in order

xii   Alvar Möller, director for Germany of the Swedish match company Svenska Tändsticksbolaget.

to arrest him. To remain a defence lawyer in this "espionage affair" would be good neither for him nor for the arrested men. I warned Langbehn of the danger threatening him and he did withdraw from the case. To replace him, Möller recommended Dr Dix, a choice that was endorsed by the Gestapo."[200]

There remained the thorny issue of Ribbentrop's cooperation. The foreign minister was currently staying at Fuschl Castle[xiii] near Salzburg. "Chance came to my assistance," Kersten recalled. "In the spring of 1943, Ribbentrop was very sick, and on Himmler's recommendation I was called upon to treat him." From the outset, Kersten observed that Ribbentrop was both physically and mentally impaired: he suffered from headaches, dizziness, abdominal spasms and digestive disorders, along with recurrent states of apathy and worrying memory losses. Unfortunately, his memory quickly returned when Kersten raised the issue of the seven Warsaw Swedes: "Ribbentrop proved most unaccommodating, stating that these people were spies and that they didn't deserve the slightest compassion. I suggested that there were other aspects to consider, [. . .] for instance the political point of view: Finland had already made representations and Sweden's peaceful policy had also to be taken into account – as well as her iron supplies . . . To which Ribbentrop retorted that he was sick and tired of reading the Swedish press, with all its anti-German statements. Sweden had a long time ago lost its right to political independence and had to be treated with severity rather than kindness. The Swedes arrested in Warsaw had deserved their punishment. He no longer wanted to hear of leniency in this matter."[201]

xiii   A castle he had appropriated by having its legitimate owner sent to Dachau, where he was to die.

Kersten apparently thought he could impress Ribbentrop by mentioning that Reichsführer Himmler held the opposite view, but that was a miscalculation. "He was very irritated and asked by what right Himmler meddled in the affairs of the foreign minister. He had better attend to police matters and stay away from politics. Ribbentrop ended the interview by assuring me that he would complain to Hitler about Himmler's interference in this case."[202]

Upon his return, Kersten had to admit to Himmler that he had failed in his attempt. "He was mainly preoccupied by the possibility that Ribbentrop would denounce him to Hitler. All things considered and properly speaking, he said, this whole affair was no business of his, and he would no longer deal with it – indeed, he washed his hands of it."[203]

It was thus with precious little support in high places that the seven Swedes confronted their judges on the morning of June 30, 1943; they could derive little comfort from the fact that the presiding officer of the Court was none other than Roland Freisler,[xiv] and that he officiated in the First Chamber of the People's Tribunal, where Hans and Sophie Scholl had been sentenced on February 22 – and beheaded a few hours later. The present trial was just as summary, and the sentence was handed down the very next day: Einar Gerge, lifetime imprisonment; Stig Lagerberg and Reinhold Grönberg, acquitted but kept in jail and at the Gestapo's disposal until further notice; Carl Herslow, Sigge Häggberg, Nils Berglind and Tore Widén, sentenced to death.

Swedish diplomacy was immediately set in motion, and King Gustav V sent a personal letter to Hitler asking him to grant a

xiv  Freisler, who had pronounced thousands of death sentences in less than three years, was the very incarnation of Nazi judicial terror.

reprieve to the four men – to no avail. But Kersten knew a better address, and he returned forthwith to Himmler's headquarters. "I found no other solution than to resort to an unabashed lie; I told him that I had received in Berlin a letter from Finnish President Ryti, who inquired about the fate of the seven arrested Swedes; he wrote that the Finns felt increasingly conscious of their Scandinavian kinship, and that they were growing impatient about this matter. [. . .] I immediately saw that Himmler had been struck by the international repercussion of this 'Swedish espionage affair', after which I had the impression that he would make a real commitment to the cause. That is what eventually happened."[204]

Just so, but it was to require much time and effort on the part of both Schellenberg and Kersten; it was yet another illustration of the latter's protracted crusades, yet the twists and turns of the *Warszawasvenskarna*[xv] affair were to cause intense emotion in Sweden – and play a decisive part in Kersten's destiny.

In the meantime, Schellenberg had spared no effort in opening secret channels of negotiation with the Allies: through such intermediaries as administrator Karl Lindemann,[xvi] consul Kurt Rieth, professor Albrecht Haushofer, lawyer Carl Langbehn and Prince Max zu Hohenlohe,[xvii] he had approached a number of British and American ambassadors, military attachés, consuls, businessmen and secret agents in Switzerland, Spain, Portugal, Sweden and Turkey; Schellenberg himself had gone to meet various people in Zurich, Stockholm and Ankara – all this with somewhat

xv   Warsaw Swedes – in their own language.
xvi   President of the German shipping company Norddeutscher Lloyd.
xvii   The most remarkable thing is that the latter three were carrying out similar missions for the secret opposition to Hitler; in fact, Prince zu Hohenlohe also did the same occasionally for Hermann Göring!

disappointing results: those contacted proved unreceptive, especially when told the name of Schellenberg's immediate superior. Admittedly, the latter was not making things any easier: in Zurich, the British consul Eric Cable had agreed to initiate negotiations, but Himmler, frightened by the rashness of the undertaking, ended up arguing that the best thing to do was to submit the whole matter to Ribbentrop – the very man whose resignation he had wanted to engineer the previous summer! Himmler did indeed report the matter to the foreign minister, with foreseeable results: on Hitler's orders, all contact with foreign nationals aimed at negotiating an end to hostilities was strictly prohibited.[205]

Himmler's inconstancy was precisely what preoccupied Schellenberg and Kersten; they deemed it impossible to open negotiations with the Allies and secure Ribbentrop's resignation – not to speak of Hitler's removal – with so little support from a dithering Reichsführer. Both men knew how dependent he was on astrologists, but which of them hit upon the idea of influencing him by producing yet another astrologist? According to Schellenberg, it was Kersten, but the choice of the candidate and the practical implementation bore the distinctive mark of Walter Schellenberg's R.S.H.A. section VI.

Their choice fell on one Wilhelm Wulff, an astrologist already well known within R.S.H.A. section IV – the Gestapo, in other words.[xviii] A native of Hamburg, Wulff had been for the last twenty years one of the most reputed practitioners of his profession, and a prime candidate for arrest during the great wave of repression that followed the departure of Rudolf Hess. His stay in the Fühlsbuttel

xviii   Where Schellenberg had worked until he was placed at the head of section VI in July 1941.

prison cum labour camp had left him with bitter memories, and although he was released four months later, he was not entirely free from surveillance. In order to keep an eye on him, the Gestapo had found him a job with a Berlin industrialist named Zimmermann, who doubled as an "honourable correspondent"[xix] for the Nazi secret service. In the spring of 1943, this man was instructed by his occasional employers to drive Wilhelm Wulff to an office located at the corner of Rüdesheimer Platz in Wilmersdorf; the large golden plaque on the door read MEDIZINALRAT FELIX KERSTEN.

Wulff's portrait of Kersten – for whom he seems to have conceived an instant dislike – is interesting in more ways than one. "Felix Kersten's stature was disproportionate; he was tall and thick-set; with his elephantine body and his colossal weight, he crushed normal chairs and armchairs. [. . .] Sunk in his furniture, an ordinary mortal was crumpled into insignificance. I myself felt diminutive in front of that Bibendum. From his bloated face emerged the avid little eyes of a child. [. . .] Despite his corpulence, he moved with agility and dexterity; his huge hands, covered with innumerable whitish scars, were constantly playing with a pencil or a small image. He was a phlegmatic with a sanguine streak, according to classic characterology. He told me point blank: 'You can tell me openly about political developments; I know a lot already, which makes me worry about the war and the situation in Germany. What do you think of Hitler's horoscope? Can you tell me something about it?' I endeavoured to describe the astral constellation with much reserve and precaution, indicating that Hitler's looked highly inauspicious; such a person could not remain durably at the head of the nation with any chance of success. [. . .]

xix   Modelled on the Soviet *sekretny sotrudnik* (secret collaborator).

Then Kersten said to me: 'Can you pass on to me Hitler's horoscope? I would like to show it to Himmler.' Having noticed my alarm, he continued: 'Dear sir, you have no reason to be afraid; Himmler won't do you the slightest harm, I'll see to it. But what you told me about Hitler's future is interesting and important; Himmler must be informed of it.' All this was said in a patronising tone . . . I then answered: 'No, no way. Please, don't mention a word of this to Himmler. I don't want to be back in security detention, courtesy of these gentlemen of the Gestapo. Himmler must not know; he would not understand and would consider it as a hostile action against the state. Please consider my statement on Hitler's horoscope as confidential information given to you only; don't cause me any trouble.' 'You really suffered that much during your security detention?' Kersten said. I replied that I had seen and known as many terrifying things as all the other internees, and added that I could supplement my statements on Hitler's unfavourable prospects with the horoscopes of other national and foreign political figures . [. . .] 'You must tell me more, Herr Wulff; it's extraordinarily useful for me and for my plans. Now that you have begun, you must not stop.' Zimmermann, who had followed the whole conversation, encouraged me to comply, but I justified my refusal with the fact that all my material had been confiscated by the Gestapo, who had surely discovered many of my predictions based on the horoscopes I had drawn up for Germany. I could only piece together a few fragments from memory – which was quite insufficient, since some of my calculations and deductions went back twenty years . . . After a most vigorous exchange, Kersten told me: 'You must meet Himmler; in fact, you'll like him. He's friendly and personable, and he can do a lot for you if you agree to it.' I thanked him for his offer. I had no desire at all to know Himmler personally; what I knew about him was quite enough for me. [. . .] Kersten concluded: 'Well then, I'm asking you to draw up a complete horoscope – on Himmler too.' [. . .] So it was that I began my work for Kersten, in return for the assurance that I would be spared all harassment by Himmler's Gestapo. In this respect, he was to keep his word. A few weeks later, I handed him a detailed horoscope, but since I lacked some data on Himmler, I could not yet carry out that part of the work. [. . .] Thus began the time when Gestapo agents regularly came to pick me up at my Hamburg residence and drive me to Hartzwalde, Kersten's estate, via Oranienburg or Ravensbrück. Jehovah's Witnesses from the Ravensbrück concentration camp worked on the estate."[206]

In describing Himmler to Wulff as "friendly and personable", Kersten had not been entirely dishonest: it was one aspect of the Reichsführer that he knew well, that of the perfect host, the merry reveller, the model family man,[xx] the animal lover, the medieval history buff, the passionate student of religions and occult sciences. But Kersten was also aware of the more sinister aspects of the slavish executor, the fanatical ideologist, the devious politician, the plodding civil servant, the cautious satrap, the bogus warlord, the indecisive potentate and the implacable executioner – all these characters sometimes blending and often clashing. "I noticed," Kersten wrote, "that Himmler feared the party leaders and had precious little power over them. He was willing to make them ample concessions in order to avoid conflicts and ruptures. [. . .] The word history was often on his lips. Not for a moment did he doubt that his place was assured in the pantheon of celebrities;

xx  Such a model, in fact, that he had two families instead of one.

he may well have lacked assurance in life, but he was quite sure that he would be honoured after his death. [. . .] He preferred to remain in the background and let others act; but that sly character was a past master at the art of using the weaknesses of his opponents and of playing one off against the other. With all his limitations, he could also be honest: once he had given his word, he kept it. Honour, History, the Führer and Comradeship – these were his great slogans."[207]

Even then, Kersten could not know all the eccentricities and contradictions of that caricatural Reichsführer: here was a man who, in the very midst of military operations in the summer of 1942, sponsored an expedition conducting zoological, anthropological, ethnological and botanical research in the Caucasus mountains;[xxi] he asked the chief of his R.S.H.A. to identify the passages of the Quran that announced the advent of Adolf Hitler; he mobilised considerable resources, thousands of hectares of land and tens of thousands of prisoners to cultivate the Russian dandelion, in the hope of producing a rubber that would be better than synthetic Buna; he initiated scientific research into the Hunza, a population of the upper Indus with a reputation for longevity;[xxii] he commissioned his Gestapo chief to produce a report on fallow lands on French soil; he manoeuvred incessantly to be entrusted by the Führer with the production and testing of the V2 missile; ever eager to increase his power, he managed to be appointed interior minister in the summer of 1943 – without either time or ability to

xxi   Under the sponsorship of his *Ahnenerbe* (Ancestral Heritage Society). Due to "military complications" in the Caucasus, this Sonderkommando Kaukasus was dissolved in February 1943.
xxii   In fact largely mythical: their average life expectancy was fifty-three years.

perform the duties required by such a function; jealously guarding his bailiwick, he clashed with Joseph Goebbels, who had sent his agents to sound out public opinion in the bars and brothels of Berlin; as self-appointed judge of the advisability of marriages within his S.S., he also took it upon himself to prohibit the divorce of Dutch pro-Nazi chief Anton Mussert; following a complaint by a submarine captain, he ordered sanctions against members of the Innsbruck Gestapo who had "insulted a woman during inter-rogation"; to the general commanding the S.S. corps in Croatia, he ordered a harsh crackdown on instructors who "in keeping with Balkan customs, shouted profanities at the mothers of recruits"[xxiii] – the same general being instructed to "have the offenders shot on the spot, and hanged in particularly serious cases"; he also commanded that those S.S. men who had assassinated Poles, Russians or Jews without an order be brought to justice – *Ordnung muss sein!*[xxiv] Yet it was that self-same Himmler who warmly thanked Gruppenführer Globocnik for "his immense and unique merit in having organised the killing of about 1.5 million men",[208] who supervised experiments of "deep refrigeration" on Soviet prisoners at Dachau, and ordered the massacre of 71,000 Jews and the deportation to Treblinka of 7,000 others during the destruction of the Warsaw Ghetto between April and May 1943.[xxv] [209]

At that time, the front had somewhat stabilised in the east, and Marshal von Manstein had even succeeded in retaking Kharkov and Belgorod. But the 2nd S.S. Panzer Korps had lost almost half

xxiii   An allusion to the ubiquitous Serbo-Croatian insult: "*Jebem ti mater!*" – I f— your mother!
xxiv   "There must be order!"
xxv   With the almost simultaneous liquidation of all other ghettos in the General Government.

its men in the operation, which put Himmler in an awkward situation vis-à-vis Hitler. More preoccupying still: whereas the German soldiers were already outnumbered seven to one, Dr Korherr, chief statistician of the S.S., informed the Reichsführer that the Red Army's reserves in men were far from exhausted.[210] Yet the situation on other fronts was even more alarming: in mid-May, the Afrika Korps capitulated in Tunisia, with 275,000 German and Italian soldiers captured; in the Atlantic, submarine losses were such that Admiral Dönitz was compelled to suspend operations.[xxvi] Two months later, Hitler tried to regain the upper hand in the east by launching Operation Zitadelle against the Kursk salient; but on July 14, 1943, after the greatest tank battle in history, the Wehrmacht was compelled to retreat before a Soviet counteroffensive north and east of Orel – which was all the more disquieting as a new front had just opened four days earlier in the Mediterranean: on July 10, Allied forces had landed in Sicily. After a fortnight of fighting and the fall of Palermo, Mussolini, outvoted at the Fascist Grand Council and disavowed by the king, was arrested and imprisoned. His successor was Marshal Badoglio, who undertook to continue fighting alongside Germany, but Hitler mistrusted him; having ordered the evacuation of Sicily and the occupation of the Alpine passes, he prepared a lightning operation to capture Rome, and ordered Himmler to find Mussolini's place of detention at any cost . . .

One month later, on August 26, Himmler was visited in the greatest secrecy by Prussian finance minister Johannes Popitz, who had been recommended to him by his lawyer friend Karl

xxvi  Five submarines sunk and seventeen damaged between May 5 and 6, 1943. Thirty-eight lost during the month of May.

Langbehn. Popitz, who belonged to the secret circle of civilian opposition to Hitler,[xxvii] had quite simply come to propose that the Reichsführer assume the leadership of a movement that would "remove" Hitler and Ribbentrop from power, before opening immediate negotiations with the United States and Great Britain! Himmler's reaction at the time is not known, but the very fact that the two men agreed to meet again soon would seem to indicate that it had not been an entirely negative one.[211]

On September 3, 1943, when the Allies crossed the Straits of Messina and gained a foothold in Calabria, Marshal Badoglio agreed to sign an armistice – whose announcement five days later triggered the launching of Operation Alarich: Marshal Rommel's divisions occupied all strategic areas of northern Italy and disarmed the Italian forces, while two airborne divisions captured Rome and Marshal Kesselring's six divisions took up positions to block any Allied progression towards Naples. And then there was the mission entrusted to Himmler six weeks earlier: to find the Duce's place of captivity at any cost. Schellenberg was deeply involved in that effort: "At this stage, we had no idea where Mussolini could be held. Himmler therefore resorted to one of his occult fantasies; he gathered together a few of the 'representatives of occult sciences' imprisoned after Rudolf Hess had left for England, and confined them to a villa by the Wannsee lake. They were seers, astrologists[xxviii] and radiesthesists, whose magic was supposed to reveal the place of detention of the disappeared Duce. Their sessions cost us an awful lot of money, for the requirements

xxvii   Particularly the *Mittwochsgesellschaft* (Wednesday Society), presided over by General Ludwig Beck.
xxviii   And among them a certain Wilhelm Wulff.

178

of these 'scientists' in good food, drink and tobacco were quite considerable. But lo and behold, a master of the sidereal pendulum established after some time that Mussolini could be found on an island west of Naples."[212]

True enough: the Duce had indeed been held captive on the island of Ponza, but he had then been transferred to that of Maddalena, then brought back to the mainland and installed in a hotel at the summit of Gran Sasso mountain. The latter fact was not discovered by the masters of the occult, but by the Roman staff of Sipo-S.D. chief Herbert Kappler, who had intercepted an Italian radio message. Thereupon, a commando of paratroopers, accompanied by S.S. Obersturmbannführer Skorzeny of R.S.H.A. section VI, succeeded in freeing the Duce and flying him to Vienna during the afternoon of September 12.

That exploit could have been credited to the chief of section VI Walter Schellenberg, but in fact, the reverse happened: the full credit for the operation went to Otto Skorzeny, a swashbuckling Austrian imposed on Schellenberg by Kaltenbrunner – who seized the opportunity to persuade Himmler to dismiss Schellenberg in favour of his protégé Skorzeny.[xxix] He would probably have succeeded but for the efforts of Kersten,[xxx] who badgered the Reichsführer for several days. Schellenberg was to recall much later: "We often cooperated, Kersten and I. When one of us was in

xxix   Though Nazi propaganda made Skorzeny the hero of the day, Operation Eiche had in fact been commanded by paratroop major Harald Mors, under the operational control of General Kurt Student – two Luftwaffe officers with no link to the S.S.
xxx   With the help of Brandt, of Chief of Staff Karl Wolff – a sworn enemy of Kaltenbrunner – and probably of General Gottlob Berger, in charge of recruitment and organisation within the S.S.

trouble, the other hurried to the rescue."[213] That is precisely what happened in the event, and Kersten won the day: Schellenberg kept his position, and was thus able to repay his debt with interest ten months later.

In the meantime, Kersten was about to leave Germany; Hartzwalde was no doubt an island of peace and well-being, with its eight horses, its twenty-five cows, its twelve sows, its one hundred and twenty chickens and its fertile fields, carefully tilled by twenty enthusiastic Jehovah's Witnesses.[xxxi] But for several months, Kersten had realised that, since Germany could no longer win the war, he would have to find a safe haven for his family in anticipation of the Reich's collapse. As a neutral country, Sweden seemed to offer excellent guarantees in this respect; besides, since the affair of the Warsaw Swedes, Kersten had in Stockholm several powerful allies[xxxii] who could readily procure him a visa, a dwelling and a licence to practise medicine. An invitation from the director of the Swedish match company Svenska Tändsticksbolaget clinched matters; but first, he had to find a way of persuading Himmler to let him go, and this was supplied by his friend Ambassador Kivimäki: the idea was to tell the Reichsführer that, as a reserve officer in the Finnish Army, Kersten had to return to Finland, but that the government in Helsinki would allow him to treat Finnish soldiers hospitalised in Sweden. In the end, Himmler reluctantly agreed, provided Kersten returned to Berlin immediately if his care were needed.

xxxi    One of them was later to state on Finnish television that "it was like passing directly from hell to heaven".
xxxii    Möller, Brandin and banker Jacob Wallenberg, who was also the main shareholder of Svenska Tändstiksbolaget.

Our Medizinalrat accordingly prepared to leave with his wife and youngest son,[xxxiii] while the two other sons were left behind, in the care of Elisabeth Lüben. Kersten intended to travel light, but his prime concern was to retrieve from the masonry of his cellar the case containing the notes he had taken of his discussions with Himmler over the past five years; tied together in one compact bundle, they were packed into the big suitcase that he could carry freely in his capacity as a Finnish diplomatic courier.[214] But a week before his departure, he learned that his friend Langbehn had been arrested,[xxxiv] upon which he went at once to Himmler's office and requested his release. The Reichsführer was not forthcoming: "He refused to let me speak to my friend, who was detained in Ravensbrück concentration camp; he also refused to let me see his case file, alleging that he no longer had it and that it had been forwarded to Hitler. In the end, he agreed to give me his word that the proceedings against Langbehn would be postponed until the end of the war."[215]

Three days later, Kersten thus wrote Himmler the following letter: "You may be assured that I shall return at the end of November to resume your treatment. Allow me to remind you once again that you have given me your word of honour that nothing will happen to Dr Langbehn, and that you will treat his case benevolently."[216] And on September 30, 1943, his mind at rest, Kersten flew off to Stockholm.[xxxv]

xxxiii   Andreas Heinrich, born the previous May. His godfather was one . . . Heinrich Himmler.
xxxiv   Langbehn was naturally accused of having spied for England; but he had indeed gone to Bern in order to meet Allen Dulles, of the O.S.S.
xxxv   Kersten says nowhere – and may not have known – that Langbehn had been the organiser of the August 26 meeting between Himmler and Popitz.

# 9

# STORM WARNINGS

In Stockholm, Kersten tasted freedom for the first time in forty months. Once settled in the modest Belfrage boarding house, he had two priorities: the first was to visit several pastry shops, since good cakes had become very scarce in Germany and our man remained prodigiously greedy; the second was to store his notes in a safe place: the "diplomatic bag" was duly sealed and deposited in a bank vault, there to await the end of the war.

Two days after his arrival, Kersten paid a visit to an old friend, Mrs Graffman; this Dutch lady, married to a Swede, was the daughter of two of his former patients in The Hague. As chance would have it, the Graffmans were also receiving an American named Abram Stevens Hewitt, who happened to be President Roosevelt's special envoy in Stockholm – and an O.S.S. agent. An interesting conversation thus resulted, and Kersten noted that day: "I am fortunate to have found a man in close touch with America. Perhaps an opportunity will arise to help Finland towards making peace. But it must be peace with honour. I had a long conversation today with Hewitt, who also speaks German, so we can understand each other very well. He would like to receive treatment from me, as his health is not very good. I will be very glad to do that."[217]

Hewitt indeed suffered from a bad back, and, while treating him, Kersten soon realised that they shared the same views on the issues at stake. "We are both of the opinion that this terrible war must be brought to an end. [. . .] However, my first thoughts are for Finland; Finland and America are not at war. Hewitt believes that it is quite possible that President Roosevelt may intervene to arrange peace between Finland and Russia, as America still has great sympathy for Finland. I told him that Finland is not altogether bound to national socialist Germany, and that the Finns themselves dislike national socialism. It was only despair over our Winter War with Russia which made us Germany's allies. Hewitt said that he could appreciate that and was prepared to act as an intermediary. But Finland had to make the first move."[218]

When Kersten flew to Helsinki on October 15, 1943 and reported to the new foreign minister Henrik Ramsay, he did not fail to mention his conversation with Hewitt. "I told Ramsay that in Stockholm I could establish contact with Roosevelt, should he so desire, as his special representative there, Mr Hewitt, was a patient of mine and I could act as a go-between. However, I advised Ramsay to conduct the negotiations through Gripenberg, the Finnish ambassador in Stockholm."[219] Kersten was obviously wary of dabbling in diplomacy: as a doctor, he did not consider himself competent to play a part in negotiations between nations, preferring to leave this to professional diplomats. But upon his return to Stockholm after October 19, he again met his American patient, and this time the conversation was by no means limited to Finland: "Hewitt too recognises the danger from the east. I offered to fly to Himmler to explore the possibilities of peace.

Hewitt declared that the first demands that the U.S.A. and England would make were the evacuation of all occupied territories, abolition of the Nazi party and the S.S., with free and democratic elections to follow under American and British control; abolition of the Hitler dictatorship; and the leading Nazis to be secured in concentration camps. Those responsible for war crimes would have to stand trial. [. . .] I told Hewitt: 'I think it possible that Himmler might accept these conditions, provided that an exception is made in his own case and his personal freedom guaranteed.'"[220]

In his report to the O.S.S., Hewitt minimised his own proposals, preferring to dwell on those of his interlocutor: "The doctor urged me to come to Germany to discuss Himmler's position with him, and to see whether a settlement might be possible. He indicated clearly that, on certain conditions, Himmler was prepared to overthrow Hitler and that he was the only man who had the power to do so in Germany."[221] Kersten apparently did not hesitate to steal a march on the Reichsführer, which is confirmed by Hewitt in a second report: "According to Kersten [. . .] Himmler knows that the war is lost and is anxious to arrive at an arrangement with the Americans and British which would leave something of Germany. [. . .] Realising it would be impossible for the Americans and the British to deal with Hitler, Himmler was now quite prepared to bring about his overthrow. [. . .] I told him that I did not represent the American government, and that I did not even know what the current policies of the American government were, and that on this account, it would be pointless for me to talk with Himmler. The doctor then suggested that I return to Washington, familiarise myself with the position of the American government, and come back to Europe.[i] [222] He [Kersten] mentioned to me that Himmler was organising his own [shadow] government within the S.S. and that his two chief advisers on foreign affairs were Oberführer Walter Schellenberg and Dr Braun,[ii] and that he would be glad to get one of these men to come to Stockholm to confirm what he had been saying to me."[223]

The S.S. chief "prepared to overthrow Hitler", "organising his own shadow government" and having "his chief advisers on foreign affairs"! Kersten clearly did not shrink from hyperbole to set the ball rolling. And on October 24, he sent the following letter to Himmler by way of the Finnish diplomatic pouch: "I have an American patient here in Stockholm; his name is Abram Stevens Hewitt (he is not a Jew)[iii] and he is in close contact with the American government. [. . .] We have had many discussions together and, in view of the ever-mounting destruction caused by the war, we have worked out proposals for peace talks. I beg of you not to throw this letter into your wastepaper basket, Herr Reichsführer, but to receive it with the humanity which resides in the heart of Heinrich Himmler. In centuries yet to come, the gratitude of the entire world will still be yours. It is not easy for me, as a Finn, to conduct peace negotiations on behalf of Germany. I ask you, therefore, to send somebody here in Stockholm who enjoys your entire confidence, so I can introduce him to Mr Hewitt.

i   More astonishing still, Kersten disclosed to Hewitt the secret proposals for a separate peace made by Stalin to Hitler in February and May 1943, of which he had learned at Himmler's headquarters: hands free for the Russians in the Balkans, Soviet expansion up to Salonica and Constantinople, annexation of the Baltic countries and of the Polish areas occupied in 1939.

ii   Clearly Dr Brandt, whom Kersten seems to have promoted to "chief adviser on foreign affairs" for the occasion.

iii   Probably a useful indication in a letter addressed to Heinrich Himmler.

Please do not hesitate, but decide at once, Herr Reichsführer – the fate of Europe hangs on it. Herr Schellenberg seems to me the person indicated, as he also speaks English."[224]

Enclosed were the "proposals for peace talks" worked out with Hewitt and Graffman. They were somewhat brazen, to put it mildly:

1. Evacuation of all territories occupied by Germany and restitution of their sovereignty
2. Abolition of the Nazi party; democratic elections under American and British supervision
3. Abolition of Hitler's dictatorship
4. Restitution of the 1914 German frontier[iv]
5. Reduction of German army and air force to a size that excludes the possibility of aggression
6. Complete control of the German armaments industry by the Americans and the British
7. Removal of the leading Nazis and their appearance before a court charged with war crimes [225]

These proposals probably took Himmler's breath away,[v] and there was no immediate reaction on his part. But Schellenberg, informed simultaneously, reacted without delay – and without permission: "I took a special plane to Sweden. [. . .] Taking all possible precautions for secrecy, I met [Mr Hewitt] in his suite at one of the largest hotels in Stockholm.[vi] [. . .] On my own responsibility

iv  A somewhat over-hasty proposal, since the 1914 German frontier included Alsace and Lorraine. The 1919 frontier would have been more to the point.
v  It is noteworthy that these demands correspond very closely to those which were to be presented at the Allied conference in Moscow a week later.
vi  Which was probably not the best guarantee for secrecy, in a capital that teemed with spies of all nationalities!

and without reservation, I told him how essential a compromise peace was to Germany."[226] Yet exactly like Kersten, Schellenberg refrained from mentioning the obvious: a compromise peace would only be possible once Hitler had been toppled, and Himmler being the only man who could bring it about, he would inevitably be the Führer's successor – a prospect the Allies were bound to find supremely unattractive.

Having introduced the two men, Kersten had quietly slipped away; once again, he must have considered that negotiations were to be left to professionals – and preferably nationals of the states directly involved. The more so as he was simultaneously being solicited for another mission, which no-one else could accomplish: soon after his arrival in Stockholm, an official from the foreign ministry had come to inform him that his minister, Christian Günther, wished to meet him unofficially – and in fact so discreetly that he would receive him in his private apartment. This highly confidential initial interview[vii] was summarised by Kersten in the following terms: "Günther's attention had been drawn to my action in favour of the seven Swedes; he had presently conceived a vast plan to help the Scandinavians who were detained in German concentration camps. Sweden's political situation [. . .] had evolved in such a way that she was henceforth compelled to undertake something,[viii] and in this respect, an action consistent with Sweden's traditional humanitarian line would be best suited to her position as a neutral country. We thoroughly discussed the advantages and

vii  Neither Kersten nor Günther gave the exact date of that meeting, both mentioning a vague "October 1943".
viii  In other words, Sweden was under strong pressure from the Allies to join the war against Germany.

the drawbacks of the proposed action [. . .] and the resistances we would encounter. The Swedish government would supply me with lists of Scandinavians and other foreigners detained in Germany, and in the course of my conversations with Himmler, I would endeavour to have them released, or at least to secure some improvement in their condition."[227]

Kersten seems to have accepted outright, which he was to explain in these terms: "This relationship with Minister Günther gave a whole new basis to my undertaking, by allowing me [. . .] to save numerous human groups from annihilation. My representations before Himmler would henceforth be made in an international context; I would thus be able to act in the name of organisations and authorities that Himmler would find difficult to disregard. [. . .] And I felt strengthened, if only by the idea that in order to help people, I would no longer have to keep on pretending that they were patients of mine. I could speak frankly in the name of a foreign nation."[228]

As for Schellenberg, he returned to Germany immediately after his talks with Hewitt. "Back in Berlin, I immediately wrote an aide-memoire on these conversations, which I intended to submit to Himmler. He was in Munich at the time.[ix] When I informed him of my meeting with Hewitt, he was both dumbfounded and absolutely appalled by my unauthorised initiative, after which he worked himself up into such a state of wrath that I deemed it preferable to wait until he calmed down before presenting him with my aide-memoire. The next day, I renewed my attempt to persuade him of the necessity of my initiative, and he listened to me in a calmer mood, but still my explanation remained

ix   For the annual celebration of the failed coup attempt of November 9, 1923.

insufficient to lift the spell that Hitler cast on his entourage in Munich."[229]

At Hochwald, near Rastenburg, the spell was still holding, as Kersten observed when he took over from Schellenberg shortly after his return from Sweden: "December 4, 1943.[x] This morning I tried to make Himmler realise that it was time for him to come to a decision about my negotiations in Stockholm with Hewitt and Graffman. [. . .] Himmler answered: 'Ach, don't torment me, give me time. I can't get rid of the Führer, to whom I owe everything. [. . .] It was he who gave me the position I now hold – and am I now to use my position as Reichsführer to overthrow the Führer? It's quite beyond me, Herr Kersten. Try to understand. Read the pledge of loyalty which I have taken as my motto. Am I to ignore all that and become a traitor? For heaven's sake don't ask that of me, Herr Kersten.' My reply was: 'I'm not asking you for anything. But the German people and Europe await your decision. You're the only man who can make it. Don't hesitate, Herr Reichsführer, grant peace to Europe, if you really want to appear before history as a great Germanic leader. In Stockholm, Mr Hewitt is waiting for your decision, so that he can take it to Roosevelt. Seize your chance – it never comes a second time.' Himmler replied: 'The conditions that Schellenberg put before me are hardly acceptable. Consider the sacrifices we have made, Herr Kersten. Are they all to be in vain? How can I take responsibility for that when faced with the leaders of the party? [. . .] I've carefully studied the letter you sent me from Stockholm; the conditions are

---

x   Here again, the date was clearly added afterwards: on December 4, Himmler was visiting Weimar, without Kersten. The first date for a treatment in his diary was December 7.

hair-raising. But perhaps one might discuss them if the situation became really grave. However, one condition is quite unacceptable: that we should accept responsibility for certain war crimes which are not crimes in our eyes. For everything that's been done in Germany under the Führer's regime has been carried out with a due regard for the law.' 'Even the annihilation of the Poles and the Jews?' I inquired. 'Certainly, that also assumed a legal form [. . .] because the Führer's orders are the supreme law in Germany. [. . .] I've never acted on my own initiative, I've only carried out the Führer's orders. So neither I nor the S.S. can accept any responsibility.'"[230]

Seeing that there was no point in further arguing along these lines, Kersten brought the discussion back to the negotiations in Stockholm, whereupon Himmler took from his wallet the letter he had received from Stockholm.

"Hmm, evacuation of all occupied territories," he said. "That's a very hard condition. You should reflect that the conquest of those lands has cost us some of Germany's best blood, Herr Kersten. But if it has to be, I might be able to agree to it. Then, for instance, you've put here: recognition of the 1914 frontiers. Mr Hewitt is not going to leave us with very much. For security's sake, we must extend a hundred miles or so further east than that. [. . .] Democratic elections in Germany under American and English supervision. I've no objection to that. Removal of the Führer and abolition of the party? What am I to do about that?"

"It's your affair what you do about it," Kersten replied, "but it's got to be done. For the Allies will never come to terms with the party nor with the Führer."

"Yes, that's the bit that's hardest to swallow," Himmler retorted. "It means cutting the ground from under my own feet. [. . .] And then this piece of nonsense," he cried, very much upset. "I'm to include in the peace terms the Allies' right to hold Germans responsible for what they're pleased to call war crimes. That's complete nonsense, Herr Kersten. We Germans aren't criminals, we've committed no crimes. We are a decent people who have fought honourably. Perhaps it's not a crime that the Allies in the last few years have been reducing our towns to ruins? Can't you realise that in the event of a German defeat, Russia – and possibly ten years later America – will dominate Europe? Next on your list comes reduction of the German army to a size which will make aggression impossible. What does Mr Hewitt mean by that? Are we to go back to an army of 100,000?[xi] We could offer no resistance to the Russians with that. Germany needs an army of at least three million if she is to protect Europe from the east."

A few minutes later, Himmler said in a tired voice:

"I can't come to a decision today. Hewitt will be in Stockholm for a few days longer. [. . .] I've got to think it over. I realise that this war is a disaster for everybody. And if I can do anything to stop it, I will. But America must also show some signs of goodwill."[231]

The sessions of treatment went on without interruption until December 15, and for eight straight days, Kersten returned to the charge – all in vain. But a fortuitous event came to his assistance: since late October 1943, the S.S. intelligence service had been receiving from Turkey some first-hand information on British and American strategy and diplomacy:[xii] "Cicero",[xiii] the rather

xi   This was one of the main conditions imposed on Germany by the Treaty of Versailles in 1919.

xii   See François Kersaudy, *L'affaire Cicéron*, Perrin, Paris, 2005.

xiii   This was the code name given to valet Elyesa Bazna by German ambassador to Ankara Franz von Papen, "since his documents were so eloquent".

indiscreet valet of the British ambassador to Ankara, was supplying the commercial attaché of the German embassy[xiv] with photographs of the most secret diplomatic correspondence between the Foreign Office and the British embassy; now it so happened that among the documents thus forwarded to Berlin, there were detailed reports on the Allied foreign ministers' conference in Moscow, as well as others concerning the recent Tehran conference between Churchill, Roosevelt and Stalin. These documents did show that major disagreements existed between the three allies, but also that they had agreed to pursue the war together until the ultimate demise of the Reich. So much for those, like Hitler and Ribbentrop, who thought they could exploit Allied disagreement! Other documents highlighted the extraordinary momentum of the enemy war effort, by quantifying the amount of war material that the Americans had already supplied to the U.S.S.R.: 189,000 field telephones, 150,000 sub-machine guns, 45,000 tons of barbed wire, 4 million pairs of boots, 2,000 tanks, 4,000 planes . . .[232]

For Schellenberg, who had been sponsoring that remarkable Turkish espionage operation from the start, it was more than a personal success: the Nazi chiefs' forecast of a split between the Allies being thus disproven and their assessment of the enemy's military potential utterly contradicted, there could be no better argument in favour of immediate negotiations. Schellenberg realised this, but he was to state much later: "As might be feared, Hitler's reaction to these documents was negative: he only deduced from them the need to pursue an all-out war, ruthlessly, with the commitment of all available forces. Himmler, on the other hand, was clearly disturbed by the examination of all this material. Shortly

xiv   S.S. Sturmbannführer Ludwig Moyzisch, an S.D. agent under diplomatic cover.

before Christmas, he sent for me and said: 'I can see that something must be done after all.' I couldn't believe my ears when he continued: 'Don't let the link with Hewitt be interrupted. Could you let him know that I'm willing to talk matters over with him?'"[233]

The about face came too late: there was to be no more contact with Hewitt, and besides, it would probably have been pointless, since the prospect of negotiations with Himmler immediately came up against the opposition of the American ambassador in Stockholm, of the State Department, of the O.S.S. and naturally of the White House; they all feared Stalin's reaction to dealings whose anti-Soviet character was readily discernible,[xv] [234] and they all knew since the Anfa declaration of January 1943 that the only Allied demand was the unconditional surrender of Nazi Germany[xvi]. Besides, President Roosevelt himself, mainly preoccupied by his re-election, could not fail to take into account the potential reaction of American voters should they find out that U.S. officials were dealing with Heinrich Himmler . . . Indeed, Hewitt was to state eight years after the war: "At that time, despite my reports, Dr Kersten was regarded in high American quarters only as Himmler's tool and was not credited with the humanitarian motives which were later so thoroughly tested and proved. I was therefore instructed to drop the negotiations."[235]

Though Schellenberg pursued his efforts to find contacts on

xv   Indeed, Schellenberg had not concealed from Hewitt that the idea was to make peace with the British and Americans, while pursuing the war on the eastern front – exactly what Admiral Canaris had proposed to Allied emissaries in Turkey and Spain a few months earlier.
xvi   At Casablanca, in the course of his concluding press conference on January 24, 1943, President Roosevelt had stated that the Allies were demanding "unconditional surrender" from Germany, Italy and Japan.

the Allied side, Kersten seemed to have given up – unless he felt that the role of go-between no longer suited him. Admittedly, that of therapist, confessor, conspirator and Good Samaritan kept him busy enough; on January 14, 1944, he noted: "Himmler was depressed and distressed because the Führer had blamed him the night before for being too soft on the German people; if one wanted to win the war, he had said, all the saboteurs and complainers had to be slaughtered. But Himmler argued that the concentration camps were already filled with two million internees; it was materially impossible to double their capacity as the Führer demanded. The annihilation of the Jews, of the people's enemies and of the saboteurs was proceeding, yet the Führer was still dissatisfied with the results, for the Final Solution was not being implemented quickly enough; according to the Führer, Himmler was too weak. He told me in a desperate voice: 'I'm at my wits' end. I do everything he asks for, but still he's not satisfied.' 'And what else can you expect from an insane paralytic?' I asked. 'That very reproach shows that the Führer is no longer normal. [. . .] In my opinion, there's only one thing to do: depose the Führer, dissolve the party and make peace with the Western powers. That is why I established the relationship with Hewitt, to restore peace – and even if the conditions were to be disadvantageous, at least you'd be able to save Germany.' Himmler cried out: 'For heaven's sake, what are you talking about? I pledged eternal allegiance to my Führer, and I can't betray my oath!'"[236]

After pointing out that when Himmler had pledged his oath to the Führer, he knew nothing of the latter's mental disorders, Kersten advised him to start by ceasing to kill Jews and other people deemed undesirable by the national socialists, then to replace all those in charge of concentration camps with trustworthy collaborators, and finally to ensure that all the internees were decently treated, before beginning to release them discreetly.

Himmler, noted Kersten, gave a little chuckle and answered:

"If I did that, the Führer would learn of it within a week, and he'd have me hanged – me and my family."

"It is high time you secured some allies within military and S.S. circles who share your inclinations. A lot of them would support you if you arrested the Führer and had him locked up in a lunatic asylum."

"Our enemies would regard that as the onset of civil war. I cannot take that responsibility. Let us leave it at that, and I'm glad no-one has overheard this conversation, my dear Kersten. You cannot understand how vulnerable I am, [. . .] and all my S.S. chiefs are no longer loyal to me. That is why I must tread carefully, in order to avoid being deposed – and perhaps see Bormann take over my position."[237]

Kersten, well aware that fear remained the Reichsführer's *primus motor,* tried another tack by pointing out that the world would ultimately hold him responsible for all the crimes that had been committed. Himmler laughed this off and reminded Kersten that on several occasions, he had shown him the letter in which the Führer claimed full responsibility for his acts and exonerated him, Heinrich Himmler, of all responsibility in the matter. A long discussion on the concept of responsibility ensued, after which Kersten renewed his recommendations: Himmler ought to stop annihilating the Jews, and treat the concentration camp internees with greater humanity. To which he added:

"After all, the Jews are human beings, like you and me."

"Yes," answered Himmler, "you've already told me this at least a thousand times, Herr Kersten. But the Führer does not share this view, and he remains convinced that there are only three living species on this earth: men, animals and Jews. The latter must be annihilated so that the other two can survive . . ."

"And you, with your faith in justice and your Germanic intelligence, you really believe that?"

"No, no, I don't believe it . . . But let's stop this discussion and not talk about it anymore."[238]

By late January 1944, Kersten was to join Himmler on his trip to The Hague. A few weeks earlier, the Reichsführer had told him: "To control all of Holland, I only need three thousand policemen and a few extra rations. With that, the police know everything." And the Reichsführer went on to boast that he had informers within all the resistance movements.[239] There had indeed been a big increase in the number of arrests recently, and on January 4, 1944, Kersten was informed by his third agent, Jan Reyers, that the diplomat Herman van Roijen himself had been arrested by the Gestapo. Once in The Hague, Kersten therefore got to work: "In the course of a dinner at the house of Reichskommissar Seyss-Inquart,[xvii] which was also attended by Obergruppenführer Rauter, I brought up the subject of Herman von Roijen. Smirking contemptuously, Rauter asked: 'Another one of your patients, I presume?' I answered: 'Yes, and even a very sick patient!' Thereupon, I was informed that van Roijen had been convicted of espionage and that his head would roll – there was nothing more that could be done about the matter. Once alone with Himmler, I beseeched him to listen to his conscience [. . .] and have van Roijen released. Himmler

xvii    On the evening of January 30, according to Himmler's diary.

explained that van Roijen had collaborated with the resistance and that, among other things, he had been seen in the company of a notorious member of the resistance. I answered that this could well have been a coincidence, and asked him to present things in this way to both Rauter and Neumann[xviii] – which he eventually promised to do."[240]

Sure enough, Jan Herman van Roijen was released two months later,[xix] and six years after the war, he was to state before a Dutch parliamentary commission of inquiry: "They just set me free. To this day, I do not know why."[241]

Meanwhile, Kersten was engaged in even more difficult under-takings: in The Hague, he was staying at the S.S. hotel behind the Peace Palace, but he commuted daily to Clingendael in order to look after the Reichsführer. As the second session of treatment was ending, Seyss-Inquart came in to report to Himmler: the next day at dawn, the Gestapo was going to arrest ten prominent people in The Hague, all of them suspected of sympathising with the resis-tance. Kersten overheard a few names, including van Vlissingen, Philips, Türkow, Roys, Doedes and Böningen... Now Frans Türkow happened to be an old friend of his, and also the man he was to join at a family dinner that same evening! Warning him would have been pointless: like all the others, Türkow was probably under police surveillance, he would not get very far and Kersten would immediately be identified as the informant. The good doctor thus spent a rather sad evening with his old friends, but when he left them at 11.30 p.m., something suddenly occurred to him and he

xviii    Brigadeführer Erich Naumann, head of Sipo-S.D. for the Netherlands and Hanns Albin Rauter's right-hand man.
xix    He was to become foreign minister in 1946.

ordered his chauffeur to drive him back to Clingendael. After passing three checkpoints, he was led to the Reichsführer's room just as he was going to bed. What followed was told by Kersten himself:

"Himmler, much surprised, exclaimed:

'You've come at the right time! My stomach cramps were just returning.'

'Just what I thought . . . That's why I came so fast.'

Five minutes later, Himmler lay down and I began my treatment. The pains stopped almost immediately and he was delighted. All of a sudden, I said:

'Herr Reichsführer, I have a great favour to ask of you. You are the only person who can help me.'

'I will gladly oblige. What is it about?'

I told him that, overhearing his conversation with Seyss-Inquart that morning, I had learned that my friend Türkow and others were to be arrested the next day. I urged him to prevent that, for my sake. Türkow and Doedes[xx] were among my dearest friends, and whatever happened to them affected me personally.

'But, my dear Kersten, [. . .] these men are traitors to the great Germanic ideal. Besides, I cannot cancel the order; it would put my men in an embarrassing situation – we must protect the rear of our combat troops.'

I argued with him for a quarter-hour; finally, he gave in and said:

'Very well, I'll speak to Rauter tomorrow.'

'That will be too late,' I answered. 'These men will be arrested in a few hours. Rauter should be called immediately.'

'But he may already be asleep,' Himmler said.

xx   Lambertus Doedes, Olympic sailing champion, 1928.

'Then he'll have to be awakened.'

'You must always have the last word, Kersten.'

'May I call Rauter?' I asked.

'Alright,' he said with a tired voice, 'go ahead and call him.'

I did so most willingly, and Himmler ordered Rauter not to arrest the ten men in question. He would decide their fate once back in Berlin; at any rate, nothing was to be undertaken in this matter for the time being, whatever the circumstances. When he hung up, I said to him:

'I thank you, Herr Reichsführer, in the name of Dutch history.'

After a moment of silence, he said to me:

'It doesn't matter whether we release one or two, for in this country, they are all traitors – Mussert included. But I promise you that, one day soon, I'll have this rascal hanged.'[xxi] [. . .]

I thought it was time to take my leave. As I was departing, Himmler called me back and told me to take a few of the apples that Seyss-Inquart had given him. I stuffed a half-dozen in my coat pocket; Himmler also gave me two chocolate bars, and added that I should not worry: nothing would happen to my friends."[242]

All this may seem astounding enough, but there was something more extraordinary to come: the day before and the day after this conversation, Kersten met his "agents" and at least one important member of the resistance! Among the former was Jacobus Nieuwenhuis,[xxii] who later recalled: "During his visit, Kersten told

xxi   Historians already knew of Himmler's contempt for Mussert, but they were probably unaware of such homicidal intentions . . .

xxii   Nieuwenhuis was the man who informed Kersten of the hostage takings, of the construction of bunkers in the middle of the Clingendael district, and of plans for the deportation of Jews, the confiscation of radio sets and the rounding up of young people for compulsory work.

me that if ever I found myself in trouble, I must absolutely try to reach him; he would then be able to help me leave for Sweden, out of the Germans' grasp."[243] Nieuwenhuis was to remember these instructions seven months later. But at the moment, Kersten was also meeting the banker and naval engineer Maurits de Beaufort, head of a resistance network that had important intelligence to pass on to the Dutch government in exile, yet had lost all contact with England; whereupon Kersten assured him that he could perfectly well carry these messages to Stockholm, whence they would be conveyed to London.

Is this all a figment of our imagination? Here was a Finnish doctor who was hated by Reich commissioner Seyss-Inquart and by the highest-ranking police officer in the Netherlands Hanns Albin Rauter, who was relentlessly spied upon by the henchmen of "Gestapo Müller", and yet could with perfect impunity meet with informants and resistance leaders? No spy novel would ever dare to come up with such a plot! Yet in this case, reality did indeed surpass fiction, because Kersten went about his business quite openly: he used a police car – driven by an S.S. non-commissioned officer – to visit his former patients and friends,[xxiii] and did so with the express permission of Himmler himself. For a Gestapo agent, picking on this fat friend of the Reichsführer, or even spying on him too overtly, could easily compromise a career, at best, within a system that was entirely built on fear, careerism and servility . . .

This was why, on the evening of February 4, 1944, Kersten could return to Berlin in the Reichsführer's private airplane with a suitcase containing some of the most secret messages of the Dutch

xxiii  Some of whom were even above suspicion as members of the collabora-tionist party N.S.B. – Kersten having seen to that!

underground movement; it was also why the same Kersten could write on February 7 to Obergruppenführer und General der Polizei Rauter, of whom he had taken leave three days earlier: "Herr Lambertus Doedes is my best friend in Holland, and I consider any accusation levelled against him or his family as a personal attack. [. . .] Himmler sent you an order not to undertake anything against Herr Doedes and his family without his written permission. [. . .] Yours is the last name on Seyss-Inquart's list of potential recipients of high distinctions; I believe this can be put right.[xxiv] Before my departure, I gave Brigadeführer Naumann a list of eight arrested people whose release I am requesting.[xxv] They are former patients and old friends." And the letter ended on this peremptory note: "You are to await the Reichsführer's decisions."[244]

Over these decisions, Kersten continued to exert a strong influence – witness the following letter he sent to Himmler on March 26: "Brigadeführer Naumann writes me that my old patient and friend Herr van Roijen has just been released. [. . .] I wish to thank you, Herr Reichsführer, for having saved my friend; with this you have given me great pleasure. Naumann informs me that three other men whose names appear on my list are unknown to the S.D. and not detained by him. I consider this out of the question. The following are the individuals concerned: G. Hintzen, Baron van Stirum from Haarlem and Dr Jan Paul Bannier. Please have these men sought by Dr Brandt. Furthermore, Naumann informs me that two men named P.I.A. Clavareau and I. Wilken are to be

xxiv  This may be called wielding the carrot and the stick: Kersten had long since discovered that promises of decorations or promotion were at least as efficient as bribes in securing the cooperation of S.S. officers and lesser officials.
xxv  Apparently a new list, since the previous ten people had *not* been arrested.

convicted of spying by a Wehrmacht tribunal. If Naumann went to a bit of trouble and showed some goodwill, I believe it would be possible to obtain from the Wehrmacht tribunal the release of the two men in question. In addition, Herr Jacob de Graeff is being detained in Buchenwald, and I would be most grateful if you ensured that he was freed. I must confess, highly esteemed Herr Reichsführer, that I fail to comprehend the harsh treatment you are imposing on Holland. Any people with a sense of honour desire their liberty, and those belonging to the Germanic race do not allow themselves to be treated as slaves. [. . .] Unfortunately, the intelligence you get from Holland only emanates from paid informers and other dubious characters. [. . .] I know you to be a man of fair judgment, otherwise I would not be sending you this letter. I appeal to your warm heart and your great Germanic spirit in begging you to adopt a humane policy in Holland. Germanic history will be grateful to you and to your descendants."[245]

At about the same time – February 11 – the Gestapo interrogation of one Wilhelm Schumann, a leading figure in the Magdeburg branch of the Jehovah's Witnesses denomination, brought to light a rather startling development. Wilhelm Schumann's statements, as recorded in the Gestapo minutes, speak for themselves; having mentioned a visit by a member of the movement called "Gertrud",[xxvi] Schumann went on: "'Gertrud' explained that Himmler had changed his attitude with respect to the Jehovah's Witnesses. A man close to Reichsführer Himmler had convinced him of the apolitical orientation of the Jehovah's Witnesses movement. [. . .]

xxvi  Gertrud Grunewald, the wife of Walter Grunewald, a member of the Berlin branch of the Jehovah's Witnesses Society, who was shot in 1943 for having refused to bear arms.

Whereupon the Reichsführer had proceeded to discuss the matter with various proficient prisoners in the Bible Students Association, and had decided that the Jehovah's Witnesses were no longer to be mistreated, even when they refused to desist from their attitude towards God. [. . .] 'Gertrud' seemed to have learned all this at an estate where Bible students from the concentration camp had been put to work."[246]

It takes only minimal acumen to guess that the estate in question was Hartzwalde, and that the man close to the Reichsführer was none other than Felix Kersten. Indeed, the way he had set about changing Himmler's mind was nothing less than amazing: he first invited the Reichsführer to Hartzwalde and showed him how diligently his Jehovah's Witnesses were working on the estate; then he described to him how in occupied regions of the Soviet Union, the disciplined and peaceful outlook of these Bible students could work wonders in pacifying the local populations and turning them away from their nationalist and orthodox dispositions.[xxvii] Of course, an essential precondition was that these prisoners henceforth be given decent treatment in anticipation of their future task. As shown by Himmler's correspondence during the next few months, it is clear that the Reichsführer had swallowed the argument hook, line and sinker; on July 21, 1944, he thus wrote to Kaltenbrunner: "We therefore have the possibility of employing the genuine Bible students held in the concentration camps in all positions of trust, and of treating them particularly well. This

---

xxvii   After the major German defeats at Stalingrad and Kursk in 1943, it took some credulity on the part of Himmler to imagine that Germany could hold on for long to Ukraine and Byelorussia, but Kersten had by then become a past master in playing on the Reichsführer's main vulnerabilities: wishful thinking and fanaticism.

will give us a starting point for the future deployment in Russia of these Bible students, thus providing us with emissaries who will enable us to pacify the Russian people through the dissemination of the Bible students' doctrine."[247]

Amazingly enough, Kersten did not stop at that: from Sweden, he brought back Jehovah's Witness publications, which his eager employees then smuggled to fellow believers in Ravensbrück and Sachsenhausen concentration camps. Kersten apparently saw to it that they were able to supply them with food as well![248]

In the meantime, the war had followed its inexorable course: in Russia, the Soviet army succeeded in lifting the siege of Leningrad, and by mid-January 1944, it was about to launch its great offensives in southern Ukraine and Crimea; south of Rome, the Wehrmacht was hard put to contain the Allied advance, while Hitler had persuaded a reluctant Mussolini to set up in northern Italy an "Italian social republic" entirely controlled by Germany; shortly thereafter, Kersten was greatly saddened to learn that his friend Count Ciano had been executed.[xxviii] By mid-February 1944, Admiral Canaris, the great protector of all opposition to Hitler, was dismissed and placed under house arrest,[xxix] and his Abwehr came under the control of Kaltenbrunner's R.S.H.A. Last but not least, Allied bombing of Berlin had reached an unprecedented intensity between January and March.

It was thus from a largely destroyed capital that Kersten flew off to Sweden with his wife on April 1, 1944. He had obtained

xxviii   Sentenced to death by a kangaroo court in Verona for having voted for the removal of Mussolini, Ciano had faced a firing squad on January 11, 1944.
xxix   This had resulted from the defection in February 1944 of a minor Abwehr agent in Istanbul, Erich Vermehren. Canaris had been held responsible for this, and in his wrath, Hitler had abruptly decided to dismiss the admiral.

Himmler's permission to leave under the same pretext as before – looking after the Finnish soldiers – and with the same proviso: he was to return immediately if the Reichsführer required his services. Upon arrival in Stockholm, his first call was for Baron van Nagell: "Dr Kersten," the baron recalled, "handed me three big envelopes with important letters for London [. . .] that had been given him in The Hague by a well-known resistance fighter, Jan Maurits de Beaufort. [. . .] I made sure that these letters were immediately forwarded to London through our courier service, after which I called on Minister Günther, who confirmed what Kersten had told me and said that he considered the man absolutely trustworthy, that he was certainly not a Nazi, and that he had already obtained some significant successes, among others the liberation of seven Swedes sentenced to death or life imprisonment in Germany. [. . .] Minister Günther then said that a new and larger rescue operation was now being prepared – about which, however, I was to keep absolutely silent – and added that in Dr Kersten, he had found the man who could carry out such a rescue mission."[249]

Indeed, Kersten then called on Minister Günther to finalise the planned rescue operation. All its aspects were examined: the need to preserve the utmost secrecy, the procedure for receiving the freed prisoners in Sweden, the support of key players to be ensured: Prime Minister Per Albin Hansson and King Gustav V in Sweden, along with Brandt and Schellenberg in Germany. Kersten accordingly promised to "get to work" on the Reichsführer as soon as he returned to Germany.

In Berlin that month, Oberführer Schellenberg was overworked; besides his regular tasks as S.S. section chief, he had three priorities: to thwart the traps set for him by Kaltenbrunner and "Gestapo

Müller", to renew contact with potential interlocutors among the Allies, and to persuade Himmler to topple Hitler. In pursuance of the latter project, he had regularly passed on all of astrologer Wulff's predictions to the Reichsführer, and, for lack of concrete results, he had decided to set up a very special interview: in late May 1944, the astrologer, having received all the necessary instructions, was driven in the greatest secrecy to Bergwald, Himmler's field headquarters in the castle of Aigen, near Salzburg. What followed was told much later by Wilhelm Wulff himself, who began with a detailed description of the man to whom he was introduced:

"Himmler was of medium height, he had the jerky movements of a very nervous man and he spoke quickly, with lively gestures. [. . .] The pallor of his complexion spoke of overwork and lack of sleep, his eyelids were reddish as from excessive reading, and his dark eyes, mouse-grey in colour, [. . .] were almost entirely covered with a typically mongoloid epicanthic fold."[250]

After the introduction came the serious topic: astrology. "His conception of it," continued Wulff, "denoted a sound knowledge of this much-derided science. [. . .] He only undertook his great actions according to some little-known astral constellations. [. . .] Then he said: 'I'm sorry that I was compelled to have you locked up, but it was no longer possible to practise astrology publicly. [. . .] We cannot tolerate the use of astrology outside our circle. In the national socialist state, astrology must remain *privilegium singulorum* – not something for the working masses.'"

Now to get to the point:

"Himmler leafed through my horoscopes for Stalin and Churchill. He made little comment on Hitler's, in which I bluntly described the disastrous outcome of his warlike undertakings, his sickness, the dangers dogging his career and his strange death. I said to Himmler: 'Hitler will not die as a result of an attempt on his life. Don't count on it! The possibility of such a major attempt is naturally obvious, but it won't kill him.' My conclusions drawn from Hitler's horoscope had already been in Himmler's hands since early in the year – Herr Kersten had passed them on to him; they pointed to the demise of Hitler in 1945.[xxx][251] I had particularly insisted on this aspect in my conclusions, in order to encourage Himmler, whose indecisiveness was well known, to undertake something against Hitler beforehand, so that he wouldn't be swept up in the maelstrom of general collapse; I thus hoped that he would feel impelled to depose Hitler and initiate peace negotiations. [. . .] Himmler asked me: 'What do you think we should do? Won't things end up turning to our advantage? We have divisions in Russia that are still intact, though not enough of them, for we must also cover the western front.' He also mentioned the 'miracle weapons', in which he placed great faith. I expressed my scepticism concerning these new weapons, I recapitulated the situation as a whole, and, to conclude, I went so far as to present Hitler's removal as the only outcome that could still save Himmler. He replied without hesitation: 'Nothing could be easier. I can just send Berger with an armoured division, and have all the key points occupied by my men.' I found this answer quite revealing; thus, Himmler had

xxx   Indeed, Schellenberg was to state to his interrogators after the war: "As regards Hitler, Wulff predicted endangerment to his life in the period around July 20, 1944, as well as a subsequent illness in November 1944. He furthermore foretold Hitler's demise before May 7, 1945, but stated that the cause of death would never be discovered, though it would be due in point of fact to alkalies (alkaloid)." Remarkably accurate predictions, of course, but Schellenberg's statements may well have been influenced by his knowledge of ulterior events. Besides, cyanide is not an alkaloid – but then, Wulff could well have been a good astrologist and a poor chemist.

already considered the possibility of a revolt against Hitler, and even contemplated directing it himself. But he immediately added, on a somewhat threatening note: 'What we are discussing here is high treason, and it could cost us our lives if Hitler were to be informed of our plans.' To which I replied:

'I know that this undertaking is difficult and dangerous, but after all, we are confronted daily with the danger of being killed by a bomb. I am convinced that attitudes abroad towards you would change radically if you brought back peace and closed the concentration camps immediately. [. . .] Hitler is blindly heading towards his own destruction. Should things continue in this way, the war will irretrievably be lost. Therefore you must act! You control the fully operative apparatus of your police, so you can easily take over. Your constellation for the next few months is favourable and Hitler's is very bad. Act before it is too late!'

Himmler looked both thoughtful and dejected:

'I only fear the mass of the population, you see. All that is not so easy to implement. In many areas of the Reich, and also in occupied territories, such a revolution would cause upheavals that I would have to crush in a bloodbath. How the rest of the masses would then act is unforeseeable.'

'But, at worst, these uprisings would be quashed in two or three months, if the cooperation of the main generals could be enlisted in time.'

'In that case, I would have to act swiftly . . . I'll give it some more thought.' [. . .]

After that, the conversation returned to the political and military situation. Himmler's views on the subject (we were in May 1944) seemed extremely naive. [. . .] He asserted that peace would soon be made with the Western powers. England was worn out; America was still intact but had not yet reached the height of her armaments potential. Once armistice and peace had been concluded with the Western powers, the war in the east could proceed. Given the favourable strategic positions occupied by the Reich, he believed that the war in the east, fought with the assistance of the Western Allies, could last for decades [. . .]."[252]

As is well known, Hitler himself was periodically prone to such ravings, and that was no coincidence. But Wilhelm Wulff went on: "After a short pause, during which he had some refreshments served, Himmler asked about his own horoscope. I had a small sketch of it dating from 1934. As he did not know his hour of birth, we both undertook to find it retrospectively, by means of comparative data."[253]

For two more hours, the two men immersed themselves in the dark mazes of the zodiac constellations. At 7 p.m., Wulff was dismissed and returned to Hamburg with understandable relief. He stopped off in Berlin to report back to Schellenberg, who was much encouraged by the length of the interview – all of five hours: "That's good, very good. So much time? That seldom happens."[254] Quite so, but with decidedly meagre results.

Hitler, on the other hand, had no use for astrology, and neither did he much care for the intelligence supplied by "Cicero" in Ankara – which mentioned a mysterious Operation Overlord to be launched after mid-May.[255] Ambassador von Papen was to write in his memoirs: "Our knowledge of Operation Overlord was limited to the name. I repeatedly suggested that in order to deceive the enemy into thinking that we knew its details, our propaganda should give the impression that we possessed considerable knowledge of Overlord. However, for some reason or other, Hitler declined to allow this."[256]

Having himself read the documents supplied by Cicero, the S.D. agent in Ankara, Ludwig Moyzisch, pushed the analysis further: "It was clear that Operation Overlord was considered by the Western Allies as one of the decisive actions of the war. Therefore, I was sure I had the answer: Overlord was the code name for the second front. I immediately sent a telegram to Berlin presenting my theory and the elements that brought me to that conclusion. Eight days later, I received this laconic response: 'Possible, but unlikely.'"[257]

In Berlin, however, the S.S. intelligence service retained a lively interest in the matter, and the translator of the documents supplied by Cicero was later to state: "The R.S.H.A. had received information about Plan Overlord as early as November 1943. It did not know the whole plan, but the documents contained several references to it, and Dr Graefe, as well as others within Amt VI,[xxxi] had deduced from them that the invasion would take place in France. [. . .] This information was passed on to Hitler's headquarters and [. . .] presented to Hitler himself, who scoffed at the idea that anyone might try to breach the Atlantic wall, and ended up saying that such a conception was extravagant."[258]

Actually, the Führer was constantly wavering between denial, fear and optimism. In January 1944, having already appointed Marshal Rommel inspector of the Atlantic wall fortifications, Hitler placed him at the head of Army Group B, defending the Channel coast. The marshal's zeal upon taking up his duties seemed to have a soothing effect in Berlin, and Goebbels entered in his diary

xxxi  R.S.H.A. section VI – foreign intelligence, headed by Walter Schellenberg.

on April 18: "The Führer is absolutely sure that the invasion will fail, and even that the Allies will be repulsed with huge losses."[259] Yet for all his bragging, Hitler was only partly reassured, all the more so as the greatest uncertainty reigned within his staff as to the possible landing place; the Führer himself had considered in turn the Pas-de-Calais, Normandy, Brittany and even the Gironde estuary, not to mention that he occasionally envisaged Belgium, Holland and above all Norway[xxxii] – whose coastal fortifications he had ordered strengthened as a matter of extreme urgency.

On June 6, 1944 at dawn, the Allies landed in Normandy.

xxxii  With some help from the British: see N.A., WO 193/822, Note on plans "Bodyguard" and "Fortitude", 30.4.44, Top Secret, p. 1.

# 10

# THE BEGINNING OF THE END

The long-awaited opening of the "second front"[i] nonetheless took the German general staff by surprise, and since any important strategic initiative required the Führer's assent, the Wehrmacht was slow in reacting during the crucial first hours of the Allied landing; and once the British, American and Canadian forces were solidly ensconced inland, the disparity of forces, especially in the air,[ii] played relentlessly against the Germans.

That same day of June 6, 1944, Kersten returned from Stockholm, and nine days later, he joined his patient at the Bergwald headquarters near Salzburg.[iii] From the very first session, our therapist entered the field with his usual weaponry of seduction, flattery, appeal to reason and . . . national socialist doctrine! After a brief allusion to the Normandy landings, he blamed Himmler

i  A "third front" would be more accurate, since as well as the eastern front, the Italian front was ablaze by then, with the Allies having entered Rome on June 4.
ii  The Luftwaffe had initially 175 fighter planes available in Normandy – versus 3,000 on the Allied side. In addition, the German fighters were short of fuel . . . Himmler, like Hitler, had counted on the destruction caused by the first V 1 missiles, but launched against London with a comparatively weak explosive charge, they were to have no effect on the strategic situation in France.
iii  In *The Man with the Miraculous Hands,* Joseph Kessel described the interview as taking place in Hochwald, East Prussia. But this does not tally with Himmler's appointment diary: from March 1 to July 13, 1944, the Reichsführer never left his Salzburg H.Q.

for killing in his concentration camps the Norwegians, the Danes and the Dutch, "last survivors of the Germanic race". Now, he added, the superior intelligence of the Reichsführer and his status as a great Germanic leader ought on the contrary to induce him to release as many as possible. Himmler replied that Hitler would never permit this, which gave Kersten an opportunity to repeat the arguments previously presented by Schellenberg and Wilhelm Wulff: should Himmler send a division of his Waffen S.S. to Berchtesgaden, he would become the next Führer . . . An appalled Himmler rejected outright the idea of a putsch, taking refuge behind the oath of allegiance inscribed on his belt buckle: *Meine Ehre heisst Treue* – "My Loyalty is my Honour". Kersten suggested he simply change his belt buckle, but the Reichsführer would not hear of it: "The sense of loyalty is sacred; I teach it to my soldiers every day."[260]

A few days later, in Berlin, Kersten met astrologer Wulff, who was later to recall: "After the beginning of the invasion, Kersten came to see me and told me with a gesture of despair: 'Himmler still does not act! He said that since all his senior officers were "unreliable", he could not contemplate the idea of a putsch.'"[261]

That, of course, was just one more excuse for inaction; at that stage, indeed, the attention of the senior officers in question was essentially absorbed by the course of the battle in Normandy, where the Wehrmacht was in great danger of being outflanked and over-whelmed south and west of Caen.[iv] Strangely enough, Himmler, who had three S.S. Panzer divisions in Normandy – and was even to have six by the end of June – appeared to take little interest in

iv There was also Ukraine, where the great Soviet offensive Bagration, launched on June 22, was beginning to shatter the whole of Army Group Centre.

the course of the battle. The Reichsführer admittedly had no say in the engagement of his divisions, which depended in theory on commander-in-chief von Rundstedt, and in practice on the Führer himself; besides, the Waffen S.S. made up only a small part of his empire: he was also in charge of the political police, the criminal police, domestic intelligence, espionage abroad, concentration camps, the new armaments factories, the Ahnenerbe, the Lebensborn,[v] the implementation of the Final Solution, the research institutes, the interior ministry, the Reich Commissariat for the Strengthening of the German Race and the Bureau for Race and Settlement.

Within the scope of all these duties – and of a few others[vi] – Heinrich Himmler devoted most of that month to studying reports on the trial of a vaccine against typhus,[vii] to the dismantling of the Lodz Ghetto,[viii] to the safekeeping of the Bayeux tapestry,[ix] to his quarrel with armaments minister Speer, whose functions he wished to usurp (after having failed to eliminate him by engineering a "medical accident"),[262] to the deportation of the Italian Jews, to the supervision of excavation work for underground factories producing the V1 flying bombs,[x] to progress in the extraction of shale oil, to modifications in the insignia on the uniforms of camp guards, to the extension of agricultural land used for growing

---

v   "Society for Genealogical Inheritance" and "Fount of Life" (institution for the creation of a pure Aryan race).

vi   Such as those linked to the function of "special representative for rubber plants".

vii   Leaving 250 dead among the prisoners used as guinea pigs.

viii   Followed by the killing of its 72,000 inhabitants.

ix   In Germany, of course; but he failed for lack of time.

x   Employing near Mittelhausen the prisoners of the Mittelbau-Dora camp, of whom 20,000 were to die.

rubber plants,[xi] to disciplinary measures against S.S. officers accused of excessive corruption or alcohol intake, to the projects for setting up new S.S. "European divisions", [xii] to propaganda tours among the S.S. regiments in occupied territories, to the deployment of prisoners to clear bomb sites in cities, to experiments on the desalinisation of sea water,[xiii] to the deportation to Auschwitz of 437,400 Hungarian Jews, to the repatriation and resettlement in the Reich of the Volksdeutsche who were supposed to colonise Byelorussia, Ukraine, Crimea and the Baltic countries, to the repression of resistance movements in Greece and Yugoslavia, and so on. This is why he had precious little time left to deal with strategic matters – for which he had not the slightest competence in any case.

Was the Reichsführer aware of what was afoot at the beginning of July 1944? Over the previous six years, plans to overthrow or assassinate Hitler had failed or been abandoned one after the other: fate, bad luck, inexperience, procrastination, foreign initiatives,[xiv] security precautions around Hitler, the Führer's legendary "sixth sense" – all had conspired to thwart the plots against him. The conspirators of the early years – former chief of staff Beck, Abwehr chief Canaris, his deputy General Oster, Marshal von Witzleben, Minister Schacht, diplomat von Weiszäcker, interior ministry official Gisevius and former mayor of Leipzig Goerdeler – were progressively joined by the civilians of the Kreisau Circle and of the

xi    The Russian Dandelion, see above, p. 175.

xii   Which would never materialise, for lack of weapons and officers.

xiii  For the benefit of the Luftwaffe and the Kriegsmarine.

xiv   Such as the September 1938 arrival of Chamberlain in Munich, which compelled the conspirators to abandon the coup they intended to stage as soon as Hitler opened hostilities against Czechoslovakia.

Mittwochsgesellschaft:[xv] Count Helmuth James von Moltke, diplomat Adam von Trott zu Solz, jurist Hans-Bernd von Haeften, former social democrat M.P. Julius Leber, Jesuit priest Alfred Delp, Professor Jens Jessen, former Prussian finance minister Johannes Popitz, diplomat Ulrich von Hassell, Count Gottfried von Bismarck, pastor Dietrich Bonhoeffer and former ambassador to Moscow Friedrich von der Schulenburg. However, all these men had gone no further than maintaining contact with the Allies and envisaging new institutions after the collapse of the Reich. But a renewed effort to bring that about required the commitment of yet another group: the officers of Army Group Centre, engaged on the eastern front.

The very soul of the resistance within that group was Colonel Henning von Tresckow; like many of his brother officers, he had been outraged by the massacres of Jewish, Russian and Ukrainian civilians committed by the Einsatzgruppen in the autumn of 1941, and he had since then managed to have appointed to his staff such opponents to Hitler as Lieutenants von Kleist and von Schlabrendorff, as well as Captain von Gersdorf.[xvi] Though he failed to enlist his successive superiors Marshals von Bock and von Kluge, he had at least established close contact as early as 1942 with the main conspirators in Berlin, namely Carl Goerdeler, Generals Oster, Beck and Olbricht, and Admiral Canaris. Together with these men, he had organised several attempts to kill Hitler; their failures caused a certain despondency, but hope returned with the arrival in Berlin of Lieutenant-Colonel Klaus Schenk von Stauffenberg, a Roman Catholic officer who was known for his resoluteness and

xv   Wednesday Society – the day on which its sixteen members usually met.
xvi  The latter two being his cousins.

idealism. Together with Generals Olbricht and von Tresckow, he drew up a plan for a coup under the code name Walkyrie,[xvii] to be launched immediately after Hitler's assassination. By early July, the success of Operation Overlord in the west and Bagration in the east spurred the plotters into immediate action.[xviii]

At this juncture, all links had been severed between Himmler and the rare members of the resistance who had approached him: the lawyer Langbehn was in jail and former minister Popitz, ostracised by the other plotters after his contact with Himmler,[xix] knew nothing more about the progress of the conspiracy. And yet the Reichsführer himself obviously knew a lot, as evidenced by what had transpired during his recent visit to Admiral Canaris; to the former chief of the Abwehr, now head of a small O.K.W. auxiliary service entitled "special staff for commercial and economic warfare", Himmler had stated bluntly that "he knew very well that influential circles within the army were hatching plans for a rebellion. [. . .] However, he would not let it get that far, and would put a stop to it in due course. He had only delayed action until he found out who was behind it. Now that he knew, he would deal with the likes of Beck and Goerdeler."[263]

Himmler was obviously well informed, since Beck was the

xvii   It was actually the diversion of an existing plan under the same code name, which was to be implemented by the reserve army in case of a surprise attack by the Allies against Berlin.

xviii   The plotters intended to negotiate with the Western Allies immediately after they had taken power, all while resisting a progression by Soviet troops in the east; this plan could therefore be compromised by an excessively quick advance from both east and west. But the spur to action also came from the fact that the Gestapo had already arrested Oster, Dohnanyi and Count von Moltke – and issued an arrest warrant against Goerdeler.

xix   For most of the conspirators, Himmler was as dangerous as Hitler and also had to be eliminated.

brains of the conspiracy and Goerdeler was its heart . . .[xx] But why would Himmler want to tell all this to the admiral, who was known to be the most dangerous opponent of the Black Order?[xxi] And was it really sensible to inform one of the presumed heads of the conspiracy that his accomplices were about to be arrested? Actually, by mid-July, General Beck was still at large and Carl Goerdeler was being sought rather half-heartedly, in connection with another case. The explanation may seem amazing, but is in fact easily understandable given Heinrich Himmler's decidedly tortuous psychology: ever since his "unavowable" conversations with Schellenberg, Kersten, Langbehn, Popitz and Wulff, the Reichsführer had never ceased to consider the possibility of a putsch – without ever making up his mind. But should a handful of amateurish plotters succeed in eliminating Hitler, then he, Heinrich Himmler, would no longer need to take the initiative: he could simply step in to "avenge the Führer" and then take power – a perfectly acceptable solution to the dilemma that had been tormenting him for almost two years . . .

Hitler having returned to Rastenburg, Himmler joined him there on July 14, and Kersten naturally followed. He thus once again experienced the harsh summer heat of East Prussia, the very relative night-time coolness of the Görlitz forest, the spartan comfort of the Hochwald headquarters and the routine of the Reichsführer's treatments – with this time a major diversion: "During the treatment this morning, Himmler told me that the

xx   But Himmler still seemed unaware that von Tresckow and Stauffenberg were its strong arm.
xxi   Whom Himmler had always refused to arrest, though he had known for a long time about his seditious activities.

Americans were at present having a lot of trouble with the Russians. This was bound to result in serious conflicts between them, and would eventually have a decisive effect on the future course of the war. That morning, I also had time for quite a long walk, and after lunch I went to have a nap. Suddenly, all hell broke loose. Sturmbannführer Lukas, Himmler's driver, burst into my sleeping car, shouting: 'Attempt on the Führer's life! Attempt on the Führer! But the Führer still lives, nothing has happened to him, he's unharmed![xxii] We have just come with the Reichsführer from the Wolfsschanze.' I leaped up, opened the door of the compartment and asked: 'Where is the Reichsführer?' Lukas answered: 'In his barracks.' I immediately put on my shoes and jacket and went to see Himmler. The guard outside his quarters had been doubled, but I showed my pass and was allowed through. I entered Himmler's office without knocking. He was standing by his desk; I looked at him for a moment and saw that he was arranging and destroying some papers. Then I asked him:

'What's really going on, Herr Reichsführer?'

Himmler answered without looking up:

'A bomb was thrown at the Führer. But Providence has saved him.'

I inquired whether he had any further information.

'Probably a Wehrmacht colonel. I'll exterminate all these

xxii   Once again, luck had played against the plotters: Colonel von Stauffenberg, with the three fingers of his one operative hand, only had time to prime one bomb and could not stuff the other one in his satchel; in addition, since work on Hitler's bunker had not been finished, the meeting was held in a wooden barracks with all windows open, thus dispersing the blast of the explosion; finally, the satchel deposited next to Hitler had been pushed behind the foot of the thick oak table by an officer who found it cumbersome. Without this conjunction of coincidences, Hitler would have had no chance of survival.

vermin. The Führer has ordered me to arrest two thousand traitors . . .'

'And who do you propose to arrest?'

'The criminals.'

'Who are these criminals? Are you sure you know who they are? I hope you won't arrest the wrong people, Herr Reichsführer.'

Himmler didn't answer; he went on rummaging frantically through his papers. [. . .] Then I continued:

'Do you remember, Herr Reichsführer, that some eighteen months ago, you showed me a report about the Führer's illness? In these circumstances, wouldn't it have been better if he had been killed? You should have acted then. Now someone else has acted for you. Look at the matter in this light before you set in motion the machinery that will destroy men whom you call traitors.'

Himmler had stopped rummaging through his papers, and he gazed at me with a look that betrayed both horror and fear. His eyes were blazing, his lips trembling. Then he shouted:

'What's that you're saying, Kersten? Is that really what you think?'

I replied slowly and categorically:

'Yes, that is exactly what I think.'

Himmler seemed desperate.

'For heaven's sake, you mustn't believe that; and I mustn't believe it either. You told me nothing and I heard nothing, Kersten! Providence has saved the Führer, and one day, History will say that his last soldier, the loyal paladin Himmler, struggled to his last breath for his Führer, the greatest man, the greatest brain in the world! [. . .] Providence has spared him so that he may bring the war to a triumphant conclusion. My place is now at his side, and I'll be ruthless in the execution of his orders. I'm flying off to Berlin immediately. Go to Hartzwalde, and stay there until I summon you!'

He gathered the last of his papers and left. I stood alone in his office, gazing at the desk that had just been emptied of all its secrets."[264]

In a frantic effort to erase all trace of past intrigues, Himmler – whom the Führer had named straight away "commander of the reserve army"[xxiii] – did indeed mete out a ruthless reprisal immediately after the collapse of the attempted coup. Once the main leaders of the conspiracy had been killed or committed suicide on the evening of July 20,[xxiv] the Gestapo took charge, and over the next six weeks, almost five thousand people directly or indirectly linked to the plot were arrested and tortured. Between August and September 1944, all officers and civilians accused of participation in the attempted coup – including Goerdeler, von der Schulenburg, von Hassell, Popitz, von Wartenburg, Generals Thomas, Halder, Stieff, Fromm, Oster, Fellgiebel and Admiral Canaris – appeared before the People's Court, presided over by the notorious Roland Freisler, who insulted and humiliated them before sending most of them to the gallows.[xxv]

xxiii  The coup attempt had been planned within that army, which was also to carry it out – without the assent, but not without the knowledge, of General Fromm, its commanding officer.

xxiv  This was the case of Beck, von Stauffenberg and Olbricht, as well as of von Tresckow, who committed suicide the next day.

xxv  The accused, though much weakened by torture, remained stoical under the insults, and General Fellgiebel even shouted to Judge Freisler after the pronouncement of the sentence: "Well, hurry up and hang us, Herr Präsident, or else you'll be hanged before us!" Schacht, Halder and Thomas were sent to concentration camps and survived the war.

That summer, however, Kersten did his very best to save some of the men caught in the broad nets cast by the Gestapo: "Among the many people accused of being linked to the 'Stauffenberg plot' were two of my friends, prefect Karl Wentzel and lawyer Karl Langbehn. [. . .] Wentzel was entered as member of the inner circle in the list of conspirators found at the home of Leipzig mayor Goerdeler; he was supposedly marked there as future minister of agriculture in the government that would replace Hitler's regime.[xxvi] [. . .] When I heard of his arrest, I went straight to Himmler and asked for his release, as well as that of Langbehn. [. . .] Unfortunately, if I may say so, the Reichsführer's health at the moment was particularly good, so he could do without me! [. . .] He told me that he was absolutely sure that Wentzel was one of the heads of the conspiracy; as for Langbehn, what Himmler told me was only too true: he had too many enemies! [. . .] All my efforts proved useless. But some time later, Himmler's health deteriorated and I was urgently summoned to treat him; this time, he gave me good grounds to hope that my friends would be acquitted. Hitherto, Himmler had always kept his word, and when he gave me his 'word of honour' that Wentzel and Langbehn would be acquitted, I was reassured."[265]

And yet, unbeknown to Kersten, he was in even greater danger than the men he was trying to save; on August 2, as he was getting ready to leave Hartzwalde for Berlin, a letter from Schellenberg, delivered by an S.S. dispatch rider, was to warn him *in extremis*:

xxvi The "supposedly" is explained by the fact that Kersten had heard "from reliable sources" that the Gestapo added names to the lists, so as to get rid of potential opponents.

Dear Mr Kersten,

During my last treatment, I suggested to you that some people – namely Obergruppenführer Kaltenbrunner and Gruppenführer Müller – are again trying to create problems for you in relation to the Langbehn Affair. [. . .] They allege to have found among Langbehn's papers some files that could be compromising for you, proving *inter alia* that you are working with the British secret service.

In the meantime, I have received confirmation of the fact that, not only do they consider you with the greatest mistrust, but they also have been keeping you for a long time under close surveillance. I would have liked to speak to you personally about all this, [. . .] but I must unfortunately leave urgently on a service trip, which is why I am having this warning note delivered to you by a particularly trustworthy messenger.

Ever since you left for Sweden [. . .], the circles in question have tried to eliminate you, even against the Reichsführer's will. Always carry a firearm, beware of strangers and above all, make no statements during conversations in the presence of people you do not know. [. . .] All your movements are being watched and your telephone conversations are listened to.

Should the opportunity arise during the next few days, take care to inform the Reichsführer cautiously that you have been made aware of the intentions of some of your enemies, so that he may again assure you of his assistance and if possible deliver you a safe conduct or something of the sort, in order to protect you from an unexpected imprisonment.

Warn also the Jehovah's Witnesses whose release you obtained from the concentration camp and who work on your estate, for one also seeks to prove that they allow you to relay information abroad concerning the concentration camps.

Please be sure to destroy this letter as soon as you have read it. [. . .] In haste and, as always, with all my gratitude and very best wishes.

Walter Schellenberg[266]

Clearly an alarming letter . . . But what its bearer said when delivering it was more alarming still: "The secret messenger," Kersten recalled, "confided to me on the same occasion that General Schellenberg advised me not to take my usual road to Berlin, [. . .] since it would be too risky for the time being."[267]

Such warnings were not to be taken lightly, and that afternoon, Kersten told his driver to take the route passing through Templin rather than Oranienburg; the subsequent events he related as follows: "I abided by Schellenberg's instructions, [. . .] after which I told Himmler that I had received 'mystical warnings' that my life was in danger. He was much upset and had an investigation carried out, which established that the warnings were perfectly well founded. Kaltenbrunner was consequently summoned to the 'special train Steiermark'[xxvii] headquarters in the vicinity of Berlin. Himmler advised me to behave in such a way that Kaltenbrunner would suspect nothing, [. . .] for he said he intended to settle this matter 'in a diplomatic way'. Upon Kaltenbrunner's arrival, Himmler invited us both to lunch in his

xxvii    A new name for "special train Heinrich".

224

dining car. Kaltenbrunner was extremely friendly, and he asked me most amiably about Sweden, and whether I had enjoyed my stay there.

'I enjoyed it not at all,' was my sombre reply.

'How so?' Kaltenbrunner asked. 'I thought Sweden was a real paradise . . .'

'That may be,' said I, 'but as for me, I lost my employment there. You must have known for a long time that I was employed by the British intelligence service. Well, imagine that they fired me! They are dissatisfied with my services because Himmler is in such good health . . .'

'Yes, the British think that Kersten is no longer any use to them,' added Himmler, who could scarcely conceal his hilarity.

Never in all my life have I seen such a dumbfounded look as that of Kaltenbrunner! He gasped for breath and was unable to say a word. Himmler burst out laughing.

'So you see, Kaltenbrunner, we really have good reasons to commiserate with Kersten!'

After which he went on more seriously:

'My dear Kaltenbrunner, if ever something were to happen to Kersten, not only would my life be in danger – yours would be too. [. . .] I fear that you would not survive him for very long. Therefore, since you are so dependent on each other, I hope that you will long remain in good health . . .'

Kaltenbrunner perfectly understood what he meant, and when Himmler proposed a toast to my health, he raised his glass with a somewhat trembling hand."[268]

Upon Schellenberg's return, Kersten learned about the details of the ambush that had been set for him: the plan was to stop his car in a small wood near the district of Ruppin and to shoot him, as well as his driver, after which the explanation would be that the car had refused to stop, so that it had been necessary to shoot – an old Gestapo trick . . . And Kersten concluded: "After that, as a precaution, I never followed this route again and always stuck to the main road, in spite of the bombings that henceforth went on almost without interruption."[269]

By August 1944, however, the roads were only secondary targets for the Allied air forces, whose attacks now concentrated on refineries and synthetic fuel plants – which produced that month only 10 per cent of their normal output. It was actually a vicious circle: the less fuel produced, the less the German fighter planes could counter the bombings and the greater the number of chemical plants destroyed – hence less fuel produced and fewer fighters available to ward off the attacks on chemical plants.[xxviii] But for the Reich, the patent loss of air superiority had even more immediate strategic consequences: in the west, the Allies had landed on August 15 in the south of France, and were meeting little serious opposition during their progression northwards up the Rhône Valley; besides, after the Battle of Normandy, which had cost the Wehrmacht 450,000 men,[xxix] German troops had been forced to evacuate Paris and head for the borders of the Reich – closely followed by the Allied armies that liberated Brussels on September 3. In the east, a huge Soviet offensive

xxviii   Other shortages were looming: that same month, Turkey severed her relations with Germany, which meant the end of the Reich's supply of chromium – a vital metal for the armaments industry. A month later, Finland in turn severed her relations with Germany and opened negotiations with the U.S.S.R. – an event whose consequences ranged far beyond the interruption of nickel supplies.
xxix   Killed, wounded or captured.

in southern Ukraine had destroyed sixteen German divisions[xxx] and caused the fall of Romanian dictator Antonescu, so his country changed sides and declared war on Germany – soon followed by Bulgaria. Almost simultaneously, the Red Army had entered Poland and set up camp on the outskirts of Warsaw, which had risen up against the Germans. Finally, at the approach of Soviet divisions, the Slovak army also turned against the Germans, and there was a marked increase in partisan activity in both Yugoslavia and Greece – two countries about to be evacuated by the Wehrmacht.

In the midst of this furious maelstrom, Himmler was fighting like the devil, armed with his arsenal of blind fanaticism, blatant cruelty, abject fear and measureless ambition. As interior minister, he presided over the fierce repression of all potential opposition within the country; as head of the Totenkopfverbände, he supervised the evacuation of all concentration camps within reach of the Soviet armies; as S.S. Reichsführer, he ordered the elimination of the Warsaw insurgents and the destruction of entire districts of the city; as newly appointed head of the Reserve Army, he was charged with securing the south-western borders of the Reich, from Switzerland to the Siegfried line; as creator and leader of the Werwolf units, he was responsible for training the recruits assigned to spread terror behind American and Soviet lines; as sponsor of the Volkssturm, the people's militia, he oversaw the training, equipping and organising of tens of thousands of novice fighters who were either too young or too old to be incorporated into the regular army; as Nazi dignitary, he was still waging a ruthless struggle against his rivals Goebbels, Göring, Rosenberg, Ribbentrop and Bormann; as chief of Sipo-S.D., he urged his henchmen to

xxx    With the loss of 380,000 men.

stamp out all outbreaks of resistance in Yugoslavia, Greece, Austria, Norway, Denmark, Slovakia, Hungary and the Netherlands.

In the Netherlands, the Gestapo and S.D. were fighting mercilessly against a widespread resistance, and over the summer, Kersten's agent Jacobus Nieuwenhuis had learned through a friend working at the police transport department that his car, bearing the licence plate X229, was subject to a search warrant. Realising the threat, Nieuwenhuis changed his licence plate and awaited the right moment to join Kersten, as the latter had instructed him to do seven months earlier.[xxxi] That moment came in early September 1944: "Our service had been ordered to move to Apeldoorn.[xxxii] In the resulting confusion, I filled in my own order of mission for Berlin, with the Dienststelle's stamp and a false signature. Having taken seventy litres of gasoline from the service warehouse, I left the same day. Miraculously, [. . .] there were practically no controls, even at the border, and on September 6, I arrived at Hartzwalde, where Kersten received me immediately. I told him all about my misadventures [. . .] and he promised to go and find out more at headquarters. [. . .] Upon his return, he confirmed that I was under grave suspicion of working for the resistance and of being an 'enemy of the people.'"[270]

Jacobus Nieuwenhuis therefore remained in hiding at Hartzwalde over the next few months; it was a very safe place, but his protector's position was hardly an enviable one at the time: on September 2, 1944, Finland had sought an armistice with the U.S.S.R. and severed its diplomatic relations with Germany. To

xxxi   See above, p. 200.
xxxii   He was still working at the S.S. Dienststelle, 2B Javastraat, The Hague. See above, p. 94.

Ambassador Kivimäki, who had just been interned himself and was concerned about the safety of his friend Kersten, the latter replied that he had no reason to worry: "Himmler's bad health is my best safe conduct."[271] But on September 8, when he joined the Reichsführer at Hochwald to resume his treatment, Kersten was greeted with these rather ungracious words: "You Finns are all traitors! [. . .] I only regret that we didn't liquidate Finland the way we did Norway, while there was still time."[272] After a few sessions of treatment, however, the old magic worked anew, so that Kersten was promised special protection for the three hundred or so Finns living in the Reich, an extraterritorial status for the Hartzwalde estate and permission to return to Sweden – under the same conditions as before. More remarkable still, he would be able to use Himmler's private telephone line – extension 145 – to call Hartzwalde or any of the Reichsführer's headquarters![xxxiii]

On September 26, Kersten flew back to Berlin in the Junkers 52 which Himmler had put at his disposal, narrowly missed being shot down on the way by an Allied plane, and left for Sweden two days later with his wife and three children. In their absence, the Hartzwalde estate would be run by the faithful "sister" Elisabeth Lüben, assisted by Kersten's secretary, the twenty Jehovah's Witnesses, a Dutch refugee and an overworked astrologist.

In Stockholm, Kersten resumed contact with Foreign Minister Günther; at the time, the Swedish government was being subjected to increasing British and American pressure, relayed locally by the representatives of the Danish and Norwegian authorities –

xxxiii  A concession that was by no means disinterested: Kersten had to be contactable at all hours, in case Himmler needed his services. At the time, mail between Berlin and Stockholm took three weeks to reach its destination.

especially since the recent arrest and deportation of Norwegian students and Danish policemen.[xxxiv] Diplomat Niels Christian Ditleff, who was working freelance at the Norwegian legation, found a precious ally in the person of Eric von Post, chief of the political section in the Swedish foreign ministry, and both had persuaded Christian Günther that the matter now brooked no delay;[273] Günther himself was to write after the war: "In the autumn of 1944, Kersten was thus given the task of negotiating with Himmler the liberation of a group of Norwegian students and Danish policemen. The Swedish government was willing to receive these poor people in Sweden, and if need be to intern them there until the end of the war, together with the Danish and Norwegian women and children who were being held in Germany. If Kersten was unable to obtain this, he had full powers to negotiate with Himmler the regrouping of all Scandinavian prisoners in a single camp, under the authority of the Swedish Red Cross – the Swedish government undertaking to provide for the maintenance of these prisoners."[274]

But soon, there was to be more to it than that, as Baron van Nagell later recalled: "I proposed to Kersten that he also include the Dutch in his rescue mission – in other words, that he undertake to save those Dutch who were still detained in German concentration camps. Dr Kersten immediately agreed, and we then discussed the technical details. Unfortunately, I could not count on the

xxxiv   In Oslo, at the beginning of 1944, Gauleiter Terboven had ordered the deportation to Germany of 644 Norwegian students accused of "moral resistance", while in Copenhagen, between September and October 1944, 1,981 Danish policemen were imprisoned at Neuengamme and Buchenwald for having refused to protect 74 firms from sabotage by the Danish resistance.

cooperation of the Dutch embassy in Stockholm,[xxxv] so that everything had to be planned and carried out with Dr Kersten alone."[275]

At the last moment, Günther was to entrust Kersten with yet another mission: the Dutch government in exile had just asked the Swedish authorities to supply food to the part of Holland that was still occupied by the Germans, who had blocked all the ports – so that it was impossible to unload supplies and famine was threatening; Kersten was thus to try to obtain from Himmler at least a partial lifting of the blockade. And of course, there were many individual requests as well, such as that of Swedish banker Jacob Wallenberg, who pleaded with Kersten to procure the release of his brother-in-law, Count Ferdinand von Arco auf Valley.

This was the first time our Medizinalrat would endeavour to obtain the liberation of very substantial groups of prisoners, as he later noted: "Impressed by the task and by the importance of the mission, I flew back to rejoin Himmler on November 28, 1944. [. . .] His headquarters was then located at Triberg, in the Black Forest.[xxxvi] [. . .] I explained to him the Swedish conditions, and on my own account[xxxvii] I also asked him to release five thousand Dutch subjects. Himmler was willing to negotiate with the Swedes,

xxxv    Apparently as a result of disagreements with Foreign Minister van Kleffens, van Nagell had been replaced as ambassador by Count van Rechteren Limpurg in May 1941, and had only remained in Stockholm as press attaché thereafter. Relations with his successor had been strained, to put it mildly.

xxxvi    The Führer having named him "supreme commander for the Upper Rhine sector", with the mission of defending an improvised bridgehead on the left bank of the Rhine, between Saarland and the Swiss border – pending the great counter-offensive in the Ardennes, to be launched in mid-December.

xxxvii    And on that of Baron van Nagell . . . Kersten himself had tried to obtain from the Dutch embassy in Stockholm a list of Dutch citizens detained in Germany, but Dutch ambassador van Rechteren Limpurg had shown no interest in the matter! See hereunder, pp. 368–69.

but when I broached the matter of the Dutch, he flew into a rage: the Dutch, he said, were no better than the Jews; they had betrayed the Germanic cause. The first day, my usual arguments were completely in vain. But the following day, his health took a turn for the worse, and when I succeeded in freeing him from his pains, he began to soften up, as usual in such situations."[276]

Indeed, on December 8, Himmler consented to release a thousand Dutch women,[xxxviii] and Scandinavia was next on the agenda. "After long days of quibbling and rehashing, Himmler eventually agreed to release fifty Danish policemen and fifty Norwegian students. He refused to do more, but added that he might later contemplate the release of a greater number of families of Danish and Norwegian children, provided the foreign press did not portray as weakness the generosity he had just demonstrated. [. . .] He was also willing to accept my suggestion that all Scandinavian prisoners be gathered into a single camp, and that it be controlled by the Red Cross."[277]

Pushing his luck, Kersten then raised the matter of the Jews, and as usual was met with a blank refusal; yet he persisted, and later noted:

"I spoke to Himmler again today about releasing the Jews. He was hesitant but did not actually refuse. He had hopes of victory, which is a good omen. 'We'll drive the English and the Americans into the Channel,' he told me. He inquired how many Jews I really wanted to have released and sent to Switzerland. I replied: 'Twenty thousand, men and women.'

xxxviii    Kersten had just learned from Secretary Brandt that there were in Ravensbrück between 5,000 and 6,000 women, of whom about 1,000 were Dutch. Actually, there were many more.

232

'Good God, I can't do that,' Himmler replied. 'Do you realise that you're giving Goebbels enough rope for the Führer to hang me?'

I made an appeal to his Germanic humanity. Towards the end of our conversation, Himmler said that I should be satisfied if, for a start, he released two or three thousand Jews and sent them to Switzerland. But he wanted to sleep on it. [...] It was particularly difficult to release Jews who were under arrest, because of Hitler's deep-rooted hatred of them."[278]

On the other hand, Himmler readily agreed to reopen the Dutch ports, so that Swedish food relief could reach the Dutch population still under German control. There also appeared to have been some haggling concerning eight hundred French, four hundred Belgian and five hundred Polish women.[279]

That same day, in the special train's dining car, Kersten met S.S. Obergruppenführer Gottlob Berger, an old warhorse who was also his patient – and who held the key position of chief of the S.S. Hauptamt.[xxxix] The man was beside himself: "Berger told me that, on Hitler's order, Himmler had instructed him to have five thousand English and American officers shot. He had refused outright: 'I am a soldier, not a murderer; a soldier does not shoot defenceless prisoners. [...] I told Himmler that the Führer could do it himself if he had the guts. I shall protect these prisoners of war, even if it costs me my life.'"[280]

Two days later, Kersten faced a Reichsführer who was just as indignant, and he had to wait until Himmler calmed down before beginning his treatment. "After a while, he confided in me that Berger had refused to carry out the Führer's order to shoot five

xxxix   And, as such, sole senior officer in charge of recruitment and organisation within the Waffen S.S.

thousand Allied officers [. . .] in retaliation for the English and American bombings of the German civilian population. I tried to calm him down by saying that one fine day he would be grateful to Berger for having refused to carry out the order. But Himmler only got more upset, and said that this was the first time one of his generals had refused to carry out an order from the Führer. 'I'll have him put before a court martial, but how can I replace him? And Berger knows it: I can't part with him at the moment.' I asked if someone else would carry out the Führer's order, to which Himmler replied: 'No, so long as General Berger is in charge of all prisoner of war camps, there's nothing I can do about it; I can't pick a fight with him now. But I won't forget that.' I said: 'In all of history, the great Germanic chieftains have never harmed defenceless people. You surely know that, Herr Reichsführer!' 'Yes, of course, that is true . . . But if you're not tough, you're perceived as being weak – which is the worst one can say of a national socialist.'"[281]

And especially of Heinrich Himmler, of course! But on December 12, Kersten received the following letter:

Dear Herr Kersten,
You will return to Sweden shortly before Christmas. On the occasion of the Christmas celebrations, I would like to ask you to take with you to Sweden the three Swedish prisoners pardoned by the Führer at my request.[282]

And so it was that the interminable affair of the Warsaw Swedes found its conclusion on the eve of Christmas 1944, with the release and repatriation of Widén, Häggberg and Berglind, the

**Der Reichsführer-SS**

(1) Berlin SW 11, den *12.* Dezember 1944
Prinz-Albrecht-Straße 8
Feld-Kommandostelle.

Lieber Herr  K e r s t e n !

Sie werden kurz vor Weihnachten wieder nach
Schweden fliegen. Ich darf Sie bitten, die drei
gefangenen Schweden, deren Begnadigung der Führer
auf meinen Vorschlag genehmigt hat, zum Julfest
mit nach Schweden zu nehmen!

Ihrer lieben Frau, Ihren Kindern und Ihnen
selbst übersende ich meine aufrichtigen Wünsche
zu Weihnachten und zum neuen Jahr und grüße Sie
herzlich

*[signature: H. Himmler]*

Lettre du Reichsführer Himmler datée du 12 décembre 1944, par laquelle il annonce à Kersten la grâce
et la libération des trois derniers ingénieurs suédois prisonniers, et le prie de les emmener en Suède
« pour les fêtes de Noël ».

*Letter from Reichsführer Himmler to Felix Kersten dated December 12, 1944,
announcing the pardon and release of the three last Swedish engineers*

235

last three men sentenced to death. This seemed all the more astounding as Himmler wrote that letter only four days before the start of the Ardennes counteroffensive[xl] – when he presumably had other concerns . . . Yet Kersten's reply on December 21 was just as remarkable; its numerous blandishments and obsequious formulations could hardly conceal the aim of setting in stone some concessions that Himmler had only made with the greatest reluctance:

Most honoured Herr Reichsführer!

I wish to thank you with all my heart for having saved the lives of my Swedish friends. I was always firmly convinced that you would help me in this matter, and you did not disappoint me! What's more, I should also like to thank you hereby for your generous concessions and to confirm our agreement of December 8, 1944. For a start, you promised me the release of one thousand Dutch women interned in concentration camps, should the Swedish government be willing to receive them and take charge of their transportation.

In addition, you agreed to release the Norwegian and Danish wives and children interned in Germany, provided that Sweden were willing to accept them [. . .] and to provide for their transportation. [. . .] Furthermore, you agreed to release the first fifty Norwegian students and fifty Danish

xl This was Operation Herbstnebel (Autumn Fog): the Führer intended to launch through the Ardennes three armies with 200,000 men and 600 tanks that would sweep before them the 80,000 widely dispersed Allied soldiers, reach the Meuse south of Liège, then make for Brussels and Antwerp – thus dividing the British-American coalition in half.

policemen. [...] Yesterday, I paid a visit to Obergruppenfüh-rer Kaltenbrunner in order to discuss the matter of their transportation. [...] I am most grateful to you, Reichsführer, for having so swiftly responded to my request, and I hope that you will now also decide to let the other Norwegian students and Danish policemen go back home as free men – after all, they too are Germans. [...] And I hope that next time I come back to treat you, you will release for me all the Dutch, Danes and Norwegians. I am confident that Sweden will accept them all, and that history will not forget your generous gesture. Upon my arrival in Sweden, I shall inform His Excellency Günther of our agreement. I take it that he will commission the Swedish ambassador in Berlin, His Excellency Richert, to negotiate with you and your people. I beg of you, Herr Reichsführer, to treat them most considerately [...] and to cause them no difficulties. I would be most pleased if you agreed to let Schellenberg take part in these talks.

Finally, most honoured Herr Reichsführer, I would like to remind you also of our discussions concerning the Jews. I had asked you to release twenty thousand of them from the Theresienstadt camp and to allow them to go to Switzer-land. Unfortunately, you told me that you could not do this under any circumstance, but that you were willing to allow two to three thousand Jews to be released and transported to Switzerland. Should the world press not consider this an admission of weakness on the part of Germany, you would be prepared to pursue our negotiations on this matter in a spirit of great benevolence. It seems to me that if you were to expel so many people to neutral countries, it would also be of benefit to Germany, given the scarcity of food.

Tomorrow, I shall be flying to Sweden with a lighter heart, since I know that you will insist on honouring the promises you made to me."[283]

And on December 22, 1944, Kersten flew back to Stockholm. Yet he was soon to return to Germany, for he considered that his mission was far from over. Indeed, it had just begun . . .

# 11

# FROM UNDER THE RUBBLE

Flying off to Stockholm, Kersten left behind him an exhilarated Reichsführer; as Hitler had predicted, his three armies, surging out from the Eiffel region, broke through the first Allied lines in the Ardennes, and in six days, they reached Stavelot, surrounded Bastogne and bypassed Houffalize and Rochefort. On December 22, 1944, von Manteuffel's 5th Panzer Army was already in sight of the Meuse, and from their "eagle's nest" at Ziegenberg, near Bad Nauheim, Hitler and Himmler were already savouring their triumph.

They had rejoiced too soon: the scarcity, exiguity and poor condition of the roads, the destroyed bridges and the shortage of fuel hampered the movement of supplies and reinforcements, which fatally compromised the offensive. On December 24, the lead divisions of the 5th Panzer Army were repelled east of the Meuse, while an American counteroffensive developing in the south threatened the whole left flank of the German spearhead; by December 24, the sky suddenly began to clear, and the panzers, troop concentrations and supply lines were targeted relentlessly by five thousand Allied planes. On December 26, when General Patton's army broke the siege of Bastogne, it was clear that the Ardennes offensive had failed.[i]

i   It had cost the Wehrmacht 100,000 men, 500 tanks and 800 planes.

Hitler refused to give up and ordered a diversion operation in the north-east of Alsace, hoping thereby to outflank the American forces engaged in the Ardennes; launched on January 1, 1945, this last organised Wehrmacht offensive in the west was halted after only twenty kilometres, long before reaching Strasbourg. But for Hitler, the worst news came from the east: on January 12, the Red Army unleashed a huge offensive on the 1,200-kilometre front between the Vistula and Oder, with 2.5 million men and 7,000 armoured vehicles storming towards Bohemia-Moravia, Silesia, Pomerania and East Prussia.

Hitler was thus compelled to leave the eagle's nest and return to Berlin; on the way, a wag in his entourage remarked that the Führer's headquarters could only be set up in Berlin, for it was the only place from which one could commute from the eastern front to the western front by taking the underground![ii] He was anticipating, of course, but not that much. At any rate, the orders given by Hitler upon his return to Berlin singularly lacked coherence: no retreat was allowed; the 6th Panzer Army, withdrawn from the western front, was assigned to the defence of Budapest instead of being rushed to the Oder front; a division of cyclists armed with grenade launchers was to be created forthwith, in order to fight the Soviet tanks; the twenty-two divisions immobilised in Courland were to stay there, as were the 350,000 men who remained idle in Norway;[iii] the generals accused of having ordered tactical retreats were dismissed; and Himmler was to be given command of a new "Vistula Army Group".

ii   This seems to have made Hitler laugh, a rare occurrence for a man who had little sense of humour – and no capacity at all for self-mockery.
iii   Because there was a large submarine base there, and "to secure our fish supplies"! Actually, Hitler still feared an enemy landing in Norway – although such an operation had obviously become strategically superfluous for the Allies.

The latter order was probably the most absurd of them all: Heinrich Himmler, a specialist in police repression without the slightest military experience, was to be placed at the head of an army group of forty divisions, on a front crucial to the defence of the capital![iv] Sure enough, whereas the Reichsführer immediately undertook to harangue the generals, forbid all retreat and order the merciless execution of all deserters, he was hard put to give orders suited to the strategic situation. Amateurism was naturally the basic cause, to which must be added that the new commander had a great many other centres of interest: he monitored the progress of oil drilling in the Bernburg area;[v] complained that Dr Richter, assistant to Hitler's dentist, had been promoted to Unterscharführer[vi] in violation of his latest directive; gave instructions for the S.S. Christmas calendar to be ready for posting on November 1, 1945; ordered an exact count of American military losses since the United States entered the war; asked Bormann whether Hitler would agree to be godfather of the eighth child of the wife of Scharführer[vii] Morgenroth; ordered that boots be reserved for combat troops; had a convoy of 2,700 Jews diverted to Switzerland "by mistake", in order to honour a promise made to his "magic Buddha";[viii] devised a new military oath-taking ceremony for Ukrainians serving in his S.S. units; awarded decorations to a dozen sharpshooters; formally authorised Standartenführer Rudolf

iv  The decision had been suggested to Hitler by Martin Bormann, who intended to keep Himmler away from Berlin – and to discredit him in the eyes of the Führer.
v  Near Magdeburg, in Sax-Anhalt. He also followed closely all research aiming to produce fuel from roots . . .
vi  Sergeant.
vii  Master sergeant.
viii  See above, p. 237.

Drape to get married; had the publication of the Ahnenerbe "scientific" journal postponed for two months; tried once again to obtain permission from Hitler to create an S.S. air force;[ix] ordered the speedier liquidation of political prisoners, with all evidence of it properly covered up; made every effort to pacify his wife, who was jealous of his mistress; issued a directive on the administration of the Tetschen-Liebwerd agronomy school, and agreed to be the godfather of the eighth child of S.S. Private Wilhelm Dolbaum.[284] Amidst all these decisions of decidedly limited strategic importance, the Reichsführer received numerous priority telephone calls from Sweden . . .

Having arrived discreetly in Sweden on the evening of December 22 with his three Swedish companions,[x] Kersten was reunited with his wife and three children in the apartment they had rented at 8 Linnégatan. After six long years, this was their first Christmas in free and peaceful surroundings; but settling in an unknown country, these destitute refugees faced a rather bleak future. To be sure, Felix Kersten had set up a medical practice next to his apartment, but the local residents seemed wary of consulting this strange Finnish therapist who did not speak their language – and had the dubious honour of being Himmler's doctor.

In truth, our practitioner had little time to devote to his patients; right after his arrival in Stockholm, he got back in touch with Christian Günther to inform him of the concessions made by Himmler. Although the minister was more than pleased, he explained to Kersten that Sweden would be unable to receive all

ix   Again in vain: Hitler wanted no trouble with Marshal Göring.
x   Discretion remained crucial, since Himmler had insisted that such releases not be presented abroad as signs of German weakness.

the refugees immediately: he, Günther, would first have to remind his parliament, his government, his prime minister and his king of all the advantages of such a rescue operation; the British, American, Danish and Norwegian authorities that were putting so much pressure on Sweden to enter the war against Germany would have to admit that the kingdom of Gustav V was far more useful to them as a neutral country, having the means to recover their nationals. But in the cabinet, as in the Riksdag and the palace, the process of persuasion might extend far beyond the New Year; and in the meantime, many more people were likely to die in German concentration camps.

Two more disappointments awaited Kersten: during his previous stay in Stockholm, he had met the Dutch ambassador and told him that he was in a position to obtain the release of thousands of Dutch nationals on a par with the Scandinavians, provided the ambassador supplied him with the names of those being held. But His Excellency Baron van Rechteren Limpurg had merely answered with a doubtful expression that he would think about it – and had left it at that.[285] Yet Kersten was not to be fended off so lightly – especially where his dear Dutchmen were concerned – so he secured the help of his friends the Graffmans and Baron van Nagell to meet Lieutenant Knulst, who was the main agent of the Dutch secret service in Stockholm. The latter was clearly more understanding and promised to supply the requested lists, but as of January 1945, nothing had come of it. More depressing still, Kersten learned that his friends Langbehn and Wentzel had been hanged; Himmler had promised to protect them, but Langbehn knew too much – particularly concerning the Reichsführer himself – and Wentzel had been executed at the express order of Hitler.

For all that, the future was not uniformly dark in early 1945; for if the miraculous return of the three Swedish engineers, followed by the release of fifty Danish policemen and as many Norwegian students a month later, took place amid the greatest discretion, it had nonetheless given rise to much comment in Stockholm society, and the name of their saviour had quickly made the rounds. This is why, in late January, Kersten received an urgent appeal from the Lutheran bishop of Stockholm, Monsignor Björkquist, in favour of Major Theodor Steltzer; this officer of the Wehrmacht transportation service in Norway, member of the Kreisau Circle and principal informant of the Norwegian resistance, had been sentenced to death four months earlier for his part in the July 20 plot. But the grateful Norwegian resistance fighters had approached the Bishop of Oslo, Eivind Berggrav, and the latter, though himself under house arrest, had contacted his Stockholm colleague Manfred Björkquist. Kersten immediately agreed to take up the case, but he could not travel to Germany at the time;[xi] to make matters worse, the ceaseless bombing had interrupted telephone communications with Brandenburg, where the new commander of the Vistula Army Group had set up his headquarters. Kersten therefore sent his secretary, Frau Wacker, with a letter for the Reichsführer personally.[xii] [286] On February 3, after a rather hectic flight, she drove through the ruins of Berlin during a spate of intense bombing by

xi   Himmler, in good health at the time, had not summoned him.
xii  Excerpts from its contents: "I beseech you, in the name of justice and humanity, to release my old friend. [. . .] You have no right to play with the lives of people in this way. If Herr Steltzer happens to have an opinion differing from yours, that is certainly no reason to kill him. [. . .] I am firmly convinced that you will spare Herr Steltzer, as you have many people at my request. One day, history will be grateful to you for this deed."

the 8th Air Force, and in five hours, she managed to reach Birken-wald, Himmler's headquarters in Birkenhain, near Prenzlau.[xiii] The Reichsführer was absent at the time, so she gave the letter to Rudolf Brandt, who let her know the next evening that his chief had agreed to postpone the execution. Unfortunately, tele-phone lines between Birkenwald-Prenzlau and the prison of Berlin-Moabit had also been cut, and the execution was due to take place the next morning at seven! There ensued a wild race against the clock: Brandt provided Frau Wacker with a car, she braved the bombings, the traffic congestions, the cratered roads and two flat tyres to reach the prison in the nick of time and deliver the order to cancel the execution. All prisoners sentenced to death were to be shot in handcuffs, and Steltzer realised that something unusual had happened when the prison director himself appeared and removed his handcuffs . . .[287]

To be sure, this was but a reprieve, but a month later, Kersten came in person to ask Himmler for Steltzer's release. This the Reichsführer eventually granted him, while adding: "One life more or less makes no difference"[288] – except of course for Theodor Steltzer, who survived the war and became minister-president of Schleswig-Holstein.

Meanwhile, however, the race against death proceeded inexora-bly, with the lives of tens of thousands of prisoners at stake. By late January 1945, the Swedish government finally adopted a plan presented by Norwegian diplomat Ditleff, with the support of von Post and Günther: a delegation of the Red Cross would be sent to Germany in order to negotiate the repatriation "by a Swedish rescue mission" of the greatest possible number of Scandinavian

xiii   See map, p. 262.

nationals.[289] But negotiate with whom? The Swedish ambassador in Berlin, upon being consulted, replied that there was no point in approaching Foreign Minister Ribbentrop, who had "lost much of his grip on events" and was "unwilling to make concessions to Sweden without compensations". And in his telegram of February 4, Ambassador Richert added that, in his opinion, "Kersten remains the only option we have left."[290]

On the afternoon of February 5, Kersten was thus urgently summoned to the office of Foreign Minister Günther, who told him the good news. As Kersten recalled: "He informed me that on the basis of my agreement with Himmler of December 1944, the Swedish government had decided to send about one hundred buses to Germany, under the flag of the Red Cross. I was to announce this by telephone to Himmler, and inform him that Count Bernadotte had been appointed principal head of transportation for this mission. His Excellency Günther had also asked me to ensure that Himmler would grant the count a favourable reception and spare him all difficulties, for the plan was now to assemble all Danish and Norwegian prisoners in a single camp. [. . .] Günther mentioned on that occasion that the Dutch, the Belgians and the French whose liberation I had secured could also be included in the transfer."[291]

Did Günther really use the German word *Haupttransportleiter* – principal head of transportation?[xiv] If so, it would be of some significance for future developments. But Kersten went on: "Back home, I saw Baron van Nagell and brought him up to date with events. [. . .] After waiting about an hour and a half, I was put through to Hartzwalde and had my adoptive sister, Miss Elisabeth

xiv   Or its Swedish equivalent: *Huvudtransportledaren.*

Lüben, on the line. She told me that Dr Rudolf Brandt had just arrived at Hartzwalde and that I could talk to him." Kersten then repeated exactly to Secretary Brandt the Swedish foreign minister's message, to the obvious satisfaction of his interlocutor: "Brandt said he was very pleased with this information and that he would report it faithfully to Himmler that very evening; he added that he would do everything in his power to support this action. Baron van Nagell, who was present in my apartment, heard the conversation."[292]

In Hartzwalde, Elisabeth Lüben was present that evening when Rudolf Brandt called Himmler.[xv] She heard him repeat Kersten's message to the Reichsführer, and also recalled the following words: "In order to avoid all difficulties that could be raised by the party, Medizinalrat Kersten proposed that Brigadeführer Schellenberg be seconded to Count Bernadotte as adjutant." And she went on: "After his conversation with Himmler, Dr Brandt told me that I could call Medizinalrat Kersten to inform him that Reichsführer Himmler was prepared to meet Count Bernadotte, and that he stuck by the agreements made with Medizinalrat Kersten."[xvi] [293]

The choice of Count Folke Bernadotte to carry out such a mission was perfectly judicious: he was the nephew of King Gustav V, well versed in the subtleties of international negotiations[xvii] and well known as the vice-president of the Swedish Red Cross – which was an additional benefit: since the Germans refused all interference in their internal affairs by foreign governments, the approach

xv   It is not known whether telephone communications with "Birkenwald" had been re-established in the meantime, or whether Brandt used a field telephone.
xvi   This may sound repetitive, but it was a sworn statement given in 1948.
xvii   Between 1943 and 1944, he had organised in Göteborg a series of prisoner exchanges between the Germans and the Allies.

could be represented as emanating from a humanitarian organisation, having no direct link with the Swedish authorities. The evolution of the situation in Germany brooking no delay, Count Bernadotte set out on February 16; he first met the head of R.S.H.A., Kaltenbrunner, and Foreign Minister von Ribbentrop, after which he could report: "When taking leave, I had good reason to believe that I would be received by Himmler. [. . .] My hopes were not disappointed: I was informed that an interview with Himmler had been granted. At 5 p.m. on February 19, Schellenberg picked me up and drove me to Hohenlychen, a big sanatorium 120 kilometres north of Berlin.[xviii] [. . .] There I met Heinrich Himmler, supreme chief of the S.S. [. . .] Seeing him there all of a sudden, with his horn-rimmed glasses and his green Waffen S.S. uniform without decorations, I felt as though I had before me a rather insignificant official. [. . .] He was remarkably and astonishingly gracious [. . .] and there was absolutely nothing diabolical in his appearance; actually, I could see no trace of the stern and icy gaze I had heard so much about."[294]

The introductions over, the two men got down to business:

"Our conversation lasted two and a half hours, in the presence of Schellenberg. As usual, I began by explaining the reasons for the anti-German atmosphere prevailing in Sweden, and Himmler immediately counterattacked by advancing a number of arguments that purported to show the innocence and humanity of German policy. [. . .] Then came the usual question: did I have concrete proposals to present? I countered by asking him if it would not be preferable that he himself propose steps that could improve the

xviii   Conveniently located near the Birkenwald headquarters, and headed by Dr Gebhardt, a former schoolmate of the Reichsführer. (See map, p. 262.)

situation, to which he replied that he had nothing to propose. I then put forward the project of internment in Sweden of the Danes and Norwegians, to which Himmler reacted violently. [. . .] He said that, at any rate, Sweden and the Allies ought to offer some compensation in exchange for such a concession, for instance in the form of an assurance that sabotage would cease in Norway. I immediately said that compensation of that kind was entirely ruled out. I had thus received an outright refusal, but the bargaining was not over, and I brought the conversation to another level by stating that the Red Cross was anxious to be permitted to work in concentration camps, particularly those that held Norwegians and Danes.

Himmler: 'An arrangement of that kind would certainly be advantageous and should pose no major problems.'

Bernadotte: 'And for practical reasons, these Norwegians and Danes should be gathered in a single camp, in order to facilitate the Red Cross' relief work. The total number of prisoners should amount to about thirteen thousand.'

Himmler: 'That number is exaggerated. I don't know the exact figures, but we should be dealing with no more than two or three thousand. However, I'll have the matter examined.'

Himmler thus agreed. He also accepted my proposal to permit the elderly, the sick and the mothers to return to Norway, after having been assembled in one camp. Nor was he opposed to the Swedish personnel of the Red Cross being given access to the camps."[295]

After another interview with Ribbentrop, who specified that the Red Cross would have to provide its own transportation means and the necessary fuel, Count Bernadotte returned to Sweden on

249

February 22 and reported to the government on the success of his mission. But in the account of that mission he was to publish a few months later, three features come across as somewhat puzzling: first, the count seems particularly proud to have obtained an interview with Himmler by dint of strenuous efforts, whereas the Reichsführer had already agreed to that interview eleven days prior to the count's arrival in Berlin. Second, it would appear that Bernadotte's undeniable talents as a diplomat had merely enabled him to obtain concessions that Himmler had already made to one Felix Kersten two months earlier. Third, the latter, who after all had enabled Bernadotte to be received by Himmler, who had induced the Reichsführer to accept the principle of gathering Norwegian and Danes into one camp supervised by the Red Cross – and even persuaded him to let Schellenberg take part in the interview of February 19,[xix] – is nowhere to be found in Count Bernadotte's account! It will take a few more months to clarify that mystery . . .

In Stockholm, meanwhile, Kersten was the subject of further solicitations, as later confirmed by Baron van Nagell: "Foreign Minister Günther went to see the king, who gave him a list of names of people he wanted to see released – hosts of counts, countesses and family members. Then I said: 'May I add a few?' Kersten said yes . . ."[296] It would appear that some releases were also solicited from abroad, as witnessed by Jacobus Nieuwenhuis, Kersten's former Dutch agent still ensconced at Hartzwalde pending his exfiltration: "When Dr Kersten was in Sweden, he made telephone calls to his secretary and presumed sister who had remained at Hartzwalde, and told her that he had spoken to Himmler about

xix   See above, p. 247.

such and such person, who 'absolutely'[xx] had to be released – after which the secretary and presumed sister got in touch with Himmler's private secretary, Dr Brandt. I was thus to witness a number of liberations."[297]

But as the situation deteriorated in Germany, the telephone soon proved insufficient for the purpose, and on February 24, Günther invited Kersten over to express his concern: on the one hand, he was continually receiving lists of people imprisoned in camps and whose lives were in peril: Danish and Norwegian Jews, Swedish spouses of political prisoners, Jews holding South American passports, resistance fighters – particularly women – whose release was requested by General de Gaulle, etc. On the other hand, all reports coming from Norway pointed to the fact that the four hundred thousand or so Germans occupying the country had orders to fight to the last man against the Allies, in which case the fighting was sure to spread to Swedish territory. To top it all, his government had received highly reliable information indicating that Hitler had issued orders to blow up all the concentration camps with their hundreds of thousands of prisoners as soon as the Allies were within a distance of eight kilometres from them;[xxi] according to some sources, the explosives were already in place . . .[298] It was no use appealing to Hitler and asking him to give up his insane project, but Günther urged Kersten to attempt one final approach to Himmler.[299]

xx   "*unbedingt*".
xxi   The order had apparently been issued for the first time ten months earlier, but instructions for carrying it out had just been transmitted in early 1945; the Swedish newspaper *Dagens Nyheter* mentioned it on February 19. After the war, this order was recalled several times by both accused and witnesses at the Nuremberg trial, and later by Albert Speer in his third book: *Der Sklavenstaat*, (*The Slave State*), DVA, Stuttgart, 1981, p. 335.

Actually, the Medizinalrat received a very similar request the next day, as he later noted: "On 25 February 1945, I was introduced in Stockholm by Ottokar von Knierem,[xxii] of the Dresdner Bank for Scandinavia, to Hillel Storch,[xxiii] one of the leading men in the World Jewish Congress of New York. The latter had received reliable information that Jewish prisoners in Germany [. . .] were in the greatest peril. The Führer had ordered that on the Allies' approach, the concentration camps should be blown up along with all their occupants, including the guards. [. . .] This order had occasioned such a deterioration in the situation that, according to Storch, it was now desperate. Storch asked me whether I was prepared to make a direct approach to Himmler so as to prevent the implementation of the concentration camp order."[300]

This was confirmed by Storch himself: "As it was known to me that Kersten had earlier intervened successfully in favour of the Finnish Jews, on behalf of the Jews who were released to Switzerland, and also in other cases, [. . .] I asked him for his help."[301]

"I agreed," Kersten wrote. "In the course of the next few days, we both decided that this intervention with Himmler should also be used to bring about a major effort on behalf of Jews under arrest in Germany, with the aim of helping them directly through the expedition of food and medicines, while also securing the transfer of as many as possible to neutral territory. We drew up the following proposals:

xxii  Scion of an old family of Baltic Germans, he was the uncle of the future Swedish prime minister Olof Palme.
xxiii  Of Latvian origin. There was obviously an association of Baltic Germans in Stockholm.

1. Dispatch of food and medicine to the Jewish prisoners.
2. Assembling of all Jews in special camps where they would be under the care and control of the International Red Cross [. . .].
3. Release of individuals on special lists.
4. Release of Jews under arrest and their transfer abroad, chiefly to Sweden and Switzerland. For Sweden, a figure of between five and ten thousand was envisaged.

"The Swedish government was behind this attempt and shared the opinion of the World Jewish Congress that the blowing up of the concentration camps would be carried out as a gesture of desperation, with the result that hundreds of thousands more people would meet their death at the very end of the war. [. . .] I received a communication from the World Jewish Congress with a memorandum of Storch's on the questions we had discussed, concluding with these words: 'We know your deep humanitarian feelings and thank you for everything you have achieved in this respect, and we hope that you will also be able to help us this time in such an extremely desperate situation.'" [302]

The German situation at the time was itself desperate: by late January 1945, the Soviet armies led by Marshals Zhukov and Koniev had reached the Oder, having taken Warsaw and Kraków; in February, the thaw and the need to regroup all forces had temporarily stabilised the front, but between February 18 and 20, a counteroffensive led by Himmler[xxiv] against the right flank of the

---

xxiv Actually, the counteroffensive was carried out by the 3rd Panzer Army, commanded by General Walther Wenck, but as head of the Vistula Army Group, Himmler naturally had to take responsibility.

1st Byelorussian front under Zhukov's command had failed dismally, whereas at the end of that month, an attack led jointly by Rokossovski and Zhukov towards the Baltic coast took the Vistula Army Group entirely by surprise, since it was deployed to defend Berlin's eastern approaches. It was therefore the whole of northern Pomerania that fell to the Red Army, and at the Reich chancellery, Himmler had to take the blame. After that, fear and overwork combined to assail the budding strategist; in early March, struck by a mild influenza, a major nervous breakdown and severe stomach cramps, the Reichsführer withdrew to the sanatorium of his friend Dr Gebhardt and urgently sent for his "magic Buddha". As a result, the triply solicited Kersten flew back to Berlin on the afternoon of March 3.

After a risky flight and a bumpy landing at Tempelhof airport, Kersten drove through the ruined capital and travelled northwards along a battered and periodically machine-gunned road that was clogged with refugees fleeing south-west in order to escape the fighting, the bombing and the abuses of the Red Army. He spent the night at Hartzwalde and arrived at Hohenlychen the next morning;[xxv] after passing through several guard posts on the approaches to the sanatorium, he was led to the rather spartan room occupied by a clearly exhausted Reichsführer, who did his best to put on a brave face. Kersten almost immediately set to work: "On March 5, 1945 at 10 a.m.,[xxvi] I began negotiations with Himmler about the concentration camps. He was much agitated and the dealings were particularly bitter and stormy, since he refused to show any clemency and relinquish his last trump card.

xxv  Hohenlychen was only 35 kilometres away from Hartzwalde.
xxvi  11 a.m., according to the Reichsführer's appointment diary.

He told me literally: 'Should national socialist Germany go under, then our enemies, the traitors to the great Germanic cause locked up in the concentration camps, will be denied the triumph of emerging victorious. They won't live to see that day, they'll croak with us. Such is the Führer's clear and logical order, and I will make sure it is carried out to the letter.'"[303]

Over the next few days, as the treatment sessions took place invariably at 11 a.m., Himmler, overwhelmed by the latest Soviet advances in Pomerania, refused all concessions to his therapist, on the release of the Jews and other prisoners entered on his lists,[xxvii] on the safekeeping of the concentration camps, on the showdown that was looming in Norway, and on the planned destruction in The Hague; for Brandt had informed Kersten that the Clingendael district, already turned into a fortress, was to be blown up at the approach of the Allies – along with all its inhabitants. When Kersten raised the question, Himmler answered: "Should we perish, the Dutch will perish with us." Two days later, when he broached the subject in another way by asking if The Hague would be defended, he received this chilling confirmation:

"Defended? You can't be serious! No, my dear Kersten, we'll blow that city of traitors to smithereens. [. . .] The Führer ordered that The Hague be razed to the ground, and I will carry out that order. The Dutch are traitors, and these parasites deserve no mercy. We have enough V2s to complete the task."[304]

And yet, there were a few glimmers of hope: on March 9, the

xxvii   In early February, after an agreement with former Swiss president Jean-Marie Musy, Himmler had authorised the transfer to Switzerland of 1,200 Jews from Theresienstadt. But Kaltenbrunner had revealed the operation to Hitler, who had prohibited any further release of Jews, under penalty of immediate execution.

news of an outbreak of typhus in the Bergen-Belsen concentration camp, reported by Storch and exploited by Kersten,[xxviii] gave rise to the following instruction, issued the very next day to all S.S. officials: "I want the epidemic to be fought without delay and with all available medical means. We cannot tolerate the propagation of epidemics in Germany. Spare neither doctors nor drugs. The prisoners are under my personal protection."[305]

The last sentence by itself bore witness to the extent of Kersten's influence. For all that, it did have its limits, as illustrated by the notes taken after the treatment of March 10:

"Today, Himmler was in a morose and meditative mood. He spoke of the losses incurred by his Waffen S.S. – more than 250,000 dead and 100,000 badly wounded. I drew his attention to the fact that the outcome of this fight could no longer be in doubt. To which he answered:

'Don't say that. We haven't yet committed our new weapons; events may yet take a new turn, even if prospects seem bleak at the moment [. . .]. I had imagined things otherwise when we took power and undertook to build the great German Reich.'

I then said:

'Let's leave this aside; now is the time to act. Please give me your written commitment that you will not carry out the Führer's order of blowing up the concentration camps with all their occupants inside. Have them hoist the white flag and be handed over to the Allies instead; I believe that these camps still contain a million human beings, and you cannot have such a dreadful bloodbath on your conscience.'

To which Himmler objected:

xxviii   Who knew perfectly well that Himmler had a mortal fear of epidemics.

256

Reichsführer-ƻƻ

1.) ƻƻ-Obergruppenführer  P o h l , Berlin
2.) ƻƻ-Gruppenführer  G l ü c k s , Oranienburg
3.) ƻƻ-Obergruppenführer Dr. Grawitz, Reichsarzt-ƻƻ u.Polizei,
4.) ƻƻ-Obergruppenführer Dr. Kaltenbrunner, Berlin    Berlin

     Mir ist gemeldet worden, daß in dem Anhaltelager Bergen-
Belsen, insbesondere unter den jüdischen Gefangenen Typhus
ausgebrochen sei.
     Ich wünsche, daß unverzüglich der Seuche mit allen
medizinischen Hilfsmitteln entgegengetreten wird. Wir
können in Deutschland keine Seuchen aufkommen lassen. Es
ist weder am Einsatz von Ärzten noch an Medikamenten zu
sparen. Die Gefangenen stehen unter meinem besonderen Schutz.

                        gez. H.  H i m m l e r .
10.3.45
Bra/H.
5.) nachrichtlich:   b.w.


     ƻƻ-Gruppenführer Prof. Gebhardt, Hohenlychen

     —————————————————————————————

6.) Herrn  K e r s t e n , z.Zt. Hohenlychen
       durchschriftlich mit der Bitte um Kenntnisnahme
       übersandt.

                    R. Brandt
                ƻƻ-Standartenführer.

Ordre du Reichsführer aux autorités supérieures de la SS susnommées, émis le 10 mars 1945.
« Il m'a été rapporté qu'une épidémie de typhus s'est déclarée dans le camp de détention de Bergen-
Belsen, particulièrement parmi les détenus juifs. Je souhaite que l'épidémie soit combattue sans délai
avec tous les moyens médicaux disponibles. Nous ne pouvons pas tolérer la propagation d'épidémies
en Allemagne. Il ne faut épargner ni médecins ni médicaments. Les prisonniers sont sous ma protection
personnelle. »

                                                        Signé H. Himmler

Pour information : 5) Au Gruppenführer SS et professeur Gebhardt, Hohenlychen. 6) À M. Kersten
actuellement à Hohenlychen.

                                        Contresigné R. Brandt, SS Standartenführer

*Reproduction of Himmler's order dated March 10, 1945*

'You must be mistaken, for there cannot be more than 800,000 people in the concentration camps.'[xxix]

I went on:

'Even that figure is considerable enough; should you allow all these people to be exterminated, Germany would be damned forever in the eyes of the world. That is why I beseech you, for the sake of World History, to give me a written confirmation that you will prevent this ultimate criminal act of Hitler's.'

Then he said:

'Yes, yes, I know you're right. You have convinced me, dear Herr Kersten, but let me think about it until tomorrow. [. . .] I can see that Norway must not become a new battleground and that The Hague must not be blown up, but we'll talk about it tomorrow or over the next few days . . . Today I no longer feel up to it.'"[306]

"Tomorrow or over the next few days" . . . Kersten had already been fobbed off five days in a row, and well knowing Himmler's irresolute character, he apparently considered that sixth day to be a failure too, which explains the project he conceived that evening, upon returning to Hartzwalde. The estate still housed his adopted sister, twenty Jehovah's Witnesses, his former agent Jacobus Nieuwenhuis and of course astrologist Wilhelm Wulff. It will be recalled that the latter had been instructed to establish detailed astrological forecasts for the Reichsführer; Wulff's main employer was Schellenberg, and together they had undertaken to persuade Himmler to topple Hitler and negotiate an armistice with the

---

xxix   It is clear that Himmler did not know, by a margin of 200,000, how many prisoners were detained in all his camps. S.S. estimates varied from 600,000 to 800,000.

Western Allies. That project was known – to the three men only – by the code name Maiplan.[xxx] But Kersten, perhaps more of a psychologist than the astrologist and the chief of intelligence combined, had by then given up all attempts to persuade Himmler to overthrow his master.

Hence the developments of that evening and of the next day, as described by a Wilhelm Wulff whose antipathy towards Kersten had evidently not abated: "On March 10, Kersten, upon his return from Hohenlychen, came up to my room[xxxi] and told me that I was to report to Himmler the next day. [. . .] Here was this Herr Kersten who was reappearing in early March 1945 with a ridiculous list of a few thousand people[xxxii] and a smaller list of a few individuals,[xxxiii] in order to, as he put it, avoid 'the worst' in the name of Humanity. [. . .] He had presented his list to Himmler and tried to obtain his assent, but by March 10 he had got nowhere. Himmler refused to release all the prisoners, since Hitler would inevitably be informed of it. He had eventually agreed to release a few people, and had gone as far as 1,800. But as for the 10,000 liberations that Kersten requested for Hillel Storch, Himmler flatly refused."[307]

The next day, March 11 at 10 a.m., the two men set out for Hohenlychen in a Kübelwagen[xxxiv] borrowed from Himmler's staff. On the thirty-five kilometres of roads passing through Menz, Fürstenberg and Ravensbrück, they came across endless

xxx   May Plan.
xxxi   Actually the room formerly occupied by Irmgard Kersten.
xxxii   Wulff, though himself a former prisoner of the Gestapo, did not seem to wonder if that list would have appeared ridiculous to those who were on it.
xxxiii   The latter probably being the one given by the king.
xxxiv   A military version of the K.D.F.-Wagen – the future Volkswagen "Beetle".

processions of refugees, wrecked cars, dead horses and countless makeshift wooden crosses by the roadside. Yet they probably saw nothing of it, so busy were they trying to get their act together. As Wulff recalled:

"I intended to hand-deliver to Himmler the astrological works ordered by Schellenberg. Among these, there was a new 'mundane horoscope'[xxxv] tracing the main events of the year 1945. Besides, I wanted to talk to Himmler once again about the necessity of over-throwing Hitler, and advise him to proceed with an immediate capit-ulation. Kersten seemed nervous when he gave me his instructions:

'Now, my dear chap, you must persuade Himmler that, accord-ing to the horoscope, my business in Sweden with Hillel Storch is important for him. You must support my action with Himmler, [. . .] so he can give me a written statement that I'll bring to Stockholm and deliver to Storch.'

In the past, Kersten had often got his way by dint of blatant lies, and a certain adroitness enabled him to reach his ends most of the time."

Wulff went on to quote Kersten's words:

"You may safely tell Himmler that the release of Jews features in his horoscope, so that Herr Storch, that mighty man, can provide him in Sweden with facilities to approach the Allies. A Jew speak-ing up for Himmler! That's the way you must present things to him. If he gives us the papers today, we'll celebrate this evening with a bottle of champagne, and we'll attend to the other problems tomorrow . . ."[308]

---

xxxv   This "mundane vedic horoscope" was supposed to retrace the influence of varying positions of the sun, moon and planets on world events; it thus comple-mented individual horoscopes, as well as those of nations.

But the astrologer stuck to his initial idea:

"Why don't you persuade Himmler to put an end to all this Hitlerian circus? The bombing that causes so much misery to the German people and claims so many lives would cease and the concentration camps would be opened anyway. [. . .] Why not convince him of the necessity of a putsch?"[309]

Wulff did not seem to realise that Kersten had been trying to do just that for three long years, had concluded that it was useless and was now trying something else. Perhaps he had told Wulff that, or perhaps he was simply tired of repeating it . . . At any rate, the astrologer went on:

"Kersten got seriously upset and insisted again that I ought to have Himmler adopt his plan first, and only present the other things to him afterwards. But I had absolutely no desire to help him in this matter, for his demands amounted to a gross falsification of the horoscope. [. . .] I told him:

'My dear Herr Kersten, I shall interpret the horoscope for Himmler as a responsible astrologer. [. . .] I'll see what I can do for you.'

The nearer we got to Hohenlychen, the more the tension increased. [. . .] We got through the checkpoints and the wire mesh gates, then we entered a sort of park where a few small isolated buildings could be made out. Our passes were checked by the S.S. guards, and Kersten, who was obviously well known here, greeted them with a *Guten Morgen!* rather than a *Heil Hitler!* [. . .] Detective Kirrmayer was waiting for us at the top of a narrow staircase leading to the first floor of a small house, and he took us to a guardroom where we were left to wait. [. . .] After which a small and plump man with the eyes of a bird of

*Hartzwalde and Himmler's successive headquarters*

prey[xxxvi] [. . .] asked us to go into the next room, where we found ourselves in Himmler's living room. [. . .] He was sitting in a cosy armchair and he offered me a seat next to him. He had just got up and smelled of soap and cheap eau de cologne. [. . .] His face looked fresher than usual and he seemed to have recovered – Kersten's massages had clearly had an effect. He wore a plain uniform, without rank insignia."[310]

So much for the setting and the introductions – after which the three men got down to brass tacks:

"The conversation," Wulff recalled, "first turned to his state of health. He immediately asked me about his personal life, his health and how long it would take him to entirely recover. All this took some time. Kersten then began to talk about his plans, whereupon Himmler started pontificating about honour, Germanic greatness and loyalty. But Kersten burst out angrily:

'In the case of my friends Wentzel and Langbehn, Herr Reichsführer, you broke your word of honour. So don't go on about the great respect of the Germans for honour.'

Himmler grinned and apologised, pleading that in that particular case the People's Court had prevailed over him, and the investigations had established that the two men were involved in the plot. [. . .] He then turned to me and mentioned the prediction in my horoscope that he would be involved in an accident on December 9, 1944.

'Think of that, Herr Wulff, on December 9, as I was driving my car in the dark, it left the road, fell about forty metres and landed

---

xxxvi   Obviously Dr Karl Gebhardt. This small man and great predator also practised in the neighbouring concentration camp of Ravensbrück, in recognition of which he was to be hanged on June 2, 1948.

on the Black Forest railway track, just as the train was coming. We only got away with great difficulty. Isn't it rather strange, how accurate the horoscope is?[xxxvii]

'Herr Reichsführer, I am now reassured. [. . .] The fact that the prediction held true seems to indicate that it was possible to retrace your exact hour of birth. [. . .] But then, you should take into account any future prediction and follow the advice given you concerning the Maiplan that we conceived.'

Maiplan was the code name agreed upon between Himmler, Schellenberg and myself. Kersten, who didn't know its meaning, pricked up his ears and gave me an inquiring look with his big childlike eyes. After that, Himmler continued:

'You must have heard of Herr Kersten's plans. What do you think of them?'

There was not much to say. From an astrological point of view, I had no reason to advise against them. I thus developed my arguments accordingly; whereupon Himmler replied:

'It is impossible for me to make such concessions to Herr Kersten. He demands the immediate transfer abroad of a great number of Jewish prisoners, which is impossible without Hitler's agreement, and the transportation of so many prisoners could not be concealed from him. The Führer was outraged at the Jewish transactions of my S.S.,[xxxviii] and gave strict orders to shoot anyone who releases Jews in the future. That is why I can only grant Kersten a part of the plan he put to me. [. . .] I don't have a free hand in this matter.'

xxxvii   Himmler, being very near-sighted, almost invariably left the road when he was at the wheel.
xxxviii   Some S.S. officials had begun to organise such transactions for their own benefit.

Then Himmler sought to divert the conversation from such a disagreeable subject:

'Herr Schellenberg told me that you wanted to inform me of the political situation according to the New World horoscope for 1945?'

The readings of the mundane horoscope were hardly encouraging for Himmler, and the horoscopes for the two first quarters of 1945 presented stellar dispositions that spelled disaster for Hitler's Reich. I explained that to him, while Kersten was sinking into his corner of the sofa and losing all interest in what I had to say. The conversation then turned to the Yalta conference, which Himmler had requested me to assess from an astrological standpoint. The constellations portrayed it in an appalling and even devastating light, which I presented to him bluntly and unceremoniously. To which I added:

'Herr Reichsführer, why not carry out our Maiplan? The worst could still be avoided, and you could improve your situation without having to worry about the Führer.'

'What you are requesting, Herr Wulff, and Herr Schellenberg with you, is no less than treason. I swore allegiance to the Führer. [. . .] And consider this: what about the eventuality of an uprising by the masses? How would they behave if I had the Führer overthrown? In case of confrontations, illegal gatherings and resistance in the cities, my S.S. would have to crush them all. Granted, worst things could happen, but as a soldier, I have sworn loyalty to Hitler and I cannot violate my oath. I owe him everything.' [. . .]

On these last words, he stared at me fixedly, then he went on:

'You were saying that the position of the stars was very negative at the moment. Can you tell me which parts of Germany will escape occupation?'xxxix [. . .]

'It seems to me that we explained to you some time ago that you ought to have entrusted one of your loyal men with the implementation of our plan . . .'

He interrupted me:

'*Ja, Ja*, who is still loyal these days? It will be extremely difficult at this stage to have the putsch implemented. As for me, I am ill and I feel weak. From a military standpoint, it could be carried off, but personally, I can't handle it. I must confess, *meine Herren*, that I simply can't do it!'

The interview was coming to an end. We had all too often in the past heard Himmler's drivel about loyalty. I increasingly felt the stifling atmosphere of the room. Himmler began to talk of [. . .] secret weapons about to be mass-produced, which encouraged him even more to postpone the moment to launch a putsch and to refrain from any decisive undertaking. At the end of the interview, he asked me once again what I thought of the world political situation, after which we took our leave. He appeared to be moved, and I thought I saw tears running down his cheeks, which I ascribed to a nervous breakdown. During that two-hour conversation, I had not uttered a word on the issues Kersten had admonished me about on the outward journey."[311]

The astrologer was clearly very proud of his feat, but it hardly improved the atmosphere during the return trip to Hartzwalde. Wulff and Kersten had both failed, and each one blamed the other for his failure. The whole scene might appear farcical, were it not

xxxix   Himmler was obviously thinking of the possibility of taking refuge in the "Alpine redoubt".

played out in the midst of one of the worst tragedies in world history, when the lives of hundreds of thousands were at stake. At any rate, the day ended on a nasty argument, and Wulff left Hartzwalde at dawn the next day with a perfectly valid excuse: his house had been demolished the day before, during the massive Allied bombing of Hamburg.

After seven days of entirely vain efforts, any ordinary person would have given up; but Kersten was no ordinary person, and his energy was truly amazing. On March 12, having returned to Hohenlychen, he was back at it: "I had no time to set down in any detail the phases of the negotiations with Himmler [. . .]. New problems and difficulties were constantly cropping up. I sat for hours at the telephone and called on all my available connections. Brandt helped me, sounded out Himmler and prepared the ground for the next negotiation. Though any outsider could see that the end was near, Himmler, quite inexplicably, still lived in fear of Hitler and his entourage, especially Goebbels and Bormann."[312]

In such circumstances, the deal finally wrung from the Reichsführer that afternoon was nothing less than an astounding feat:

1. Himmler will not pass on Hitler's order to blow up concentration camps on the Allies' approach; none is to be blown up and no prisoner is to be killed.
2. On the Allies' approach, concentration camps are to hoist a white flag and be handed over in an orderly manner.
3. Further execution of Jews is suspended and prohibited. The Jews are to be treated in the same way as other prisoners.

4. The concentration camps will not be evacuated. Prisoners are to be left where they are at present and will be allowed to receive food parcels.[313]

Did Heinrich Himmler really sign such a compromising document? Did Kersten actually countersign it "in the name of humanity"? Our Medizinalrat was to certify it in a book published in 1952, yet he had made no mention of it in his two previous books, written five years earlier. The most likely explanation is that the agreement had been a purely verbal one; but that it existed, and that Himmler undertook to abide by it on that fateful day of March 12, 1945, is a fact attested to by at least six witnesses.[xl] [314] Now should the Reichsführer really refrain from passing on Hitler's deadly command, then a thrombosis would clog the infernal Nazi machinery, thus saving some 800,000 unfortunate prisoners . . . Kersten, having often observed that the Reichsführer insisted on keeping his word once he had given it, felt confident at the end of that decisive day.

Yet nothing seemed to justify such confidence: Kaltenbrunner, Bormann and "Gestapo Müller" would certainly not make things easier for him; Himmler was dominated by fear, and that fear could still lead him to commit the irreparable; Hitler could step in at any moment and call everything into question; British and American bombings constantly threatened to remove all the actors in this tragedy – including Kersten himself; and the Russians, who

xl    Brandt, Schellenberg, Masur, Storch, Ambassador van Nagell and Swedish foreign minister Günther. Hillel Storch, who clearly did not believe in the signatures *per se*, was quick to add: "What is important, however, is that the content of the agreement is correct."

by then were only sixty kilometres from Hartzwalde, might easily reserve for him the very fate that had befallen Raoul Wallenberg two months earlier.[xli] Nothing could be ruled out in the midst of such an inferno, and at this stage, Kersten might easily have echoed the wise advice of an illustrious contemporary:[xlii] "The reader of these lines must realise how dark and baffling is the veil of the unknown."

xli   Wallenberg, who had saved between 15,000 and 20,000 Jews in Budapest, had been freed by the Red Army on January 13, 1945, after which he disappeared forever into the depths of the Gulag.
xlii   And winner of the Nobel Prize in Literature 1953.

# 12

# HIGH-RISK MISSION

By mid-March 1945, the Führer, ensconced in his bunker eight metres below ground, was predicting that the Soviet army would suffer the greatest defeat in history; though careful not to contradict him, his henchmen Bormann, Rosenberg, Göring, Ribbentrop and Himmler were discreetly seeking a way out of the inevitable Armageddon; senior officers Kesselring, von Rundstedt, Dönitz, Keitel, Jodl and chief of staff Guderian kept on mechanically directing a campaign on two opposing fronts that were rapidly closing in on them; their soldiers, lacking arms, equipment and officers, but knowing full well that to retreat was as dangerous as to advance, were fighting desperately in every single theatre of war; the refugees from Silesia, Pomerania and East Prussia, turned out of their homes by the ravages of the Red Army, were fleeing westwards by forced marches; the innumerable prisoners, crowded into concentration and labour camps, fearfully awaited the outcome of the confrontation, be it deliverance or apocalypse; and one solitary man, apparently spurning all danger, was trying to save as many people as possible from the imminent disaster . . .

In six years, he had saved hundreds; henceforth, it could be hundreds of thousands! But one can become a wholesaler without ceasing to be a retailer: indeed, during the fifteen sessions of treatment he gave in March 1945, Kersten kept on presenting the Reichsführer with new names of inmates to be released: Count von Bismarck, the Norwegian painter Reidar Aulie,[i] Polish princess Zofia Sapieha,[ii] Jewish Professor Alfred Philippson with wife and daughter, Swedish author Sara Uthaug, Count Julius Tarnowski, Swedish entrepreneur Milan Richter and his whole family, French Countess Tatiana Claret de Fleurieu,[iii] Oslo police chief Kristian Welhaven and his wife, former Austrian president Karl Seitz,[iv] Count Anton von Arco auf Valley, Beatrice Borch née Ramsay, the Norwegian lawyer Johann Hjort,[v] his wife and six children. All of them were eventually released.[315]

However, Kersten was concerned above all by the fate of the Jews, for they were obviously the most threatened. On March 14, 1945, he noted the following: "I conducted in-depth negotiations on the release of the Jews imprisoned in Bergen-Belsen camp [. . .] and I asked Himmler to allow them to be transferred to Sweden. I pointed out that the World Jewish Congress attached great importance to their release. [. . .] I was more successful on another point: Himmler was inclined to permit the dispatch of food and medicines to concentration camps; they were to be addressed

i   Because the Germans disliked his pictures – particularly the one representing the invasion of Norway in April 1940 – he had been interned in Grini detention camp near Oslo.

ii   Future grandmother of Queen Matilda of Belgium.

iii   An intelligence agent in the Castille network, this intrepid French resistance fighter had been deported to Ravensbrück in January 1944. As General de Gaulle had asked the Swedish government to intercede on her behalf, King Gustav V added her name to his personal list.

iv   The judges had received directly from Hitler an order to sentence him to death.

v   One of Quisling's first lieutenants, he had joined the resistance after the German invasion.

in the first instance to particular individuals, namely Jews, Dutch, Norwegians, Danes, French, English or North Americans."

March 15: "I took the opportunity to propose to Himmler the assembling of all Jews in special camps under the control of the Red Cross, which would also be responsible for their care and sustenance, or at least supervise it. Himmler was very well disposed towards this proposal."

March 16: "I again discussed with Himmler the release of certain categories of Jews to Sweden and Switzerland; I went through with him the list given me concerning the release of various individuals. Himmler was very open-minded about it and promised me that the question of releases would be given serious consideration. I had the impression that he was prepared to make bigger concessions. He raised the question of transportation himself and remarked that Sweden or Switzerland would have to take care of it. I took advantage of this favourable situation to talk to Himmler again about the treatment of Jews in concentration camps. He drew up a special order in my presence which forbade any sort of cruelty to Jewish prisoners and prohibited killing them."

And March 17: "Having once again raised with Himmler the question of releasing certain categories of Jewish prisoners, I obtained from him [. . .] the assurance that 5,000 of them would be set free, and that they could be transported either to Sweden or Switzerland. Our discussion was interrupted by an urgent telephone call. I took this opportunity to tell Brandt of the results and to ask him if it was at all possible, once the principle had been accepted, to raise the figure of those to be released. Brandt agreed and said that with time and discretion that figure could easily be doubled."[316]

This must have been highly satisfactory to Kersten – a gambler at heart who always sought to double the stakes; indeed, he noted that same day:

"I took advantage of Himmler's favourable disposition to put before him a plan which had occurred to me today, as I was considering the best way of securing more releases. My idea was to arrange a meeting between Himmler and the representative of the World Jewish Congress. [. . .] At first, he refused outright:

'I can't receive a Jew. If the Führer were to hear of it, he would have me shot dead on the spot.'

I had expected it – again that fear of the Führer – but on the other hand, it was a positive sign, for he had not refused on his own account. Taking advantage of this, I acted as if he had himself given his assent and stated that in his position as head of the German police responsible for border control, he had every facility for preserving complete secrecy about flights in and out of the country. If he gave the right instructions, neither Goebbels, nor Bormann, nor Hitler could possibly hear of it. This made sense to Himmler. I suggested that the talks take place at Hartzwalde and that he decide himself who was to take part in them. Himmler said that only Brandt and Schellenberg could be considered. I replied that this seemed quite satisfactory to me, and asked if I could pass on the information that he agreed to a personal negotiation with Herr Storch, the representative of the World Jewish Congress. Himmler hesitated a moment before giving his answer, then said: 'Yes, Herr Kersten, you may do that.'"[317]

The most amazing thing is perhaps that Kersten always seemed to have several irons in the fire; four days earlier, he had been badgering the Reichsführer regarding another matter: "I asked Himmler for the release of the French women in the Ravensbrück camp, which he had already promised me in December 1944. I pointed out to him that [. . .] since France was no longer under German occupation, the reasons for their arrest no longer made any sense. I thought this would be relatively easy to obtain, but I found out to my astonishment that Himmler was not inclined to grant the request. Some of the prisoners were apparently being detained on higher orders, so that Himmler feared complications. After much delay and a few angry exchanges, he finally authorised the liberation of eight hundred French women and their transfer to Sweden. He explained that he wanted to keep some in order to have a bargaining chip vis-à-vis France. He apparently intends to select women whose release involves no danger. I will get in touch with Brandt at once concerning the steps to be taken in order to secure their immediate liberation."[318]

Indeed he did; the very next day, he wrote to Brandt: "After some stormy negotiations, the Reichsführer has finally granted me the release of eight hundred French women from Ravensbrück concentration camp and their transportation to Sweden. [. . .] Now please, dear Dr Brandt, do ensure that Ravensbrück is informed without delay, so that Sturmbannführer Suren no longer treats these French women as captives and that he releases them immediately when the Swedish buses arrive to take them away. In addition, please make sure that the number of eight hundred is considerably rounded upward. Also, as the Reichsführer informed you last week in my presence, he granted me the release of one thousand Dutch women, four hundred Belgian women and five hundred Polish women. The removal of these unfortunate women must proceed without a hitch and swiftly enough to prevent Kaltenbrunner from interfering."[319]

Yet this was only the tip of the iceberg; for there was also the insane order to destroy The Hague, which Kersten was determined to have annulled. On March 14, he had also tackled the Reichsführer on that subject: "I had another long talk this morning with Himmler about the fate of The Hague, Clingendael and the closure dyke.[vi] I put my point of view to him again and appealed to him, in the name of humanity, not to implement Hitler's secret order. Then I got straight to the point and asked Himmler if it was possible to give a direct order to those in charge not to blow up anything. Himmler replied that Germany's military position had so seriously deteriorated that priority had to be given to military considerations. I pointed out to him that military considerations were not relevant here. Whether Clingendael was blown up or not would not affect the course of the war one way or the other; but he could not turn a blind eye to tens of thousands of innocent men, women and children being exterminated; he could not answer to history for such a crime. History would view Hitler's order as the ravings of a madman, which he had obeyed only because he had himself lost his mind. I could see that Himmler was hesitating. He seemed to be wondering whether he dared to contravene Hitler's direct order. [. . .] I urged him to listen to his conscience and heed his own humanitarian feelings. I would have understood his attitude if such measures could have had the slightest effect on the course of events, but in the present case, they were incomprehensible. I could see that I was slowly gaining ground. Himmler

vi   The German plan was also to blow up the closure dyke, thereby flooding the city.

took up his pencil, jotted down a few lines on a piece of paper, then called Brandt and in my presence gave the order that, if the situation arose, The Hague, Clingendael and the closure dyke were to be left undamaged. Then he turned to me and said: 'Then The Hague will not be destroyed, but the Dutch certainly don't deserve it. They have done everything to undermine the victory over Bolshevism.'"[320]

In accordance with the instructions of Minister Günther, Kersten also raised the question of occupied Norway, and pointed out that a last stand there could only lead to Swedish intervention or to the invasion of all of Scandinavia by the Red Army. Himmler began by reminding him of the Führer's words – "If we lose this war, the enemy will only be left with a field of ruins in Norway. I owe it to the German soldiers who fell there" – but on March 20, Himmler finally promised to give the necessary orders to prevent hostilities and prepare a surrender. Of course, such strategic decisions were not his to make, but as only his S.S. could force the Wehrmacht to fight at this juncture, a promise of that kind was not without value.

In the midst of it all, Kersten had also to support the action of Count Bernadotte, to whom Himmler had indeed given permission to assemble all the Scandinavian prisoners in the Neuengamme camp, though not to transfer them to Sweden. Kersten, who had met the count for the first time on March 8 at the Swedish embassy, was almost immediately called upon to help him out, as Jacobus Nieuwenhuis, still holed up at Hartzwalde, was later to recall: "In mid-March 1945,[vii] Mr Kersten was absent from Hartzwalde when a car bearing a Swedish flag arrived. [. . .] An

vii    On March 17 to be precise.

officer stepped out, [. . .] introduced himself as Count Bernadotte and asked if Kersten was at home. I answered that he was visiting a neighbouring farm, but that I could call him on the telephone – which I did. [. . .] The count then picked up the phone and I heard him ask for Kersten's assistance in a case involving twenty or so Frenchmen, Norwegians and Poles. Bernadotte said that he was getting nowhere, that Kaltenbrunner was putting obstacles in his way and that he could no longer gain access to Himmler. He asked Kersten if he could raise the matter with Himmler. Mr Kersten came back half an hour later. I was not present during their conversation, but after Bernadotte had left, Mr Kersten returned to see Himmler, and the next evening he told me that the people concerned were free."[321]

This was confirmed by Kersten, who added: "Bernadotte had also asked me to arrange another meeting for him with Himmler. The latter agreed, and so it came about."[322] Indeed it did, but only sixteen days later – for the Swedish relief operation was coming up against numerous obstacles, which the count did his best to overcome by negotiating with Kaltenbrunner and Schellenberg. The three hundred men and women of the Swedish Red Cross[viii] reached Friedrichsruh in their "White Buses"[ix] on March 12, and they began to commute between Neuengamme and Sachsenhausen concentration camps three days later; however, they were denied access to the Neuengamme camp itself, although this was where they were to deposit the Scandinavian prisoners who had

viii  Aside from about thirty Red Cross nurses and doctors, the rest of the staff was made up of volunteers from the Swedish army, bearing only Red Cross insignia.
ix  The British had demanded that the thirty-six buses be painted white, in order to be recognised by Allied fighter aircraft. There was nonetheless to be a tragic accident before the end of April.

(1) Berlin SW 11, den 21. März 1945.
Prinz-Albrecht-Straße 8

Feld-Kommandostelle

Lieber Herr  K e r s t e n  !

Sie schrieben mir vor einiger Zeit einen
Brief, in dem Sie sich im Namen schwedischer Freunde
für das Schicksal des früheren Bundeskanzlers  S e i t z
verwendeten. Durch die viele Arbeit der vergangenen
Wochen kam ich nicht dazu, Ihnen früher zu antworten.
Der frühere Bundeskanzler Seitz hat sich leider trotz
seiner 75 Jahre in sehr unglücklicher Form in Dinge
eingemischt, die ihn praktisch bei exakter juristischer
Erfassung des Tatbestandes vor den Volksgerichtshof
gebracht hätten. Ich habe trotzdem bereits vor einigen
Wochen verfügt, dass Herr Seitz in Anbetracht seines
Alters aus der Haft entlassen wurde. Die Behörde war
ihm auch behilflich beim Auffinden einer Privatwohnung.
Er befindet sich in einem kleinen thüringischen Städt-
chen, das ich Ihnen noch bekanntgebe. Eine Ausreise
nach Schweden kann ich verständlicherweise, da es sich
bei Herrn Seitz um einen deutschen Staatsangehörigen
handelt, nicht genehmigen. Es besteht jedoch derzeit
die Möglichkeit, dass Herr Seitz in seinem neuen Auf-
enthaltsort private Besuche empfängt.

Mit vielen Grüssen

H. Himmler

Lettre de Himmler à Kersten en date du 21 mars 1945, l'informant de la libération de l'ancien chancelier autrichien Karl Seitz.

*Letter from Himmler dated March 21, 1945, informing Kersten of the release
of the former Austrian chancellor Karl Seitz*

been set free. Actually, they knew next to nothing about this "second class camp",[x] except that its mortality rate was one of the highest in Germany . . . So it was that during the next two weeks, the brave crews of the White Buses picked up prisoners from Dachau and Mauthausen to drive them to a camp that was even more dreadful than the one they had left behind.[xi] Moreover, Max Pauly, the Neuengamme camp commander who was directly answerable to "Gestapo Müller", did absolutely nothing to make things easier for Count Bernadotte.[xii]

Nonetheless, however atrocious the conditions prevailing in prisoner camps of all classes, the Reichsführer did indeed appear to have kept the promise made to Kersten on March 12; Obergruppen-führer Oswald Pohl[xiii] was thus to declare at Nuremberg: "I saw Himmler for the last time in March 1945. [. . .] On that occasion, he ordered me to make the rounds of all the camps and tell the commanders to stop harming the Jews. [. . .] I thus saw the commanders of the following nine concentration camps: Neuengamme, Oran-ienburg [Sachsenhausen], Gross-Rosen, Auschwitz,[xiv] Flossenbürg, Buchenwald, Dachau, Mauthausen and Bergen-Belsen."[xv] [323] This was confirmed by former Auschwitz commander Rudolf Höss, who accompanied Pohl on five of these visits: "[Pohl] was to deliver

x    The worst category of camp, after that of death camps. After the war, it was estimated that 52,000 out of 87,000 prisoners had died there.

xi    This considerably affected their morale, to such an extent that half the staff returned to Sweden in early April. They were replaced by Danish volunteers.

xii    Tried by the British for war crimes in March 1946, Pauly was hanged six months later.

xiii    See above, pp. 57 and 164.

xiv    Entirely ruled out: Auschwitz had been liberated by the Soviet army on January 27.

xv    It is noteworthy that Ravensbrück, though in close proximity to Hohenlychen, was not mentioned.

personally to the camp commanders the order to stop killing Jews and to do their utmost to lower the prisoners' mortality rate."[324] There was also the following report by Buchenwald prisoner Otto Kipp: "In March 1945, we received a letter from the S.S. command ordering that the sick be treated better. [. . .] The letter also included a ban on shooting prisoners, and from that day on, there were no more lethal injections either. The letter also specified that, from then on, the Jews were to be better treated, on a par with the Soviet war prisoners" – which was confirmed by Louis Gimnich, his *Blockältester*:[xvi] "In March 1945, the central command of the S.S. ordered that sick prisoners receive better treatment, and criticised the unduly high mortality rate – a complete reversal of the January 1945 order."[325] Those who received such instructions could of course have no inkling of who was behind them.

The man who had ordered such a drastic reversal in policy was about to resign from his most recently acquired function; as conditions in Himmler's headquarters appeared to be growing increasingly chaotic, Chief of Staff Hans Guderian decided to drive there himself. "Once at his headquarters near Prenzlau, [. . .] I was told that Himmler was suffering from influenza and was being treated by his personal physician, Professor Gebhardt, in the Hohenlychen sanatorium. I drove there immediately, and found Himmler in apparently robust health. [. . .]. I then pointed out to this S.S. potentate that he held, on his own, a whole series of the highest appointments in the state: he was national leader of the S.S., chief of the German police, minister of the interior, commander-in-chief of the reserve army and, finally, he commanded the Vistula Army Group. Each of these posts required the

xvi Block chief.

full-time activity of one man, [. . .]. And no matter what respect I might have for his ability, such a plethora of offices was bound to be beyond the strength of any one individual. Meanwhile, he must have realised by now that the command of troops at the front is no easy matter. I therefore proposed to him that he give up his command of the army groups and concentrate on his other offices."[326]

Himmler, who had lost much of his self-confidence and still trembled before Hitler, replied hesitantly: "I can't go and say that to the Führer. He wouldn't approve of my making such a suggestion." But Guderian offered to make it for him, and Himmler agreed – apparently with some relief. The chief of staff later commented dryly: "It was complete irresponsibility on his part to wish to hold such an appointment; it was equally irresponsible of Hitler to entrust him with it." That evening, at any rate, Guderian proposed to Hitler that the Reichsführer be replaced at the head of the Vistula Army Group by Colonel-General Heinrici, commander of the 1st Panzer Army in the Carpathians. "Hitler disliked the idea, but after a certain amount of grumbling, he finally agreed. Heinrici was appointed on March 20."[327]

Though an excellent officer, Gotthard Heinrici could not work miracles: the Red Army, repulsing all counter-attacks, was relentlessly tightening its grip on Pomerania, East Prussia and Upper Silesia. As usual, Hitler took it out on the army commanders in the field – in this case on General Busse, whom he accused of having failed to relieve Küstrin and of contemplating a retreat westward. But Chief of Staff Guderian, lacking the submissiveness of his predecessors, vigorously defended Busse and a violent quarrel ensued, with foreseeable results: on March 28, Guderian was dismissed "for reasons of health". His successor as chief of staff was to be General Hans Krebs, who was young, intelligent, diplomatic, highly professional and under no illusions; taking up his new duties, he confided to his aide-de-camp: "The war will be over in four weeks."[328]

In view of the situation in the field, this was a reasonable forecast: having crossed the Rhine in mid-March, eighty-five British, American and Canadian divisions fanned out between Mainz and Wesel, and by the end of the month, western Germany was witnessing an updated version of the blitzkrieg: the Americans took Mannheim, Frankfurt am Main, Fulda and Cassel, the Canadians occupied Arnhem and progressed methodically towards northern Holland, while the British broke through in the direction of Bochum, thence to encircle the Ruhr from the north – jointly with the 1st American Army coming from the south. As usual, Hitler forbade all retreat and ordered a dogged resistance in the "Ruhr Fortress", thus condemning the whole of his army group to destruction or captivity.[xvii]

Whether it was due to the alleviation of his duties or to a fortnight of diligent medical care, Himmler had entirely recovered, so that Kersten was able to return to Stockholm on March 21.[xviii] Upon his departure, he was handed a letter from Himmler beginning thus: "Please accept my thanks for your visit. As always, I rejoiced that you came as an old friend to enable me to benefit from your great medical talent. Over the years, we have discussed

xvii 340,000 German soldiers were to be captured there – three times more than at Stalingrad.
xviii Without knowing it, he had just escaped a second assassination attempt engineered by Kaltenbrunner. (C.Z.A., 4/570-79, Hillel Storch to Kersten, 5/10/55.)

a number of issues, and your attitude has always been that of a doctor who, far from all politics, has striven to foster individual welfare and that of humanity as a whole."[329]

"Far from all politics" was necessarily a relative concept: whether Kersten liked it or not, it was politics that persisted in closing in on him. As he was flying back to Stockholm, Ambassador Richert in Berlin wrote to Eric von Post at the foreign ministry: "Kersten informed Bernadotte and Brandel [. . .] that the 'Jewish list' was ready, that the Swedish prisoners would be released – with the exception of those sentenced to death, for whom Himmler was not in a position to make a definite decision, but had committed himself to further discussion in the best possible spirit – and that most of the special cases had also been settled. It is now sincerely to be hoped that the promises made to Kersten will be honoured before it is too late. [. . .] Kersten seems to have interceded for Jews other than those on our list, with, he believes, good results."[330] And Richert added: "Concerning the Danish and Norwegian internees, Kersten has been insisting on their transfer from Neuengamme to Sweden. According to his own statements, it would appear that Himmler has been won over to this idea, but getting it done requires collaboration from other quarters."[331]

This was clearly a reference to Kaltenbrunner and "Gestapo Müller", whose cooperation was indeed far from assured – which is why Count Bernadotte was getting nowhere in his attempts to negotiate, so he too flew back to Sweden on March 22. Like all the other officials of the Swedish Red Cross, he had failed to obtain permission to visit the camp at Neuengamme, to where his White Buses were still bringing all Scandinavian prisoners released from the other camps. Bringing them back to Sweden was an even more distant prospect: as is known, the count had met with a blank refusal during his interview with Himmler on February 19, and nothing had really changed since then.

The day after his arrival in Stockholm, Kersten reported back to Foreign Minister Günther, who expressed his amazement at what he was told:

"I can't believe that you were able to obtain Himmler's cooperation on all these points. Convincing him not to blow up the concentration camps is a historic achievement. How many people do you think there are in the camps, Herr Kersten?"

"They say about 800,000."[xix]

Kersten went on to raise another major issue: Count Bernadotte had told him on March 8 that his mission was to accept only the freed Scandinavian nationals in his White Buses; now he, Kersten, had obtained a promise from Himmler to release a number of Dutch, Belgian, French and Jewish prisoners as well, provided the White Buses be responsible for their transport. He was particularly concerned about the Jewish women in Ravensbrück, and asked Günther to give Bernadotte the necessary instruction for the conveying of all released prisoners without exception – to Neuengamme initially, and on to Sweden as soon as possible.[xx] Had not Minister Günther promised him four months earlier that all prisoners released would be allowed to enter Sweden? Kersten added that time was of the essence, since he had seen for himself

---

xix   Kersten could not know the exact number – and as we have seen, Himmler did not know it either.

xx    And to inform Colonel Björk accordingly, since he was responsible for convoying operations on the spot.

that road traffic in northern Germany was increasingly chaotic. Günther then asked:

"How many releases do you think you can secure?"

"Between twenty and twenty-five thousand, including some five thousand to six thousand Jews. The figure Himmler allowed me was somewhat lower than that, but General Schellenberg and Dr Brandt promised me that they would have it raised when the prisoners left the camps."

Günther thanked Kersten most warmly for his efforts and assured him that all the people whose liberation he could secure would be welcomed in Sweden. [. . .] He added that he had just been informed that Kaltenbrunner was being "extremely disagreeable" and was trying to prevent the relief operation. He asked Kersten whether he would be prepared to go back to Berlin in order to request Himmler's intervention should this situation persist, to which Kersten answered that he was quite prepared to return to Germany if serious difficulties were to crop up. Günther agreed that it would be important for Himmler to meet Storch, but confessed he did not believe the Reichsführer would agree to receive a Jew – and even less so to negotiate with him. [. . .] Over the years, the Jews had indeed tried to contact representatives of the Nazi authorities, and they had always failed. But Kersten replied that he believed it should be possible to arrange a meeting between Storch and Himmler. At which Günther exclaimed:

"That would truly be the Eighth Wonder of the World!"[332]

Two days later, Kersten wrote to Storch and updated him on his talks with Himmler: the prospects for the release of certain categories of Jewish prisoners; the possibility of sending food parcels to others, even without precise names of addressees being

Der Reichsführer-𝕊𝕊

(1) Berlin SW 11, den 19.April 1945
Prinz-Albrecht-Straße 8

Herrn
Medizinalrat Felix K e r s t e n
S t o c k h o l m
Linnegatan 8

Sehr geehrter, lieber Herr Kersten !

Der Reichsführer-SS hat angeordnet, dass an die jüdischen
Häftlinge in den deutschen Lagern Liebesgabenpakete sowie
Medikamente geschickt werden dürfen. Die Versendung müsste
am besten über das Internationale Rote Kreuz vorgenommen
werden.

Ich bitte Sie, sich mit der zuständigen schwedischen
Roten-Kreuz-Stelle in Verbindung zu setzen, damit von dort
aus alles Notwendige veranlasst werden kann.

Mit freundlichen Grüssen

Brandt

Rudolf Brandt à Kersten, 19 avril 1945 :

« Le Reichsführer SS a ordonné qu'il soit permis aux prisonniers juifs dans les camps allemands de
recevoir des colis et des médicaments. La Croix-Rouge internationale devrait de préférence se charger
de l'expédition. Je vous prie de vous mettre en relation à ce sujet avec les instances responsables de la
Croix-Rouge suédoise, afin qu'elle initie toutes les démarches nécessaires. »

*Rudolf Brandt to Kersten, April 19, 1945 re parcels and medicine*

286

given; the probability that parcels with medicines would also be accepted; Himmler's agreement in principle to the regrouping of Jews into special camps where medical care and supplies would be dispensed by the Red Cross; the Reichsführer's promise to prohibit henceforth any ill-treatment or slaughter of Jews. But Kersten added the following qualification: "You will understand that I cannot vouch for the effective implementation of all these measures," as well as a caveat: "The possible release of Jews, as well as the improvement in their welfare already underway, would be suspended forthwith if the world press were to mention them and if they were portrayed as evidence of weakness on the part of Germany." And Kersten concluded: "I must also tell you that, at my suggestion, the Reichsführer would be willing to negotiate with you on issues still outstanding."[333]

This was a bit much to ask of a representative of the World Jewish Congress, but Storch declared himself ready to take his chance – though not without some understandable misgivings, which Kersten did his best to allay; on March 29, he wrote back: "Let me repeat word for word what Herr Himmler said on the matter of your voyage: 'I guarantee on my life and on my honour that nothing will happen to Herr Storch.' As a result of years of acquaintance with Herr Himmler, I know that he stands by his word, but in order to offer you the greatest possible security, I shall naturally accompany you on your trip to Germany, [. . .] and vouch for the fact that you, most honoured Herr Storch, will not only be received in the best possible way, but will also return to Sweden safe and sound."[334]

That sounded convincing, but Storch had more pressing concerns: on March 31, he wrote to Kersten that according to his information, new guards had been dispatched to the concentration camps, bearing some rather disquieting orders.[335] Kersten replied that Himmler had always kept his word once he had given it, but as the Allies approached Theresienstadt, Buchenwald and Bergen-Belsen, Storch grew increasingly worried. Finally, on April 7, he was informed that the next day at 6 a.m., a squad of Croatian S.S. were to blow up Bergen-Belsen camp on orders from Kaltenbrunner.[336] As Storch himself later reported: "On the night of April 7, having heard that, in spite of promises made to Kersten by Himmler, Kaltenbrunner had ordered that Bergen-Belsen camp be blown up,[xxi] Herr von Knierem and I went over to Kersten's place. We sat there for several hours waiting for a telephone call to be put through to Himmler's headquarters. Dr Kersten spoke that night with several people, including Dr Brandt.[337] [. . .] At first, Brandt did not believe it was true, [. . .] but he promised to contact Himmler.[338] He called back Herr Kersten later in the night to inform him that all necessary orders had been given to prevent Kaltenbrunner from blowing up the camp."[339] Which is indeed what happened.[xxii]

By early April 1945, Kersten's humanitarian activity was reaching new heights – to such an extent that one wonders how he still found time to look after his patients: there were always new prisoners to be released, and information gained from Brandt

---

xxi  It would appear that Kaltenbrunner had given that order in reaction to news published in the Western press concerning the appalling state of Buchenwald camp at the time of its liberation.

xxii  So it was that a French prisoner named Simone Veil, future cabinet minister and president of the European Parliament, owed her life to Felix Kersten – which she probably never knew. Bergen-Belsen camp was to be liberated by British troops a week later.

and Schellenberg to be exploited without delay. Kersten thus learned that Ernst Hepp, the press attaché of the German legation in Stockholm, was to be arrested by the Gestapo as soon as he returned to Germany – and that a similar fate awaited Ottokar von Knierem, the director of Dresdner Bank for Scandinavia and one of Kersten's patients. The two men were duly warned and remained in Sweden. Olof Palme, von Knierem's nephew and future Swedish prime minister, recalled a visit to his uncle at the time: "I was invited to tea at my uncle's house. Among the other guests were Felix Kersten and Hillel Storch. Kersten was enormously fat, and I remember how greedily he ate orange marmalade direct from the bowl. [. . .] The conversation revolved around how one could save Jews from concentration camps and if Kersten could influence Himmler in this direction. Himmler was considered to be greatly dependent upon Kersten."[340]

Indeed he was . . . And among the other people to be saved, there was Jacobus Nieuwenhuis, the trusty Dutch agent who had been holed up in Hartzwalde for the last six months, and whom his former "employer" had not forgotten: "Kersten succeeded in obtaining a Swedish safe conduct for my wife and myself. He also provided us with an exit visa to leave Germany, [. . .] which cost him 10,000 marks and four pounds of coffee; he did not consider this too expensive: the marks were worthless and coffee was cheap in Sweden . . ."[341] Thanks to which Nieuwenhuis could land in Stockholm with his wife on April 3, 1945 – and relate what followed: "Mr Kersten told me: 'Go and see Knulst,[xxiii] he'll give you a list of Dutch people whom I'll try to have Himmler release.' I thus obtained a list of ninety-four people, all Dutch Jews, men

xxiii   The head of Dutch intelligence in Stockholm. See above, p. 243.

and women, some well known, some even very well known – at the time at least. I gave this list to Mr Kersten, who was very disappointed that it was so short. [. . .] He extended it himself by adding names, and all these people were released. [. . .] I often found him in telephone conversation with Minister Günther; they were invariably talking about the release of people held in Germany, and about instructions to be received by Count Bernadotte concerning the transfer of people set free."[342]

That is indeed what it was all about, for in this White Bus operation, Kersten was engaged on two fronts simultaneously: on the one hand, he had to urge Brandt and Schellenberg to remove the obstacles that Kaltenbrunner and "Gestapo Müller" were constantly putting up to counter Count Bernadotte's rescue operation; and on the other hand, he had to urge the Swedish authorities to instruct the very same Count Bernadotte to include Dutch, Belgians, French and Jews in that rescue operation. In the latter respect, he was to be successful, since on March 27, an instruction issued by the Swedish foreign ministry slightly modified the count's mission, in anticipation of his second interview with Himmler. The revised instruction was as follows:

"First of all, request is now once more to be made for permission to transfer to Sweden all the Danish and Norwegian men and women interned in Germany (Neuengamme). Subsidiary issues: 1. Request presence of Swedish Red Cross personnel in entire Neuengamme camp (approximately 50,000 internees). 2. Offer of Swedish Red Cross buses for use as transport to Neuengamme camp or to other suitable camp of non-Scandinavian internees in Germany. Should mainly concern approximately 25,000 French women who, in conjunction with the German retreat from France, were removed to Germany and placed in a camp there.

The above has been supplemented today with a communication to Bernadotte whereby, inasmuch as it is convenient and no impediment is to be feared for the tasks mentioned above, he request the transfer to Sweden of a number of Jews."[343]

Actually, the count was to obtain only minimal concessions at his April 2 meeting with Reichsführer Himmler. Having finally gained access to Neuengamme camp three days earlier, Bernadotte had seen for himself the appalling state of the premises – even in the so-called "privileged section" hastily set up for the Scandinavian prisoners. This he reported to Himmler straight away, while drawing the obvious conclusions: "I demanded once again that all Danish and Norwegian prisoners be permitted to go to Sweden. Himmler answered that, personally, he would be happy to accede to my request, but that it was impossible for him. Hitler was evidently behind it all."[344] Nevertheless, Bernadotte was promised that women and invalids would be released and transferred to Sweden – progressively and in small groups – and that this would also apply to a small fraction of the 461 Norwegian students interned at Neuengamme. And the count added in his report: "After that, I found that I had been swept into the vortex of high politics."[345]

How was this to be understood? In fact, Schellenberg had just enlisted him in his personal campaign to persuade Himmler to negotiate with the Western Allies: "Schellenberg drove me back to Berlin and told me that after my departure Himmler had continued to raise the issue of capitulation in the west, and that, were it not for Hitler, he would have had no qualms about asking me to go and see Eisenhower. However, he intimated that the situation could change: Hitler's position might well be weakened, and this could happen at any moment. Himmler had instructed Schellenberg to tell me that, if this were to arise, he hoped that I would immediately go to Allied headquarters. He added that Himmler was in an awkward position, torn between his desire to preserve Germany from chaos and his loyalty to the Führer."[346]

This was hardly new: it reflected the Reichsführer's state of mind over the last three years, during which period Schellenberg, Kersten, Wulff, Popitz and Langbehn had successively and vainly urged him to act. But Schellenberg considered that the military situation had become so serious that there was no time left for procrastination, and he later recalled:

"On April 13, Himmler asked me to go and see him at Wustrow.[xxiv] He took me for a walk in the forest, during which he said:

'Schellenberg, I believe that nothing more can be done with Hitler. Do you think de Crinis could be right about him?'[xxv]

'At any rate,' I replied, 'everything seems to point to it, and I believe that now is the time for you to act.'

He remained silent. I then reminded him of Kersten's plan to come to Germany in the course of the next few days with Hillel Storch, a representative of the World Jewish Congress of New York, who wanted to talk about the Jewish problem with Himmler

xxiv   His new headquarters between Berlin and Hamburg.
xxv   Max de Crinis, an S.S. psychiatrist and neurologist, had diagnosed the symptoms of Parkinson's disease simply by observing Hitler on the newsreels.

personally. Once again, Himmler was unable to give a definite reply. [. . .] Receiving a Jew was obviously a difficult step for him to take. He thought it would provoke a definitive break with Hitler. [. . .] He was afraid that if Kaltenbrunner found out, he would immediately report the matter to Hitler. I reassured him, pointing out that as Kaltenbrunner was going to Austria, he would not hear about it. Besides, the meeting could take place at Kersten's estate. After much hesitation, he finally agreed."[347]

Yet Schellenberg was in for another surprise: "Suddenly, he began to talk about how things would go once he took power in Germany and became Hitler's successor." This was but a fleeting mood, however: "[Himmler] was very greatly troubled about his break with the Führer, which by this time was almost complete. [. . .] He told me that I was the only one, apart from Brandt, whom he could completely trust. What should he do? He could not shoot Hitler; he could not poison him; he could not arrest him in the Reich chancellery, for then the whole military machine would come to a standstill. I told him that none of this mattered and that only two possibilities lay before him: either he should go to Hitler and tell him frankly all that had happened during the last few years and compel him to resign; or else he should remove him by force. Himmler objected that if he spoke to Hitler like that, the Führer would have a fit of rage and shoot him out of hand. I said: 'That is just what you must protect yourself against – you can still count on enough higher S.S. leaders, and you are in a strong position to have him arrested.'"[348]

It is astonishing that after so much pointless quibbling, Schellenberg still entertained the illusion that Himmler could be turned into a putsch leader. Yet this conversation did leave its mark, as astrologer Wilhelm Wulff was to bear witness: on April 13, he had been summoned urgently to Hartzwalde, but owing to the chaotic state of the roads, it took him two whole days to reach his destination – only to find himself in the midst of a veritable maelstrom: "In the early morning of April 15, we arrived at Hartzwalde, where the manageress of the estate[xxvi] told me right away that I was to prepare for an important discussion at the behest of Herr Schellenberg; I was also given a secret letter containing the questions asked by Schellenberg and Himmler about Bernadotte's journey and about possible negotiations with Churchill, Eisenhower or Montgomery, whose horoscopes I had already established. [. . .] At about 10 a.m., Schellenberg and Dr Rudolf Brandt arrived, and the latter gave me a list of national socialists who could be proposed for the formation of a new government:

1. Reichsleiter Martin Bormann, born 17.6.1900 in Halberstadt
2. Reichsminister and Professor Albert Speer, born 19.3.1905 in Mannheim
3. Reichsminister Dr Arthur Seyss-Inquart, born 22.7.1892 in Stannern bei Iglau
4. Reichsminister Count Schwerin von Krosigk, born 22.8.1887 in Rathmannsdorf
5. Generalfeldmarschall Ferdinand Schörner, born 12.6.1892 in Munich[349]

Whatever the verdict of the stars, it would have been difficult to find a more baroque government than that – even when headed

xxvi   Obviously Elisabeth Lüben.

by such an unlikely chief of state as Heinrich Himmler.[xxvii] However, the house astrologist had little time to meditate upon the flaws inherent in this decidedly hypothetical constitutional process, for his taskmasters were both demanding and in a hurry: "The astrological work was most tiring, and constantly interrupted by calls from the command post and from headquarters."

But the unfortunate Wilhelm Wulff had seen nothing yet, for on April 18, he was informed that the S.S. chiefs, including Himmler and Schellenberg, intended to take refuge in southern Germany: "This was the so-called Obersalzberg Plan.[xxviii] Himmler wanted to remain in the vicinity of General Schörner's army, which was still intact, and I was to be included in the transfer. [. . .] For the time being, I was to assess the plan of a breakthrough southwards from an astrological point of view – a task that took me even more time." One can only sympathise with the stellar craftsman – particularly as on that very day, another piece of news further disturbed his astral labours: "Felix Kersten called from Stockholm to announce that he would be arriving with President Hillel Storch."[350]

This was the meeting from which Kersten expected so much; it was supposed to convince the Reichsführer to commit himself firmly to saving the surviving Jews, by agreeing to release them all – or at least to entrust them to the care of the Red Cross, at a time when their camps were no longer supplied and famine threatened

---

xxvii   Quite apart from the fact that the first man on the list was his sworn enemy, and that Himmler himself had tried to have the second one killed . . .

xxviii   Ever the mirage of the *Alpenfestung*, the Alpine fortress – a largely fanciful concept: the south-western extremity of the Bavarian Alps, facing Switzerland, did indeed have some defensive structures and S.S. garrisons, but the northern and north-eastern slopes were not fortified, and there were no supplies, armaments or munition depots – and no mountain troops to defend it.

their terribly debilitated condition. In Germany, Schellenberg had at long last managed to overcome Himmler's reluctance to attend the meeting, and he was able to inform Kersten that an airplane would be placed at his disposal on April 19. In Sweden, the prospects were hardly brighter: Storch initially considered the trip to be superfluous, since Kersten had already obtained all the necessary commitments from Himmler, but he had changed his mind after the Bergen-Belsen episode;[351] the World Jewish Congress had then baulked at the apparent incongruity of having one of its representatives take part in discussions with the most notorious malefactor of the Jewish people; after which it considered that Hillel Storch was not the appropriate person to pull off such a venture: "He is unaccustomed to diplomatic negotiations, and his hot temper could be fatal in a face-to-face with Himmler." And once the World Jewish Congress finally relented, it was the Swedish foreign ministry that refused to give Storch a passport.[xxix] Yet Kersten succeeded in overcoming this obstacle by obtaining a pass the likes of which had never been seen in all of Nazi Germany: "Please let Herr Medizinalrat Kersten and the man travelling with him cross the border without demanding their identity papers. Signed: Schellenberg, S.S. Brigadeführer, Brigadier-General of the S.S. and the police."[352]

Everything thus appeared to have been settled – but for a last-minute hitch, as recounted by Gösta Engzell, head of the Swedish foreign ministry's legal department: "At ten o'clock on the morning

xxix Christian Günther apparently feared that Hillel Storch, known as a stateless refugee, would do more harm than good by presenting a passport of convenience to the Germans. But Günther seems above all to have yielded to pressure from American and British diplomats, who considered that Storch was not qualified for the task – and were generally opposed to dealing with Himmler.

Der Chef der Sicherheitspolizei
und des SD

Amtschef VI

<small>Über in der Narrpart enthaltenen Geschäftszeichen u. Datum anzugeben</small>

Berlin SW 11, den **19. April** 194 5.
Prinz-Albrecht-Straße d
Fernsprecher 120040

Geheime Reichssache

### Bescheinigung:

        Es wird gebeten, Herrn Medizinalrat
Felix   K e r s t e n   und den in seiner Begleitung
reisenden Herren ohne Vorzeigung der Ausweispapiere
die Grenze passieren zu lassen.

        In Vertretung:

*Schellenberg*

        SS-Brigadeführer, Generalmajor
        der Waffen-SS und Polizei

f.d.Richtigkeit:

*Brandt*

        SS-Standartenführer.

Le chef du Sipo et du SD, section VI., Berlin, 19 avril 1945.

ATTESTATION

Prière de laisser passer la frontière à M. le Medizinalrat Felix Kersten et à l'homme qui voyage en sa compagnie, sans réclamer leurs papiers d'identité.

Par délégation :
Signé Schellenberg,

SS Brigadeführer, général de brigade de la Waffen SS et de la police

*The pass cited in the text opposite*

297

of April 19, Felix Kersten stormed into my office. He was terribly upset and told me that Storch had just said to him on the telephone that he no longer wanted to go. I can still see Kersten standing in front of me in his tracksuit, saying: 'The plane is here and waiting for us. It's taking off at twelve!'"[353]

What had happened? Quite simply that Hillel Storch's wife, Anja, coldly assessing the chances of survival of a Latvian Jew without a passport meeting the head of the Gestapo in war-torn Nazi Germany under conditions of very relative secrecy,[xxx354] had made a dreadful scene to her husband during the night – and Storch had finally given in.[355] What could be done? Storch advised Kersten less than two hours before departure time that his right-hand man, one Norbert Masur, was prepared to replace him;[356] this Swedish businessman, a Jew of German origin, was reputedly "a born diplomat, even-tempered, who made a strong impression without being pompous or creating turbulence in his wake"[357] – and obviously a brave man as well, since he agreed to embark at a moment's notice on such a suicidal venture . . . But Kersten remained pre-occupied: would not the Reichsführer use this last-minute replacement as an excuse to cancel the meeting?

Actually, there was a far more serious reason to be worried, for the eastern front was ablaze once again: all along the Oder and the Neisse, twenty-two Soviet armies had gone on the offensive beginning April 16; in the north, Marshal Rokossovski's 2nd Byelorussian Front quickly broke through the first German line of defence near Stettin; in the centre, Marshal Zhukov's 1st Byelorussian Front attacked Seelow and Prötzel, in order to approach

xxx  Bernadotte had already informed Peter Kleist, Ribbentrop's representative in Sweden, of Storch's imminent journey to Berlin.

the capital by the north-east; more to the south, Marshal Koniev's 1st Ukrainian Front had taken Cottbus and was heading north-west towards Potsdam and Berlin. But above all, the Soviets were seeking to reach the Elbe, so as to isolate Berlin and cut Germany in half. They had the means to do so: two million men, 6,250 tanks, 42,000 cannons and 7,500 planes. To counter this formidable war machine, Heinrici's Vistula Army Group and Schörner's Army Group Centre could only field various remnants of divisions that were short of fuel, practically without artillery or air cover, and threatened from behind by the British and American armies. In such circumstances, the Soviets could reach Berlin in a few days, and even sooner gain control over the whole area north of the capital – including of course the Hartzwalde estate ... .

It therefore took an exceptional courage and a superior motivation for Kersten to leap once again into the lion's den; should the Soviets capture Himmler's doctor, a Finn of Estonian origin and former officer of an anti-Bolshevik army, he would never be heard of again. Yet Kersten arrived at Bromma airport at the appointed time and boarded the German plane that was about to cross a Baltic Sea patrolled day and night by Russian, British and American fighter planes. Norbert Masur thus began the tale of a journey from which he did not expect to return: "At 1400 hours in the afternoon of April 19, a German plane bearing the swastika took off from Bromma, with Kersten and myself as sole passengers."[358]

Masur and Kersten had never met before, but having no time to waste on small talk, they quickly agreed on the concessions to be obtained from Himmler:

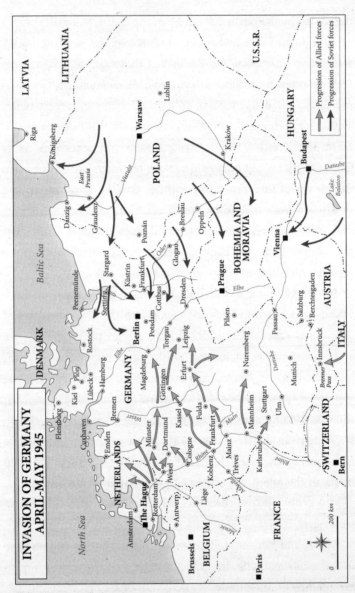

*The invasion of Germany, April–May 1945*

1. All Jews in Germany to be left where they are and none to be forcefully evacuated.
2. Each time a transfer of Jews to a neutral country is feasible, for instance under the aegis of the Red Cross, it must be allowed.
3. The camp commanders must be ordered to treat the Jews decently, and to surrender their camps to the Allies once the front reaches them.

Himmler was also to be presented with a new list of Swedish, Norwegian, French, Dutch and Jewish prisoners whose immediate release was requested by the Swedish foreign ministry. [359] And Günther had entrusted Kersten with an additional mission: get the Reichsführer to order the capitulation of the 350,000 men of the Wehrmacht, Kriegsmarine, Luftwaffe and S.S. stationed in Norway, and whose last-ditch stand could yet drag Sweden into the war.

God favours the reckless: during that four-hour flight, no Allied plane took an interest in the solitary Junkers 52, which thus landed safely at Tempelhof airport shortly before 4.30 p.m. The German policemen, who had obviously received instructions, saluted politely, but the S.S. men charged with driving them to Hartzwalde were nowhere to be seen, and the massive bombing of the capital invariably began at dusk. When the car sent by Himmler's head-quarters finally arrived a little after 8 p.m., there began a mad race through the ruins so as to leave the capital as quickly as possible, followed by a northward journey with all lights out that took them through Oranienburg, Sachsenhausen and Gransee – interspersed with frequent stops in the forest to evade marauding Allied planes. It was almost midnight when the two men finally reached

Hartzwalde; there, along with Elisabeth Lüben, Frau Wacker and Wilhelm Wulff, they were to wait for the Reichsführer's arrival.

The wait was likely to be a long one. Schellenberg, on duty at Hohenlychen headquarters that night, took up the story: "In the meantime, a message had come that Kersten and Norbert Masur had arrived at Tempelhof airport and had driven to Kersten's estate at Hartzwalde. As Count Bernadotte was expected in Berlin at the same time, there was a great danger that these two meetings might overlap, especially in view of the difficult military situation. Himmler therefore asked me to drive to Kersten's estate that very night in order to conduct preparatory negotiations with Herr Masur, and also to arrange a time for Himmler to meet him. [. . .] Contrary to his usual custom, Himmler suddenly ordered a bottle of champagne, so as to drink a toast to Hitler's birthday at the stroke of midnight."[360]

That Himmler could celebrate with moist eyes the birthday of a man whose elimination he had contemplated a few hours earlier will come as no surprise to those who have begun to know him. Schellenberg did seem rather appalled, but his opinion was not invited and he set out to accomplish his task: "It was a bright moonlit night, but we were held up on our way for quite some time by aircraft dropping flares over Berlin. We arrived at Hartzwalde at 2.30 a.m. to find the whole place fast asleep."[361]

Not quite, actually, as Wilhelm Wulff saw him enter and later recalled: "Kersten immediately took him aside and showed him his programme, as well as the list of people whom the Swedish government wanted to retrieve. The discussions were conducted by candle-light.[xxxi] [. . .] I understood that the Reichsführer refused to make

xxxi   Oranienburg having been bombed the day before, the whole sector was without electricity.

any significant concessions to the Swedes before a meeting with Eisenhower could be arranged. [. . .] Schellenberg, who had not slept for days, seemed exhausted."[362] This was confirmed by the Brigade-führer himself, who added: "I talked to Kersten until four o'clock in the morning. He was extremely disheartened by Himmler's changes of mind. 'I doubt,' he said, 'whether a meeting between Himmler and Masur still has some chance of success.'"[363] Indeed, Schellenberg's words gave no grounds for optimism, as Kersten was quick to note: "Schellenberg explained to me [. . .] that due to the strong pressure being applied by several party chiefs who had expressed their indignation at the release of concentration camp prisoners, Himmler was unwilling to make concessions at the moment."[364]

On the morning of April 20, Schellenberg was introduced to Norbert Masur, who had probably never imagined that he would one day breakfast with an S.S. general. Yet he went along with it, particularly as this one seemed quite out of the ordinary, as Masur himself was later to recall: "A young man in civilian dress, who made a good impression and seemed almost sensitive, with no apparent trace of the hardcore Nazi type I had expected to meet. He looked very depressed, considered the war as lost and feared the worst for Germany's future."[365] Such was also the impression of Wilhelm Wulff, who witnessed their conversation: "Masur having set out his requests, Schellenberg acquiesced, under certain conditions." But the Brigadeführer realised above all that Masur wished to see Himmler without delay, as he wanted to leave Berlin by the next day at the latest – which was quite understandable, since the din of the explosions meant that the fighting was getting ever closer. However, giving him satisfaction would be no easy task. "I knew," Schellenberg recalled, "that Himmler intended once again to put off meeting with him, and that I had to do everything in my power to bring it about as quickly as possible."[366]

But even before that, Schellenberg had another matter to settle with the astrologer, who reported the following: "We constantly heard the thunder of cannons coming from the Oderbruch,[xxxii] which often sounded like a barrage of drumfire. Schellenberg told me that he had avoided attending the grotesque celebration of the 'madman's'[xxxiii] birthday, [. . .] but that he had nonetheless to return to Himmler's headquarters at Wustrow, and that I therefore had to give him at least part of the evaluations requested by the Reichsführer. They concerned the following matters: 1. Himmler attaches a great importance to the Führer's death. At what date can it be expected? 2. Are Himmler's efforts to initiate armistice talks likely to be successful? 3. Is Hartzwalde threatened due to the proximity of the fighting and to the presence of the 'muna'?[xxxiv] 4. Should all the residents of Hartzwalde be evacuated?"[367] Wulff was given another list of people whose horoscopes Himmler required – evidently other potential ministers for his future government.[xxxv]

At 5 p.m. that same day, Schellenberg left for Wustrow, there to wait for Himmler who was in Berlin to attend the Führer's birthday celebrations. Every year on April 20, processions of Nazi dignitaries and foreign diplomats came to the chancery and lined up to extend their best wishes to the Führer; but on that particular

xxxii  The swampy area north of Frankfurt on the Oder, where Marshal Zhukov's 1st Byelorussian Front was trying to force a breakthrough towards Berlin.

xxxiii  As early as 1943, Kersten had noted that the name "Hitler" caused Schellenberg such distaste that he refused to pronounce it.

xxxiv  A vast ammunition depot situated close to the estate.

xxxv  Among them: Baldur von Schirach, Erich von dem Bach-Zelewski and Ludolf von Alvensleben – all three highly unsavoury individuals.

day of 1945, celebrations seemed out of place, all was quiet around the chancery, and Hitler's inner circle only came to attend the situation con-ference inside the bunker: Keitel, Jodl, Göring, Himmler, Dönitz, Speer, Kaltenbrunner, Bormann, Ribbentrop and Chief of Staff Krebs. A week earlier, the Führer had savoured a brief moment of triumph upon learning of President Roosevelt's death: being totally ignorant of American institutions, he had imagined that this would cause the United States to exit the war. But since then, he had lapsed back into lethargy, and Dönitz's aide-de-camp, Walter Lüdde-Neurath, described him as "broken, puffy, stooped, exhausted and nervous".[368] Armaments minister Albert Speer also recalled that "no-one quite knew what to say. In view of the circumstances, Hitler received our congratulations coolly and almost unwillingly".[369]

The circumstances were indeed rather bleak: already subjected to daily air raids by the Allied air forces, the capital was now under-going the sporadic shelling of Soviet long-range artillery as well; to the north, the British were approaching Bremen and Emden; to the south, the Americans had just entered Nuremberg, the French were encamped in the suburbs of Stuttgart and the Russians were in Vienna; in the centre, General Busse's 9th Army had been routed on the Oder, between Frankfurt and Küstrin;[xxxvi] south-east of Berlin, the Red Army had passed Cottbus and was heading north towards Postdam, while in the south-west, American forces had occupied Leipzig that very morning. In other words, the last route to Bavaria and Austria along the Elbe would be cut off before long . . .

xxxvi   Hitler had forbidden him all retreat, though he had long since been over-taken by the enemy.

This was indeed what most troubled Göring, Himmler, Bormann and Ribbentrop, whose sole concern during that situation conference was to save their own skins. "The night before," wrote Speer, "the idea had been raised of not defending the metropolis and transferring instead to the Alpine redoubt. But overnight, Hitler had decided to fight for the city in the streets of Berlin. At once, everyone began clamouring that it was essential to shift the headquarters southwards to the Obersalzberg, and that now was the last moment to do so. [. . .] Hitler was indignant: 'How can I call on the troops to fight the decisive battle for Berlin while I myself withdraw to safety? [. . .] I shall leave it to fate whether I die in the capital or fly to Obersalzberg at the last moment!'"[370]

Göring nevertheless succeeded in wrangling permission from the Führer to leave for Bavaria, on the grounds that "the situation there called for a unified command of the Luftwaffe"; but Himmler, emerging from the bunker, realised that he, for one, would be unable to escape the Brandenburg deathtrap, unless he took a snap decision by himself – a prospect which he found deeply repugnant.

At 11.30 p.m., having narrowly escaped a bombing raid, the Reichsführer was back in Wustrow, there to be informed by Schellenberg that both Masur and Bernadotte had announced their intention to leave the very next day. Schellenberg then explained to his chief that seeing the count was imperative if he wanted to meet Eisenhower, and that a meeting with Masur was no less so if he wanted to project a better image of himself to the outside world – at the price of a few last-minute humanitarian gestures. Himmler eventually gave in: he would go and see Masur at Hartzwalde straight away, and then meet Count Bernadotte at six in the morning at the Hohenlychen sanatorium![xxxvii] At 1.15 a.m., Himmler, Brandt, Schellenberg and a driver therefore left Wustrow for Hartzwalde, where they arrived at 2.30 a.m., having sought refuge in a wood to escape the attentions of a night fighter on the prowl.

At Hartzwalde, they were greeted with some relief by Kersten, for whom it had been a long and uncertain wait. As Brandt and Schellenberg entered the house, Kersten took Himmler aside. "We conferred alone in the garden. I begged Himmler to understand what was at stake. [. . .] It was to show the world that humanity had not entirely disappeared in Germany. [. . .] Once again, I appealed to his respect for the verdict of history, for I had often noted how receptive he was to such an argument. Himmler promised me to do his best [. . .] and added these exact words: 'I would like to bury the hatchet between the Jews and us. Had it depended on me alone, many things would have been done differently. But the Führer demanded that I be ruthless.'"[371]

After a few more inconclusive exchanges,[xxxviii] the two men entered the house. Himmler came face-to-face with Masur at the entrance to the salon, which was dimly lit by a wood fire and a few candles. He said "*Guten Tag!*",[xxxix] stepped forward and extended his hand. Masur cleared his throat, replied "*Guten Tag!*" and shook

---

xxxvii   Thus in the opposite direction. Once again, sleep was not provided for.
xxxviii   Kersten again raised the question of the capitulation of German forces in Norway, but Himmler replied that this was for the Führer to decide. Himmler asked Kersten if the Swedes would allow the German troops in Norway to cross their territory in order to be redeployed in Germany, but Kersten, duly instructed by Günther, answered that Sweden would only agree to intern them. Himmler then asked Kersten if he had a means of contacting General Eisenhower, but received a predictable reply – and probably the advice to raise the matter with Count Bernadotte.
xxxix   No doubt suspecting that "*Heil Hitler!*" would have been inappropriate.

his hand; after which Himmler made the introductions: "I presume that you already know Brigadeführer Schellenberg; and this is Standartenführer Brandt." Masur nodded towards Schellenberg and shook hands with Brandt, about whom he had heard so much during the last forty-eight hours. Astrologist Wilhelm Wulff, having witnessed these social niceties, was not invited to take part in the discussions to follow – admittedly, he had much work to do.

"Herr Reichsführer, please make yourself comfortable," Kersten said, pointing to the tea table in the centre of the room. Everyone moved forward, except Himmler, who did not budge and kept staring at the fire; then he said slowly, as if talking to himself:

"Germany is a country that has not known peace for at least a generation. When the Great War broke out, I was fourteen years old; it was scarcely over when the civil war erupted, and the Jews played a leading role during the Spartacist uprising."

Himmler turned around, looked fixedly at Masur, then took a seat. The others followed; Kersten slumped into a large armchair next to Himmler, Masur sat opposite, while Schellenberg and Brandt took seats on either side. Masur noted that "Himmler was dressed in a perfectly tailored uniform, displaying all his medals and rank insignia; despite the late hour, he seemed well groomed, well rested and wide awake, giving an impression of calm and self-restraint."

That the Reichsführer was an excellent comedian is well known at this stage. There was a tense silence as he bent forward and took a piece of cake. Kersten signalled the cook to serve coffee, and Himmler resumed talking with a professorial tone.

"The Jews are a foreign element in Germany, it has always been so – a foreign element that causes irritation. [...] On several occasions, they were expelled from Germany, but they always came back. You see, after we took power, we sought to solve this problem once and for all. With Heydrich, I set up an emigration organisation. [. . .] But even those countries that declared themselves best disposed towards the Jews refused to take them in!"[372]

Masur, who had hitherto struggled to contain himself, could bear it no longer.

"Herr Himmler . . . Brutally expelling people from their parents' and grandparents' country has never been reconcilable with international law and established legal rules!"

Himmler continued his monologue without appearing to have heard.

"The war brought us into contact with the proletarian Jewish masses of eastern Europe. There was no way we could tolerate having such an enemy in our rear. The Jewish masses were infested with diseases, they spread dangerous epidemics, especially typhus. I myself lost thousands of my best S.S. men through these epidemics.[xl] [373] [. . .] Besides, these eastern European Jews helped the partisans by creating underground resistance movements, and they shot at Germans from within their ghettos."[374]

Kersten glanced anxiously at Masur, who had remained impassive, while Himmler continued to elaborate on the eastern campaign, the ferocity of Soviet soldiers and the sufferings of the German people. But time was running out, and Masur finally interrupted him.

---

xl    During the inward journey between Wustrow and Hartzwalde, Schellenberg had tried to dissuade Himmler from embarking on an attempt at self-justification, and advised him to focus rather on the future. But Himmler had only promised to "think about it".

"Herr Himmler, I actually wanted to talk about the concentration camps."

After a moment's hesitation, Himmler said:

"The concentration camps . . . Their bad reputation is due to the name that was given them, which was poorly chosen. They should have been called re-education camps. [. . .] Of course, the prisoners had to work hard, but so did all the German people. In the camps, these prisoners were treated harshly but fairly."

In the face of such blatant lies, Masur could no longer contain himself, and he replied icily:

"Herr Himmler, I lost a large part of my family, of my friends' families and many comrades from my younger days in your . . . re-education camps!"[375]

But Himmler went on undeterred:

"I must admit that mistakes were made, but when I was told about them, I meted out harsh punishment to those who were to blame."

Kersten, who admired Masur's self-restraint, also realised that things were going wrong, that forty-five minutes had already been lost and that something had to be done:

"Let's not talk about the past, since there's nothing we can do about it. Let us rather talk of the present and of what can still be salvaged."

Clearly encouraged, Masur echoed his words:

"If we want to help reconcile our peoples, we must at least secure the lives of the Jews remaining in Germany."

And he urged Himmler to set them all free.

The Reichsführer then launched into a long diatribe; in keeping with the promise made to Kersten, he had ordered that the Bergen-Belsen and Buchenwald camps be surrendered intact to the Allies,[xli] but he had been poorly rewarded for it: the international press had excoriated him once again.

"No-one has been slandered more than I have over the past twelve years, and I didn't much care about it. [...] But these foreign publications were used to wage a heinous propaganda campaign against us, and this has not particularly encouraged me to continue surrendering camps to the Allies."[376]

To which Masur retorted that it was impossible to dictate to the international press what it should write, and that the Jews exerted absolutely no influence over it. The conversation then moved on to Ravensbrück and to the prisoners whose release Himmler had promised Kersten in December 1944 and March 1945. "Kersten and I," Masur recalled, "repeated time and again that he had to allow the evacuation towards Sweden of the Ravensbrück prisoners." The problem was that each time a new issue was raised, Himmler launched into another self-justifying rant.

Glancing at his watch, Masur realised that this candlelight gathering to the sound of explosions had already gone on for an hour and a half, without the slightest concrete results, whereas none of the five men in the room had slept for the last forty-eight hours! Masur looked at Kersten, who nodded in return, took out his list from the Swedish foreign ministry and asked Himmler to browse through it with him;[377] there was a cross next to the names of people to be released as a priority.[xlii] After a moment, Himmler rose and said:

xli    Buchenwald had been liberated by the Americans on April 11, and Bergen-Belsen by the British on April 15.
xlii   Himmler actually agreed to release them all: fifty Norwegian Jews, thirteen Swedes, fifty Dutch Jews, fifty Dutch women, three French women, one Frenchman and several Swedes sentenced to death.

"I need to talk in private with Herr Brandt and Herr Kersten."

Schellenberg and Masur glanced at each other, got up and left the salon. Kersten then said to Himmler that he should stand by the agreement they had reached in March and make a clear offer to Masur:

"Now that you stand for the first time before a representative of Judaism, you cannot refuse to show him the same goodwill that you showed me before."[378]

Masur and Schellenberg were called back twenty minutes later; they found Himmler standing in the middle of the living room, flanked by Kersten and Brandt. The Reichsführer solemnly announced:

"I am willing to release a thousand women from Ravensbrück concentration camp, and you can have them carried off by the Red Cross. But calling them Jews is out of the question. It's very important![xliii] Let's call them, say . . . Poles."[379]

Himmler added that he was also prepared to release the women from Ravensbrück who were on the Swedish foreign ministry's list, as well as fifty Jews from the Norwegian camps and some of the Dutch Jews from Theresienstadt – if the Red Cross could transport them. And he concluded:

"As for putting an end to forced evacuations and surrendering the camps to the Allies, I will do my best to give you satisfaction."[380]

It was now 4.30 in the morning; Wilhelm Wulff saw Himmler and Masur go out together into the garden, as later confirmed by Masur: "I was alone with him for about half an hour, a Jew face to face with the frightening and ruthless Gestapo chief who had about five million Jewish lives on his conscience." But of course,

xliii   An abject fear of Hitler's reactions, as always.

none of this was discussed just then, and Himmler cautioned Masur: "It is essential that your visit here remain secret, and the same goes for the arrival of the Jewish women in Sweden."[381] As they re-entered the house, Wulff thought he heard the Reichsführer say: "*Ja, ja*, Herr Masur, had we known each other ten years earlier, this war would never have happened."[382] Such words might seem absurd, but at this stage, Himmler no longer shied away from anything, even the most outrageous statements.

In the meantime, Kersten was having a private conversation with Schellenberg and Brandt, who promised him to see to it that the figure of a thousand women be substantially increased, and that the Reichsführer's pledge to deliver the camps intact be honoured. Shortly before five o'clock, Himmler's car crunched to a halt on the gravel drive in front of the house; as Brandt, Schellenberg and Masur remained behind, Kersten accompanied the Reichsführer to his car and asked him to confirm that The Hague, Clingendael and the dyke would not be blown up.

"You have my word of honour, Herr Kersten, that I have already prevented that. [. . .] The Hague is a Germanic city; it will not be destroyed. [. . .] But the Dutch have not deserved it. [. . .] My dear Kersten, you have always been more Dutch than Finn, and you have never believed in our victory. I now realise that in many cases you were right."

"How could I have believed in a German victory, when you showed me Hitler's medical file? Germany has been ruled by a madman."

Himmler answered *mezza voce*:

"*Ach ja*, Herr Kersten, we have made great mistakes. If I could start all over again, I would surely do many things differently. But it's too late now. Besides, my life is almost at an end. We wanted to build a great and strong Germany, and all we're leaving behind us is a heap of ruins. [. . .] All the best for your life in Sweden, and pass on my greetings to your family. I always wanted to act for the best, but I was often compelled to act contrary to my own convictions. Believe me, Herr Kersten, it was hard and bitter going at times. The Führer demanded it of me, and Bormann and Goebbels were his evil advisers. As a loyal and disciplined soldier, I had to obey; for without discipline and obedience, no state can endure. I shall decide for myself how long I still have to live, for my life is now meaningless. And what will History say of me? [. . .] I shall be held to blame for many of the misdeeds perpetrated by others. [. . .] With us disappears the best part of the German people. What remains no longer concerns us; the Allies can do what they like with it."[xliv] [383]

The two men had by now reached the car; Himmler got in, sat down and put out his hand to the man who had probably been his sole confidant.

"Herr Kersten, I thank you from the bottom of my heart for having so selflessly given me the benefit of your vast medical science for so many years. Whatever happens, you must not think ill of me. Do try to help my poor family if at all possible. Farewell!"

"When Himmler uttered these last words," Kersten remembered, "he had tears in his eyes."[384] Schellenberg climbed in beside the Reichsführer, the car started up and moved away in the first light of dawn, under Kersten's incredulous gaze. And Masur recalled: "After Himmler's departure, we slept for a few hours – or

xliv    Perhaps without realising it, Himmler was once again repeating Hitler's drivel word for word.

314

at least we tried to." As for Kersten, he did not even try. "Once Himmler had left, I visited for the last time all the familiar places in and around the house where I had spent so many years. I took leave of this estate where a small part of history had just played out, and of this garden where the first primroses were just emerging. It was only on returning to my room that I mentally relived all the events of the years gone by; I revisited them all, as if in a book, page after page. But each time, my mind returned to those hours when I was lying, sick among the sick, in the bed of a field hospital, and then to those when, working as the doctor's assistant, I discovered the healing power of my hands. Ever since then, it had been my lot to care for people and to assist them when they were imperilled by a tyrannical regime. I gave thanks to the Lord who had granted me that favour."[385]

At ten o'clock on the morning of April 21, Kersten left Hartzwalde for the last time; with Masur, he headed for Berlin, whose contours were already discernible from afar under the pall of black smoke that enveloped it. And a few hours later, taking off from Tempelhof airport and flying into an airspace largely controlled by the Soviet air force, Felix Kersten once more put his life on the line.

315

# 13

# THE TWILIGHT OF THE GODS

At dawn on April 21, 1945, as Count Bernadotte was about to meet Heinrich Himmler at the Hohenlychen sanatorium, he did not expect much from the discussion: over the last two days, his White Buses had been transferring to Denmark the 5,500 Scandinavians assembled at Neuengamme,[i] after which the whole staff had orders from Bernadotte to return to Sweden – a clear indication that the count did not expect to rescue any more prisoners.

At 6 a.m. on the dot, Bernadotte saw the Reichsführer enter the breakfast room. "He looked tired and even exhausted. [. . .] He told me that he had hardly slept for several nights."[386] Himmler apparently did not tell Bernadotte the reason for his latest bout of insomnia, and neither did Schellenberg – perhaps because the mission of an S.D. chief was to gather intelligence rather than provide it . . . At any rate, the count went on with his story: "The breakfast table was well laden, and Himmler ate with appetite. He occasionally tapped on his front teeth with his fingernail, which betrayed his nervousness, according to what Schellenberg had told me. This time, we talked only of humanitarian measures; I requested once again that the Scandinavian prisoners on their way

i  A risk-free concession from Himmler, as Denmark was still under German occupation at the time.

to Denmark be allowed to continue their journey on to Sweden, but Himmler once more refused. [. . .] He gave in on other points, however, and expressed great interest in my proposal to let the Red Cross handle the transfer of all the French women held in Ravensbrück concentration camp. He added that not only did he agree to this, but he even invited us to take charge of the women of all nationalities, since the camp was soon to be evacuated. I promised him that I would give my staff the necessary orders without delay."[387]

Apparently convinced that his talents as a negotiator had been instrumental in achieving these results, Count Bernadotte later strove to have the whole world share his view. Yet what he had just obtained boiled down basically to what Himmler had promised Masur and Kersten two hours earlier – with a further concession that Schellenberg had most likely suggested to him on the way from Hartzwalde to Hohenlychen: since Ravensbrück camp had to be evacuated before the Soviet advance in any case, why not put on a show of generosity by handing over all the women to the Red Cross?[ii] Actually, it was not even Bernadotte who first ordered the drivers of the White Buses already at the Danish border to turn around, but Franz Göring,[iii] Schellenberg's assistant![388]

S.S. Hauptsturmführer Franz Göring was already on the spot when the first convoy of fifteen Danish ambulances arrived at Ravensbrück early in the afternoon of April 22. His presence was to prove providential for the women detained there, for camp

ii    It will be recalled that Schellenberg had promised Kersten that he would seek to obtain a substantial increase in the number of women released.

iii   Dubbed by his colleagues "the little Göring" in order to distinguish him from "the fat Göring" (no known kinship). All the White Buses were accompanied by Gestapo agents, who passed on to the drivers the order to turn around.

commander Fritz Suhren adamantly refused to release anyone. Göring managed to contact Rudolf Brandt and explained the situation to him; shortly thereafter, Himmler's secretary called the camp commander and reiterated the Reichsführer's order to release all the women. According to Göring, Suhren then confided in him that "he no longer knew where he stood, since he had received through Kaltenbrunner the Führer's express order to keep all the prisoners in the camp and to liquidate them on the approach of enemy forces".[389] And Fritz Suhren had yet another problem: he had in his camp seventy-one *Kaninchen*[iv] – French and Polish – whom Professor Gebhardt was using for medical experiments, and whom he had ordered liquidated a few weeks earlier in order to conceal his misdeeds. But as too many women had been earmarked for execution,[v] all the *Kaninchen* were still alive and he, Suhren, no longer knew what to do with them.

This was to be the start of a high-risk salvage operation: over the next three days, the Swedish and Danish ambulances, buses and trucks, driving along roads that were clogged with refugees, machine-gunned by British planes and bombarded by Soviet artillery, conveyed to Denmark 2,904 women[vi] – Polish, French, Belgian, Dutch, German, British, Hungarian and Jewish of various nationalities. On Brandt's order, Franz Göring even succeeded in requisitioning at the last moment a Reichsbahn train that brought back an additional 3,989.[vii] [390] A Swedish bus from the last convoy

iv   Rabbits.
v    Until April 21, sixty to ninety prisoners were gassed each day in Ravensbrück.
vi   Including the *Kaninchen*.
vii  More than 20,000 women, mainly German and Russian, were to remain in Ravensbrück. Those who were unable to leave the camp were liberated on April 30 by the Red Army, with tragic results.

even managed to venture as far as Hartzwalde, where it picked up "a couple of unidentified people of Swedish descent"[391] – apparently Elisabeth Lüben and Irmgard Kersten's brother.[viii]

The day after his return to Stockholm, Kersten reported to Minister Günther on the results of his mission; it had been a half-success, and therefore half a failure: he had been unable to persuade Himmler to order the capitulation of German troops in Denmark and Norway – which could have been expected, since this did not fall under the Reichsführer's remit. Günther was certainly aware of it when he entrusted him with the mission, but he had probably grown used to seeing Kersten perform miracles. On the other hand, our Medizinalrat had succeeded in obtaining the release of all prisoners on the Swedish foreign ministry's list;[ix] but the day after, he added in a memorandum addressed to the minister: "Concerning the figure of 350,000 Jews still living in Germany that was given to me in early March, [. . .] I am now convinced that we are in fact dealing at best with 50,000 to 100,000 Jews. Personally speaking, I am strongly under the impression that the German authorities themselves do not know the exact figure."[392]

That was more than likely; but the other person who needed reassuring was Hillel Storch, about whom Kersten commented at the time: "Storch still fails to grasp the importance of what we have obtained from Himmler. He particularly doubts that Himmler will stick to the agreement and refrain from giving contrary orders

viii    This somewhat mythical descent probably being designed to justify the diversion in reports to the Red Cross administration. The same bus apparently picked up some Jehovah's Witnesses as well, though certainly not all of them.
ix    "Fifty Norwegian Jews, thirteen Swedes, fifty Dutch Jews (men), fifty Dutch Jews (women), three French women, one Frenchman, several Swedes sentenced to death."

at the last moment, which would result in the annihilation of all Jews in the concentration camps. Knowing Himmler's mentality, I assured him that it would not happen."[393] This was perhaps placing undue reliance on Heinrich Himmler's commitment to the given word – even though on April 21, Kersten had secured the cooperation of his two accomplices Brandt and Schellenberg, who had promised him that they would see to it that the Reichsführer stood by his commitment. But in Germany, things had reached such a point that no-one controlled anything any longer . . .

Adolf Hitler less than any other; that same April 22, deep down in his subterranean bunker, the Führer was still counting on "operational group Steiner", positioned west of Eberswalde, to launch a major counteroffensive south-eastwards and loosen the Soviet grip that was tightening inexorably on Berlin. But that unit was made up essentially of garrison troops, elements of the Luftwaffe and young recruits with no fighting experience, no heavy weapons, tanks short on fuel, no air cover and none of the expected reinforcements from the Wehrmacht and the S.S. Its counteroffensive was therefore slow to materialise, and Hitler continually harassed the O.K.W. to get it moving, yet nothing happened. The Soviets had already reached the suburbs of the capital, and the Führer's nerves finally snapped; shortly before midnight, General Koller, air force chief of staff, went to Krampnitz barracks near Potsdam, where General Jodl[x] apprised him of the situation: "Hitler has given up. He has decided to stay in Berlin, to command the defence of the city and to put a bullet through his head at the last moment. He said he could not fight for physical reasons, and also because he did not want to risk being wounded and falling

x   Head of the O.K.W. operational section.

into enemy hands. [. . .] The latest developments in the military situation have affected him considerably and he keeps on talking of betrayal, abandonment and corruption within the command and the troops. Even the S.S. were betraying him, even Sepp Dietrich;[xi] Steiner failed to intervene, and that was the *coup de grâce*."[394]

Hermann Göring was immediately informed of this new development, which led him to believe that his hour had come. Himmler was informed too,[xii] which plunged him into depths of uncertainty; indeed, he was still wavering between blind obedience to the Führer and the temptation to negotiate behind his back with the Western Allies – each alternative raising in turn innumerable problems, which he endeavoured to overcome through a mixture of double-dealing, ferocity, subservience and escapism. In an effort to placate Hitler, he ordered that all deserters and soldiers trying to surrender be hanged in public, he launched his Werwolf against any town mayor who collaborated with the Allies,[xiii] had political prisoners executed and ordered that the inmates of Dachau, Flossenbürg and Sachsenhausen be evacuated and sent on forced marches upon the enemy's approach – thereby breaching a number of his commitments to Kersten. And yet he was well aware that the Führer was at the end of his tether, and as early as April 14, he had confided to Gruppenführer Jürgen Stroop his impression that "Hitler was behaving in a strange way"[395] – something of a

xi   Who had ordered the retreat of his 6th Panzerarmee from Budapest, contrary to orders received from Berlin.

xii   In the evening of April 22, by Hermann Fegelein, his liaison officer with the Führer.

xiii   Thus perished on March 25 lawyer Franz Oppenhoff, who had accepted the position of mayor of Aachen from the Americans.

euphemism, which a telephone call in the evening of April 22 had entirely confirmed.

Conversely, Himmler saw himself at times as the Führer's successor, negotiating a compromise of sorts with the West that would enable him to pursue his war against the Soviet Union. But this would only happen if Hitler agreed to step down, for he, Himmler, was by no means brave enough to topple the Führer. Of course, there was that terrible nervous breakdown in the chancery bunker on April 22, but everyone in Hitler's inner circle knew that he always regained his composure – which is precisely what was happening at the moment. Besides, negotiating with the Allies raised a number of equally intractable problems: on the one hand, even grossly overestimating the value of his cooperation in British and American eyes, he had to admit that their representatives were not particularly keen to deal with him; on the other hand, he did not quite know how to proceed: was it reasonable to offer an anti-Soviet alliance to the British and Americans who had just reaffirmed at Yalta their resolve to win the war hand in hand with Stalin? And assuming for one moment that he did propose a surrender, would he be deemed an acceptable interlocutor? Which in turn created yet another dilemma: was it better to show goodwill by releasing a great number of prisoners, or to force the Allies to take him seriously by holding as many hostages as possible? Up until then, he had played both cards, by authorising Count Bernadotte's White Bus mission, while on the other hand ordering on March 27 Baldur von Schirach, Gauleiter of Vienna, to transfer all the Jews from Vienna to Linz and Mauthausen, since they were his "most valuable assets".[396] And behind it all lay that abject fear of Hitler, Bormann, Goebbels and Kaltenbrunner that sapped his morale and paralysed all initiative – with in parallel the dire necessity of saving his own skin once the Führer had left this world. The Hamlet dilemma? A mere trifle compared to the storm that was raging inside the Reichsführer's shaved head.

In the end, it was Walter Schellenberg who spurred him into action. "I spoke to him again of the possibility of a final exchange with Bernadotte, though I did not know where he could be reached at the time. Perhaps he was still in Lübeck. Himmler decided to send me there forthwith." Once on the spot, Schellenberg was told that Bernadotte was in Denmark, but he managed to contact him and to arrange a discussion with Himmler at the Swedish consulate in Lübeck. It finally took place on April 23 at 11 p.m. "The electricity was cut off," Schellenberg recalled, "so the discussion proceeded by candlelight, and hardly had it begun when the alarm sounded, followed by a powerful air attack against a neighbouring airfield. It was already midnight when we managed to leave the shelter and resume our conversation."[397]

This was confirmed by Count Bernadotte, who added: "Himmler, who seemed extremely tired and very much on edge, was clearly making a great effort to appear calm. The Gestapo chief began by saying that it was quite possible that Hitler was already dead, and that if he wasn't yet, his number would be up in the next few days. [. . .] Berlin was surrounded and it was only a question of days before the city fell. [. . .] He recognised that the situation was desperate, that the war would soon come to an end and that Germany had no choice but to admit defeat, yet he had been unable to betray his oath of loyalty to the Führer. Now, things were different. Hitler could well be dead already."[398]

The repetition revealing his desire as well as his uncertainty, Himmler went on:

"With the situation now as it is, I consider that I have a free rein. In order to safeguard the greatest possible part of Germany from a Russian invasion, I am willing to capitulate on the western front, so as to enable the forces of the Western powers to advance eastward as quickly as possible. On the other hand, I am unwilling to capitulate on the eastern front. I have always been and I will always be a sworn enemy of Bolshevism. [. . .] Would you agree to transmit this message to the Swedish minister of foreign affairs, so that he may inform the Western powers accordingly?"

Bernadotte: "It seems to me that it is quite impossible to implement a capitulation on the western front while still fighting on the eastern front. It is all but certain that England and America will refuse to make any kind of separate deal with Germany."

Himmler: "I understand how difficult it is, but at any rate, I want to try to save millions of Germans from a Soviet occupation."

Bernadotte: "I'm not willing to transmit your message to the Swedish foreign minister, unless you promise to include Denmark and Norway in the capitulation."

And the count noted: "Himmler answered unhesitatingly that he would agree to that, and that he had no objections to American, British and Swedish troops occupying Denmark and Norway, [. . .] but only provided the Soviet troops did not participate. [. . .] Having again expressed my scepticism as to the likelihood of reaching an agreement with the Western powers, I suggested he write a brief letter to Foreign Minister Günther. [. . .] Himmler did so at once."[399]

The Reichsführer then alluded to a possible meeting with Eisenhower, and avowed that this was "the darkest day of his life", after which it was agreed that Bernadotte would return to Sweden post-haste and update Schellenberg on the "success" of his mission. It was 2.30 in the morning when the three men left the consulate, and Himmler got behind the wheel – with foreseeable results. "He set off so quickly," recalled Schellenberg, "that we landed in a ditch. All of us, including Count Bernadotte, had to struggle for a quarter of an hour to get the car going again."[400] To which Bernadotte added: "On witnessing this departure, our legation secretary Torsten Brandel and our attaché Count Axel Lewenhaupt agreed with me that there was something symbolic in the way Himmler had made his departure."[401]

Most assuredly . . . All day on April 24, at any rate, Schellenberg sought to reassure the Reichsführer, who was already alarmed by the boldness of his proposal to the Allies.[xiv] That same day, in Stockholm, Minister Günther received Bernadotte's report together with Himmler's letter; he informed Kersten and passed on the offer of capitulation to the American and British embassies. Three weeks earlier, Churchill had written to Eden: "No truck with Himmler,"[402] but what the Reichsführer was now proposing could mean an early end to the war, and that was not to be dismissed lightly. Initially attracted by the prospect, Churchill thus dispatched a long message to Supreme Commander Eisenhower, who could no longer bear to hear the name of Himmler ever since his visit to a concentration camp two weeks earlier[xv] – and also realised the extent of the complications that a partial capitulation would cause

xiv    But also gave at long last the necessary orders for the transfer to Sweden of all the prisoners who had been freed by the Red Cross: 20,937 men, women and children of twenty-two nationalities.

xv    At Ohrdruf, a satellite camp of Buchenwald. He was later to write: "I am certain that I have never at any other time experienced an equal sense of shock."

with Stalin. He therefore replied to Churchill that he viewed the offer as "a last desperate attempt to split the Allies".[403] The British war cabinet being in full agreement, Churchill was already more reserved when he telephoned the new American president, Harry Truman.[xvi]

Churchill: "Have you received the report from Stockholm by your ambassador?"

Truman: "Yes, I have."

Churchill: "On that proposal?"

Truman: "Yes. I have just a short message saying that there is such a proposal in existence."

Churchill: "Yes, it's of course . . . We thought it looked very good. [. . .]"

Truman: "What has he to surrender: does that mean everything, Norway, Denmark, Italy and Holland?"

Churchill: "They mentioned Italy and Yugoslavia.[xvii] We mentioned everything and have included that to take in Denmark and Norway. Everything on the western front, but he hasn't proposed a surrender on the eastern front. So we thought perhaps it would be necessary to report it to Stalin; that is, of course, to say that in our view the surrender must be simultaneous to agree to our terms."

Truman: "I think he should be forced to surrender to all three

---

xvi  This was their first transatlantic telephone conversation since Truman's accession to power eleven days earlier; it was recorded at the time.

xvii  This is one of the curiosities of the conversation: nothing in Bernadotte's report concerned Italy or Yugoslavia. Besides, Churchill mentioned that Schellenberg (whom he called "General Finisberg", then "Herr Stinsberg") said to Bernadotte that Hitler had suffered a "haemorrhage of the brain" – here again, nothing of the sort appears in the writings of either Schellenberg or Bernadotte.

governments, Russia, you and the United States. I don't think we ought to even consider a piecemeal surrender."

Churchill: "No, no, no. Not a piecemeal surrender to a man like Himmler."[404]

The conversation thus ended in complete agreement: there could be no other possibility than simultaneous and unconditional surrender to the representatives of the three major powers, and it was decided that after Stalin's approval had been received, ambassadors Johnson and Mallet in Stockholm would be instructed to inform Bernadotte of this decision – for transmission to Himmler's liaison officer. The members of the anti-Hitler coalition naturally felt in a position of strength: on April 25, the armies of Zhukov and Koniev had completed the encirclement of Berlin, while American and Soviet troops made their junction at Torgau, on the Elbe, thus effectively cutting Germany in half.

On the evening of April 26, American ambassador to Stockholm Hershell Johnson invited Count Bernadotte to his office to take cognisance of President Truman's answer, which was laconic enough: total and unconditional capitulation on all fronts to the three powers, with the surrender of German forces in the field to the Allied commanders in their respective operational theatres – along with this warning: "In the event of further resistance anywhere, Allied attacks will be pursued until final victory." Bernadotte then went to the foreign ministry and conferred with Günther. "The minister told me that if I delivered the answer in person, a breakdown in negotiations could possibly be avoided, thus permitting the pursuit of negotiations concerning a German capitulation in Norway and Denmark. On April 27, I thus flew to Odense, where I met with Brigadeführer Schellenberg."[405]

As could be expected, Schellenberg received the news with no particular pleasure at 5 p.m. that day; not only did the Allies refuse to negotiate with Himmler, but it was also rumoured that his offer of capitulation had been leaked to the press.[xviii] When Schellenberg called the Reichsführer shortly after midnight to inform him of the Allied refusal, he added that the count wanted to see him again in order to discuss the matter of German forces in Denmark and Norway. Himmler refused outright: that proposal had been no more than a ploy on his part to negotiate a surrender – or even an alliance – with the Western powers; no negotiation, no capitulation of German forces in Scandinavia – *ausgeschlossen!*[xix] A disappointed and furious Himmler summoned Schellenberg to Lübeck forthwith.

Well acquainted with his chief's mentality, the Brigadeführer felt more than a little worried: "I had henceforth to consider that Himmler would point to me as the instigator of his peace initiative and would hold me responsible for its failure. He might even have me liquidated. To protect myself, I hit upon the idea of arranging for an astrologer to accompany me: one whom Himmler knew personally and of whom he thought very highly."[406]

There could be little doubt as to the identity of the astrologer in question; Wilhelm Wulff was indeed summoned to Lübeck on the morning of April 28 and immediately hustled into a requisitioned bright red Mercedes, complete with chauffeur and S.S. escort. His travel impressions: "The trip to Lübeck amounted to a veritable tour of the front line. On country roads, we overtook the remains

xviii   It initially passed unnoticed, since rumours of that kind had been circulating for weeks.
xix   Out of the question!

328

of cars that had been riddled with bullets and set on fire by dive bomber attacks; injured people had been hauled out of burning cars and were sprawled on the roadside or laboriously trudging on. [. . .] Behind Ahrensburg station, one could glimpse uprooted railway tracks, derailed trains, bombed-out, shredded and mangled carriages. [. . .] The spring sunshine cast a pallid glow over this Dantesque spectacle."[407]

Wulff nonetheless managed to reach Lübeck that evening and was put up at the Danziger Hof Hotel, where the staff of R.S.H.A. section VI and Schellenberg's office were quartered. The latter arrived a few hours later, and Wulff could resume his narrative: "Schellenberg greeted me with these words: 'Make sure that Himmler sends me to Stockholm! Have you brought the documents with you?' He looked stressed and obviously lacked sleep. He held out a trembling hand and smiled to conceal his fear. While the telephones rang and the adjutants, the S.S. soldiers and the orderlies kept coming and going, he told me about his concerns: 'The Western powers persist in rejecting any negotiation with Himmler; an unconditional surrender of the Wehrmacht and an armistice are unacceptable to us. How can we get out of this mess? Public opinion abroad is informed by Reuters of our connection with the Swedes and of Himmler's proposal.[xx] What should I tell the Reichsführer? He will blame me for having put him in an awkward position, since Hitler will relieve him of his duties. [. . .] I still have a chance: if the Reichsführer sends me to Stockholm

xx Quite true: during the San Francisco conference, Eden had mentioned Himmler's proposal to the British director of the Information Service, who had confided it to a journalist working for Reuters. The news was broadcast by the B.B.C. and relayed by Swedish radio in the afternoon of April 28.

with the task of negotiating the return of our troops from Norway, [. . .] I will try to arrange something with Bernadotte. [. . .] The Reichsführer will put you in the picture; he's looking for a way out.'"[408]

The strategy was perfectly clear: Wulff was to let the stars speak once again, this time in favour of the plans – and of the salvation – of Walter Schellenberg. The astrologer withdrew for an hour to prepare his assortment of files, cards, pendulums and spell books, after which the two men set out together for Himmler's campaign headquarters, located in a barracks at some distance from Lübeck. They arrived shortly after midnight and were shown into a cavernous waiting room. After a while, Himmler entered the room, puffing on a cigar, and Wulff noted: "He had a swollen and ruddy face, his eyelids looked heavy. He had just dined, and his breath smelled somewhat of schnapps. He greeted us with a grimace of a smile. To begin with, he asked Schellenberg to give him an update on events. He had been annoyed no end by the news that appeared in the press, and he was convinced that Hitler would relieve him of all his duties and have him arrested. He asked me what his stars had to say about all this. I was arranging the necessary instruments on the table, when Himmler began to speak: 'I now recognise, Herr Wulff, that you warned me sincerely, by advising me to have Hitler deposed and to open armistice negotiations with the British. It is too late for that now; Hitler will have me arrested. [. . .] Whatever can I do, whatever can I do?'"[409]

Both Wulff and Schellenberg did their best to steer the conversation towards the matter that interested them, but Himmler was greatly excited and kept raving on. Having at length leafed through his horoscope, Wulff finally interrupted him: "I pointed out to him that he still had a chance, provided he sent Schellenberg to Sweden so that he could resume negotiations with Bernadotte and the Swedish foreign minister; then, after receipt of a message agreed with Schellenberg, he could escape from Germany [. . .]. After I had reported on the alignment of the planets, he simply responded: 'Is that all?' Next, Schellenberg started to outline his proposal and the new opportunities to negotiate that would arise if he had a mandate from Himmler to work out an agreement with Sweden concerning the withdrawal of German troops from Norway – which would give him an opportunity to ask Bernadotte to arrange a meeting between Himmler and Eisenhower."[410]

At dawn on April 29, this was of course pure fantasy; yet the Reichsführer was prepared to grasp at the slightest straw, as Schellenberg observed with great relief: "Against all odds, the meeting turned out quite well. My astrologer partner helped me as best he could [. . .] and Himmler even mandated me to negotiate with Count Bernadotte on the termination of the German occupation of Norway and the internment in Sweden of the German occupation forces for the remainder of the war. [. . .] Finally, he expressed his readiness to appoint me as his personal representative to the Swedish government, in order to negotiate a peace agreement for the whole of Scandinavia. At that stage, he was still convinced that he would soon become Hitler's successor."[411]

Thus, Himmler was both terrified at the idea of being arrested by Hitler, and simultaneously convinced that he would succeed him. Actually, this was not entirely unreasonable – provided of course that the Führer consented to put an end to his life, as he had intimated on April 22. There was, however, every indication that he had pulled himself together since then, as Marshal Göring had just found out the hard way: indeed, on the afternoon of April 23, he had cabled Hitler from Berchtesgaden proposing to "assume henceforth the leadership of the Reich, with full powers inside and outside the country". Egged on by Martin Bormann, the Führer had immediately stripped Göring of all his offices, deprived him of his right to succession and ordered his arrest.[412] This explains why Himmler could still consider himself the only possible successor to the Führer – as reflected in his confidences to Minister Albert Speer: "I've already been in touch with various people I intend to bring into my cabinet. [. . .] Europe will not be able to manage without me in the future. It will continue to need me as minister of police, to maintain law and order. It'll take me no more than an hour to convince Eisenhower of that fact."[413]

Meanwhile, Hitler, leaning over a map of Berlin, had returned to his favourite exercises of theoretical strategy: General Busse's 9th Army – virtually surrounded after the Führer had ordered it to hold fast – was to move west and join Wenck's 12th Army in launching an offensive northwards to break the siege of Berlin. In the meantime, the capital itself would muster its forces to halt the advance of the hordes from the east: with 44,600 exhausted soldiers, a few tanks short of fuel, 42,500 elderly, untrained and poorly equipped volunteers from the Volkssturm, 2,700 adolescents from the Hitler Youth and a few hundred workers from Organisation Todt, it would keep in check the two million men of Marshals Zhukov, Koniev and Rokossovski, supported by inexhaustible reserves of tanks, planes and heavy artillery.

Three days later, Germany was admittedly cut in half, but Hitler, having anticipated such an eventuality, had already set up one military administration for northern Germany under Admiral

Dönitz,[xxi] and another for southern Germany under Marshal Kesselring.[xxii] As for the defence of Berlin, there could be one supreme commander only: the Führer himself. With the Red Army advancing cautiously towards the centre of the capital in ruins, Hitler was still pinning his hopes on a breakthrough by Wenck's 12th Army; advancing from the west, it was already reported to be in the vicinity of Potsdam, and Busse's 9th Army was once again ordered to disengage in the east and reinforce Wenck's offensive – while in the north, General Holste's forces were expected to blaze a path south and link up with Wenck's Army on the outskirts of Berlin.

And so it was that from the depths of his subterranean hideout, to the deafening sound of huge explosions that continually shook the bunker, amid clouds of concrete dust and suffocating odours of perspiration, tobacco,[xxiii] sulphur, diesel and clogged toilets, Hitler was still claiming that the encirclement of Berlin would be broken, and that the Soviets would suffer a historic defeat on the approaches to the capital of the Reich! The aviator Hanna Reitsch, who had managed to reach the bunker during the evening of April 26,[xxiv] described the beleaguered Führer in these terms: "All day long on April 27 and 28, he was mentally planning the tactics that Wenck might use to free Berlin. He would stride about the

xxi   With authority over northern Germany, the Netherlands, Denmark and Norway.
xxii   In command of southern Germany, Italy, Bohemia-Moravia and Hungary.
xxiii   The staff had begun to smoke at will in the bunker, as Hitler no longer paid attention.
xxiv   In the same plane as General Ritter von Greim, whom Hitler had just appointed commander-in-chief of the Luftwaffe to succeed Marshal Göring. Von Greim had been seriously wounded in the foot by Soviet anti-aircraft fire while flying over the city.

shelter, waving a roadmap that was fast disintegrating from the sweat of his hands, and planning Wenck's campaign with anyone who happened to be listening. When he became overly excited, he would snatch the map from where it lay, pace with a quick, nervous stride about the room, and loudly 'direct' the city's defence with armies that no longer existed. [. . .] The rest of the time, he sat stooped and crumpled at his table, moving buttons to represent his non-existent armies back and forth on a sweat-stained map."[414] Indeed a purely unreal exercise: Wenck's Army now comprised only three infantry divisions, without tanks or artillery; Busse's 9th Army, with thirteen severely battered divisions left, was now entirely surrounded west of the Oder, and no-one really knew the whereabouts of Holste's forces.

The news broke around 9 p.m. on the evening of April 28, when Heinz Lorenz, deputy head of the press service, entered the bunker with news from Reuters, broadcast by the B.B.C.: Reichsführer Heinrich Himmler had proposed to surrender to the Allies, who had refused.[xxv] The effect was devastating: "Hitler," recalled Hanna Reitsch, "raged like a madman. His colour rose to a heated red and his face was virtually unrecognisable. [. . .] After his lengthy outburst, Hitler sank into a stupor."[415] It was to be of short duration, for that night the Führer embarked on a frenzy of activity: just before midnight, he ordered Hermann Fegelein, Himmler's liaison agent, to be shot on the spot;[xxvi] at 1.30 in the morning on April 29,

xxv   This news was already being relayed by Swedish radio during the afternoon, but Hitler had refused to believe it.
xxvi   This rather sinister character, married to Eva Braun's sister, had been arrested the day before while trying to escape with his mistress. In the evening of April 28, an improvised court martial sentenced him to death for high treason: he was to pay for Himmler.

he went to see the newly appointed and badly wounded Marshal Ritter von Greim, whose mistress Hanna Reitsch recalled the scene in the following words: "Hitler, with a chalk-white face, [ . . . ] slumped down on the edge of the bed. [. . .] 'Every available plane,' he said, 'must be called up by daylight, therefore it is my order to you to return to Rechlin and muster your plans from there. It is the task of your aircraft to destroy the positions from which the Russians will launch their attack on the chancery. With Luftwaffe help, Wenck may get through. That is the first reason why you must leave the shelter. The second is that Himmler must be stopped.' And as soon as he mentioned the S.S. Führer, his voice became more unsteady and both his lips and hands trembled. The order to von Greim was that if Himmler had actually made the reported contact[xxvii] and could be found, he should immediately be arrested. 'A traitor must never succeed me as Führer! You must get out to ensure that he will not.'"[416] Ritter von Greim and Hanna Reitsch indeed managed to leave Berlin that night at the controls of an Arado 96 training aircraft – no mean feat in itself, considering Soviet air supremacy over the capital.

But for Hitler, the night was far from over; around 2.30 a.m., immediately after his perfunctory marriage to Eva Braun, the Führer dictated a "political testament" whereby he named as his successor Grand Admiral Dönitz[xxviii] in lieu of Hermann Göring, and then announced: "Before my death, I expel from the party and from all his offices the former Reichsführer S.S. and Reich Minister

xxvii   An interesting expression, which shows that in spite of everything, Hitler was not quite sure of the information – or still refused to believe it.
xxviii   And even formed his government for him, with Goebbels as Reich chancellor, Bormann as party minister and Seyss-Inquart as foreign minister.

of the Interior Heinrich Himmler" – this to be followed by an ultimate, stammering condemnation of his two former henchmen: "Göring and Himmler, by their secret negotiations with the enemy, without my knowledge or approval, and by their illegal attempts to seize power in the state, quite apart from their treachery to my person, have brought irreparable shame on the country and the whole people."[417]

All day long on April 29, Hitler prepared to take leave of this world; he put his affairs in order, sent three emissaries to deliver copies of his testament to Dönitz, Schörner[xxix] and the Brown House in Munich respectively,[xxx] burned his remaining papers, thanked his staff, chatted with a few officers who were about to attempt a breakout, gave instructions for the disposal of his body and had his dog Blondi poisoned. And yet, at 11 p.m., he was still sending the following message to the O.K.W's temporary headquarters in Dobbin:[xxxi] "To Chief O.K.W. Operations Staff, Colonel-General Jodl. 1. Where is Wenck's advance guard? 2. When will he arrive? 3. Where is 9th Army? 4. Where is Holste's Group? 5. When will he arrive?"[418] The reply was received in the bunker shortly after 3 a.m. on April 30: "Wenck's Army still engaged south of Schwielow Lake outside Potsdam and unable to continue its attack on Berlin. 9th Army encircled. Group Holste forced onto the defensive."[419]

Even Hitler had to face the evidence: there was no hope left. During the situation conference just before midday, Generals

---

xxix   Ferdinand Schörner, freshly promoted to marshal, was still fighting near Prague with remnants of his Army Group Centre.

xxx   None of the three men were to reach their destination.

xxxi   In Mecklenburg, near Rostock.

Weidling and Mohnke, commanders of Berlin and of "the Citadel", reckoned that the battle for Berlin would be over that evening. The Soviets had already occupied Alexanderplatz, Potsdamerstrasse and Wilhelmstrasse, and were only three hundred metres from the bunker. The time had come: shortly before 3.30 p.m., the Führer and his wife put an end to their lives. Three hours later, while their corpses were still burning in the chancery garden, Goebbels and Bormann cabled Admiral Dönitz that he had been appointed Hitler's successor; but that the Führer was no longer among the living was nowhere mentioned in the telegram.

Since taking leave of Wulff and Schellenberg at dawn on April 29, Himmler had resumed the tortuous course of his activities: repeated exhortations to hang all deserters and defeatists in order to placate the Führer; reduction of Werwolf activities so as to avoid provoking the Allies; offers of negotiations over Scandinavia in an effort to seduce them; gathering of all prisoners who could be used as bargaining chips with a view to securing his own future. But in the midst of this haphazard policy, one thing at least was left unchanged: despite Hitler's frenzied calls to order and the best efforts of Kaltenbrunner and "Gestapo Müller", the concentration camps were *not* being blown up and their hundreds of thousands of prisoners were still alive. Why was that? Because the Reichs-führer had not ordered it! And why had he not? Because he wanted to keep a promise once made to his "magic Buddha"? Because he had nothing to gain from it – not even the Führer's esteem, which he had forfeited two months earlier? Because it would not be the best way of opening negotiations with the Allies? Because he had other preoccupations – ensuring his own survival and safety to start with? There was probably some truth in all that, but the fact remained that between April 22 and April 30, Sachsenhausen, Flossenbürg, Dachau, Ravensbrück and hundreds of their satellite camps were abandoned "intact" to American, British and Soviet troops.

At this stage, Himmler was still holed up in the sprawling police barracks near Lübeck; as he had not been arrested, he assumed that Hitler was henceforth cut off from the outside world, unable to exercise his authority, or even already dead. The Reichsführer therefore got back to work forming his government,[xxxii] and also acted as informal adviser to Admiral Dönitz, based in Plön[xxxiii] and still in charge of military administration in northern Germany. The admiral, who remained entirely loyal to Hitler, needed a man with Himmler's stature and experience to maintain law and order in his sector and to ward off enemy attacks: after all, the Reichsführer was minister of the interior, head of the Gestapo, of the intelligence service, of thirty-eight S.S. divisions, of the reserve army and of the Feldgendarmerie; besides, pursuant to Marshal Göring's arrest six days earlier, no-one in military circles entertained the slightest doubt that Heinrich Himmler would be Hitler's successor. Hence the admiral's utter amazement when, in the late afternoon of April 30, 1945, he read the cable from the chancery informing him that he, Karl Dönitz, had been appointed the Führer's successor.

Dönitz had naturally been informed by Bormann and von Greim of the arrest order issued against Himmler, but in common with practically all German officers, he had not the slightest

xxxii   Among the many people approached were Speer, Seyss-Inquart, Dönitz and even Belgian Rexist Léon Degrelle – for the post of foreign minister!
xxxiii   Thirty-seven kilometres north-west of Lübeck.

confidence in Bormann, and the von Greim/Hanna Reitsch pair must have seemed to him more than a little hysterical; anyway, how could he go about arresting the Reichsführer? Dönitz's authority in northern Germany existed on paper only, the Wehrmacht was under the O.K.W.'s exclusive command, the Kriegsmarine had no police authority, and the police only answered to . . . Heinrich Himmler. Arresting the Reichsführer was therefore out of the question, but the admiral did have to inform him of the news he had just received. How would Himmler react? Late in the evening of April 30, Dönitz therefore called him on the telephone and requested that he come to Plön forthwith; as a precaution, the admiral hid a pistol with the safety catch off under a pile of papers on his desk . . .[420]

It was to remain unused; Himmler arrived at Plön around midnight – escorted by six S.S. officers armed to the teeth – and was taken to the admiral, who politely offered him a chair. "I handed Himmler the telegram announcing my appointment. 'Please read this,' I said. I watched him closely. As he read, an expression of astonishment, indeed of consternation, spread over his face. All hope seemed to have abandoned him. He turned very pale. Finally, he stood up and bowed. 'Allow me,' he said, 'to become the second man in your state.'"[421]

To Himmler, the offer seemed perfectly logical: Admiral Dönitz being politically inexperienced, he could not dispense with the backing of a seasoned politician, armed with all the apparatus of intelligence and policing necessary for governance. Yet Dönitz had sense enough to refuse the inclusion in his future government of such a compromising man as Heinrich Himmler – though he no doubt worded his refusal far more cautiously than he later claimed in his memoirs.[422] For all that, Schellenberg found the next morning a Reichsführer "who was in the worst possible mood. He was toying with the idea of resigning, and even spoke of suicide".[423] Late in the morning of May 1, shortly after Admiral Dönitz but six hours before the German people, they both learned of Hitler's death.[xxxiv]

What followed was brief and simple: with an uncertain legitimacy,[xxxv] a fragile power[xxxvi] and a government of individuals only marginally complicit in the crimes of the previous regime, Admiral Dönitz attempted the impossible: continue to resist militarily, while negotiating the terms of a surrender that would enable the evacuation of millions of Germans threatened by the advance of the Red Army. But after the fall of Berlin, with the British in Hamburg, the Soviets in Rostock and the Americans in Wittenberg, the areas under Dönitz's control were shrinking inexorably, and he was forced to move the seat of his government further north to Flensburg, close to the Danish border. Himmler himself had to evacuate his Lübeck headquarters in all haste, just a few hours before the arrival of British forces. On the road to Kiel, he met the Belgian Rexist chief Léon Degrelle under decidedly unceremonious circumstances – as Degrelle himself later recalled. "In the

xxxiv An initial and partially explicit radiogram was sent at 7.30 a.m. on May 1 and received in Plön at 10.53: "Testament is now in force." The second one, sent from the bunker that same day at 3.30 p.m. and signed Goebbels, specified: "The Führer died yesterday at 15.30."

xxxv Based on three radiograms, none of which was signed by the Führer; in fact, no-one at the time had seen the text of Hitler's political testament.

xxxvi The Wehrmacht had sworn loyalty to Hitler only, and its attitude since the disappearance of the Führer was difficult to ascertain. Himmler, on the other hand, still had an escort of 150 men and S.S. regiments stationed all over Schleswig-Holstein.

middle of the night of May 2, 1945, we were bogged down in the mud of a pitch-dark field; some five hundred metres ahead of us, a thousand Allied planes were finishing off Kiel. Everything was exploding into luminous debris like so many patches of molten metal, which by contrast made still darker the night in which we were cowering. '*Mein Lieber Degrelle*,' said Himmler, 'you must survive. Everything will change quickly. You must hold on for six months. Just another six months . . .' His small, beady eyes were scrutinising me from behind his spectacles, which glowed with each burst of explosions."[424] Even this late in the day, Himmler was still anticipating the confrontation between Soviets and Americans that would make him indispensable![xxxvii]

Walter Lüdde-Neurath, aide-de-camp to Admiral Dönitz, later wrote: "Himmler returned several times to our headquarters, for instance to take part in our discussions on the issue of occupied countries on May 3 and 4. On May 4, he still held the view that Norway and Bohemia were solid guarantees and valuable cards to play in the surrender negotiations. [. . .] He considered himself to be uniquely qualified to deal with Montgomery and Eisenhower. If he was to be believed, the latter expected no-one else but him. With his S.S., he represented an indispensable 'element of order in central Europe'. The conflict between east and west would deteriorate so rapidly that he and his S.S. would become the pivotal element within three months."[425]

During the evening of May 4, Admiral von Friedeburg, representing Dönitz, signed with Marshal Montgomery an act of partial surrender involving all German forces stationed in north-west

xxxvii   Once again under the influence of the Führer, who had been predicting such a confrontation for the last three months.

Germany, Denmark and the Netherlands. In Flensburg, meanwhile, the Reichsführer had become a largely unheeded and increasingly cumbersome adviser, until that day of May 6 when Admiral Dönitz officially relieved him of all his duties; and Himmler bowed out: with Hitler gone, his S.S. scattered, his police powerless, his saviour far away, his enemies quite close and the stars desperately silent, he felt drained of both resilience and willpower.

But Walter Schellenberg could still be of use; Count Schwerin von Krosigk, foreign minister in Admiral Dönitz's provisional government, sent him to Stockholm as minister plenipotentiary in order to negotiate the surrender of the German occupation army in Norway. He could thus fly to Stockholm at last and resume his relations with Count Bernadotte. But the negotiations proved difficult, for Schellenberg's authority was questioned by the Swedes, the British, the Norwegians and even by General Boehme, the commander of German troops in Norway. Finally, on May 7, Schellenberg was informed that General Jodl, dispatched to Reims by Admiral Dönitz, had signed that very morning the capitulation of all German forces; it was to take effect the next day at 11 p.m., and naturally included the Wehrmacht in Norway. "From then on," Schellenberg soberly concluded, "my services were no longer required."[426]

May 7, 1945 was a day of jubilation in Stockholm; after six terribly long years, the war in Europe was over at last. Felix Kersten, who had experienced it more closely than any Swede, was about to join in the popular celebrations, when shortly before midday, he received a telephone call; it was from Count Bernadotte, who informed him that Walter Schellenberg was a guest at his house and would like to see him. Kersten took a taxi to the count's estate, located on the exclusive island of Djurgården. Their reunion was more than cordial; at dawn on April 21, Kersten and Schellenberg had parted company after a historic gathering at Hartzwalde, and the storm had raged furiously over Germany during the following fortnight; yet it had finally delivered them both safe and sound to Swedish shores. The two men went out into the grounds of the estate for a chat, and Schellenberg, having updated Kersten on his most recent adventures, mentioned that Count Bernadotte had promised to help him settle in Sweden and protect him against any attempt by the Allies to have him extradited.[xxxviii] He then enquired about Kersten's plans for the future.

"I intend to remain in Sweden and practise medicine here. It's a nice country and I like it a lot."

Schellenberg remarked that after all Kersten had done for Sweden and for Holland, he should be welcome in both countries. After which he added:

"Would you be prepared to testify that during the war, I was always willing to help you conduct your humanitarian relief operations on behalf of Finland, Holland, Sweden, Norway, France, Belgium, Luxembourg among others, and that I always did so selflessly?"

To which Kersten replied without hesitation:

"I could always swear to that; your help and that of Brandt were invaluable to me in saving the seven Warsaw Swedes, and later on,

xxxviii  Apart from the fact that he had been head of the foreign intelligence service of an organisation deemed criminal by the Allies, Schellenberg had taken part in the Venlo affair in November 1939, when two British agents, Best and Stevens, were kidnapped and imprisoned in Germany.

343

you were of great assistance to me when Kaltenbrunner tried to obstruct the transfer of the 20,000 prisoners from the concentration camps. [. . .] Besides, I shall never forget that your letter of August 1944 saved my life when Kaltenbrunner set up an ambush for me on the road to Berlin."[427]

After reminiscing a little more about the perils they had braved together, Schellenberg asked Kersten if he would agree to treat him again, as his stomach pains had returned. The response being self-evident, the two men parted company on the best of terms, and on his way home, Kersten had to struggle through huge crowds celebrating the return to peace. For Schellenberg as for Kersten, this was a saga of dangers, rescues, courage and friendship that ended well – or so it seemed . . .

# 14

## DEFERRED GRATITUDE

In Stockholm, on May 8, 1945, Schellenberg went to Kersten's office at 8 Linnégatan to resume a long-interrupted treatment. To his therapist, who was also a tried and tested friend, he opened his heart: Count Bernadotte, he explained, had promised to help him settle in Sweden with his family, and to protect him against any request for extradition; the countess had even hinted at the possibility of taking him to the United States and presenting him to some influential people.[i] Kersten, whom life had robbed of many an illusion, asked him if he believed that all these promises were entirely disinterested, but Schellenberg hastened to reassure him:

"Actually, Bernadotte only wants me to confirm that he was the sole planner and implementer of the rescue operation in Germany."

Kersten: "This is no small requirement; besides, it would be a gross misrepresentation of the facts, for this rescue operation was the work of the Swedish state through Foreign Minister Christian Günther, with my support. Bernadotte played only an ancillary role in all this."

Schellenberg seemed embarrassed.

i Countess Bernadotte, née Estelle Manville, came from an extremely rich and influential American family; she was highly ambitious for her husband, and clearly eager to add fame to fortune.

"Yes, I'm aware of that. I was with you in this affair from the start, and I know that no-one could have seen it through had you not persuaded Himmler of the importance of cooperating with Christian Günther. Without your influence over Himmler, nothing could have been achieved. But I am in a difficult situation, Herr Kersten, and I can see no other way out."[428]

Thus, beggars cannot be choosers and necessity makes law . . . During the following day's treatment, Schellenberg also told Kersten that Bernadotte was about to write a book on the White Buses, to be published in about six weeks, since the count believed in "striking while the iron was hot". He, Schellenberg, would help in the writing and add his own testimony to bolster the credibility of Bernadotte's version of events. Kersten asked him if he was really well advised to support such a lie, since the truth would come out sooner or later, but Schellenberg reassured him: Bernadotte was a member of the royal family, he had excellent connections in Swedish society, and he "controlled" more than a few politicians and journalists; moreover, his wife was very wealthy and quite well connected too. He would be thanked and honoured world-wide for what he had done. Kersten inquired as to whether he had already written the testimony requested by Bernadotte.

"No, not yet; but think it over, Herr Kersten, and keep all this to yourself; it will be safer for you. It would be unwise to go against Count Bernadotte, as he could make life difficult for you. Even if you are a Finn, your situation in Sweden is not as secure as you might think. That is what Bernadotte told me, at any rate."[429]

In the meantime, Kersten had discovered that his patient's ailments were far from benign, and indeed, Schellenberg was complaining of severe abdominal pains when he returned the next day. Having been duly briefed by Count Bernadotte, however, he insisted on carrying out his mission and took up his plea: Kersten would be well advised to follow his example by acknowledging that Bernadotte had been the sole planner and executor of the rescue operation; this would spare him a lot of trouble in the future, as he could very well be expelled from Sweden. Kersten asked whether he was telling him all this at Bernadotte's behest, to which Schellenberg replied that this was the way he had understood things, so he was taking the liberty of giving him some sound advice. Having thanked him for his solicitude, Kersten nonetheless reiterated that the rescue operation had been undertaken by Christian Günther on behalf of the Swedish people, and that "it would be difficult to represent it as a private expedition carried out by the head of a transport organisation, even if his name happened to be Count Bernadotte." Though he was perfectly aware of that, Schellenberg preferred to view the issue from a different perspective: Kersten ought to keep in mind how precarious his situation was, and also consider that Bernadotte was an influential person, whose recommendations could be useful to him in obtaining new patients. To which Kersten responded with a laugh: "Don't worry about my future, dear Schellenberg; I trust that even in Sweden my work will be appreciated without any recommendation from Bernadotte."[430]

When Schellenberg returned the next morning, he was still bubbling with enthusiasm; Bernadotte had once more promised to look after his future and to put everything right. This he was in a position to do, for the British and the Americans were grateful to him and trusted him implicitly. Besides, his friends had already assured him that he would be awarded the Nobel Peace

Prize – preliminary moves to that effect were already afoot.[ii] "The higher Bernadotte rises," Schellenberg concluded, "the safer I will be."

That day, shortly before the end of the treatment, Count Bernadotte arrived to drive Schellenberg back to his estate. He began to stroll around the living room, peering at the pictures on the wall, then he said to Kersten:

"Herr Medicinalråd,[iii] these pictures were of course offered to you by Himmler, who had stolen them from Dutch museums."

Surprised at the remark, Kersten replied that he had never received anything of value from Himmler; then he added:

"I bought these pictures before the war – with my own money."

This was obviously not what the count wished to hear, and before taking his leave, he observed sarcastically:

"I wasn't aware that one could earn that much money in your profession!"[431]

A brief exchange that left Kersten with a disagreeable impression – and was but a portend of what was to come.

Schellenberg returned for further treatment on May 13; he no longer lived at the count's estate, but occupied a small flat in the Stockholm suburb of Saltsjö-Duvnäs – and was as confident as ever: the count and the countess had promised to take him with them to the United States in the autumn. Kersten, who had probably conferred with Minister Günther in the meantime, endeavoured to temper Schellenberg's enthusiasm: whatever Bernadotte

---

ii   An interesting statement – and quite probably the key to Bernadotte's past and subsequent behaviour.

iii   A Swedish version of the Finnish title Lääkintöneuvos and of the German Medizinalrat.

might have led him to expect, it was highly unlikely that the Americans would grant an entry visa to one of Himmler's closest collaborators, a member of a criminal organisation and head of an espionage service to boot. Imagining anything to the contrary would be extremely naive, and Schellenberg ought not to believe everything that Bernadotte told him.

There was wisdom in this warning, for on June 17, 1945, in spite of every promise and without having had time to pack his bags, the former Brigadeführer was hustled into a Dakota aircraft and delivered to Allied headquarters at Frankfurt am Main,[432] thence to be swiftly transferred to Great Britain. At Latchmere House in south-west London, he was interrogated without excessive courtesy and introduced to the rudimentary conditions of comfort offered by prisoner-of-war camp 020.[iv] Kersten was never to see him again, to the great regret of both the friend and the doctor – who had noted at the time: "His duodenum and gallbladder are in very poor condition;[433] he could develop a cancer if he is not treated regularly by me."[434] And unhappily for Walter Schellenberg, Dr Kersten's diagnoses were always disturbingly accurate.

Bernadotte's campaign plans were no less so: with the help of Schellenberg and of his ghostwriter Ragnar Svanström,[435] the count had been moving rapidly ahead, and on June 16, a mere five weeks after the end of the war in Europe, his book was published under the title *Slutet* (*The End*), with a subtitle as modest as it was succinct: *My humanitarian negotiations in Germany in the spring of 1945 and their political consequences.* An English translation

iv  Schellenberg apparently considered that he had been betrayed by Count Bernadotte, but that seasoned intelligence officer was betrayed above all by his own naivety in imagining that Sweden could refuse to deliver him to the Allies.

appeared simultaneously in Britain, entitled *The Curtain Falls*[v] – naturally accompanied by high-profile advertising and excerpts published in the *Daily Telegraph*. The book's contents largely reflected what Schellenberg's confidences to Kersten had foreshadowed: Bernadotte had been the sole organiser, negotiator and transporter of the White Bus operation that saved the lives of at least twenty thousand people. At the mission's planning stage, Ditleff's name was only mentioned cursorily, whereas Hillel Storch's had disappeared entirely.[vi] [436] As for the expedition itself, Gottfried Björk, who commanded the whole operation on the ground, did earn a mention, but not a word was to be found of Hans Arnoldsson, Sven Frykman, Harald Folke and Gerhard Rynberg, the four men who had led the convoys to the various concentration camps and displayed exceptional courage and diplomacy in having the prisoners handed over. Finally, with respect to the negotiations conducted in Germany, Ambassador Richert, Norbert Masur and Rudolf Brandt were simply erased from the picture, as was the man who had given the Swedes access to Himmler, persuaded the latter to receive Bernadotte and obtained from the Reichsführer nine-tenths of the concessions that the count was presently attributing to himself: the reader will doubtless have recognised Medizinalrat Felix Kersten. To be sure, had all these actors received their due, the reader in question might have wondered what the book's author had actually done.[vii] But a mere

v   With however a somewhat more discreet subtitle: *The last days of the Third Reich.*
vi   Swedish historian Sune Persson reckoned soberly that "Bernadotte clearly played a modest role during that phase". The other phases would doubtless have justified a similar observation . . .
vii   Apart from his representational role – the most valuable at this stage for Sweden in general and for the royal family in particular.

glance at the introduction would suffice to see Bernadotte reach fresh heights of duplicity: "It is with much hesitation that, after many requests, I have written an account of my experiences during my work in connection with the activity of the Swedish Red Cross in Germany during the last months of the Second World War. I have overcome my hesitation in the hope that what I have described may throw some light on the dramatic events at the time of the collapse of the Third Reich."[viii]

To publicise his exploits, the unassuming count had neglected absolutely nothing – not even potential contradictors: indeed, just two days before the publication, Kersten received a telephone call from Bernadotte, who warned him bluntly that he was to refrain from criticising the forthcoming book if he did not want to be expelled to Finland.[ix] Following that conversation, the count boasted to Schellenberg that he had dealt Kersten "a knock-out blow".[437] Felix Kersten was indeed devastated; his wife recalled that he was "beside himself" and felt "hounded like a wild animal".[438] In desperation, he appealed for support to Baron van Nagell, who promptly took things in hand: he obtained an assurance from Prime Minister Günther that extraditing Kersten was absolutely out of the question, then he made a personal call on Bernadotte. "I was only allowed to see him for five minutes in the Swedish Red Cross office, but that was enough. I reminded him straight away

viii    Folke Bernadotte, *The Curtain Falls,* Alfred A. Knopf, N.Y.,1945, p.5. *Sidste Akt,* Gyldendalske Boghandel, Copenhagen, 1945, is the Danish version of *Slutet,* in all respects consistent with the Swedish version. On the other hand, the English version diverges at times from the original, appears to have been hastily translated and is often unreliable. Thus "at five o'clock in the afternoon of February 19" becomes in the English version "at five o'clock in the afternoon of February 12" (p. 19).
ix    Under predominantly Soviet influence at the time.

that Dr Kersten had done all the work and that he [Bernadotte] had only been charged by the Swedish government with transporting the released prisoners to Sweden. [. . .] He told me that the activities of Dr Kersten were of no interest to Sweden, [. . .] but he recognised without demur that it was Dr Kersten who had saved all those people, and that he himself had only organised their transportation to Sweden.[x] He even admitted that, had Kersten not succeeded in obtaining the release of the concentration camp prisoners, the Red Cross buses would have returned empty to Sweden."[439] Baron van Nagell was later to give a more detailed account of Bernadotte's answer: "He finally admitted that the relief operation to which his name was attached actually consisted of two different actions, to wit: 1) The liberation of the prisoners held in the German detention camps, which Dr Kersten *alone* had obtained, and 2) His (Bernadotte's) transportation of the released prisoners, which naturally could not have taken place without the first action; but without his help, that first action would have been fruitless."[440]

But what was the value of a private verbal acknowledgement, compared to a deluge of advertising? In Sweden alone, 67,000 copies of *Slutet* were sold during the first ten days, and there were to be twenty reprints before the end of 1945. The book was translated into eighteen languages, and Bernadotte, crowned "Prince of Peace", became world famous. Over the next few months, he was made successively Commander and Grand-Cross of the Swedish

---

x   Even that was a generous estimate of his role in the affair, since the organiser of transportation on the ground was Colonel Gottfrid Björck. That any competent officer or diplomat could have done Bernadotte's work in Berlin, whereas none could have done Kersten's, probably did not escape Bernadotte at the time.

Order of the Northern Star, Grand-Cross of the Order of the Belgian Crown, Grand-Cross of the Polish Order Polonia Restituta, Commander of the American Legion of Merit, Grand-Cross of the Danish Order of Dannebrog, Grand-Officer of the French Legion of Honour, Knight Grand-Cross of the Dutch Order of Orange-Nassau, Commander First Class of the Norwegian Order of Saint Olaf, Grand-Cross of the Finnish Order of the White Rose, and he received a laudatory scroll from Stockholm's rabbi, "for having saved 10,000 Jews". He was showered with doctorates *Honoris Causa* from countless European and American universities, and received floods of tributes and presents from former Polish, Norwegian, Danish, Yugoslav, Dutch, Romanian, Belgian and French prisoners alike – all genuinely convinced that they owed him their liberation. On top of it all, he was appointed president of the Swedish Red Cross on January 1, 1946, thus succeeding his uncle Prince Carl Bernadotte to unanimous applause.

Felix Kersten, for one, was light years away from all that hulla-baloo; for months, he had been targeted by former Nazis,[xi] communists, social democrats[xii] and followers of Count Bernadotte. This unholy alliance produced a formidable barrage of disinformation aimed at utterly discrediting Kersten in the eyes of public opinion: here was Himmler's former doctor, who was not a Finn but a German; he was rumoured to have been seen in S.S. uniform

xi   Joseph Goebbels' agents of influence, with excellent connections in the Swedish media, had been instructed as early as 1943 to denounce Kersten – whom Goebbels considered Himmler's man in Sweden. After the defeat of the Reich, these agents of influence had apparently recycled themselves by changing sponsors – while keeping certain habits.

xii   The communists were still holding Kersten's participation in anti-Bolshevik operations against him twenty-six years after the event; and after 1945, the Swedish social democrats were largely under communist influence.

during the war; his Hartzwalde estate had been given to him by the Reichsführer; his rescue missions had made him a rich man; he owned paintings by Dutch masters that had been stolen from Dutch museums between 1941 and 1942. And the list of his supposed infamies did not stop at that: he had also "been called to Berchtesgaden in order to knead the Führer's body";[441] he was a quack with a fake doctor's degree who practised medicine illegally; the Nuremberg archives held incriminating documents on him; Marshal Göring[xiii] had given him some land to extend his estate, and so on.[442] It was of course difficult for any man to defend himself against such absurd allegations, relayed as they were by a noisy press campaign and often accepted uncritically by people who should have known better; thus Sven Grafström, deputy director of the political section in the Swedish foreign ministry, made the following entry in his diary: "I consider Kersten to be a war criminal, no more, no less"[443] – not to mention His Majesty's Ambassador Sir Victor Mallet, who wrote in a report to the Foreign Office: "Kersten is known to me as a Nazi and a thoroughly bad man."[444] Whence that knowledge came he failed to disclose.

For Kersten, this was all the more disastrous as in January 1945, he and his family had applied for Swedish citizenship, and they had still received no reply. Kersten could therefore be expelled, just as Count Bernadotte had threatened – the latter indeed using all his influence to ensure that the application for citizenship was rejected.[xiv][445] It is easy to understand the count's logic – though not necessarily his morality: once a Swedish citizen, Kersten would

xiii   Whom Kersten had never met.
xiv   Which appears clearly in a letter from the Dutch ambassador in Helsinki to his foreign minister dated October 18, 1948.

surely have no compunction in denouncing the deception behind his best-seller *Slutet*, and *The Curtain Falls* would then take on a very different meaning . . . Folke Bernadotte could naturally count on the unmitigated support of his uncle the king, even though Kersten had previously obtained the release of various people featured on a certain royal list.[xv] But what could past services weigh, compared to the present interests of King Gustav V's kingdom – and to the future glory of his nephew?

For all that, there remained Christian Günther, on whose service Kersten had worked with such zeal since 1943; could not the minister intercede on behalf of his former agent? Actually, he had already done so on several occasions,[xvi] [446] but he no longer exerted much influence; for in July 1945, the coalition government in which Günther was foreign minister had fallen from power and been replaced by an exclusively social democrat government, whose foreign minister was former Rector Östen Undén. The latter proceeded to make a clean sweep of his ministry: Günther was appointed ambassador to Rome, Boheman was sent to Paris and von Post to Ankara, while Ambassador Richert was relegated to the Stockholm Chamber of Commerce. In fact, Undén, who belonged to the left wing of the Social Democrat Party, claimed that the Soviet Union had "a rule of law", often spoke of the "so-called free world" and wanted above all to establish privileged ties with the Soviet comrades. Within the framework of a rather subservient

xv  See above, pp. 250 and 259.
xvi  For instance with this letter to Gösta Engzell, dated November 4, 1948: "There can be no doubt that Kersten accomplished an absolutely incredible mission by saving so many people from the Nazi exterminators. [. . .] Besides, it can be said without any exaggeration that it is thanks to his intervention only that the great rescue mission headed by Bernadotte could be implemented."

foreign policy, he even refused to demand from Moscow the release of Raoul Wallenberg, hero of Budapest and member of one of the most distinguished families in Sweden.[xvii] It was therefore not hard to imagine the new foreign minister's eagerness to have this inconvenient Finnish therapist extradited, should the Soviets demand it; but as luck would have it, Stalin, who was very busy elsewhere, displayed not the slightest interest in Felix Kersten. Which is probably why the head of Dutch intelligence in Sweden, F.Th. Dijkmeester, could write to his headquarters on November 22, 1945: "Kersten's presence in Stockholm is tolerated, at least as long as he keeps a low profile."[447] The meaning could not be clearer.

To seek safe haven in Finland was not an option either, for ever since the September 1944 armistice, the country was largely kept in check by a "control commission" dominated by the Soviets,[xviii] and the new Finnish "strongmen" – Prime Minister Paasikivi, Justice Minister Kekkonen and (communist) Interior Minister Leino – had no choice but to conduct an essentially pro-Soviet policy. Of the Finnish statesmen with whom Kersten had worked so diligently during the war, Foreign Minister Witting had died, whereas, at Soviet insistence, President Ryti, Prime Minister Rangell and Ambassador Kivimäki had been put on trial, charged with "crimes against the peace", convicted and sentenced to several years in prison. Should Felix Kersten return to Finland, he would certainly have been treated likewise – if not worse . . .

xvii    He even went further, by denouncing members of the Wallenberg family who had publicly declared that the Soviets were lying when they asserted that they did not know the whereabouts of the young diplomat.
xviii   Headed by Stalin's henchman – and future organiser of the Kominform – Andrei Zhdanov.

But then, if Kersten was held in such low esteem in Sweden and considered *persona non grata* in Finland, why did he not settle in the Netherlands, as had been his dream all through the war? The answer is simple: his reputation there was worse even than in Sweden, and his life would have been at risk. Indeed, the Dutch were convinced that Felix Kersten, who had been welcomed in Holland for twelve years, had gone on to betray them during the war by collaborating with the Moffen:[xix] had he not been seen around the country in company with Himmler, Rauter, Mussert and Seyss-Inquart? Had he not joined in their banquets and confabulations? How was it that such a man had not yet been shot like Mussert, or "suicided" like Rost van Tonningen?[xx] Of course, they had no way of knowing that each one of Kersten's visits was followed by the release of scores of prisoners – who themselves had no idea who their saviour was, as Professor Gerke and diplomat Herman van Roijen were later to testify: their gaolers had not taken the trouble to explain the reasons for their release – which they could not know anyway; they had simply told the prisoners to pack their belongings, clear off and make themselves inconspicuous. As for Kersten's agents among the collaborationists and the enemy forces, such as Schijf and Nieuwenhuis, to whom so many members of the Dutch underground owed their lives, they were still being prosecuted: had they not been members of the hated N.S.B.? In all the newly liberated countries of Europe, countless anonymous heroes were struggling against the same infernal

xix   A derogatory nickname for Germans, akin to the French "Boches", the American "Krauts" and the British "Jerries".

xx   Who had jumped from the second floor of Scheveningen prison on June 6, 1945. Many Dutchmen at the time believed that he had in fact been pushed because he knew too much.

spiral; such was the case of the Belgian resistance fighter Hélène Moszkiewiez, who had infiltrated the Gestapo and was very nearly lynched after the liberation of Brussels, or of the Swedish-Norwegian actress and double agent Sonja Wigert, who was only rehabilitated twenty-five years after her death. As for Felix Kersten, Dutch Ambassador van Nagell wrote this to a friend: "I have warned him several times *not* to go to Holland unless invited to do so. [. . .] He must be 'cleansed'[xxi] first."[448]

Such was the exact intent of Maurits de Beaufort, one of the very few Dutchmen who knew what Kersten had been doing during the war – and who, as a distinguished figure of the underground movement, had every right to be heard. In early 1946, de Beaufort, knowing that Crown Princess Juliana was to visit Stockholm in the spring, sent to her secretary twenty-nine pages of documents, all translated into Dutch, to acquaint her with the activities of Kersten on behalf of Holland during the war.[449] His efforts were less than successful: neither the secretary nor the princess had any time to read the documents; thus, when the latter eventually decorated 193 individuals at the Grand Hotel in Stockholm on April 9, 1946, Felix Kersten, after witnessing the solemn presentation of the Grand-Cross of the Order of Orange-Nassau to Count Bernadotte, had to be content with the medal of the Red Cross in silver – which he had already received from Prince Hendrick twelve years earlier! For the princely family of the Netherlands, it was a simple case of oversight; for Swedish high society, it was the scathing disavowal of a controversial figure; but for Kersten, it was, in his own words, "a virtual death sentence".[450]

A severely depressed and frustrated Kersten had to cope

xxi  "*Gezuiverd.*"

simultaneously with serious financial problems; he had a family to support, costly rent to pay and precious few Swedish patients to take care of. He asked the authorities to reimburse his travel expenses to and from Germany on behalf of the Swedish foreign ministry, which was the very least they could do for their wartime emissary at Himmler's headquarters; and yet, since Tage Erlander's social democrat government did not recognise the secret obligations contracted by its predecessor, Kersten's request was simply turned down. After that, he undertook to write his memoirs, on the basis of the hastily scribbled notes he had brought back from Germany.[451] The result was a Swedish-language version, *Samtal med Himmler* (*Dialogue with Himmler*), published in 1947,[xxii] and a Dutch version, *Klerk en Beul* (*Clerk and Henchman*), published in Amsterdam a year later; though by no means contradictory, these two versions were often confused, occasionally whimsical,[xxiii] [452] but always fascinating and remarkably documented. For all that, they met with little success in either Sweden or Holland.

For this rather exceptional saviour and survivor, the war was not a completely closed case; reading the press, he learned the fate of some of the worst actors in the drama he had just witnessed:

xxii    There was also an early American edition, *The Memoirs of Felix Kersten*, New York, 1947, ghostwritten by Herma Briffault, with many mistakes and a sensationalist style that was swiftly disavowed by Kersten himself.
xxiii   Particularly when dealing with the 1941 plan for the deportation of the entire Dutch population, which Kersten supposedly persuaded Himmler to abandon. The aim of that historical forgery was obviously to ingratiate himself with the Dutch authorities – although the real services he had rendered ought to have been more than enough for that purpose. On the other hand, Kersten failed to mention some of his proven and documented exploits, such as his April 7, 1945 call to Himmler that saved the Bergen-Belsen concentration camp – hence the above-mentioned confusion in the narratives.

the capture and suicide of Heinrich Himmler,[xxiv] the hanging of
Kaltenbrunner, Ribbentrop and Seyss-Inquart, the disappearance
of "Gestapo Müller",[xxv] the suicide of Glücks, the arrest of Pohl and
the endless trial of Rauter.[xxvi] But as some of his wartime friends,
acolytes and agents were also held accountable in court, Kersten set
out to help them; he thus testified in favour of Nieuwenhuis, Flick
and Gottlob Berger – whom he probably saved from the gallows
by evoking his refusal to shoot five thousand Allied airmen.[453]
Admittedly, some of his other intercessions were more difficult
to comprehend, such as those in favour of General Friedrich Chris-
tiansen, former Wehrmacht commander-in-chief for Holland, of
military doctor van Nieuwenhuyzen and of Petrus Hamer, former
police commissioner for The Hague – all three having unquestion-
ably been complicit in war crimes. But Kersten also campaigned
energetically in support of Rudolf Brandt, one of the accused in
the 1947 "Doctors' Trial",[454] and he even appealed to President
Truman to grant him a reprieve[455] – all in vain, for the little secretary, without whose help Kersten could have achieved nothing at
all, was hanged in Landsberg prison in June 1948: his signature
appeared at the bottom of some of the most compromising documents dictated by the Reichsführer.[xxvii]

Three months later, Kersten learned of the disappearance of yet
another player in one of the greatest tragedies in history: after the
phenomenal success of *The Curtain Falls* and the glorification of

xxiv   Arrested by the British near Luneburg on May 22, 1945, he swallowed a
cyanide capsule the next day, after having been identified.
xxv   Who was never found.
xxvi   Who was finally shot at Scheveningen in March 1949.
xxvii   Particularly concerning medical experiments conducted in concentration
camps.

its author, Folke Bernadotte was named United Nations mediator for Palestine. Hardly had the state of Israel proclaimed its independence than it was confronted with a coalition of Egyptian, Syrian, Iraqi and Transjordan military forces; Bernadotte, who had landed in Cairo on May 25, 1948, succeeded in getting the belligerents to accept a truce, and all summer, he conducted heated negotiations with the parties involved, in order to reach a comprehensive settlement of the conflict. But on September 17, 1948, the count was assassinated in Jerusalem by Jewish extremists belonging to the "Stern Gang" – a crime that Prime Minister Ben Gurion denounced before the Knesset as "the work of gangsters".[xxviii] As a result of this wanton murder,[xxix] the "Prince of Peace" was raised to the status of "Martyr of Humanity", and merely three months after his death, British journalist Ralph Hewins wrote in an impassioned hagiography that "Folke Bernadotte came about as near to being a saint as an ordinary human being can", and went on to add that "it is characteristic of Bernadotte's generosity that [. . .] he never stole another's credit"[456] – surely the one virtue to avoid mentioning when paying tribute to the immortal author of *The Curtain Falls*!

After that, friends and followers of the count, nostalgics for the Third Reich and left-wingers of all hues redoubled efforts to make life difficult for Felix Kersten – who still failed to obtain Swedish nationality. But the most unexpected being usually the most sure to happen, it was from Holland that finally came the first signs of salvation: in late 1947, Professor Posthumus, member of the Dutch

xxviii   Later qualifying the Lehi or Stern Gang as "a terrorist organisation" and announcing its dissolution.
xxix   It was triply useless: the settlement plan was far from complete, the state of Israel had already announced that it would not be bound by it, and under its own charter the United Nations had no means of imposing it.

Academy of Sciences and founder of the new Nederlands Instituut voor Oorlogsdokumentatie,[xxx] examining *ex officio* the case of "Nazi collaborator" Felix Kersten, sensed that something was not quite right in the whole affair; he shared his doubts with Prime Minister Willem Drees, who asked him for a preliminary report on the case, and also instructed him to set up a special commission to enquire into the facts of Kersten's role during the war.[xxxi] At that time, the Dutch parliament itself was establishing a commission of inquiry into the wartime efforts of the royal government and its agents to assist and rescue Dutch nationals in occupied Netherlands and in German prisons; this would perforce involve the commission in scrutinising Kersten's case as well.

Professor Posthumus, for one, took his mission quite seriously;[xxxii] he travelled to Sweden, Finland and Germany, and visited Nuremberg jail to interview Brandt, Berger, Schellenberg,[xxxiii] [457] Ohlendorf and even Harster – Rauter's right-hand man, who was still furious with the "confounded Finnish doctor" for having snatched so many prisoners from him.[458] The professor also contacted former members of the Dutch, Norwegian, Belgian and Danish resistance movements, as well as Swedish representatives of the World Jewish Congress, who had just certified that "Kersten

xxx    Netherlands Institute for War Documentation.

xxxi    It was to include three members: the former secretary-general of the Dutch foreign ministry, Snouck-Hurgronje (president), the first secretary of the Dutch embassy in Paris, van Schelle, and Professor Rüter of Leiden University.

xxxii    Something of a wartime hero himself, Posthumus had placed Jewish children among Dutch families for safety during the occupation. He was much later recognised as a "Righteous among the Nations".

xxxiii    Who described Kersten as "an excellent psychologist" and peerless therapist, adding with a touch of nostalgia: "We often cooperated, Kersten and I. When one of us was in trouble, the other rushed to the rescue."

saved some 100,000 people of various nationalities, including about 60,000 Jews [. . .] at the risk of his life. [. . .] He also succeeded in getting Himmler to agree to the expedition of food parcels to the Jews in the concentration camps, which saved numerous lives. [. . .] Kersten never refused us his help, whatever the difficulties of the situation."[459] In October 1948, the highly scrupulous Posthumus went as far as to submit a sample of Kersten's handwriting to a Dutch "psycho-graphologist" by the name of Rose Raake, whose expertise on the profile of a man only known to her as "*Heer X*" was to prove most informative: "At the moment of writing these lines, the author feels very depressed, as if the ground were slipping away from under his feet. [. . .] There is something subtle in him, almost feminine. It is this dedication, this natural impulse to give of himself, to help others, to reach out in order to assist, that gives such an impression of femininity."[460] Though hardly compatible with the present American ramblings known as gender studies, this assessment may well reconcile more than one reader to graphology.

Be that as it may, Posthumus duly delivered his preliminary report to Prime Minister Drees on September 2, 1948. This extensive document retraced Kersten's past relations with Himmler, Schellenberg and Brandt, but also went into his dealings with Günther, Bernadotte,[xxxiv] Knulst and Ambassador van Rechteren Limpurg. Its conclusion: "The accomplishments of Dr Kersten deserve our admiration. In the midst of an increasingly terrifying environment, Kersten tirelessly sought the triumph of humanitarianism"; and after having recalled all the services he had rendered

xxxiv   With this interesting observation on p. 14: "Bernadotte, it could be said without excessive amiability, was the errand boy of Felix Kersten – a man unknown to Bernadotte in his book."

M e m o r a n d u m

rörande Medicinalrådet Felix Kersten.

Undertecknad World Jewish Congress får härmed göra följande uttalande rörande Medicinalrådet Felix Kerstens insatser vid räddningen av judar m.fl. ur de tyska koncentrationslägren m.m.

1) Kersten har oegennyttigt ställt sig till förfogande vid våra strävanden att rädda i de tyska koncentrationslägren internerade judar. Sålunda har genom Kerstens bemödanden under de gångna krigsåren 3.500 judar frigivits och kunnat överföras till Sverige.

2) Den tyske riksledaren Hitler hade befallt, att de tyska koncentrations-lägren skulle sprängas i luften med samtliga fångar och vaktpersonal, då de allierade trupperna närmade sig. Vi vädjade till Kersten att söka förhindra detta. Med användande av sitt inflytande över riksledare Himmler, som skulle verkställt ordern, lyckades Kersten övertyga Himmler om, att icke utföra denna ohyggliga order. Härigenom räddades 100.000-tals människor av olika nationaliteter, däribland omkring 60.000 judar. Vi veta vidare, att det lyckades Kersten hos Himmler genomdriva att de i koncentrationslägren befintliga judarna icke vidare finge skjutas; utan skulle behandlas lika med andra fångar, detta med undantag för ett visst mindre antal judar vilka på order av Kaltenbrunner blevo deporterade.

3) Med fara för eget liv har Kersten lyckats rädda otaliga medborgare i Sverige, Danmark, Norge, Österrike, Frankrike, Holland och Belgien.

4) Kersten har utverkat av Himmler tillstånd att skicka livsmedelspaket till judarna i koncentrationslägren, som har räddat många människors liv.

5) Slutligen vilja vi nämna, att Kersten aldrig har vägrat oss sin hjälp huru svår situation än varit och hans räddningsinsatser ha varit av mycket stor betydelse i de svåraste tider av lidande i vår historia.

Stockholm, den 18 juni 1947.

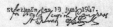

*Memorandum from the Swedish representatives of the World Jewish Congress*

to Holland – from obtaining the release of resistance fighters to saving the district of Clingendael – the report concluded soberly: "Our government and people are highly indebted to him."[461]

A week later, Posthumus forwarded his report to the Parliamentary Inquiry Commission, whose hearings had already begun. One of the first people called to testify was Baron van Nagell, who described his first encounter with Felix Kersten in the following terms: "He struck us as a curious character who wanted to help everybody and get people out of concentration camps. [. . .] Lieutenant Knulst made enquiries about him with the Secret Service, as well as with the French and the Americans, [. . .] and he ended up by telling me that Kersten was neither a Nazi nor a spy, that he was absolutely dependable and could be used to save people."[462]

But the Parliamentary Commission was interested above all in the wartime activities of Dutch diplomats and civil servants when it called upon Kersten himself to testify on September 15, 1948; indeed, the members of the sub-committee specifically wanted to know why their Stockholm embassy had been unable to supply him with full lists of Dutch prisoners to be released, or to send food parcels to all the others. Kersten began by confirming that Lieutenant Knulst could only give him ninety-four names, and had told him, after enquiring with the embassy, that it was impossible to send food parcels.

*The president*: "And he didn't say why?"

*Mr Kersten:* "He told me that they had no money [. . .]."

*Mr Hoogcarspel:* "But in London, there would necessarily have been money available for such purpose."

*Mr Kersten:* "Of course, it wasn't all that expensive. [. . .] A food parcel for the Jews cost from thirty to forty crowns."

*The president:* "It is therefore your opinion that the Dutch could perfectly well have sent food parcels?"

*Mr Kersten:* "Yes, and that is what I wanted them to do."

*The president:* "And you believe that more people could have been released, had their addresses been available? Besides, was it possible to send these parcels to Dutch prisoners without having their names?"[xxxv]

*Mr Kersten:* "Yes, this was done for the Jews,[xxxvi] and it could just as easily have been done for the Dutch. If you bear in mind that for the Nazis, the greatest enemies were the Jews, and that nonetheless Himmler agreed to have them sent food parcels, it stands to reason that he would have done the same for the Dutch."

*The president:* "You mean that since he had agreed to let the Jews receive parcels, even without their names being indicated, he would have done likewise for the Dutch?"

*Mr Kersten:* "That goes without saying; he had given the same permission for the Norwegian and the Danes."

*The president:* "With or without names?"

*Mr Kersten:* "With and without names."

*Mr Hoogcarspel:* "In the Jews' case, it would seem that Himmler had given his agreement on April 19, 1945, whereas for the Norwegian and Danes, he had given it earlier. Therefore, in the case of the Dutch, this could also have been organised much earlier."

---

xxxv  The whole session was dealing with two different but related matters: the addresses of prisoners to be released and the names of prisoners who could receive food parcels.

xxxvi  The efforts of the Swedish Red Cross had been considerable in delivering these parcels, but they had been paid for through a subscription opened by a relief committee of three (Storch, Spivak and Lapidus), independently of the World Jewish Congress. In all, 70,000 parcels weighing 3 kilograms each had been sent.

*Mr Kersten:* "Of course, but we are talking specifically of April 19; most of the people in the concentration camps died towards the end of April, and the parcels for the Jews arrived just in time. Before that, it was not as important. Of course, it was still important and necessary, but less so than in April." [xxxvii] [463]

The president then asked Kersten if he had concerned himself with the ulterior fate of the people whose release he had secured.

*Mr Kersten:* "No, once they were in Sweden, it was no longer my concern."

Which led quite naturally to the role played by Count Bernadotte[xxxviii] in the whole affair.

*The president:* "So you asked Himmler to receive Bernadotte?"

*Mr Kersten:* "Yes, I asked Himmler to receive him courteously, and to grant him everything that we had agreed upon together."

*The president:* "But could not Bernadotte have got in touch with Himmler by other means? Through the Swedish embassy, for instance?"

*Mr Kersten:* "No foreign ambassador ever spoke to Himmler. He was a very secluded person in Germany."

*The president:* "Why was that?"

*Mr Kersten:* "He was withdrawn by nature, he was afraid of people. [. . .] He wanted above all to remain inconspicuous."

*The president:* "Therefore, Bernadotte could never have got in touch with him without your help?"

*Mr Kersten:* "No, that was not possible."[464]

However, this was by no means the main concern of the members of the commission of inquiry; hearing after hearing, they had

xxxvii  Because the camps were no longer supplied by that time.
xxxviii  Who had only forty-eight hours left to live at the time of that hearing.

begun to suspect that a certain degree of nonchalance – if not negligence – had prevailed within the ranks of their diplomats in Stockholm during the war: lists with names and addresses of Dutch prisoners that had disappeared somewhere between London and Stockholm, food parcels that could have been sent but were not sent, a Finnish doctor with excellent connections in both German and Swedish circles whose services had been declined. All this seriously disturbed the honourable members of parliament, and on August 19, 1949, Count Willem Constantijn van Rechteren Limpurg, former Dutch ambassador to Sweden, was called before the commission.

*The president:* "The lists to which I am referring contained the names of thousands of concentration camp prisoners, and they were addressed to you. What we would like to know at present is: did you receive them or not?"

*Mr Stokvis:* "At any rate, it would seem that this matter did not make a sufficient impression on you for you to keep it in mind."

Such was the conclusion of a rather gruelling cross-examination about the issue of food parcels and lists of prisoners. Hailing from the oldest Batavian nobility and lavishly decorated, Count van Rechteren Limpurg was clearly unaccustomed to such arraignments and felt somewhat destabilised; but worse was to come.

*The president:* "I would like you to tell us what grudge you had – or possibly still have – against Dr Kersten."

*Mr van Rechteren Limpurg:* "I only met Kersten once, and I do not quite recall what we talked about. The encounter was very brief. [...] The fact that he was Himmler's doctor made us cautious. [...]"

*The president:* "You did know all along that he was working with the Swedish authorities in order to have people released?"

*Mr van Rechteren Limpurg:* "Yes."

*The president:* "And in spite of that, you didn't want to cooperate with him. Why didn't you, since the Swedes were doing it and there was a chance that it might save thousands of Dutchmen? [. . .] What were your reasons? That question has been troubling us for years. [. . .]"

*Mr Stokvis:* "So you saw him once, and on that occasion Kersten told you to check up on him with Minister Günther. Did you do so?"

*Mr van Rechteren Limpurg:* "He said that?"

*Mr Stokvis:* "Yes, he said it under oath. Did you or did you not consult Minister Günther to enquire about him? Yes or no?"

*The president:* "Should it not seem obvious to you that even if Heer Kersten had not told you to do so, you had to seek information from Günther, given that thousands of Dutch lives were at stake?"

*Mr van Rechteren Limpurg:* "Of course, one could not know what degree of power he wielded; one could only surmise."

*The president:* "That should have been one more reason to go and enquire with Heer Günther, to ask him what he thought of Kersten. I believe that this is what you did not do."

*Mr van Rechteren Limpurg:* "I do not recall having talked about it with Minister Günther. [. . .]"

*Mr Stokvis:* "Did this whole matter hold all your attention at the time?"

*Mr van Rechteren Limpurg:* "Yes, of course it did."

*Mr Stokvis:* "This could hardly be deduced from the information you are providing us at present."[465]

The hearings were to go on for another two years, but on January 12, 1950, after eleven months of inquiry, the commission set up by Professor Posthumus[xxxix] delivered its report to the prime minister, the foreign minister and the members of parliament. In seven solidly argued and thoroughly documented points,[xl] its three authors entirely refuted the accusations aimed against Kersten and proceeded to confirm most of his past undertakings on behalf of the Netherlands: the release of numerous Dutch nationals arrested for acts of resistance; the lifting of the ban on the unloading in Dutch harbours of Swedish ships bearing food during the famine of the winter 1944–45; the conveyance to Stockholm of important messages from the Dutch resistance to be forwarded to the government in exile in London; the liberation of Dutch women detained in Ravensbrück concentration camp; the rescue of 2,700 Jews transferred to Switzerland, that of 3,700 Jews transported to Sweden and that of 63,000 other Jews saved from annihilation "among whom there were necessarily a great number of Dutchmen"; the non-implementation by Himmler of the Führer's order to blow up the concentration camps with all their prisoners – Dutch included – on the approach of the Allies; the counterorder obtained from Himmler concerning the destruction of Clingendael and the dynamiting of the dykes around The Hague.[466] To back their contention, the authors of the report invoked "trustworthy testimonies", "authentic documents" and

xxxix  See above, p. 362.

xl  The authors of the report had collected testimonies and evidence from most of the people encountered during this narrative: Ramsay, Ryti, Kivimäki, Günther, Richert, Engzell, von Post, Steltzer, Seip, Harster, Brandt, Schellenberg, Berger, Storch, Masur, de Beaufort, Nieuwenhuis, Schijf, Knulst, van Nagell, Posthumus, Roëll and many others.

"overabundant evidence".[467] As concerns some other facts adduced, such as preventing the deportation eastwards of the entire Dutch population in 1941, the commission was more reserved, noting with both caution and diplomacy that "it is impossible to prove that such plans would indeed have been implemented had Heer Kersten not intervened".[468]

But with that report, the case was settled: on August 17, 1950, to the amazement of all the Dutch who had not followed these three years of discreet enquiries and closed hearings, Prince Bernhard, the husband of Queen Juliana, solemnly awarded Felix Kersten the Cross of Grand Officer of the Order of Orange-Nassau,[xli] a reparation as belated as it was deserved. And the prince declared on that occasion: "It is difficult to find words to thank you for all you have done for the Netherlands."[469]

xli   It was admittedly one rank below that of the Knight Grand-Cross awarded to Count Bernadotte – perhaps to avoid upsetting the Swedes . . .

# 15

# EARLY DEPARTURE

Felix Kersten was not one to disdain honours, but he had another priority – the same as before: obtaining Swedish citizenship for himself and his family. He had been living in Stockholm with his wife and children for the last five years, the faithful Elizabeth Lüben also resided there, and Kersten had acquired a small estate south-east of the capital: Stensäter, near Strängnäs. In Sweden as in the Netherlands, there were a few individuals who had every reason to know him and were more than willing to defend his interests; among them were Baron von Nagell, Hillel Storch, Norbert Masur, Ottokar van Knierem, Maurits de Beaufort, Christian Günther, Arvid Richert, Jacob Wallenberg and Nicolaas Posthumus. On November 24, 1950, the latter even wrote a letter to Swedish foreign minister Östen Undén, informing him of the conclusions reached by the three-man commission of inquiry after two years of research – which, in a nutshell, were that Medizinalrat Kersten had proved to be "a saviour of men and a benefactor of great magnitude"; the research, Posthumus added, had also disproved every accusation levelled against Kersten, and had established that, far from profiteering from his rescue work, he had used the greater part of his personal fortune to accomplish his missions. The professor ended his letter by mentioning that Kersten had recently been made Grand Officer of the Order of Orange-Nassau.[470] But when ideology coincided with national interest, even the Swedes' legendary sense of justice and fair play had to give way: Östen Undén did not even bother to acknowledge receipt of the letter. Undaunted, Professor Posthumus pursued his crusade on Kersten's behalf: in 1951, he even proposed him for the Nobel Peace Prize – and continued to do so for the next seven years.

In the meantime, after undergoing three months of "debriefing" at 020 Interrogation Centre near London, Schellenberg was flown back to Nuremberg, where he was first called to appear as a witness for the prosecution at the Kaltenbrunner trial. His own turn came in early 1947, when he appeared in court with twenty co-defendants at the so-called "Wilhelmstrasse trial". Thanks to numerous testimonies and affidavits in his favour produced by Bernadotte, by the head of the Swiss intelligence service Henri Masson and his compatriot Jean-Marie Musy, by French General Giraud and by Rabbi Isaac Sternbuch,[471] he was condemned on April 14, 1949 to only six years' imprisonment. The sentence was the more lenient since it ran from June 17, 1945, and, even then, he was not to serve it out in full: since 1947, the state of his health had considerably deteriorated, and during the trial, he had spent most of his time at Nuremberg General Hospital; when sentenced, in fact, he had just undergone a major operation to remove a cancerous growth on his gallbladder. On account of this, he was granted a medical pardon by American High Commissioner for Germany John J. McCloy on March 27, 1950 – which at least allowed him to change hospitals, then to stay in Switzerland for specialist consultations. Schellenberg thereafter settled in

Torino, where he died following a second operation on March 31, 1952.[i]

Kersten only learned of his death six months later, and was deeply affected by it.[472] It is not known why he had not been contacted by Schellenberg's lawyers, or called upon to treat him – which would probably have been more useful.[ii] But in the spring of 1952, Kersten was entirely absorbed by his application for citizenship, soon to be examined by the Swedish authorities. After five years of research and hearings, the Dutch parliamentary commission had just released a 512-page report that was decidedly favourable to Kersten, merciless to Count van Rechteren Limpurg and fairly embarrassing to the Swedish authorities.[473] Kersten could thus hope that its publication would have a positive influence on those who were to decide his fate – the more so as some Swedish diplomats remembered him quite well; thus Gösta Engzell, former head of the foreign ministry's juridical section, wrote from Warsaw in reply to an enquiry: "I am quite prepared to attest that Kersten did not let any difficulty get in his way. [. . .] For all I know, there was never any question of his expenses, though I often wondered how he covered them. That he did have considerable expenses is obvious; during his many trips from Stockholm to Germany, he always brought vast amounts of 'bribe material' with him."[474]

But that was without counting on the political leanings of the Swedish government – and particularly on those of its foreign

i   He was aged only forty-two.
ii  This would have required a special permission from the treating physicians and another one from American military authorities – both of which would probably have been denied him. After Schellenberg's release in March 1950, his state of health probably no longer fell within Kersten's competence.

minister. Indeed, Östen Undén, who wrote in his diary that Kersten was "an adventurer",[475] instructed the director of his ministry's archive, one Uno Willers, to draft an aide-memoire with a definite political slant – towards the left, needless to say. He could not have found a better man for the job, since Willers had much to atone for: a former Nazi, a great admirer of Germany and long-standing member of the fascist Sveriges Nationella Förbund,[476] Uno Willers had quickly leapt from the extreme right to the extreme left; now resorting mostly to insinuation, he wrote that "Kersten's profession gives an impression of quackery", and that the testimonies in his favour, though eloquent as to his past services, were hardly convincing as to his vocation to become a Swede. Carried away, Willers then showed his true colours: Kersten, he wrote, had expressed "strong anti-communist views", and his having joined anti-Bolshevik volunteers in Estonia during the period 1918–19 could have given him "a specific political orientation that might be very close to some post-war fascist political currents".[477] Such ideological contortions were apparently enough to convince the members of the government, and on October 17, 1952, Kersten was refused Swedish citizenship.

Out of disappointment and desperation, Kersten made an extraordinary move: convinced that agents of Bernadotte had torpedoed his citizenship application, Kersten proceeded to circulate a letter that the count had supposedly addressed to Himmler on March 10, 1945: "The presence of Jews is as unwelcome in Sweden as it is in Germany. This is why I quite understand your position on the Jewish question. Medizinalrat Kersten informs me that you have authorised the release and transfer to Sweden of 5,000 Jews. This I deem unsatisfactory, for I do not wish to transport Jews.

375

But since I cannot refuse officially, I beg of you, Herr Himmler, to do it yourself! Medizinalrat Kersten has no mandate to negotiate the release of Jews, and he did it in a private capacity. My position is identical concerning the transportation to Sweden of French, Dutch and Belgian nationals."[478]

All this was of course disastrous, not for Bernadotte's reputation, but for Kersten's, as the document was obviously a crude forgery: no letterhead, no signature, a style that was not the count's, a syntax that was clearly Kersten's, and an antisemitism attributed to Bernadotte that was totally alien to him: he had indeed refused on March 8, 1945 to transport non-Scandinavian prisoners,[iii] but this was only because his essentially military training had taught him to follow instructions to the letter;[iv] when the Swedish foreign ministry adjusted its instructions on March 27, Bernadotte proceeded to implement them as well, without restriction or recrimination. To claim that there were antisemitic motives behind his actions was thus nothing but base defamation that could only be explained by Kersten's acute state of desperation, at the time. But this forgery seems to have horrified his friends, as Hillel Storch confided to Gösta Engzell thirty years later: "Knierem and I repeatedly said to Kersten: 'With all your good deeds, you're now attacking Bernadotte with lies – and you are discrediting yourself in the process.' Knierem practically begged him on bended knee to renounce the use of this forgery."[479]

To no avail: Kersten did not give up, and he even showed his document to a number of journalists and members of parliament –

iii   See above, pp. 284 and 290.
iv   Which could at worst be interpreted as a certain lack of boldness and personal initiative.

including Deputy James Dickson, who warned him against what might be considered an attempt at blackmail. Since Kersten insisted, Dickson, who also had the honorary title of chamberlain, asked him for a copy of the document and showed it to King Gustav V Adolph[v] on March 12, 1953. The latter, who was perfectly familiar with his late cousin's style, decreed unhesitatingly: "It's a fake!"[480]

This might have cost Kersten dearly, but for once, the Swedish political situation played in his favour: the monarchy and the Social Democrat Party were embroiled in the deplorable Haijby affair,[vi] at a time when the Dutch parliamentary commission's report had made some impression on Swedish public opinion. And then, from beyond the North Sea, another polemicist entered the fray: obviously alerted by Professor Posthumus, British historian Hugh Trevor-Roper wrote in the American magazine *Atlantic Monthly* a withering article condemning the refusal to grant Kersten Swedish citizenship; drawing on a wealth of supporting evidence, he denounced Count Bernadotte's subterfuges to take all the credit for the rescue operation of April 1945, and he went on: "What were Bernadotte's motives in thus suppressing all credit but his own? His own work was perfectly reputable: why did he think it necessary so busily and – it must sometimes appear – so unscrupulously to inflate its significance? Possibly it was personal vanity; perhaps Swedish politics. At all events it was successful, and

---

v   Who had succeeded his father Gustav V two years earlier.
vi   Kurt Haijby – real name Kurt Johansson – was a notorious hoodlum, who had been sentenced for murder in Germany and for paedophilia in Sweden. He claimed to have had intimate relations with King Gustav V, whom he had clearly black-mailed, and he wrote in 1950 a *roman à clef* about the affair. Revelations about the payments made to him by the palace for decades to buy his silence had precipitated the scandal.

by its success stifled the less privileged voice of truth. For who knew the facts? A few Swedes – but Bernadotte had got in first in Sweden, and why should they publicly challenge that formidable claim? A few Germans – but why should they advertise the fact that they had been Himmler's counsellors? A few Jews – but Bernadotte was murdered by Jews and a sense of guilt inhibits them from further censure.[vii] All these have given private testimony, but publicly they have not spoken out. Fortunately, there is a fourth category of those who knew. In Holland, there are no such inhibitions and so it is there that the truth has gradually emerged." And the historian concluded by deploring that Kersten had not been awarded the Nobel Peace Prize. [481]

A skilfully crafted indictment, no doubt, to which must be added that Professor Trevor-Roper was not just any historian: as an officer of the British intelligence service M.I.6 during the war, he had been tasked in the autumn of 1945 with investigating the circumstances of Hitler's disappearance; his detailed report, submitted to the Allied authorities two months later, had subsequently been published as a book that soon became famous: *The Last Days of Hitler*. Coming from a historian of such stature, the article in *Atlantic Monthly* caused something of a sensation, and compelled the Swedish foreign ministry to issue an official communiqué. It was an attempt to refute Trevor-Roper's conclusions, but as it quoted no evidence of any kind, it proved unconvincing. In an attempt to calm things down, the ministry eventually chose

vii   This remains true to this day, and that sense of guilt explains why the saviour of 60,000 Jews has still not been recognised as "Righteous among the Nations". But a sense of decency naturally demanded that Count Bernadotte not be recognised either.

to publish the "politically slanted" aide-memoire drafted by Director Uno Willers that had hitherto remained confidential.

It was a major mistake: the right-wing parties, allied to the liberal Folkparti, seized on the document to attack social democrat minister Ingvar Lindell, who had been the government rapporteur for Kersten's citizenship application. A subcommittee of the Riksdag, charged with investigating the background of the process that had led to the rejection of that application, ended with the striking conclusion that "there can be no doubt that steps were deliberately taken to ensure that Kersten's participation in the Swedish operation [in the spring of 1945] was forgotten, so that Count Bernadotte, and perhaps Sweden, could reap all the credit for it".[482]

During the ensuing debate in the Second Chamber of the Riksdag on April 29, 1953, the "politically slanted" aide-memoire was itself subjected to devastating attacks; for in the meantime, the international situation had left its mark: the Korean War, Stalin's threats against Norway and Finland, the entry of Denmark and Norway into N.A.T.O., the recent discovery of a Soviet military espionage network in Sweden and the multiplicity of naval and aerial incidents in the Baltic had considerably dimmed the attraction of communism and somewhat tempered official Sovietophilia. But in the Riksdag, the social democrat speaker – and pastor[viii] – Halvard Hallén defended the government's position by insinuating that Kersten had not resided in the country long enough to

viii   A somewhat special deputy and pastor, who at least once in 1954 went directly from a secret session of the Riksdag committee on foreign affairs to the Soviet embassy, in order to inform his red comrades of the tenor of the debates! Whether he had asked for the Lord's forgiveness beforehand remains unknown.

claim Swedish citizenship, and that he was not "a real Finn"[ix] but "a Balt,[x] a German, a foreigner anyway". This did not go down well, while the spokesman for the Folkparti was rather more successful when he expressed the hope that "Mr Hallén's allegations will eventually sink into the sea of oblivion, where they obviously belong"; he went on to praise Kersten, "a man who undeniably accomplished a host of quite remarkable actions, partly on behalf of Sweden, and partly, one might say, on behalf of all mankind. A man who, in my view, [. . .] did not receive from the Swedes the gratitude and the esteem he rightfully deserved." He then dealt with the aide-memoire penned by Uno Willers, which he described as "riddled with vague and erroneous formulations and conclusions. [. . .] It is a sort of commissioned scribble that superbly disregards all the affidavits concerning this matter, in Sweden and abroad."

Next to speak was Deputy James Dickson,[xi] representing the conservative Högerparti: "It seems to me that, when later in life Mr Hallén reads his words as recorded in the register of debates, he will come to regret many things that he has said today. [. . .] It would be interesting to see what precise instructions Mr Willers had received when he was commissioned to write this aide-memoire." That was getting dangerously close to the root of the matter, after which three other opposition members took the floor

ix   Finns could apply for Swedish citizenship after only five years of residence.
x    A devastating argument, since Sweden had already extradited Baltic refugees to the U.S.S.R. immediately after the war, in the hope of propitiating Stalin.
xi   This flamboyant figure, successively or simultaneously agricultural engineer, aviator and explorer, had volunteered to fight in the Finnish army during the Winter War, after which he served until 1945 in the C-byrån, the Swedish army's intelligence service.

and bitterly reproached the authorities for having "refused Swedish nationality to a benefactor of humanity".[483] The government narrowly escaped a vote of no confidence, but its position was clearly untenable; on October 30, 1953, Felix Kersten was granted Swedish citizenship.[xii]

From then on, our Medizinalrat was able to devote himself to his three great passions: family, medicine and agronomy. He commuted regularly from his Stockholm office to the small estate of Stensäter – at least during his stays in Sweden, for if he had few patients in Stockholm, he had many abroad. Kersten had finally realised his dream by reopening an office in The Hague; but as his German patients – and their families – had not forgotten him either, he opened another office in Düsseldorf. And then there was Paris, as his son Arno Kersten later explained: "The problem was that, as a matter of principle, many people were unwilling to go to Germany after the war and preferred to be treated in Paris. In the first place, there were many Jewish patients, such as members of the Rothschild family, captains of industry from Latin American countries, artists, actors and actresses. The most famous was Greta Garbo, who came to Paris for treatment several years in a row; she often went shopping with my mother. Grace Kelly also wanted to come, but she cancelled her appointment at the last moment. By the late fifties, [Kersten's] year was divided into

xii    Three years later, Sweden officially did justice to Felix Kersten in a White Book about the eponymous buses: *1945 års Svenska Hjälpexpedition til Tyskland*, Ny Serie II: 8, Stockholm, 1956. From beginning to end, it looked more than anything like an attempt to refute Trevor-Roper's arguments, but there was on page 19 this grudging admission: "It is incontestable that in December 1944, Dr Kersten made energetic and successful representations to Himmler regarding the Danish and Norwegian internees in Germany. The importance of the work thus done by Dr Kersten in preparing the way for the Swedish expedition is clear and important enough."

four periods: winter in Stockholm, spring in Düsseldorf, early autumn in The Hague and late autumn in Paris."[484]

For all that, the past could not be erased altogether: old friendships were rekindled, and Kersten treated such long-standing acquaintances as Christian Günther, Hillel Storch, Gottlob Berger[xiii] and industrialist Friedrich Flick, whose life Kersten had saved three times,[xiv] and who expressed his gratitude by offering him a brand-new, custom-made Mercedes. Banker Jacob Wallenberg, deeply grateful to his brother-in-law's saviour[xv] and eager to make up for his country's ingratitude, had him paid an indemnity of 55,000 crowns – and made a point of ordering his accountant to make sure that the sum was tax-free.[485]

In 1952, the former "magic Buddha" published a new version of his memoirs in Germany, this time in the shape of a diary – which he had not kept at the time, thus rendering the book unreliable in places; and when a more comprehensive English version appeared four years later, it was hardly more reliable.[xvi] Nonetheless, be it orally or in writing, Kersten was to reminisce more than once

xiii   Who had benefited from an early release in 1951.

xiv   By treating him before and during the war, by intervening with Himmler to save him from deportation to a concentration camp, then by testifying in his favour during the Nuremberg trial of 1947. At the end of the latter, Friedrich Flick – who after all had employed during the war 10,000 forced workers under inhuman conditions and pillaged the resources of several occupied countries – received the comparatively light sentence of seven years in prison, then was released early in 1950, which enabled him to rebuild a colossal fortune – and to be awarded the Order of Merit by the Federal Republic of Germany in 1963.

xv   See above, pp. 231 and 271.

xvi   *Totenkopf und Treue*, Robert Mölich Verlag, Hamburg, 1952, and *The Kersten Memoirs*, Macmillan, London, 1956. This may explain the contempt of British historians for Felix Kersten's memoirs: they only read the English version – and perhaps the German version for the bravest – but none of them took any interest in the initial Swedish and Dutch versions.

during those post-war years: "Himmler nurtured the idea of going down in history as a great man – one of the greatest of all times; so that, even with primitive means, great successes could be achieved";[486] "Goebbels had his spies, who were more efficient than Himmler's spies, because he paid them better. [. . .] He had spies in Himmler's entourage, but Himmler too had his spies, who spied on Goebbels and on Goebbels' spies, as well as on Göring and Ribbentrop, who also had their spies, spying on Himmler; but these Himmler quickly detected, and he had them sent to the front, where they died a hero's death";[487] "Ribbentrop was the stupidest by far; never in my whole life have I been witness to such stupidity";[488] "Himmler's relations with the Wehrmacht were abominable. He considered all the generals to be traitors and wanted them all hanged: 'After the war,' he used to say, 'none of these scoundrels will remain alive'";[xvii][489] "The maxim 'The Führer is always right' had a mystical justification for Himmler. He would have had his own brother shot without the slightest hesitation, or even had himself shot, if the Führer had ordered it. For Hitler, Führer of the great Germanic Reich, necessarily knew the whys and wherefores of his decisions, even if he, Himmler, could not always understand them, or even disapproved of them."[490]

In 1959, journalist Elie Wiesel, an Auschwitz survivor and future Nobel Laureate, interviewed Kersten in Stockholm: "The man's name, Felix Kersten, was familiar to me. I had read somewhere that Heinrich Himmler had been among his patients. [. . .] Kersten treated him often, sometimes daily. What did the S.S. Reichsführer talk about as his healer massaged his pain-racked

xvii  Many German generals who had fought bravely during the war were thus never to know that they owed their lives to Germany's defeat . . .

body? According to Kersten, everything, including the Jews. And their extermination? Rarely. But let me quote from our conversation:

'Did Himmler confide in you, Mr Kersten?'

'Yes.'

'Did he sleep during massages?'

'Sometimes.'

'So it would have been possible for you to press a little harder on his neck, for instance?'

'Yes, that possibility was open to me. Although . . . the hallway and nearby offices were full of S.S. men.'

'But you could have killed him?'

'Yes.'

'Why did you spare his life? Because you were afraid to lose yours?'

'No, it wasn't that. I told myself I could have some influence over him.[xviii] And in fact, I did save human lives. [. . .]'

Kersten was a strange man. I felt uncomfortable in his presence, perhaps because he was the only man I knew who had maintained close relations with Himmler. What did he leave unsaid?"[491]

Probably as much as he said . . . But at about the same time, Kersten entrusted many of his memories and documents to German priest and professor Achim Besgen, as well as to French reporter and novelist Joseph Kessel; the former gathered them in a mystical hagiography, and the latter turned them into a

xviii The other obvious answer naturally being that had Kersten done so, Himmler would have been instantly replaced by either Kaltenbrunner or "Gestapo" Müller – an unsavoury prospect, and certainly a death warrant for the 60,000 Jewish survivors . . .

masterpiece of fiction.[xix] But at that late stage, Kersten was more concerned with passing on his medical experience, which he summarised in a short and highly pedagogical book: *Die Heilkraft der Hand* (*The Therapeutic Power of the Hand*), in which Himmler's name is nowhere to be found.

"We did not always understand," his son Arno Kersten was later to write, "that our father was somewhat stressed by his financial situation. He wanted to ensure family circumstances in such a way that if something happened to him, his family would not end up on the streets."[492] Alas! Unbeknown to Arno, his father had long had yet another source of stress: back in 1943, astrologer Wulff [xx] had already noted that "Kersten suffers from a thyroid disease and from a fatty degeneration of the heart"[xxi] [493] – which he had not deduced from the alignment of the planets, but from the confidences of Irmgard Kersten. Yet Arno did remember one of his father's habits: "When we were just children, and later teenagers, we noticed the increasing number of multicoloured pills that appeared on his breakfast menu. We naturally wanted to know why he took all these remedies, and we were told that they were meant to improve his heart function."[494]

In early 1960, a mere fifteen years late, France recognised the eminent services once rendered to her imprisoned nationals by Himmler's therapist, and decided to award him the Legion of

xix   Achim Besgen, *Der stille Befehl*, Nymphenburger Verlag, Munich, 1960; Joseph Kessel, *Les Mains du Miracle*, Gallimard, Paris, 1960.

xx   It is interesting to note that Wilhelm Wulff appears nowhere in the four versions of Kersten's memoirs – either because the latter deemed that Wulff had been unequal to his task, or because he feared to arouse the reader's incredulity by introducing the planets in a historical narrative.

xxi   A pathological process whereby the muscle cells of the myocardium are progressively replaced by fatty cells. Obesity would appear to be the triggering factor.

Honour. Kersten accordingly set out for Paris with his wife, but in the vicinity of the German town of Hamm, he suffered a heart attack followed by an embolism, and died on the next day, April 16, 1960. After a moving ceremony in Düsseldorf, attended by many of his former patients, his ashes were transferred to Länna cemetery, near the estate of Stensäter – his second Hartzwalde.

The Jewish lawyer and philosopher Gerhart Riegner[xxii] was to say thirty-six years later: "Kersten was undeniably an extraordinary man, and the fact that he had this power to influence Himmler was a gift of the Almighty! I can see no other explanation."[495] An assertion that is perfectly plausible, but not easily verifiable – and that is bound to remain so as long as the archives of the Lord remain impenetrable . . .

xxii   Gerhart Riegner, secretary of the World Jewish Congress in Berne during the war, was the man who sent a telegram to London on 10 August 1942, disclosing "a Nazi project to exterminate 3.5 to 4 million Jews."

# NOTES

## CHAPTER 1

1   Felix Kersten, *Klerk en Beul,*
    J.M. Meulenhoff, Amsterdam, 1948,
    p. 24.

2   Ibid.

3   N.I.O.D., Map D 6. *Mein
    Lebenslauf,* Stockholm, 30/9/45.

4   Arno Kersten, *S.S.-Ledaren
    Himmlers innersta hemligheter,*
    Vaktel Förlag, Eskilstuna, 2016,
    p. 20.

5   Felix Kersten, *Klerk en Beul,* op. cit.,
    p. 26.

6   Arno Kersten, *S.S.-Ledaren,* op. cit.,
    p. 21.

7   Tapio Tamminen, *Himmler a jeho
    Finsky buddha,* C Press, Brno, 2020,
    p. 56.

8   Felix Kersten, *Klerk en Beul,* op. cit.,
    p. 27.

9   Achim Besgen, *Der stille Befehl,*
    Nymphenburger Verlagshandlung,
    Munich, 1960, p. 18; Joseph Kessel,
    *Les mains du miracle,* Gallimard,
    Paris, 1960, p. 37.

10  Felix Kersten, *Die Heilkraft der
    Hand,* Karl Haug Verlag, Ulm,
    1958, pp. 80–1; 121.

11  Ibid., pp. 122; 128.

12  Herbert Petersen, "Bericht über den
    gebürtigen Dorpatenser Felix
    Kersten", in *Jahrbuch des Baltischen
    Deutschtums,* Bd. 13, 1966, p. 2.

13  Felix Kersten, *Die Heilkraft der
    Hand,* op. cit., p. 170.

14  Joseph Kessel, *Les mains du miracle,*
    op. cit., pp. 40–1.

15  Felix Kersten, *Jeg var Himmlers lege,*
    Gyldendal, Oslo, 1947, p. 18; *Klerk
    en Beul,* op. cit., p. 29.

16  Ibid.

17  N.I.O.D., Map A. Doc. I. 878,
    Bedankbriefje van prinz Hendrik
    aan Kersten voor behandeling,
    27/10/1928.

18  Idem, Map D 6, Mein Lebenslauf,
    30/9/45, Stockholm, p. 3.

19  Idem, Map E 15, Antekening van
    gesprek met J.L. Doedes, L. de Jong,
    28 oct. 47.

20  Felix Kersten, *Jeg var Himmlers lege,*
    op. cit., p. 18; *Klerk en Beul,* op. cit.,
    p. 30.

21  Ibid., p. 31.

22  Felix Kersten, *Jeg var Himmlers lege,*
    op. cit., p. 68.

23  N.I.O.D., Map F 1, Gesprek prof.
    Posthumus met Medisinalrat
    F. Kersten op 1 sept. 47, p. 17.

24  *Enquêtecommissie Regeringsbeleid
    1940–1945,* Deel 6 C, Verhoren,
    Staatsdrukkerij, The Hague, 1952,
    p. 132.

## CHAPTER 2

25  N.I.O.D., Map F 1, Gesprek prof.
    Posthumus met Medisinalrat
    F. Kersten op 1 sept. 47, p. 6.

26  Felix Kersten, *Jeg var Himmlers lege,*
    op. cit., p. 20.

27  Ibid., p. 21.

28  Felix Kersten, *Totenkopf und Treue,*
    Robert Mölich, Hamburg, 1952,
    p. 389. N.I.O.D., Map F 1, Gesprek
    prof. Posthumus met Medisinalrat
    F. Kersten op 1 sept. 47, p. 8; Felix
    Kersten, *Jeg var Himmlers lege,*
    op. cit., p. 21.

29  Felix Kersten, *Totenkopf und Treue,*
    op. cit., p. 389.

30  Felix Kersten, *Jeg var Himmlers lege,*
    op. cit., p. 22.

31 N.I.O.D., Map F 1, Gesprek prof. Posthumus, op. cit., pp. 6–7.

32 Felix Kersten, *Jeg var Himmlers lege*, op. cit., p. 23.

33 Ibid.

34 N.I.O.D., Map H 8, Zusatz zum Memorandum für Holland von 12 juin 1945, 26/9/45, p. 1.

35 Achim Besgen, *Der stille Befehl*, op. cit., p. 22.

36 N.I.O.D., Map E 44, P.J. Schijf, Waarom ik lid der Beweging werd, 27/5/48.

37 *Enquêtecommissie Regeringsbeleid 1940–1945*, Deel 6 C, Verhoren, op. cit., p. 132.

38 Arno Kersten, *S.S.-Ledaren*, op. cit., p. 33.

39 *Enquêtecommissie Regeringsbeleid 1940–1945*, Deel 6 C, Verhoren, op. cit., p. 134.

40 Joseph Kessel, *Les mains du miracle*, op. cit., p. 79.

41 Arno Kersten, *S.S.-Ledaren*, op. cit., p. 34.

42 Ibid., p. 35.

43 Felix Kersten, *Jeg var Himmlers Lege*, op. cit., pp. 53–4.

44 N.I.O.D., Map F 1, Gesprek prof. Posthumus met Medisinalrat F. Kersten op 1 sept. 47, p. 12.

45 Felix Kersten, *Totenkopf und Treue*, op. cit., p. 406.

46 Walter Hubatsch, *Hitler's Weisungen für die Kriegsführung 1939–1945, Dokumente des O.K.W.*, Bernard und Graefe, Frankfurt,1962, p. 32; Erich Kern, *Verrat an Deutschland*, Schütz, Göttingen,1963, p. 225.

47 *Enquêtecommissie Regeringsbeleid 1940–1945*, Deel 6 C, Verhoren, op. cit., p. 133.

48 François Kersaudy, *Stratèges et Norvège 1940*, Hachette, Paris, 1977, pp. 110–15.

49 C.Z.A., C4/570-26, Affidavit by Henrik Ramsay, 13/6/1949.

50 Felix Kersten, *Totenkopf und Treue*, op. cit., pp. 290–1.

51 Ibid., p. 236.

52 *Enquêtecommissie Regeringsbeleid 1940–1945*, Deel 6 C, Verhoren, op. cit., p. 133; Felix Kersten, *Klerk en Beul*, op. cit., pp. 34–5.

53 Ibid., p. 35.

54 *Enquêtecommissie Regeringsbeleid 1940–1945*, Deel 6 C, op. cit., p. 133.

55 Felix Kersten, *Klerk en Beul*, op. cit., p. 35.

## CHAPTER 3

56 Felix Kersten, *The Kersten Memoirs*, New York, Macmillan, 1956, p. 88.

57 Ibid., pp. 88–9.

58 N.I.O.D., Map F 1, Gesprek prof. Posthumus. met Medisinalrat F. Kersten op 1 sept. 47, p. 13. Map F 5 A, p. 1.

59 Ibid., Map F 1, p. 10.

60 Joseph Kessel, *Les mains du miracle*, op. cit., pp. 108–10.

61 *Enquêtecommissie Regeringsbeleid 1940–1945*, Deel 6 A en B, Verslag, Bijlagen, Memorandum opgesteld door Jacobus Nieuwenhuis, Stockholm, 7/3/1948, pp. 171–2.

62 N.I.O.D., Map E 43, affidavit by J.P. Schijf, as noted by D.D. Vallgraaf, 21/9/48.

63 *Enquêtecommissie Regeringsbeleid 1940–1945*, Deel 6 a en B, Verslag, Bijlagen, op. cit., pp. 113–14.

64 Ibid., Memorandum opgesteld door Jacobus Nieuwenhuis, Stockholm, 7/3/1948, p. 172.

65 N.I.O.D., Map H 7, F. Kersten tot M. de Beaufort, 30/1/46.

66 Arno Kersten, *S.S.-Ledaren*, op. cit., p. 170.

67 S.R.A., Advokat Knut Littorin Samling, vol. 1, F. Kersten to K. Littorin, 17/9/49, p. 1.

68 Felix Kersten, *Jeg var Himmlers lege*, op. cit., pp. 68–9.

69 Felix Kersten, *Klerk en Beul*, op. cit., p. 89.

70 Eugen Dollmann, *The Interpreter*, Hutchinson, London, 1967, pp. 178–80.

71 Felix Kersten, *Jeg var Himmlers lege*, op. cit., p. 70.

72 Felix Kersten, *Klerk en Beul*, op. cit., pp. 89–90.

73 Ibid., p. 90.

74 Galeazzo Ciano, *Diario*, Rizzoli, Milan, 1963, vol. I, pp. 372–80.

75 Eugen Dollmann, *The Interpreter*, op. cit., p. 181.

76 Felix Kersten, *Jeg var Himmlers lege*, op. cit., p. 71.

77 *Enquêtecommissie Regeringsbeleid 1940–1945*, Deel 6 A en B, Verslag, Bijlagen, op. cit., p. 179, note 2.

78 Arno Kersten, *S.S.-Ledaren*, op. cit., pp. 13–14.

79 Peter Longerich, *Himmler*, Héloïse d'Ormesson, Paris, 2008, pp. 432–46.

80 Joseph Kessel, *Les mains du miracle*, op. cit., p. 140.

81 Gerhard Engel, *Heeresadjutant bei Hitler, 1938–1943*, D.V.A., Stuttgart, 1974, p. 105. Otto Dietrich, *Hitler*, Chicago, Regnery, 1955, p. 63. Hans Frank, *Im Angesicht des Galgens*, Beck Verlag, Munich, 1953, p. 411.

82 Arno Kersten, *S.S.-Ledaren*, op. cit., pp. 98–9; Felix Kersten, *Jeg var Himmlers lege*, op. cit., p. 60.

**CHAPTER 4**

83 Arno Kersten, *S.S.-Ledaren*, op. cit., pp. 91–2.

84 Alfred Rosenberg, *Journal 1934–1944*, Flammarion, Paris, 2015, pp. 395–7.

85 Felix Kersten, *Klerk en Beul*, op. cit., pp. 44–5.

86 Felix Kersten, *The Kersten Memoirs*, op. cit., p. 302.

87 Ibid., pp. 303–4.

88 Felix Kersten, *Klerk en Beul*, op. cit., p. 47; *The Kersten Memoirs*, op. cit., pp. 305–6.

89 N.I.O.D., Map E 45, Ausführungen zum Umsiedlungsplan, 28/9/48, Den Haag.

90 Karl Wolff, "Eichmanns Chef Heinrich Himmler", *Neue Illustrierte* no. 17, 23/4/1961, p. 22.

91 N.I.O.D., Map F 1 Gesprek mat Med. F. Kersten, op. cit., p. 11.

92 *Der Dienstkalender Heinrich Himmlers 1941/42*, Hans Christians Verlag, Hamburg, 1999, p. 195.

93 Felix Kersten, *Klerk en Beul*, op. cit., p. 79.

94 See for instance Staffan Thorsell, *Warszawasvenskarna*, Bonniers Förlaget, Stockholm, 2015, p. 238.

95 Felix Kersten, *Klerk en Beul*, op. cit., p. 59.

96 Felix Kersten, *The Kersten Memoirs*, op. cit., pp. 119–20.

97 N.I.O.D., Map E 44, P.J. Schijf, Waarom ik lid der Beweging werd, 27/5/48.

98 Arno Kersten, *S.S.-Ledaren*, op. cit., pp. 110–11.

99 Clara von Arnim, *Der grüne Baum des Lebens*, Knaur, Munich, 2002, p. 260.

100 Felix Kersten, *Klerk en Beul*, op. cit., pp. 78–9.

101 *Enquêtecommissie Regeringsbeleid 1940–1945*, Deel 6 A en B, Verslag en Bijlagen, op. cit., p. 172.

102 *Der Dienstkalender Heinrich Himmlers 1941/42*, op. cit., p. 183.

103 Eugen Kogon, *Der S.S. Staat*, Nachdruck, Munich, 1974, p. 375. *Der Dienstkalender Himmlers*, op. cit., p. 283.

104 Felix Kersten, *Jeg var Himmlers Lege*, op. cit., p. 51.

105    Arno Kersten, *S.S.-Ledaren*, op. cit., p. 125.

## CHAPTER 5

106    Mario Dederichs, *Heydrich*, Tallandier, Paris, 2007, p. 133.

107    Felix Kersten, *The Kersten Memoirs*, op. cit., pp. 90–1.

108    Arno Kersten, *S.S.-Ledaren*, op. cit., pp. 133–4.

109    François Kersaudy, *Hermann Göring*, Perrin, Paris, 2009, p. 187.

110    Wilhelm M. Carlgren, *Svensk Utrikespolitik 1939–1945*, Allmänna Förlaget, Stockholm, 1973, pp. 340–1.

111    Ibid., p. 341.

112    Idem.

113    François Kersaudy, *Vi Stoler paa England*, Cappelen, Oslo, 1991, pp. 120–6.

114    Felix Kersten, *Jeg var Himmlers Lege*, op. cit., p. 34.

115    N.I.O.D., Map B1, Kersten tot Brandt, 5/3/42.

116    Ibid., Map B2, Kersten tot Himmler, 15/6/42.

117    N.I.O.D., Map F7, Gedeelte van het verhoor van Harster door L. de Jong over Kersten, 7 maart 1949, p. 38.

118    C.Z.A., C4/570-16, Eidesstattliche Erklärung von S.S. Standartenführer Sepp Tiefenbacher, 1 August 1954.

119    Walter Schellenberg, *Aufzeichnungen des letzten Geheimdienstchefs unter Hitler*, Moewig, Gütersloh, 1981, p. 311.

120    Ibid., p. 314.

121    André Brissaud, *Canaris*, Perrin, Paris, 1970, p. 549.

122    François Kersaudy, *Les secrets du IIIe Reich*, Perrin, Paris, 2013, ch. 3.

123    Walter Schellenberg, *Memoiren*, op. cit., pp. 314–15.

124    N.I.O.D., Map F1 Gesprek mat Med. F. Kersten, op. cit., p. 21.

125    Martin Broszat, *Kommandant in Auschwitz*, D.V.A., Stuttgart, 1958, p. 182.

126    Ibid., pp. 183–4.

127    *Der Dienstkalender Heinrich Himmlers 1941/42*, op. cit., p. 259.

128    Felix Kersten, *Klerk en Beul*, op. cit., p. 80; *Jeg var Himmlers Lege*, op. cit., pp. 94–5.

129    Ibid., p. 81.

130    Idem.

## CHAPTER 6

131    Felix Kersten, *Jeg var Himmlers Lege*, op. cit., p. 102.

132    Arno Kersten, *S.S.-Ledaren*, op. cit., p. 164.

133    Felix Kersten, *Klerk en Beul*, op. cit., pp. 92–3.

134    Ibid., p. 93.

135    Ibid., pp. 93–4.

136    Felix Kersten, *Samtal med Himmler*, CKM förlag, Stockholm, 2010, p. 140 (a new edition of the book published in 1947).

137    Arno Kersten, *S.S.-Ledaren*, op. cit., p. 169.

138    Olli Vehviläinen, *Finland and the Second World War*, Palgrave Macmillan, London, 2002, p. 85.

139    Felix Kersten, *Klerk en Beul*, op. cit., p. 95.

140    C.Z.A., C4/570-34, Kivimäki to Kersten, 5/12/1948; C4/570-26, Affidavit by Henrik Ramsay, 13/6/1949.

141    Felix Kersten, *Totenkopf und Treue*, op. cit., p. 181.

142    Felix Kersten, *Samtal med Himmler*, op. cit., pp. 126–7.

143    Ibid., p. 128.

144    Elke Fröhlich, Ed., *Die Tagebücher von Josef Goebbels*, Teil II, Bd. 5, Munich 1998, pp. 353–4.

145    Ibid., Teil I, Bd. 3, p. 55, 23 Feb. 1937.

146 Otto Dietrich, *Hitler*, Regnery, Chicago, 1955, p. 71.

147 Felix Kersten, *Totenkopf und Treue*, op. cit., pp. 157–63.

148 Ibid., p. 163.

149 Ibid., pp. 127–8.

150 Felix Kersten, *Totenkopf und Treue*, op. cit., pp. 128–9.

151 André Brissaud, *Canaris*, op. cit., p. 512.

152 Ibid., p. 513.

153 François Kersaudy, *Les secrets du IIIe Reich*, op. cit., pp. 75–81.

154 André Brissaud, *Canaris*, op. cit., p. 511; Walter Schellenberg, *The Labyrinth*, Da Capo, London, 2000, p. 193.

155 Walter Schellenberg, *Aufzeichnungen*, op. cit., p. 339.

156 Der Dienstkalender Heinrich Himmlers 1941/42, op. cit., pp. 514–15.

157 Walter Schellenberg, *Aufzeichnungen*, op. cit., p. 331.

158 Felix Kersten, *Klerk en Beul*, op. cit., p. 127.

159 Walter Schellenberg, *Aufzeichnungen*, op. cit., p. 332.

160 Achim Besgen, *Der stille Befehl*, op. cit., p.155.

161 Reinhard R. Doerries, *Hitler's Last Chief of Intelligence*, Routledge, London, 2003, p. 283.

## CHAPTER 7

162 Elke Fröhlich, *Journal de Joseph Goebbels, 1939–1942*, Tallandier, Paris, 2009, p. 628.

163 Albert Speer, *Erinnerungen*, Propyläen Verlag, Berlin, 1971, p. 252.

164 Alfred Rosenberg, *Journal 1934–1944*, Flammarion, Paris, 2015, p. 467.

165 *Der Dienstkalender Heinrich Himmlers 1941–1942*, op. cit., pp. 541–69.

166 Felix Kersten, *Klerk en Beul*, op. cit., pp. 144–5.

167 Didrik Arup Seip, *Hjemme og i Fiendeland*, Gyldendal Norsk Forlag, Oslo, 1946, pp. 445, 453; 457–65.

168 Ibid., pp. 467; 477–80.

169 Ibid., p. 471.

170 Felix Kersten, *Klerk en Beul*, op. cit., p. 145.

171 Idem.

172 Idem.

173 *Enquêtecommissie Regeringsbeleid 1940–1945*, Deel 6 A en B, op. cit., pp. 172–3.

174 Felix Kersten, *Klerk en Beul*, op. cit., p. 61.

175 F.K., *Jeg var Himmlers Lege*, op. cit., p. 101.

176 F.K., *Klerk en Beul*, op. cit., pp. 60–1.

177 F.K., *Samtal med Himmler*, op. cit., p. 116.

178 F.K., *Klerk en Beul*, op. cit., p. 90.

179 Ibid., p. 91; *The Kersten Memoirs*, op. cit., p. 158.

180 Galeazzo Ciano, *Diario 1939–1943*, vol. II., Rizzoli, Milan, 1963, p. 225.

181 F.K., *Jeg var Himmlers Lege*, op. cit., p. 89.

182 Ibid., p. 91.

183 François Kersaudy, *Stalingrad*, Perrin, Paris, 2013, p. 61.

184 F.K., *The Kersten Memoirs*, op. cit., pp. 126–7.

185 Ibid., pp. 127–8.

186 Ibid., p. 128.

187 F.K. *Jeg var Himmlers lege*, op. cit., pp. 155–7.

188 Ibid., p. 159.

189 F.K., *The Kersten Memoirs*, op. cit., pp. 166–7.

190 Ibid., p. 167.

191 Ibid., pp. 167–8.

192 David Irving, *Wie krank war Himmler wirklich?*, Heyne, Munich, 1980, p. 39.

193 F. Kersaudy, *Les secrets du Troisième Reich*, Perrin, Paris, 2013, ch. 5, "L'homme à femmes".

194 David Irving, *Die geheimen Tagebücher des Dr Morell*, Goldmann, Munich, 1983, p. 41.

195 F.K., *The Kersten Memoirs*, op. cit., p. 170.

**CHAPTER 8**

196 F.K., *Klerk en Beul*, op. cit., pp. 38–9.

197 N.I.O.D., Map B3, op. cit., Kersten tot H.H., 21/3/43.

198 F.K., *Jeg var Himmlers Lege*, op. cit., pp. 110–11.

199 Ibid., p. 111.

200 Idem.

201 F.K., *Samtal med Himmler*, op. cit., pp.157–8.

202 Ibid., p. 158.

203 Ibid., p. 159.

204 Idem.

205 Reinhard R. Doerries, Ed., *Hitler's Last Chief*, op. cit., p. 101; Walter Schellenberg, *Aufzeichnungen*, op. cit., pp. 352–3.

206 Wilhelm Th. Wulff, *Tierkreis und Hakenkreuz*, Bertelsmann, Gütersloh, 1968, pp. 117–26.

207 F.K., *Samtal med Himmler*, op. cit., pp. 57–8.

208 *Der Dienstkalender Heinrich Himmlers 1943–1945*, Piper Verlag, Munich, 2020, pp. 128; 260; 274; 390; 430; 461; 511; 513–4; 537; 553.

209 Ibid., pp. 162; 246.

210 Ibid., p. 175.

211 Allen W. Dulles, *Germany's Underground*, Little & Ives, N.Y., 1947, pp. 157–60.

212 Walter Schellenberg, *Aufzeichnungen*, op. cit., p. 360.

213 N.I.O.D., Map F4, Verslag van gepreek van K.W. Swart met W. Schellenberg in het Duitse Hospitaal te Nurenberg, 18/10/48.

214 F.K., *The Kersten Memoirs*, op. cit., p. 188. In other versions, he gave the bag to another Finnish diplomatic courier; see F.K., *Jeg var Himmlers Lege*, op. cit., p. 37; *Samtal med Himmler*, op. cit., p. 48.

215 F.K., *Jeg var Himmlers Lege*, op. cit., p. 131.

216 N.I.O.D., Map A, Kersten 29–47, Kersten an Himmler, 25/9/43.

**CHAPTER 9**

217 F.K., *The Kersten Memoirs*, op. cit., p. 188.

218 Ibid., p. 189.

219 Ibid., p. 191.

220 Ibid., pp. 189–90.

221 U.S. N.A.R.A., RG 226, Microfilm 1642, Roll 23, Frames 782–800, A. Hewitt: "Contact with Himmler", in William Donovan's Memorandum for the President, March 20, 1944, quoted in John H. Waller, *The Devil's Doctor*, John Wiley & Sons, N.Y., 2002, pp. 146–7.

222 P.R.O., F.O. 371/29085, Aide memoire from the U.S. Dept of State, 22/1/44, quoted in John H. Waller, *The Devil's Doctor*, op. cit., p. 147.

223 Ibid.

224 F.K., *The Kersten Memoirs*, op. cit., p. 190.

225 Ibid., p. 191.

226 Walter Schellenberg, *The Labyrinth*, Da Capo, London, 2000, pp. 370–1; *Aufzeichnungen*, op. cit., p. 380.

227 F.K., *Klerk en Beul*, op. cit., p. 116.

228 Ibid., p. 117.

229 Walter Schellenberg, *Aufzeichnungen*, op. cit., p. 380.

230 F.K., *The Kersten Memoirs*, op. cit., pp. 192–3.

231 Ibid., pp. 193–4.

232 François Kersaudy, *L'affaire Cicéron*, Perrin, Paris, 2005, pp. 48–9.

233 Walter Schellenberg, *Aufzeichnungen*, op. cit., p. 382.

234 François Kersaudy, *Les secrets du Troisième Reich*, op. cit., pp. 227–9.

235 R.A., Advokat K. Littorin Samling, vol. 3, PM by A. Hewitt, 3/5/53, N.Y.

236 Arno Kersten, *Himmlers innersta Hemligheter*, op. cit., p. 235.

237 Ibid., p. 236.

238 Ibid, p. 237.

239 Idem.

240 N.I.O.D., Map H8, F. Kersten, Zusatz zum Memorandum für Holland von 12/6/45, p. 5.

241 *Enquêtecommissie Regeringsbeleid 1939-1945*, Deel 6C, Verhoren, op. cit., p. 899, Verhoor van Dr Jan Herman van Rojien.

242 F.K., *The Kersten Memoirs*, op. cit., pp. 265–7; Arno Kersten, *Himmlers innersta Hemligheter*, op. cit., pp. 238–40.

243 *Enquêtecommissie Regeringsbeleid 1939-1945*, Deel 6A en B, Verslag, Bijlagen, op. cit., p. 174, Memorandum opgesteld door Jacobus Nieuwenhuis, Stockholm, 7 Maart 1948.

244 N.I.O.D., Map B6, F. Kersten an S.S. Obergruppenführer und General der Polizei Rauter, 7/2/44.

245 F.K., *Klerk en Beul*, op. cit., pp. 148–9.

246 Manfred Gebhard, Ed., *Die Zeugen Jehovas*, Urania Verlag, Leipzig, 1970, pp. 206–7.

247 Friedrich Zipfel, *Kirchenkampf in Deutschland 1933 bis 1945*, Walter de Gruyter, Berlin, 1965, p. 200.

248 Detlef Garbe, *Between Resistance and Martyrdom*, Univeristy of Madison Press, Madison, 2008, p. 724.

249 C.Z.A. C4/570-28, Van Nagell. Memorandum über meine Zusammenarbeit mit F. Kersten, 3/10/1949, p.1.

250 Wilhelm Th. Wulff, *Tierkreis und Hakenkreuz*, op. cit., p. 161.

251 Ibid., p. 162.

252 Ibid., p. 166.

253 Idem.

254 Idem.

255 François Kersaudy, *L'affaire Cicéron*, op. cit., p. 60.

256 Franz von Papen, *Memoirs*, André Deutsch, London, 1952, p. 518.

257 Ludwig C. Moyzisch, *Der Fall Cicero*, Presse Verlag, Sarrebrück, 1949, pp. 176–7.

258 N.A., KV 6/8, Extract from P.F. 66886, Y box 6174, Molkenteller, Serial 12a. Sent by H.Q. O.O.S./S.C.I., Ist U.S. Army, APO 230 to A.C. of S., G-2, 13 May 1945, p. 2.

259 Joseph Goebbels, *Journal 1943-1945*, op. cit., p. 420.

## CHAPTER 10

260 Joseph Kessel, *Les Mains du Miracle*, op. cit., pp. 249–50.

261 Wilhelm Th. Wulff, *Tierkreis und Hakenkreuz*, op. cit., p. 167.

262 Albert Speer, *Erinnerungen*, op. cit., p. 343.

263 Fabian von Schlabrendorff, *The Secret War against Hitler*, Hodder & Stoughton, London, 1966, p. 273.

264 Felix Kersten, *Klerk en Beul*, op. cit., p. 150–1; Arno Kersten, *Himmlers innersta hemligheter*, op. cit., pp. 259–60; *The Kersten Memoirs*, op. cit., pp. 201–2.

265 Felix Kersten, *Jeg var Himmlers Lege*, op. cit., pp. 167–8.

266 Felix Kersten, *Klerk en Beul*, op. cit., pp. 104–5 (the letter is reproduced in facsimile).

267 Felix Kersten, *Samtal med Himmler*, op. cit., p. 256.

268 Ibid., pp. 261–2.

269 Ibid., p. 262.

270 *Enquêtecommissie Regeringsbeleid 1940–1945*, Deel 6 A en B., Verslag, Bijlagen, op. cit., p. 174.

271 Felix Kersten, *Jeg var Himmlers Lege*, op. cit., p. 191.

272 Felix Kersten, *Klerk en Beul*, op. cit., p. 155.

273 Sune Persson, *Escape from the Reich*, Frontline Books, London, 2009, pp. 38–40.

274 Felix Kersten, *Klerk en Beul*, op. cit., p. 193 (the minister's affidavit is reproduced in facsimile).

275 C.Z.A., C4/570-28, Van Nagell. Memorandum über meine Zusammenarbeit mit F. Kersten, 3/10/1949, p. 2.

276 Felix Kersten, *Jeg var Himmlers Lege*, op. cit., p. 195.

277 Felix Kersten, *Klerk en Beul*, op. cit., p. 118.

278 Felix Kersten, *The Kersten Memoirs*, op. cit., p. 204.

279 *Enquêtecommissie Regeringsbeleid 1940–1945*, Deel 6 C, Verhoren, op. cit., p. 141; Arno Kersten, *Himmlers innersta hemligheter*, op. cit., p. 279.

280 Ibid., p. 278.

281 Ibid., pp. 280–1.

282 Ibid., p. 325 (the letter is reproduced).

283 Felix Kersten, *Klerk en Beul*, op. cit., pp. 119–21.

## CHAPTER 11

284 Mathias Uhl, Ed., *Der Dienstkalender Heinrich Himmlers*, op. cit., pp. 991, 993, 995, 1001, 1026, 1030, 1036, 1040, 1053, 1061.

285 *Enquêtecommissie Regeringsbeleid 1940–1945*, Deel 6 B, Bijlagen, op. cit., p. 175.

286 Achim Besgen, *Der stille Befehl*, op. cit., p. 38.

287 Theodor Steltzer, *Sechzig Jahre Zeitgenosse*, List Verlag, Munich, 1966, p. 171.

288 Felix Kersten, *Jeg var Himmlers lege*, op. cit., pp. 169–70.

289 Sune Persson, *Escape from the Third Reich*, op. cit., pp. 57–8.

290 Ibid., p. 69.

291 *Enquêtecommissie Regeringsbeleid 1940–1945*, Deel 6 B, Bijlagen, op. cit., p. 174.

292 Idem.

293 Ibid., p. 175.

294 Folke Bernadotte, *Sidste Akt*, Gyldendal, Copenhagen, 1945, p. 33.

295 Ibid., p. 38–9.

296 *Enquêtecommissie Regeringsbeleid 1940–1945*, Deel 6 C, Verhoren, op. cit., p. 92.

297 Ibid., p. 453.

298 Arno Kersten, *Himmlers innersta hemligheter*, op. cit., p. 290.

299 Affidavit from Minister *Günther* in *Klerk en Beul*, op. cit., pp. 193–4.

300 Felix Kersten, *Totenkopf und Treue*, op.cit., pp. 339–41.

301 C.Z.A., C4/554-50, Storch to Rundfunk Köln, 11/3/1958.

302 Felix Kersten, *Totenkopf und Treue*, op.cit., pp. 339–41, and C.Z.A., C4/570-14, Storch to Kersten, 2/3/45.

303 Arno Kersten, *Himmlers innersta hemligheter*, op. cit., p. 331.

304 Felix Kersten, *Klerk en Beul*, op. cit., p. 169.

305 Arno Kersten, *Himmlers innersta hemligheter*, op. cit., p. 327.

306 Ibid., pp. 329–30.

307 Wilhelm T. Wulff, *Tierkreis und Hakenkreuz*, op. cit., pp. 185–6.

308 Ibid., pp. 187–9.

309 Ibid., p. 189.

310 Ibid., pp. 189–90.

311 Ibid., pp. 193–202.

312  *Felix Kersten, Totenkopf und Treue,*
op. cit., p. 344.

313  Ibid., p. 343.

314  Sune Persson, *Escape from the Third
Reich,* op. cit., p. 264, note 14.

**CHAPTER 12**

315  I.f.Z., F 44 / 1 – 110, Dem
Reichführer zur Entlassung und
Ausreise vorgelegt. Bewilligt 7 März
1945.

316  *Felix Kersten, Totenkopf und Treue,*
op. cit., pp. 345–51.

317  Ibid., pp. 351–2.

318  Ibid., p. 345.

319  I.f.Z., F 44/1 – 118, Kersten an
Standartenführer Brandt, 14 März
1945.

320  Felix Kersten, *Totenkopf und Treue,*
op. cit., pp. 330–1.

321  *Enquêtecommissie Regeringsbeleid
1940–1945, Deel 6 C, Verhoren,* pp.
453–4.

322  *Enquêtecommissie Regeringsbeleid
1940–1945,* Deel 6 B, Verslag en
Bijlagen, p. 174.

323  *Nazi conspiracy and aggression,*
Supplement B (Red Series),
U.S.G.P.O., Washington 1948, p.
1593.

324  N.A., WO 309/217, Depoisition of
R.F.F. Hoess, OC 92, Field security
section, 14/3/46, p. 6.

325  David A. Hackett, Edit., *Der
Buchenwald-Report,* Munich, 1996,
pp. 360; 363.

326  Heinz Guderian, *Panzer Leader,*
Futura, London, 1974, pp. 421–2.

327  Ibid., p. 421.

328  Bernd Freytag von Loringhoven,
*Dans le bunker de Hitler,* Perrin,
Paris, 2005, p. 149.

329  Felix Kersten, *Klerk en Beul,* op. cit.,
p. 160–161 (Himmler's letter is
reproduced).

330  R.A., U.D. 1920, HP, vol. 1692,
Richert til von Post, 22/3/45.

331  Ibid.

332  Arno Kersten, *Himmlers innersta
hemligheter,* op. cit., pp. 299–300.

333  Felix Kersten, *Klerk en Beul,* op. cit.,
pp. 166–8 (Kersten's letter is
reproduced).

334  I.f.Z., F 44 /1 – 136, Kersten an
Herrn Hillel Storch, 29 März
1945.

335  Sune Persson, *Escape from the
Third Reich,* op. cit., p. 154.

336  Eleanora Storch Schwab, "A
Daughter Remembers", in Gertrude
Schneider, *The Unfinished Road,*
Praeger, NY, 1991, p. 179.

337  C.Z.A., C4/570-70, Hillel Storch
an Professor Posthumus, 1/8/1955,
p. 3.

338  C.Z.A., C4/552-67, Storch till
Kanslirådet A. Kromnow, UD,
4/9/1963.

339  C.Z.A., C4/570-70, Hillel Storch
to Professor Posthumus, 1/8/1955,
p. 3.

340  *Stockholms Tidningen,* 30/4/1983,
quoted in Eleanora Storch Schwab,
"A Daughter Remembers", in
Gertrude Schneider, *The Unfinished
Road,* op. cit., pp. 181–2.

341  N.I.O.D., Map H9, J. NIeuwenhuis:
Memorandum over mijn
verksamhed tijdens de
Oorlogsjahren in de
informatiedienst van Dr Kersten,
p. 12.

342  *Enquêtecommissie Regeringsbeleid
1940–1945,* Deel 6 C, Verhoren,
p. 454, Verhoor van Jacobus
Nieuwenhuis, 2/2/49.

343  *1945 års svenska hjälpexpedition till
Tyskland. Förspel och Förhandlingar,*
Ny serie II:11, Stockholm 1956,
p. 25.

344  Folke Bernadotte, *Sidste Akt,*
op. cit., p. 62.

345  Ibid., p. 61.

346  Ibid., p. 64.

347 Walter Schellenberg, *Aufzeichnungen*, op. cit., p. 426.

348 Ibid., pp. 426–7.

349 Wilhelm T. Wulff, *Tierkreis und Hakenkreuz*, op. cit., pp. 204–5.

350 Ibid., p. 205.

351 C.Z.A., C4/570-117, Kersten an Norbert Masur, 21 März 1956.

352 Lena Einhorn, *Handelsresande i liv*, Prisma, Stockholm, 1999, p. 398.

353 Ibid., p. 395.

354 C.Z.A., C4/549-42, Storch an Lev Zelmonovits, 26/5/1945.

355 Eleanora Storch Schwab, "A Daughter Remembers", in Gertrude Schneider, *The Unfinished Road*, op. cit., p. 178.

356 I.f.Z., F 44/1 – 175, Kersten an Minister Günther, 23 April 1945, and C.Z.A., C4/483-20, ditto.

357 Ibid., p. 138.

358 Norbert Masur, *En Jude Talar med Himmler*, Bonniers, Stockholm, 1945, p. 7.

359 R.A., U.D. 1920 års HP 1051, Masurs rapport til UD, 24/4/45.

360 Walter Schellenberg, *Aufzeichnungen*, op. cit., pp. 427–8.

361 Ibid., p. 428.

362 Wilhelm T. Wulff, *Tierkreis und Hakenkreuz*, op. cit., p. 208.

363 Walter Schellenberg, *Aufzeichnungen*, op. cit., p. 429.

364 Felix Kersten, *Klerk en Beul*, op. cit., p. 182.

365 Norbert Masur, *En Jude Talar med Himmler*, Bonniers, Stockholm, 1945, p. 12.

366 Walter Schellenberg, *Aufzeichnungen*, op. cit., p. 429.

367 Wilhelm T. Wulff, *Tierkreis und Hakenkreuz*, op. cit., pp. 208–9.

368 Walther Lüdde-Neurath, *Les derniers jours du Troisième Reich*, Berger-Levrault, Paris, 1963, p. 24.

369 Albert Speer, *Erinnerungen*, op. cit., p. 477.

370 Idem.

371 Felix Kersten, *Klerk en Beul*, op. cit., p. 184.

372 Lena Einhorn, *Handelsresande i liv*, op. cit., p. 408.

373 Arno Kersten, *S.S.-ledaren Himmlers innersta hemligheter*, op. cit., p. 304.

374 Idem.

375 Idem.

376 Idem.

377 I.f.Z, F 44 /1 – 175, Kersten an Minister Günther, 23 April 1945, p. 2.

378 Arno Kersten, *S.S.-ledaren Himmlers innersta hemligheter*, op. cit., p. 304.

379 Norbert Masur, *En Jude talar med Himmler*, op. cit., pp. 17–26.

380 Lena Einhorn, *Handelsresande i liv*, op. cit., p. 411.

381 R.A., U.D. 1920 års HP 1051, Masurs rapport til UD, 24/4/45; Lena Einhorn, *Handelsresande i liv*, op. cit., p. 411. Norbert Masur, *En Jude talar med Himmler*, op. cit. pp. 26–30; Arno Kersten, *S.S.-ledaren Himmlers innersta hemligheter*, op. cit., p. 306.

382 Wilhelm T. Wulff, *Tierkreis und Hakenkreuz*, op. cit., pp. 211–12.

383 Arno Kersten, *S.S.-ledaren Himmlers innersta hemligheter*, op. cit., p. 306; Felix Kersten, *Klerk en Beul*, op. cit., p. 188; Lena Einhorn, *Handelsresande i liv*, op. cit., pp. 412–13.

384 Felix Kersten, *Klerk en Beul*, op. cit., p. 188.

385 Ibid., p. 189.

## CHAPTER 13

386 Folke Bernadotte, *Sidste Akt*, op. cit., p. 70.

387 Ibid., p. 71.

388 N.A., K.V. 2/98 Fritz Göring report to M.I.5 in Sarah Helm, *Si c'est une*

*femme,* Calmann-Levy, Paris, 2016, p. 981.

389  Ibid., p. 982.

390  Sune Persson, *Escape from the Third Reich,* op. cit., pp. 216–17.

391  Ibid., p. 213.

392  Felix Kersten, *Totenkopf und Treue,* op. cit., p. 386.

393  Ibid., p. 387.

394  Karl Koller, *Der letzte Monat,* Norbert Wohlgemuth Verlag, Mannheim, 1949, p. 31.

395  Kazimierz Moczarski, *Entretiens avec le bourreau,* Gallimard, Paris, 1979, p. 313.

396  I.M.T., Nuremberg trial proceedings vol. XIV, Testimony of Baldur von Schirach, 24 May 1946, p. 439.

397  Walter Schellenberg, *Aufzeichnungen,* op. cit., pp. 433–4.

398  Folke Bernadotte, *Sidste Akt,* op. cit., p. 74.

399  Ibid., pp. 76–7.

400  Walter Schellenberg, *Aufzeichnungen,* op. cit., p. 435.

401  Folke Bernadotte, *Sidste Akt,* op. cit., p. 78.

402  F.O. 954/23, Eden to Churchill, April 1, 1945, Churchill's comment April 5; also in Steven Koblik "No truck with Himmler", *Scandia,* vol. 51, 1985, p. 185.

403  Dwight D. Eisenhower, *Crusade in Europe,* Heinemann, London, 1948, p. 462.

404  Harry Truman, *Year of decisions,* Doubleday, N.Y., 1955, pp. 89–93.

405  Folke Bernadotte, *Sidste Akt,* op. cit., pp. 80–1.

406  Walter Schellenberg, *Aufzeichnungen,* op. cit., p. 437.

407  Wilhelm Wulff, *Tierkreis und Hakenkreuz,* op. cit., p. 217.

408  Ibid., pp. 218–19.

409  Ibid., pp. 223–4.

410  Ibid., pp. 225.

411  Walter Schellenberg,

*Aufzeichnungen,* op. cit., pp. 437–8.

412  François Kersaudy, *Hermann Göring,* Perrin, Paris, 2009, pp. 606–21.

413  Albert Speer, *Erinnerungen,* op. cit., p. 489.

414  B.A.C.M. Research – Paperless archives.com, Hanna Reitsch interrogation, 8 October 1945, pp. 8–10.

415  Ibid., p. 11.

416  Ibid.

417  Hugh R. Trevor-Roper, *The Last Days of Hitler,* Macmillan, London, 1947, pp. 194–5.

418  Walter Warlimont, *Inside Hitler's Headquarters,* Weidenfeld, London, 1964, p. 516.

419  Ian Kershaw, *Hitler,* vol. II, Penguin, London, 2000, p. 826.

420  Karl Dönitz, *10 Jahre und 20 Tage,* Athenäum, Frankfurt, 1963, p. 346.

421  Ibid., pp. 347–8.

422  Idem.

423  Walter Schellenberg, *Aufzeichnungen,* op. cit., p. 440.

424  Léon Degrelle, *Hitler pour mille ans,* La table ronde, Paris, 1969, p. 185.

425  Walter Lüdde-Neurath, *Les derniers jours du troisième Reich,* Berger-Levrault, Paris, 1963, pp. 148–9.

426  Walter Schellenberg, *Aufzeichnungen,* op. cit., p. 446.

427  Arno Kersten, *S.S.-Ledaren,* op. cit., pp. 308–9.

**CHAPTER 14**

428  Arno Kersten, *S.S. Ledaren,* op. cit., pp. 309–10.

429  Ibid., p. 310.

430  Ibid., p. 311.

431  Idem.

432  Sune Persson, *Vi åker til Sverige,* Rimbo, Fischer & Co, 2003, p. 441.

433  C.Z.A., C4/554-31, Gespräch mit Schellenberg,10/5/45.

434  N.I.O.D., Map D 4,
Aufzeichnungen, 6/7/46, p. 5.

435  Sune Persson, *Vi åker til Sverige*,
op. cit., p. 141.

436  Ibid., p. 499.

437  Gerald Fleming, "Die Herkunft des
'Bernadotte Briefs' an Himmler
vom 10 März 1945", in Walter
Schellenberg, *Aufzeichnungen*,
op. cit., p. 484.

438  Louis de Jong, "Hat Felix Kersten
das Niederländische Volk gerettet?",
in *Schriftenreihe der
Vierteljahrshefte für Zeitgeschichte*,
No. 28, Stuttgart, DVA, 1974,
p. 139.

439  N.I.O.D., Map E 41, Verklaring van
Nagell 29/8/1948.

440  C.Z.A., C4/570-28, Van Nagell,
Memorandum über meine
Zusammenarbeit mit F. Kersten,
3/10/1949, p. 5.

441  *Trots Allt*, 2–8/2/45.

442  *Enquêtecommissie Regeringsbeleid
1940–1945*, Deel 6 B, op. cit., p. 181;
N.I.O.D., Map E 41, Von Hentig
aan de redacteur de Volkskrant,
30/8/48. Ibid., Map H 8, Posthumus
aan Östen Undén, 24/11/50, p. 2.

443  Lena Einhorn, *Handelsresande i liv*,
op. cit., p. 447.

444  . F.O. 371/48026, Mallet to F.O.,
25/2/45, quoted in Steven Koblik,
"No truck with Himmler", op. cit.,
p. 175.

445  *Enquêtecommissie Regeringsbeleid
1940–1945*, Deel 6 B, Bijlagen,
op. cit., p. 180, note 6, Schrijven van
Van der Vulgt aan de minister van
Buitenlandse Zaken van 18/10/48.

446  RA, UD 1920 års HP 1692, Brev
från Günther till Engzell, 4/11/48.

447  *Enquêtecommissie Regeringsbeleid
1940–1945*, Deel 6 B, op. cit., p. 177,
Brief van F. Th. Dijkmeester aan de
hoofden van de bureaus
inlichtingen.

448  N.I.O.D., Map I 17, Van Nagell aan
Amici, 19/4/46.

449  Ibid., Map I 18, Secretaris van
prinses Juliana, 11/2/46.

450  Ibid., Map F 1, p. 29, Gesprek
Prof. Posthumus med Med. F.
Kersten, op. cit.

451  Ibid., Map H 7, Kersten aan de
Beaufort, 30/1/46.

452  Louis de Jong, "Hat Felix Kersten
das Niederländische Volk gerettet?",
op. cit., pp. 79–141.

453  N.I.O.D., Map E 51, Testimony of
F. Kersten au TMI IV, cas 11,
Gottlob Berger, 18 Oct. 48.

454  Freek Van Rijsinge, *Het Kersten
spiel*, Amsterdam, Boom, 2006,
pp. 71–81.

455  RA, Advokat K. Littorin Samling,
vol. 4, 22/7/47.

456  Ralph Hewins, *Count Folke
Bernadotte*, London, Hutchinson,
1948, pp. 122, 190.

457  N.I.O.D., F 3 – F 4, Verslag van
gesprek [. . .] met W. Schellenberg
in het Duitse Hospitaal te
Nuremberg 18/10/48, p. 2.

458  N.I.O.D., Map F 7, Harster over
Kersten, 2/5/48, p. 38.

459  Felix Kersten, *Klerk en Beul*,
op. cit., p. 190.

460  N.I.O.D., Map E 48, Rose Raake,
verslag over Heer X, 5/10/48.

461  *Enquêtecommissie Regeringsbeleid
1940–1945*, Deel 6 B, op. cit., p. 171,
Nota van 2 sept. 48 van Prof. N.W.
Posthumus over de Heer E.A.F.
Kersten. Copie dans N.I.O.D.,
Map G 2, 2 Sept. 48.

462  *Enquêtecommissie Regeringsbeleid
1940–1945*, Deel 6 C, op. cit., p. 91;
Verhoor van Mr J.E.H. Baron van
Nagell, 28/7/48.

463  Ibid., pp. 139–40, Verhoor van
Medizinalrat E.A.F. Kersten,
15/9/48.

464  Ibid., p. 143.

465  Ibid., pp. 559–60, Verhoor van
     Mr W.C. Graaf van Rechteren
     Limpurg, 19/8/48.

466  *Enquêtecommissie Regeringsbeleid
     1940–1945*, Deel 6 B, op. cit.,
     p. 181–184, Bijlage 63, Zakelijke
     inhoud van het op 12 januari 1950
     aan de Minister van Buitenlandse
     Zaken uitgebrachte rapport van de
     Commissie [. . .] over de Heer
     E.A.F. Kersten.

467  Ibid., pp. 183–4.

468  Ibid., p. 184.

469  Freek Van Rijsinge, *Het Kersten
     spiel*, op. cit., p. 7.

## CHAPTER 15

470  N.I.O.D., Map H 8, Prof.
     Posthumus aan Östen Undén,
     24/11/50.

471  Reinhard R. Doerries, *Hitler's
     Last Chief of Foreign Intelligence*,
     op. cit., p. 53.

472  Freek Van Rijsinge, *Het Kersten
     spiel*, op. cit., p. 88.

473  *Enquêtecommissie Regeringsbeleid
     1940–1945*, Deel 6 A, Verslag,
     op. cit., pp. 333–6, 344–7.

474  R.A., U.D. 1920, H.P., vol. 1692,
     G. Engzell till Buråchef
     U. Back-Holst, 17/1/51.

475  Östen Undén Dagbok, 6/10/52,
     quoted in Sune Persson, *Vi åker
     til Sverige*, op. cit., p. 507.

476  Tapio Tamminen, *Himmler a jeho
     finsky buddha*, op.cit., p. 291.

477  R.A., U.D. 1920, HP, vol. 1692,
     VPM rörande Felix Kersten
     och hans ansökan om Svensk
     medborgarskap. Uno Willers,
     14 Juni 1952.

478  Letter quoted in Gerald Fleming,
     "Die Herkunft des 'Bernadotte
     Briefs' an Himmler vom 10. März
     1945", op. cit., p. 465.

479  Lena Einhorn, *Handelsresande i liv*,
     op. cit., p. 450.

480  Gerald Fleming, "Die Herkunft
     des 'Bernadotte Briefs' an Himmler
     vom 10. März 1945", op. cit., p. 487.

481  *The Atlantic Monthly*,
     February 1953.

482  Bihang til Riksdagens Protokoll år
     1953, Stockholm, 1954, p. 17.

483  Riksdagens Protokoll no 27,
     29/4/53, pp. 6, 7, 11–23.

484  Postface by Arno Kersten in Felix
     Kersten, *Samtal med Himmler*,
     op. cit., p. XXVII.

485  R.A., Advokat K. Littorin Samling,
     vol. 1, Littorin till Wallenberg,
     9/2/53.

486  N.I.O.D., Map H 7, Kersten aan
     M. de Beaufort, 30/1/46.

487  Ibid., Map D 5, "Die fünfte
     Kolonnen", 20/9/48.

488  Ibid., Map F 1, p. 19.

489  Ibid., p. 20.

490  Felix Kersten, *Totenkopf und
     Treue*, op. cit., p. 395.

491  Elie Wiesel, *All Rivers run to the
     Sea*, Schocken, N.Y., 1996,
     pp. 312–13.

492  Postface by Arno Kersten in Felix
     Kersten, *Samtal med Himmler*,
     op. cit., p. XXVII.

493  Wilhelm Th. Wulff, *Tierkreis und
     Hakenkreuz*, op. cit., p. 119.

494  Postface by Arno Kersten in Felix
     Kersten, *Samtal med Himmler*,
     op. cit., p. XXVII.

495  Lena Einhorn, *Handelsresande i liv*,
     op. cit., p. 455.

# SOURCES

## ARCHIVES

**N.I.O.D., Amsterdam** (Instituut voor Oorlogs, Holocaust en Genocidestudies)
Dossier Kersten, 248-0878

    Map a (1–11) Stukken betreffende de periode 1928 – 24 nov. 1947

    Map b (1–50) Stukken betreffende de periode 5 maart. 1942 – 27 apr.1945

    Map c (1–17) Stukken betreffende de periode 1 maart 1941 – 28 sept. 1949

    Map d (1–6)  Stukken betreffende de periode 12 juni 1945 – 30 sept. 1945

    Map e (1–70) Stukken betreffende de periode 1 juni 1945 – 9 dec.1954

    Map f (1–7)   Stukken betreffende de periode 17 sep. 1947 – maart 1949

    Map g (1–4)  Stukken betreffende de periode 18 aug. 1948 – 11 okt. 1948

    Map h (1–9)  Stukken betreffende de periode 6 mei 1944 – 9 juli 1976

    Map i (1–19) Stukken betreffende de periode 22 juli 1942 – 2 okt. 1972


**R.A., Stockholm** (Riksarkiv)

    U.D.: Utrikesdepartementet (Foreign Ministry)

        HP 21 I. Judefrågan. Allmänt. Hjälp åt Flyktingar

        HP 39 D. Hum. Hjälpverksamhet 1944–45. HP 1591

        HP 39 N Spec. Felix Kersten. HP 1692

    Advokat Knut Littorins Arkiv: Samling gällande Medicinalrådet Felix Kersten

        Vol. 1 Korrespondens

        Vol. 2 Warszawasvenskarna m.fl.

        Vol. 3 Ordnar. Pressurklipp.m.m.

        Vol. 4 Korrespondens med Günther / Samling gällande Himmler


**I.f.Z., Munich** (Institut für Zeitgeschichte)

    F 44/1 Felix Kersten (1–291)

    F 44/7 Kersten. Verschiedenes, III und IV, 1945–168

**N.A., London** (National Archives, Public Record Office)

    KV 6/8

    FO 954/23 Scandinavia

    WO 309/217, WO 193/822


**C.Z.A., Jerusalem** (Central Zionist Archives)

    C4/495 Franz Goering 1945

    C4/519 Case Bernadotte – Kersten 1977 / 76

    C4/524 Ditto – 1957 / 56

    C4/525 Case of Kersten 1956 / 56

    C4/535 Saving Jews 1975 / 72

    C4/544 Dr Kersten 1948 / 46

    C4/545 Case of Bernadotte 1955 / 49

    C4/547 Case of Bernadotte – Kersten 1956

    C4/548 Ditto – 1956 / 46

    C4/549 Case of Kersten – Bernadotte 1957 / 45

    C4/550 Saving Jews 1982 / 45

    C4/552 Case of Bernadotte – Kersten 1960 / 79

    C4/554 Ditto – 1949 / 77

    C4/558 Attempts to save Jews 1950 / 57

    C4/558-1t Correspondence. Robert Kempner

    C4/570 Felix Kersten 1945 / 77

    C4/627 Hillel Storch 1978 / 79

    C4/631-1t Storch's memorandum 1955

# SELECTED BIBLIOGRAPHY

Kersten's memoirs are the primary sources. The first two volumes – the most interesting – are in Swedish and Dutch respectively:

Felix Kersten, *Samtal med Himmler*, CKM förlag, Stockholm, 2010 (a reprint of the book published in 1947 by Ljus Förlag, Stockholm). A contemporary Norwegian translation also used by this author: Felix Kersten, *Jeg var Himmlers lege*, Oslo, Gyldendal, 1947.

Felix Kersten, *Klerk en Beul*, J.M. Meulenhoff, Amsterdam, 1948.

(Both versions are complementary and rarely contradictory. No English translation of either book is available.)

The next two volumes, in German and English, are belated attempts by Kersten to reconstruct a diary that – for obvious reasons – he had not kept during the war:

Felix Kersten, *Totenkopf und Treue*, Robert Mölich, Hamburg, 1952.

Felix Kersten, *The Kersten Memoirs*, Macmillan, New York, 1956.

(Based on wartime notes, but quite unreliable as diaries.)

The practitioner's medical experience is largely summed up in:

Felix Kersten, *Die Heilkraft der Hand* (*The Healing Power of the Hand*), Ulm, Karl Haug Verlag, 1958.

(Remarkably pedagogical, with not a single mention of Heinrich Himmler.)

Kersten's last surviving son, Arno, has delved deep into his father's archives to write a Swedish-language survey of the whole affair:

Arno Kersten, *SS-Ledaren Himmlers innersta hemligheter*, Vaktel Förlag, Eskilstuna, 2016.

(No English version available, only an Estonian translation, which may not be much help to the average reader).

The next best sources are the memoirs of Kersten's wartime accomplice, Walter Schellenberg:

Walter Schellenberg, *Aufzeichnungen des letzten Geheimdienstchefs unter Hitler*, Moewig, Gütersloh, 1981.

Walter Schellenberg, *The Labyrinth*, Da Capo, London, 2000.

(The British and German editors seem to have selected different parts of Schellenberg's handwritten text. But where the former S.S. Brigadeführer's relations with Felix Kersten are concerned, there are no noteworthy discrepancies between the two versions.)

An interesting compilation of Schellenberg's post-war interrogations by the Allies:

Reinhard R. Doerries, Ed., *Hitler's Last Chief of Intelligence*, Routledge, London, 2003.

(Includes a summary of Schellenberg's relations with Kersten and of their joint undertakings.)

Another indispensable source: the memoirs of astrologer Wulff, employed by both Kersten and Schellenberg as purveyor of horoscopes to the Reichsführer during the last two years of the war:

Wilhelm Th. Wulff, *Tierkreis und Hakenkreuz*, Bertelsmann, Gütersloh, 1968. English translation: *Zodiac and Swastika*, Coward, N.Y., 1973.

(An account that is all the more fascinating as Wulff clearly hates Kersten, whom he describes as deceitful and manipulative. That Kersten saved tens of thousands he does not deny, but clearly considers it a piffling detail. Had Wilhelm Wulff written a whole book on Felix Kersten, he might well have entitled it *Schwindlers Liste* – Swindler's List.)

Among the other witnesses to Kersten's wartime exploits, Norbert Masur, who accompanied him on his last and most perilous journey to Berlin:

Norbert Masur, *En Jude Talar med Himmler* (*A Jew Talks to Himmler*), Bonniers, Stockholm, 1946.

(There are Dutch and German translations of the book in the archives of Amsterdam, Stockholm and Munich, but no published English version is available.)

Folke Bernadotte's account is of interest, inasmuch as it studiously avoids any mention of Kersten's part in the count's negotiations with Himmler:

Count Folke Bernadotte, *Slutet*, Nordstedt, Stockholm, 1945; *The Fall of the Curtain*, Cassell, London, 1945. *Sidste Akt*, Gyldendal, Copenhagen, 1945.

(The English translation is unreliable. The Danish version is a perfect rendition of the Swedish original – the latter written jointly by Schellenberg and the count's usual ghost-writer, Ragnar Svanström.)

The following authors wrote of their acquaintance with Kersten during or after the war:

Eugen Dollmann, *The Interpreter*, Hutchinson, London, 1967.

Clara von Arnim, *Der grüne Baum des Lebens*, Knaur, Munich, 2002.

Eleonora Storch Schwab, "A daughter remembers" in Gertrude Schneider, *The Unfinished Road*, Praeger, N.Y., 1991.

Elie Wiesel, *All Rivers Run to the Sea*, Schocken, N.Y., 1996.


Among the very few who learned that their saviour was Felix Kersten:

Didrik Arup Seip, *Hjemme og i Fiendeland*, Gyldendal Norsk Forlag, Oslo, 1946.

Theodor Steltzer, *Sechzig Jahre Zeitgenosse*, List Verlag, Munich, 1966.


Two authors in whom Kersten confided before his death wrote noteworthy hagiographic accounts:

Achim Besgen, *Der stille Befehl*, Nymphenburger Verlagshandlung, Munich, 1960.

Joseph Kessel, *Les mains du miracle*, Gallimard, Paris, 1960. (English translation: *The Man with the Miraculous Hands*, Burford Books, Ithaca, N.Y., 2004.)

Main works by historians or journalists dealing with the Kersten–Himmler relationship:

Tapio Tamminen, *Himmler ja hänen Suomalainen Buddansa* (*Himmler and His Finnish Buddha*), Atena, Helsinki, 2018.

(An interesting analysis, with useful references to Finnish archives. Unfortunately, there is no published English translation, but for readers who are unfamiliar with the Finnish language – such as this author – a Czech translation is available: Tapio Tamminen, *Himmler a jeho Finsky buddha*, C Press, Brno, 2020.)

John H. Waller, *The Devil's Doctor*, John Wiley & Sons, N.Y., 2002.

(The author, a former C.I.A. official, has delved deep into O.S.S. and diplomatic archives, with conclusive results.)

Sune Persson, *Vi åker til Sverige*, Fischer & Co, Rimbo, 2003.

(A highly detailed account of the White Buses odyssey, by a noted Swedish historian. Bernadotte's and Kersten's roles in the affair are discussed at length. The book has been at least partly translated: Sune Persson, *Escape from the Reich*, Frontline Books, London, 2009.)

Lena Einhorn, *Handelsresande i liv*, Prisma, Stockholm, 1999.

(An extensively documented book that centres on the life of Hillel Storch, one of Kersten's Swedish "overseers" during the last months of the war. Much information on the background of the perilous April 20 expedition, and on some of Kersten's postwar tribulations. No English translation so far.)

Louis de Jong, "Hat Felix Kersten das Niederländische Volk gerettet?", in *Schriftenreihe der Vierteljahrshefte für Zeitgeschichte*, Nr. 28, D.V.A., Stuttgart, 1974.

(German translation of a Dutch article proving conclusively that Kersten did not and could not have dissuaded Himmler from carrying out the massive eastward deportation of the entire Dutch population, since no project of that kind had ever been seriously contemplated.)

Freek Van Rijsinge, *Het Kersten spiel*, Boom, Amsterdam, 2006.

(The author discovered a batch of letters written by Felix Kersten that might lead one to the conclusion that the latter suffered from post-war Stockholm Syndrome – a condition that would be fully understandable, considering that the original Swedish hostages of the Stockholm bank robbers had been held only six days, whereas Felix Kersten had been detained six years.)

Ian Buruma, *The Collaborators*, Atlantic Books, London, 2023.

Based on nine books (including a novel), five journal articles and four archival documents, this indictment includes much innuendo, innumerable question marks and a few grievous mistakes; Buruma thus confuses Second Lieutenant Rudolf Brandt with the notorious Major General Karl Brandt and presents Himmler's utterances as Kersten's own. Altogether an attempt at debunking that vastly overshoots the target.

Werner Neuss, *Menschenfreund und Mörder* (*Philantropist and Killer*), Projekte-Verlag Cornelius, Halle, 2010.

(Easily the oddest book about Felix Kersten: Werner Neuss, a retired German brain surgeon, set out to prove his father's hunch that Felix Kersten was none other than one Felix Huberti, a German murderer who had fled to Finland in 1919 in order to escape retribution. How the young Huberti, a native of Halle in central Germany, managed to learn Finnish, Russian and medicine simultaneously, all the while impersonating the real Felix Kersten in front of the latter's family and friends, is unfortunately left unsaid. In a sequel to his book, Werner Neuss intends to prove that Kersten-Huberti was guilty of yet another murder: that of Count Bernadotte . . . No comment.)

On Himmler himself:

Peter Longerich, *Heinrich Himmler*, Siedler Verlag, Munich, 2008. (*Heinrich Himmler,* OUP, Oxford, 2012.)

Peter Padfield, *Himmler, Reichsführer SS*, Macmillan, London, 1990. (Probably the best written and most informative.)

Richard Breitman, *The Architect of Genocide*, Alfred A. Knopf, N.Y., 1991.

For the political and military background of the events mentioned, see above all:

Albert Speer, *Erinnerungen*, Propyläen Verlag, Berlin, 1971. (*Inside the Third Reich,* Weidenfeld & Nicolson, London, 1995.)

(With a useful corrective by Martin Kitchen: *Speer, Hitler's Architect*, Yale UP, New Haven, 2015.)

Gerhard Engel, *Heeresadjutant bei Hitler, 1938–1943*, D.V.A., Stuttgart, 1974. (*At the Heart of the Reich*, Greenhill Books, London, 2005.)

Otto Dietrich, *Hitler*, Regnery, Chicago, 1955.

Walter Warlimont, *Inside Hitler's Headquarters*, Weidenfeld, London, 1964.

Karl Dönitz, *10 Jahre und 20 Tage*, Athenäum, Frankfurt, 1963. (*Memoirs, Ten Years and Twenty Days*, Naval Institute Press, Annapolis, 1990.)

Finally, a number of invaluable printed documents:

Walter Hubatsch, *Hitler's Weisungen für die Kriegsführung 1939–1945, Dokumente des OKW*, Bernard und Graefe, Frankfurt, 1962. (Hitler's directives for the conduct of the war, 1939–45.)

*Der Dienstkalender Heinrich Himmlers 1941/42*, Hans Christians Verlag, Hamburg, 1999. Second volume: *1943–1945*, Piper Verlag, Munich, 2020. (Himmler's appointment diaries, 1941–45.)

Wilhelm M. Carlgren, *Svensk Utrikespolitik 1939–1945*, Allmänna Förlaget, Stockholm, 1973. (An analysis of documents on Swedish foreign policy during the war.)

*1945 års svenska hjälpexpedition till Tyskland. Förspel och Förhandlingar*, Ny serie II:11, Stockholm 1956. (Definitive Swedish Foreign Ministry report on the White Buses expedition.)

*Enquêtecommissie Regeringsbeleid 1940–1945*, Deel 6 A en B, Verslag, Bijlagen. Deel 6 C, Verhoren, Staatsdrukkerij, The Hague, 1952. (A huge, two-volume report by the Dutch Parliamentary Inquiry Commission on government policy and assistance to Dutch nationals during the war.)

# INDEX

References to images and maps are in *italics*.

407